(SES)

Maternal Ed   p. 85, 342, 370

Siblings p. 87

Multiple risks, pp. 90, 93

Cronbach's α, NLSCY, p. 113

Dichotomous variables, maternal
   smoking & drinking during pregnancy p. 134

eg. sample design p. 135   **VULNERABLE CHILDREN**

Substance abuse variables (parent) p. 134

Depression pp. 217-8.   Cut-off
   Scale

Limitation of Multiple Regression p. 280.

Friends factor p. 322

Stability model, p. 357

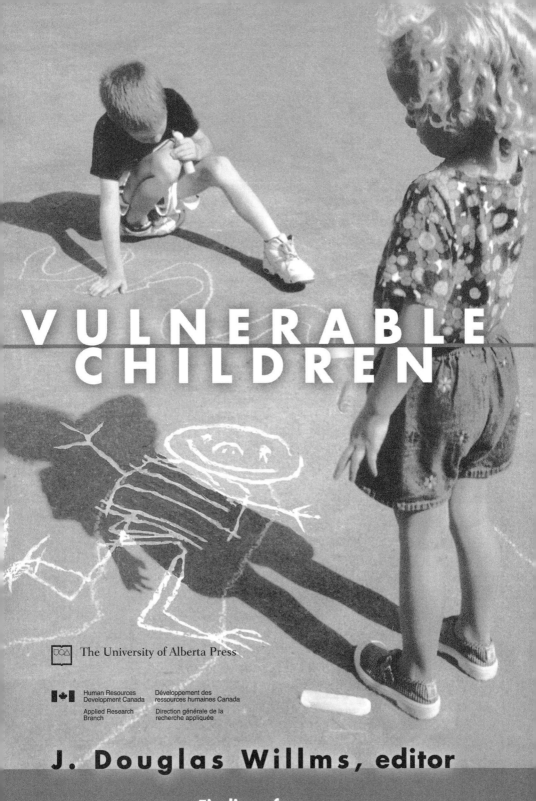

VULNERABLE CHILDREN

The University of Alberta Press

Human Resources
Development Canada

Développement des
ressources humaines Canada

Applied Research
Branch

Direction générale de la
recherche appliquée

J. Douglas Willms, editor

Findings from
Canada's National Longitudinal Survey of Children and Youth

Copyright this volume © The University of Alberta Press 2002

Published by   and
The University of Alberta Press   Applied Research Branch
Ring House 2   Human Resources Development Canada
Edmonton, Alberta   T6G 2E1   165 Hôtel de Ville, 7th floor
www.uap.ualberta.ca   Hull, Quebec   K1A 0J2
                                      www.hrdc-drhc.gc.ca/arb

The Applied Research Branch of Human Resources Development Canada generates policy-relevant research, of which the publication of *Vulnerable Children* is a part.

NATIONAL LIBRARY OF CANADA CATALOGUING IN PUBLICATION DATA

Main entry under title:
Vulnerable children

   Includes bibliographical references.
   ISBN 0–88864–399–3 (bound). — ISBN 0–88864–331–4 (pbk.)

   1. Children—Canada—Social conditions. 2. Children—Canada—Longitudinal studies.
3. National Longitudinal Survey of Children and Youth. 1. Willms, Jon Douglas.
HQ792.C3V84 2002   362.7'0971   C2002–910639–7

Printed and bound in Canada by Friesens, Altona, Manitoba.
∞ Printed on acid-free paper.
Proofreading assistance by Tara Taylor.

The University of Alberta Press acknowledges the financial support of the Government of Canada through the Book Publishing Industry Development Program for its publishing activities. The Press also gratefully acknowledges the support received for its program from the Canada Council for the Arts.

THE CANADA COUNCIL | LE CONSEIL DES ARTS
FOR THE ARTS | DU CANADA
SINCE 1957 | DEPUIS 1957

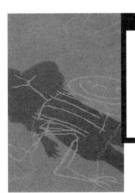

Contents

SECTION THREE • Life in the Family

SECTION FOUR • Life at School

SECTION FIVE • Investing in Children

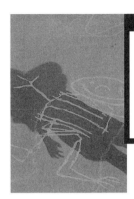

Foreword

FOR THOSE OF US WHO CARE about Canada's children, this is a very important book. We know that many children in our country are vulnerable and we are concerned that the number seems to be growing. But how many are there? Where are they to be found? Why are they vulnerable? And, most important, what can we do to help them grow up healthy, stay in school, and engage with life in a positive and constructive manner? These are questions that have long preoccupied us. Now, thanks to the National Longitudinal Survey of Children and Youth (NLSCY) and the thoughtful and intelligent analyses of remarkable academics like Doug Willms and the others whose work he has brought together in this fascinating volume, we have some clear answers. We also have a new framework for understanding our responsibilities as service providers, policy-makers, program designers, community leaders, and legislators.

Since the NLSCY is a longitudinal study, its results are encouraging researchers to define vulnerability by outcomes over time rather than by factors that put children at risk at any particular moment. This places new emphasis on processes that are open to change. Putting in place the necessary supports for a low birth-weight baby, for example, should enable underweight infants to catch up with their contemporaries and be neither more nor less vulnerable than the rest to poor school outcomes or behavioural problems.

This way of looking at vulnerable children shifts the focus from static to dynamic factors. From this perspective, the data show that it is the relationships and the activities within the family environment that are the strongest determinants of childhood vulnerability. The benefits of good parenting skills, a cohesive family group, and parents in good mental health have been demonstrated to outweigh the negative effects associated with poverty. The material poverty in which children live matters, of course, particularly when poverty is deep and prolonged. However, many children from poor families do well, and most vulnerable children live in families that are not poor, so making sure that the family income is adequate, while highly desirable, will not on its own substantially reduce the number of vulnerable children. Success will come, according to the evidence collected in this book, when we have managed to put in place the elements of a family-enabling society, including income support, of course, but much else as well.

The last two chapters of *Vulnerable Children* contain a blueprint for a family-enabling society. To construct it will require four corner posts. The first is collaboration. In Canada, because of our constitutional division of powers, constructive collaboration is necessary among all levels of government to set the conditions for improving outcomes for children. Collaboration is also necessary among businesses and social agencies, schools and other institutions in the communities in which children live. At the same time, collaboration must be encouraged among parents, teachers, and children themselves. The Early Childhood Development (ECD) Accord between the provinces and the federal government, signed in September 2000, with its four areas of cooperation, is an example of the way to go. Under the ECD Accord, provincial and territorial governments have committed to the following four priority areas: promoting healthy pregnancy, birth and infancy; improving parenting and family supports; strengthening early childhood development, learning and care; and strengthening community supports.

The second corner post is investment in human capital based on life-long learning. To start with, we need a seamless and universal system of support for families from the time a child is conceived until he or she enters kindergarten designed to promote learning and human development. Older children, strongly influenced by classroom and school environments, require ongoing educational and social supports to stay in school. But learning should never cease. Opportunities for continuing education should be available for every age group so that the generations will reinforce one another's strengths and not weaknesses.

The third corner post is social inclusion. The research suggests that successful communities are those that succeed in bolstering outcomes for their least advantaged children. We need to design programs and policies that integrate children of all backgrounds and abilities rather than segregate them from one another.

The fourth corner post is an increased capacity for program evaluation, monitoring, and research. The NLSCY has already proved itself invaluable as a source of reliable data. We need to continue and expand it as well as examine policies derived from the results to see if they are making the intended difference.

For a structure to be stable, however, its corner posts must be erected on a solid foundation, and there can be no better foundation for a family-enabling society than the United Nations Convention on the Rights of the Child, ratified by Canada in 1991. Respect for children is implicit in the research that is collected in this book and also in the conclusions that have been drawn from the findings. However, respect for children must be made explicit if the family-enabling society we would like to see constructed is to have positive results for vulnerable children. In its Preamble, the Convention recognizes "that the child, for the full and harmonious development of his or her personality should grow up in the family environment, in an atmosphere of happiness, love and understanding" and also "that the family, as the fundamental group of society … should be afforded the necessary protection and assistance so that it can fully assume its responsibilities within the community." The Convention goes on to affirm that children have inherent rights as human beings and that they are individuals with a growing need for autonomy.

Families need to understand the deep commitment they owe the children under their care and use their authority wisely; the rest of us must recognize our own obligations. For only when their rights are fully respected will the most vulnerable of children be able to grow up "prepared for responsible life in a free society, in the spirit of understanding, peace, tolerance, equality of the sexes, and friendship among all peoples" (UN Convention on the Rights of the Child, art. 28).

—THE HONOURABLE LANDON PEARSON
The Senate of Canada Advisor on Children's Rights

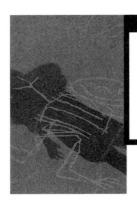

Acknowledgements

VULNERABLE CHILDREN is part of an ongoing and evolving research program concerning Canadian children, a program that is only partially represented by the papers in this volume. Work on this volume began more than four years ago with a training program at the University of New Brunswick. The program aimed to teach scholars who were in the early stages of their careers some of the more advanced statistical methods applicable to analyzing data from the National Longitudinal Survey of Children and Youth (NLSCY). These scholars worked closely with members of the NLSCY Expert Advisory Committee to bring together a set of papers about the factors that affect children's development, funded by the Applied Research Branch of Human Resource Development Canada (HRDC). This work engendered a strong network of scholars who are dedicated to conducting policy relevant research on issues affecting the lives of Canadian children.

I am greatly indebted to the Applied Research Branch at HRDC, which provided funding for this research program. When the analyses for this volume were at an early stage, HRDC held a workshop that brought together many of the people who are at the forefront of developing social policy for children in Canada. Later, when the work was close to completion, HRDC sponsored a national conference to showcase NLSCY research on Canadian children and families. These meetings included representatives from the federal government, provincial and municipal governments, non-government and voluntary organizations, social workers, educators, parents, and youth. I am grateful for their feedback, which contributed immensely to this work.

I am especially grateful to Allen Zeesman, who provided continuous support for this project since its inception. He provided feedback on the work at every stage and contributed many key ideas that have helped to bring the findings more directly to bear on Canadian social policy. He focussed our attention on a simple question: "How many vulnerable children are there in Canada?" This led to the development of a "vulnerability index" for Canadian children. The index, which considers a child to be vulnerable if he or she had poor outcomes in either the cognitive or behavioral domains, has proven a useful policy tool because it provides a means of describing the extent of variation in childhood vulnerability among provinces, communities, and neighbourhoods, as well as a way to monitor children's outcomes over time. The NLSCY and the development of the Canadian research network have stemmed from Allen's leadership in the area of child development.

Several other people at HRDC also contributed to this research. Satya Brink, Cindy Cook, and Susan McKellar deserve special thanks. They provided detailed critiques of each chapter and were particularly helpful in drawing out the policy implications of the findings.

The staff in the Special Surveys Division at Statistics Canada played a key role in collecting the NLSCY data and producing a final data set. Thanks are due especially to Gilles Montigny and Sylvie Michaud, who were charged with managing the operations of the survey. I am also grateful to Margo Shields, who helped me develop the measure of socioeconomic status, and to Scott Murray and Michael Wolfson, who gave helpful advice and considerable encouragement as this work was progressing.

I also appreciate the support received from the Spencer Foundation to study community and school effects on children's outcomes. The Foundation's support was key to developing an infrastructure for research on child development at the University of New Brunswick, which enabled our researchers to examine community effects in more detail and begin a research program that brings geomatic techniques to bear on questions about community and school effects.

The Canadian Institute for Health Information also provided funding in support of research relevant to understanding variation among communities in health outcomes. This support, through the Canadian Population Health Initiative, helped to cast this work in a broader context and led to similar work concerned with health outcomes, particularly childhood obesity. I am grateful for their support of our research in this area.

I am also grateful to the Canadian Institute for Advanced Research for its support of the NB/CIAR Chair in Human Development at the University of New Brunswick. This support afforded me the time and opportunity to work with colleagues from across Canada. I also want to thank my colleagues in the Human Development Program of the CIAR, who offered invaluable advice on this project.

Many of the staff at the Canadian Research Institute for Social Policy contributed to this volume in many ways: offering advice, editing drafts, and providing technical assistance. Thanks are owing especially to Sandy Harris, Marie-Andrée Somers, and Elizabeth Sloat, who helped with this volume from start to finish. Their support has not only been invaluable to this work but has also contributed to the training activities of the network and to the development of a long-term research program on child development at the University of New Brunswick.

I would also like to thank Leslie Vermeer for her careful editing of this volume, and the other staff at the University of Alberta Press who contributed to its publication.

My wife, Ann, contributed to this work in many ways. As an artist and teacher, she knows well the anguish and joys of the creative process and understands my enthusiasm for academic work. And as the mother of our three children, Alison, Maya, and Andrew, she appreciates the many challenges that parents face every day. Thus, after listening to the ideas and reading drafts of the chapters, she was able to provide suggestions that helped ground this work in the lives of the mothers and teachers who participated in our survey, and of all those dedicated to giving our children the best possible start. I am ever grateful for her encouragement and support.

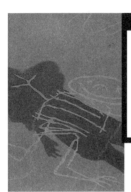# Contributors

RAYMOND BAILLARGEON is Research Scientist at the Centre de Recherche de l'Hôpital Sainte-Justine and Department of Psychiatry, Université de Montréal.

MICHAEL H. BOYLE is Professor, Department of Psychiatry and Behavioural Neurosciences, and a member of Canadian Centre for Studies of Children at Risk, McMaster University.

SUSAN DAHINTEN is an Assistant Professor in the School of Nursing and Canadian Child and Youth Research Network Scholar at the University of British Columbia.

RUTH CHAO is an Assistant Professor in Psychology at the University of California, Riverside.

SARAH CONNOR is a Senior Analyst with the Health Analysis and Measurement Group at Statistics Canada.

CYNTHIA COOK is a Research Data Centre Analyst for Statistics Canada and is a member of the HRDC Canadian Child and Youth Research Network.

WENDY M. CRAIG is an Associate Professor in the Department of Psychology at Queen's University.

MARTIN D. DOOLEY is Professor of Economics at McMaster University, and is affiliated with the Canadian Centre for the Study of Children at Risk.

GEORGE FREMPONG is an Assistant Professor of mathematics education at York University.

CLYDE HERTZMAN is Director of the Human Early Learning Partnership at UBC, a CRC Chair in Population Health and Human Development, and a Fellow of the Canadian Institute for Advanced Research.

CHRISTA JAPEL is a researcher at the Research Unit on Children's Psychosocial Maladjustment at the Université de Montréal.

JENNIFER JENKINS is a Professor in the Department of Human Development and Applied Psychology at the University of Toronto.

DAN KEATING is the Atkinson Professor of Early Child Development and Education, Department of Human Development and Applied Psychology, Ontario Institute for Studies in Education, University of Toronto; and Fellow and Director of the Human Development Program, Canadian Institute for Advanced Research.

DAFNA KOHEN is an Assistant Professor in the Department of Health Care & Epidemiology, University of British Columbia and a Senior Research Analyst at Statistics Canada.

JANE LAW is a Research Associate at the University of Cambridge.

ELLEN L. LIPMAN is a member at the Canadian Centre for Studies of Children at Risk and Associate Professor in the Department of Psychiatry and Behavioural Neurosciences at McMaster University.

PIERRE MCDUFF is a Research Analyst for PRIMASE at the Psychology Department, Université de Montréal.

LYNN MCINTYRE is Professor and Dean of the Faculty of Health Professions at Dalhousie University.

FIONA MILLER is a Staff Psychologist in the Child Psychiatry Program at the Centre for Addiction and Mental Health, Clarke Division.

CLAUDE L. NORMAND is a freelance research scientist who collaborates regularly with the Research Unit on Children's Psychosocial Maladjustment at the Université de Montréal.

DAVID R. OFFORD is the Director of the Canadian Centre for Studies of Children at Risk and Professor Emeritus, Psychiatry and Behavioural Neurosciences, at McMaster University.

RAY DEV. PETERS is Professor of Psychology and Research Director of the Better Beginnings Better Futures Research Coordination Unit at Queen's University.

YVONNE RACINE is Research Co-ordinator of the Canadian Centre for Studies of Children at Risk and a Research Associate in the Department of Psychiatry and Behavioural Neuroscience at McMaster University.

ELIZABETH SLOAT is a Researcher with the Canadian Research Institute for Social Policy and Assistant Professor in the Faculty of Education at the University of New Brunswick. She is is a member of the HRDC Canadian Child and Youth Research Network.

MARIE-ANDRÉE SOMERS is a Researcher at the Canadian Research Institute for Social Policy at the University of New Brunswick. She is currently completing graduate studies in applied statistics at the University of Oxford.

RICHARD E. TREMBLAY is the Canada Research Chair in Child Development, the Director of the Centre of Excellence on Early Childhood Development, and the Molson Fellow of the Canadian Institute of Advanced Research.

J. DOUGLAS WILLMS is the Canada Research Chair in Human Development and the Director of the Canadian Research Institute for Social Policy at the University of New Brunswick. He is the NB/CIBC Fellow of the Canadian Institute of Advanced Research.

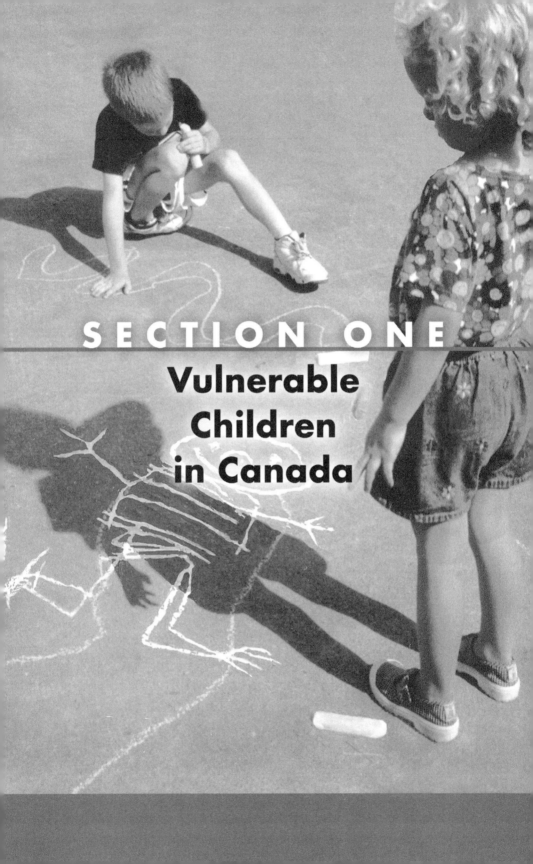

SECTION ONE

Vulnerable Children in Canada

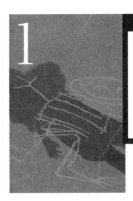

A Study of Vulnerable Children

J. DOUGLAS WILLMS

ALL CHILDREN IN CANADA LIVE WITH RISK. They are susceptible to disease and injury, and as they grow and learn they face numerous challenges that threaten their mental and physical well-being. Some children face greater risk because they must cope with unduly negative life experiences, such as racial and ethnic prejudice, inadequate parenting, family violence, and poverty. Considerable research has been done to identify and quantify the prevalence and importance of these risk factors. However, despite the existence of such risks, most children grow up healthy in most respects. Even among those children who face multiple risks, most do well in terms of the cognitive, behavioural, social, and health outcomes that concern parents, educators, and the broad policy-making community.

For the first time in Canada, the National Longitudinal Survey of Children and Youth (NLSCY) has made it possible to measure and analyze a wide range of developmental outcomes. Thus, we can begin with the empirical observation that a child has a significant problem in some developmental domain. We have decided to refer to children who are experiencing an episode of poor developmental outcomes as *vulnerable*. These children are vulnerable in the sense that unless there is a serious effort to intervene on their behalf, they are prone to experiencing problems throughout their childhood and are more likely to experience unemployment and poor physical and mental health as young

3

adults. Then, knowing that we have identified a group of children of great interest to Canadians, we proceed to look at the main determining factors of vulnerability.

Although the NLSCY is the first national survey to provide such a wide range of developmental outcomes and determinants, it builds on previous research inspired by the same approach. The Ontario Child Health Study, conducted in the early 1980s, gives us some indication of the number of Canadian children who are vulnerable. Its aim was to estimate the prevalence of various types of emotional and behavioural disorders among children in Ontario (Boyle et al., 1987). It found that 16.5 percent of children aged 4 to 11 were classified as having some form of psychiatric behaviour disorder (Offord et al., 1987). In addition to anti-social behaviours, children who suffer from behaviour disorders tend to have associated impairments such as poor school performance and difficulties in getting along with their parents, peers, and teachers (Offord & Waters, 1983).

Moreover, studies that have followed children with behaviour disorders into adulthood estimate that about 40 percent of them continue to suffer from psychological and social difficulties as adults (Offord & Bennett, 1994). The children in the Ontario study who were identified as vulnerable are now young adults. We expect that many of them continue to have social and psychological problems, and that their difficulties constitute one of the major challenges that their children now face. But children growing up today also face other challenges. Even more than the generation before them, they must adapt to environments that are continually changing: because the structure of families is becoming more diverse, because the nature of work is being transformed, because the roles of schools and the church have been called into question, and because our institutions are being restructured brought on by technological advances. Children with psychological and social difficulties find it more difficult to cope in this changing environment, and thus the prevalence of vulnerable children may be greater than it was two decades ago.

This book asks whether we can significantly improve the quality of life for vulnerable children and ensure that all children achieve their potential. Can we help them meet the challenges they face? Can we provide avenues for success, so that more children will lead healthy, productive lives? Can we identify schools and communities that are more successful in improving the life chances of vulnerable children, and determine what it is that they are doing differently?

The aim of this book is to provide information that will help parents, teachers, social workers, administrators, and other professionals address these questions. It provides reviews of the research on these questions and attempts to address them by analyzing data from the NLSCY. The analysis establishes how many children in Canada are vulnerable and determines where the majority of them reside. It also identifies the main aspects of family, school, and community life that contribute to healthy child development.

■ Canada's First National Longitudinal Study of Children and Youth

The overall purpose of the NLSCY is to develop a national database on the characteristics and life experiences of Canadian children as they grow from infancy to adulthood. The NLSCY provides for the first time a single source of data for the study of child development in context, including the diverse life paths of normal development. The study was developed to support evidence-based policy and is building a human-development view of the early decades of life. The Applied Research Branch of Human Resources Development Canada directs and funds the NLSCY in partnership with Statistics Canada. The Branch plays a leadership role in supplying information to the federal government for both the formulation of policy relating to children and initiatives such as the National Children's Agenda.

The analyses in this book use data from the base year of the study, which were collected between December 1994 and May 1995. The target population comprised all Canadian children from newborn to age eleven. The participating households were selected from the sampling frame of Statistics Canada's Labour Force Survey, which is representative of Canada's population.[1] The achieved sample included 22,831 children from 13,439 households. The survey is being repeated every two years, following the 1994/95 cohort. In addition, children aged 0 to 23 months are added for each new cycle and followed until age 4–5, in order to continue studying the early years.

One of the distinguishing features of the NLSCY is that it has particularly good data on the age, sex, and marital status of all members of the household, and how these factors are related to each other, as well as on the income and employment of the children's parents or guardians. Thus, the final data set includes much more accurate information on family background than is typically available in most large-scale studies. Also, as in any study of this type, the people who elect to participate tend to differ somewhat in their demographic

Figure 1.1

Survey instruments of the NLSCY

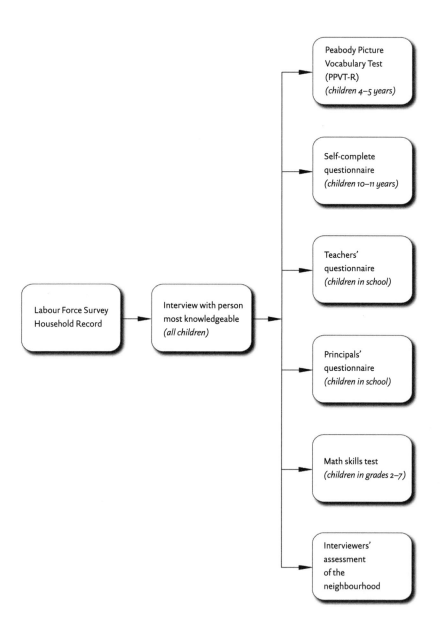

characteristics from those who decline. However, because prior information was available on the Household Record, Statistics Canada could accurately estimate the bias due to non-response and construct sampling weights that can be used to adjust for this bias.

An overview of the survey instruments used in the NLSCY is displayed in Figure 1.1. The principal instrument was an interview in the home with the person most knowledgeable (PMK) about the children in the family. In the vast majority of cases, the PMK was the child's mother. Interviewers followed a closed-format schedule to collect extensive data on the health and well-being of the children, the physical and mental health of the parents, parenting styles, family functioning, and characteristics of the neighbourhood. During the home interview, children aged four or five were administered the Peabody Picture Vocabulary Test, a test of receptive vocabulary. Children aged ten and eleven were asked to complete a self-administered questionnaire, which included items pertaining to their friendships and family relations, and their experiences in and out of school. Following the home visit, if permission was received from the PMK, a questionnaire was administered to the principals and teachers of school-age children, and a brief mathematics skills test was given to children in grades two through seven. Further details of the NLSCY survey are provided in the *NLSCY Overview of Survey Instruments for 1994–95, Data Collection, Cycle 1* (Statistics Canada, HRDC, 1995).

Another distinguishing feature of this study is its nested design. The sampling strategy identified households with a child of the targeted age. For the selected households, the sample included the target child and all other children who were newborn to age eleven, up to a maximum of four children. In families with more than four children, four were randomly selected. Because of the nested design, we were able to examine variation in outcomes among children within the same families. For example, we could ask whether certain outcomes tend to "run in families"; for example, if one child is physically aggressive, is it likely that other children in the family will also be physically aggressive? The families studied in the NLSCY are also nested within neighbourhoods and wider communities. Although the sampling design did not explicitly sample families within neighbourhoods or communities, it is possible to locate families within enumeration areas (small census areas that comprise about 400 families) and merge the data describing children and their families with data from the 1991 census. This provides a means to examine neighbourhood and community effects.

■ Socioeconomic Gradients and Childhood Vulnerability

One of the most persistent and pervasive findings of the research on human development is that people's health and well-being are related to socioeconomic factors such as income, occupational prestige, and level of education. A *gradient* exists: people at the lower end of the social hierarchy tend to have a greater frequency of illness and disease and a shorter life span than those further up the social hierarchy (Hertzman, 1999; Kunst & Machenbach, 1992; Marmot et al., 1991; Power, Manor & Fox, 1991; Wilkinson, 1992). Similarly, children and youth growing up in families of lower socioeconomic status tend to do less well in academic pursuits, are less likely to complete secondary school, and tend to be less successful in entering the labour market than those from more advantaged backgrounds (e.g., Raudenbush & Kasim, 1998; Willms, 1986). The relationship between children's outcomes and family income is so firmly entrenched in our understanding of human development that the term "children at risk" has almost become synonymous with "children living in poverty." It is easy to presume that the majority of children with behaviour problems or with poor academic results are from low-income families; or conversely, that children with model behaviour and strong academic skills are predominantly from affluent families. Yet this is not always the case. Although there may be a gradient associated with family income, we often encounter children from poor families who have been remarkably resilient, and children from affluent families who have behavioural or academic difficulties.

Our strategy for studying childhood vulnerability is through an analysis of *socioeconomic gradients*. A socioeconomic gradient is simply the relationship between some developmental outcome and socioeconomic status (SES). It can be depicted as a line on a graph with some developmental outcome on the vertical axis and SES on the horizontal axis. Thus, a gradient can be described by its *level*, its *slope*, and the *strength* of the outcome–SES relationship. In this study, the analysis of gradients entails an examination of the relationships among a wide range of children's educational and health outcomes, and a number of socioeconomic factors, including family income, parents' occupational status, and parents' level of education. In adopting a gradient perspective, we attempt to integrate two dominant approaches to the study of childhood vulnerability in a way that captures the strengths of each approach.

One approach, which tends to be characteristic of the line of inquiry taken by psychologists and economists, emphasizes the independent actions of individuals, particularly parents. It assumes that parents make independent decisions to achieve what they perceive to be best for their family—what economists call "maximizing utility" (Coleman, 1988). For example, parents with more resources are more likely to play often with their children, buy them more educational toys, read to them more often—generally provide them with a richer environment—than are parents with fewer resources. The focus of research in this vein is on identifying "risk factors" associated with vulnerability, such as poverty or growing up in a single-parent family.

Another approach, more characteristic of the work of sociologists, stresses the importance of social context in shaping, constraining, and redirecting individuals' actions (Coleman, 1988). Researchers following this line of inquiry maintain that people's individual choices depend on the norms of their immediate community and the kind of social support available to them. Taking the example above, the amount of time parents spend with their children would be shaped by the culture of the neighbourhood, friendship networks, and the nature of support in the workplace and wider community. Much of the research on social context has been ethnographic. It has striven to describe the "culture" of workplaces and communities in which people interact, and to determine whether this culture supports or discourages individual and group actions. Work following this line of inquiry has also attempted to uncover the structural and organizational features of schools, workplaces, and communities that contribute to the relationship between developmental outcomes and social class.

■ An Example of Socioeconomic Gradients

When data from the first cycle of the NLSCY were being collected, Canada participated in the International Adult Literacy Survey (IALS), a large international study conducted by the Organization of Economic Cooperation and Development (OECD) and Statistics Canada, with support from the OECD, the European Union Task Force for Human Resources, and the United Nations Educational, Scientific and Cultural Organization (UNESCO). The aim of the IALS was to determine the level and distribution of literacy among the adult populations of participating countries, and to investigate and compare the factors relevant to literacy. The study entailed intensive testing and interviewing of a representative sample of adults in each country.

The IALS embraced a broad definition of literacy, which is reflected in the literacy test. The test covers three domains of literacy: prose, document, and quantitative. Prose literacy refers to people's ability to read, understand, and use information from written texts such as stories and editorials. Document

Figure 1.2

Quantitative literacy scores for youth aged 16–25

International Adult Literacy Study, 1994

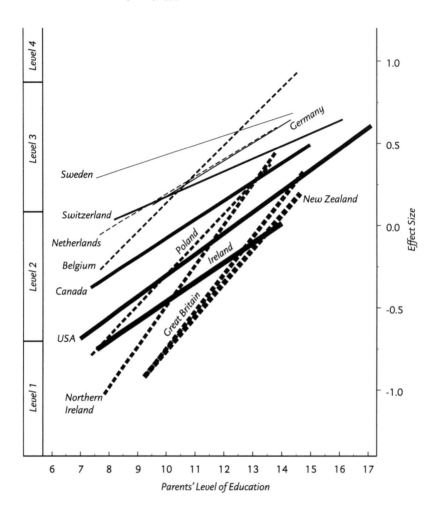

literacy entails locating and using information from texts such as job applications, transportation schedules, and maps. Quantitative literacy requires the ability to find, understand, and use mathematical operations embedded in texts: weather charts found in the newspaper, for instance, or the calculation of interest using a loan chart.

As part of the IALS research program, I examined the socioeconomic gradients for youth aged 16–25 in 12 of the participating countries. The socioeconomic gradients for quantitative literacy skills are displayed in Figure 1.2. The achievement test scores for each participant were expressed as a scaled score, which were grouped into five literacy levels ranging from simple tasks at Level 1 to complex literacy tasks at Level 5. The y-axis indicates these levels of literacy skills. The x-axis indicates the level of education of the youth's parents. (For more detail, see Willms, 1999a).

This simple analysis shows that countries vary considerably in their literacy skills, and that each country has a socioeconomic gradient—a significant relationship between literacy skills and parents' education. But the analysis also reveals an important pattern: the countries with high levels of literacy skills tend to be those with shallow gradients; that is, the gradients converge at higher levels of SES. This pattern indicates that youth from advantaged backgrounds tend to have relatively strong literacy skills in every country, whereas youth from less advantaged backgrounds tend to vary considerably in their skills. This pattern of converging gradients is also evident among provinces in Canada (1997), states in the US (Willms, 1999a), and to some extent, among communities within Poland (Willms, 1999b).

An analysis of gradients within countries is also concerned with the gaps in social outcomes between minority and majority groups, and between males and females. A study of the IALS data for youth in Northern Ireland, for example, indicated that Catholic youth lagged behind Protestant youth in their literacy skills, but this inequality was especially pronounced for males from lower socioeconomic backgrounds (Willms, 1998). Similarly, within Canada, the gap between males and females is fairly small in most provinces, but in two provinces, British Columbia and New Brunswick, there is a disproportionate number of males from lower socioeconomic families with inadequate literacy skills (Willms, 1997).

■ **Research Questions**

These findings from the IALS, and other research on socioeconomic gradients, raise a number of questions that underlie this study.

1. At what age do socioeconomic gradients for children's outcomes become evident? Do gradients become stronger as children get older? For example, are there gradients in the prevalence of children with

low birth weight? Are gradients evident in children's early temperament? Do gradients become stronger as children progress through
school?

2. Are gradients stronger for some outcomes than for others? Is the relationship with socioeconomic status stronger for behavioural outcomes
than it is for cognitive outcomes, at each age, from birth to age eleven?

3. Are gradients linear or curvilinear? In Canada and the US, the relationship between health outcomes and income is curvilinear. Studies
based on large samples of US adults have revealed that among people
earning less than $20,000, an increase in income is associated with
markedly better health outcomes; but among those earning more than
$20,000, an increase in income has only a marginal effect on their
health status (Epelbaum, 1990; House et al., 1990; Mirowsky & Hu,
1996). Canadian data indicate that the income gradient is also curvilinear, but the change in slope appears to be more gradual (Boyle &
Willms, 1999; Wolfson, Rowe, Gentleman, & Tomiak, 1993; Wolfson
et al., 1999). We know relatively little about the form of the relationship between family income and children's behavioural and cognitive
outcomes. This question is particularly relevant to policies
concerning the redistribution of income through income transfers to
targeted groups.

4. Are there groups within our society whose children are particularly
vulnerable? This study examines several issues pertaining to single
parents and teenage mothers. The analyses determine whether the
prevalence of vulnerability is higher in these groups, and if so,
whether it is related to the income and education of the mothers. The
book does not address issues pertaining to the challenges facing
immigrant families; however, the principal analyses include measures
of immigrant status as statistical controls. The sample sizes in the
NLSCY are too small to examine adequately the effects associated
with being an immigrant. Also, participation rates for immigrants may
have been affected by the challenges associated with learning a new
language and living in a new culture, and if so, it is likely that the
sample of immigrant families was not nationally representative. For
similar reasons, we do not examine differences associated with race
or ethnicity, and nor do we examine issues concerning Aboriginals,
because the NLSCY sample did not include Aboriginals living on
reserves.

5. Which components of SES are most strongly related to children's social and cognitive outcomes? Previous research on gradients has emphasized family income, but other factors, especially the level of parents' education and their occupational status, have been shown to play an important role. This study attempts to unpack SES into its constituent components and determine the relative importance of these components for a range of outcomes at different ages.

This set of five questions underpins economic "investment theory." It posits that parents invest resources in their children's development, which yield returns in their children's future well-being (Becker, 1981; Becker & Tomes, 1986). The investments include expenditures on homes in certain neighbour-hoods, quality daycares and schools, books and educational materials, nutrition, and health care. Thus, we expect that socioeconomic factors such as family income and parents' level of education will be related to children's develop-mental outcomes. Previous research has emphasized the importance of these factors; however, few studies have been able to examine the magnitude of the socioeconomic effects or their functional form. Although socioeconomic factors influence children's outcomes, they do not tell us much about why some children do better than others. Therefore, we need to understand the role of parenting and other influences to understand socioeconomic gradients. This need leads us to a second set of five questions, concerned with what actu-ally happens within families, schools, and communities that affects children's outcomes.

1. What factors mediate the relationships between childhood outcomes and socioeconomic status? *Mediating factors* describe the underlying processes through which one variable influences another (Baron & Kenny, 1986). For example, suppose we observe a relationship between academic achievement and family income. Our goal then would be to uncover the underlying processes through which income influences achievement. For example, do parents in low-income families tend to be less engaged with their children on a daily basis than parents in high-income families? If so, do levels of engagement explain, at least partially, why there is an income gradient? If this is the case, then engagement would be considered a mediating factor.

A dominant theory about why there are socioeconomic gradients in children's outcomes is that unemployment and low family income lead to stress and depression, and these factors affect parents' ability to provide adequate care and guidance to their children. Another theory, to which we do not subscribe, is that a "culture of poverty" exists among parents of lower SES. The argument follows that children from disadvantaged backgrounds have poor behaviour and academic achievement because their parents have values and norms for behaviour that make them bad role models (see Mayer, 1997). In this study, the analyses examine the potentially mediating effects of four major factors: parenting styles, engagement, family functioning, and maternal depression.

2. Do children's outcomes vary among communities? Recall that gradients are comprised of a *level,* a *slope,* and a measure of their *strength.* This question pertains to average levels of children's outcomes and to the prevalence of vulnerability. We are concerned whether some communities are more effective than others. The term *community* is notoriously difficult to define. We use it in this study to refer to a group of citizens who are collectively concerned about the health and well-being of their children. From this perspective, there are multiple and overlapping communities, such as neighbourhoods, church communities, municipalities, classrooms, schools, and school districts. The data do not allow us to examine variation in outcomes for all of these types of communities, but we are able to examine whether the prevalence of childhood vulnerability varies among neighbourhoods, schools, cities, and provinces.

3. Does the relationship between childhood outcomes and socioeconomic status vary among communities? This question pertains to the *slopes* of the socioeconomic gradients. Are some communities particularly successful in abating inequalities in children's outcomes? The analysis is especially concerned with testing the *hypothesis of converging gradients.* If the hypothesis holds, it would indicate that children from affluent backgrounds tend to fare well in any community, whereas children from disadvantaged backgrounds are more prone to vulnerability in certain communities.

4. Are there characteristics of communities that account for observed differences in average levels of outcomes or prevalence rates? If some communities do have better developmental outcomes for children, or a lower prevalence of childhood vulnerability, what factors contribute to this difference? An important question is whether children are

more vulnerable if they live in low SES communities, other factors being equal. Our hypothesis is that children from poor families who live in especially poor communities are more likely to be vulnerable than children from poor families living in communities with average or above-average levels of income. This is the *hypothesis of double jeopardy*. Another pertinent question is whether communities vary in their outcome because of varying levels of social support. Our hypothesis is that some communities are successful in reducing childhood vulnerability because a higher level of trust and co-operation exists among their citizens, and because there are formal and informal networks that support parents in raising their children.

5. Are there characteristics of communities that account for observed differences in the relationship between childhood outcomes and socioeconomic gradients? Two communities could have the same average level of outcomes but differ in the slopes of their gradients. This is the case, for example, for Ireland and Northern Ireland in Figure 1.2. Ireland has a shallower gradient, indicating fewer inequalities among youth from advantaged and disadvantaged backgrounds. We want to know at a more local level—for example, at the levels of schools, cities, and provinces—whether certain policies and practices lead to a more equitable distribution of outcomes.

■ An Index of Vulnerability

During the course of this study, I had the opportunity to present preliminary findings to some of the provincial and federal leaders who are responsible for developing public policies that affect Canadian children. They asked a seemingly simple question: "How many vulnerable children are there in Canada?" Answering this question is not so simple: it requires us to classify children as either "vulnerable" or "not vulnerable." In doing so, we must decide which outcomes are relevant, and for each outcome where the cut-off score should be set to define vulnerability. We can easily see that the answer to this question depends on which outcomes comprise the index and where we arbitrarily set the cut-off score on the various scales used to characterize these outcomes.

Nevertheless, I attempted to establish reasonable criteria for each of the scales across the age range and provide estimates of the number of vulnerable children. This led to the development of a "vulnerability index": a summary measure of the prevalence of vulnerable children. This measure turns out to be a useful device. First, in the same way that a composite measure of SES is useful for examining and describing the relationships between outcomes and a broad array of socioeconomic indicators, a vulnerability index is useful for examining the relationships associated with childhood vulnerability. Second, the vulnerability index provides a means of describing the extent of variation in childhood vulnerability among communities and among provinces. Third, the index provides a means for making general comparisons of the effects of various factors across studies and across ages. Fourth, it provides a means of monitoring children's outcomes over time. When the vulnerability index is used for these purposes, I am less concerned that its construction requires rather arbitrary decisions concerning the cut-off points. As long as the same criteria are used across studies, and from year to year, it does not matter so much whether the cut-off points yield relatively low or high estimates. Also, in the same way that the factors comprising economic indices (such as the consumer price index or the TSE 300) are modified periodically, the content of the vulnerability index can be changed as the NLSCY evolves.

■ Summary of This Book

Vulnerable Children is made up of five sections. Chapter 2 discusses some of the theories underlying the two dominant approaches to the study of childhood vulnerability and identifies some of their shortcomings. It then provides a review of the literature on social class gradients, with an emphasis on recent research pertaining to educational and health outcomes. Finally, it provides a summary of the statistical methods employed in the book and an expository discussion about the issues pertaining to the assessment of socioeconomic gradients.

Chapter 3 begins with a description of the measures used to characterize children's outcomes and define vulnerability. It then gives estimates of the prevalence of vulnerable children for Canada and each of the ten provinces.

Chapter 4 presents the main findings regarding the nature and magnitude of socioeconomic gradients in children's outcomes. The analyses examine the shape of the distribution across various outcomes and determine the extent to which gradients vary across outcomes and age groups. Further analyses discern the extent to which the prevalence of vulnerable children varies among neighbourhoods and communities. It then tests the two hypotheses described above, the hypothesis of converging gradients and the hypothesis of double jeopardy. Finally, it asks whether measures of social support can explain some of the variation in prevalence rates among neighbourhoods and communities. The concepts of "relative risk" and "attributable risk" are introduced, which are used to assess the relative importance of the various factors comprising socioeconomic status.

In the analysis in Chapter 4, I wanted to address the question of *where* the majority of vulnerable children in Canada live. However, the data available for individual neighbourhoods and for most cities are too sparse to provide accurate estimates, and in some cases, providing these estimates might compromise the confidential nature of the data. Therefore, we took an indirect approach. We used information on the relationship between children's outcomes and SES to identify a set of key predictors that influence children's outcomes. We then classified the more than 40,000 Canadian enumeration areas used in the 1991 Census into eight "types," based on the set of key predictors. We linked the NLSCY and Census data, and estimated the prevalence of vulnerable children in each "type" of community. Finally, we displayed the community types on colour maps of the provinces and five major cities. Although these maps do not directly display the prevalence of vulnerable children in each area, they provide an indication of the *expected* prevalence, given the socioeconomic characteristics of the area. These are presented in Appendix B: Provincial Maps Depicting Neighbourhood Types (see pp. 389–406).

■ Early Signs of Vulnerability

The NLSCY is the first national study to collect data from a large representative sample of mothers on their perceptions of their children's behaviour. For children up to age three, the interviewers asked the PMK—usually the mother—a series of questions about their child's temperament (e.g., fussy/irritable, unresponsive, or unadaptable). The analyses in Chapter 5 determine the dimensions of temperament that parents find difficult and examine how reliably these traits can be measured. This discussion also determines how strongly these aspects of temperament are correlated with other markers of vulnerability.

One of the special features of the NLSCY is that up to four children from the same family were selected and then assessed on a number of different behavioural and emotional characteristics. Siblings from two to eleven years of age were assessed on anxiety, emotional disorder, hyperactivity, inattention, and physical aggression. Most studies of children's behaviour problems, except for twin studies, have targeted only one child per family. Chapter 6 is concerned with whether childhood behavioural problems, such as physical aggression, tend to "run in families." The analyses describe the concentration of physical aggression among siblings in Canadian families and evaluate the extent to which the level at which a younger child manifests physically aggressive behaviours can be predicted from an older sibling's level of physical aggression.

Recent research has demonstrated that there is a relationship between a family's socioeconomic characteristics and the peri- and post-natal outcomes of their children. Chapter 7 provides a profile of the pregnant women in Canada who drink or smoke during pregnancy and determines whether certain characteristics, such as age, education, or income, are related to whether women use these substances during pregnancy. The analysis then examines the relationship between the peri- and post-natal outcomes and SES, and determines the extent to which the use of alcohol and cigarettes during pregnancy mediate these relationships.

Life in the family

A number of studies have demonstrated a link between schooling outcomes and "parenting styles": children tend to have superior schooling outcomes if their parents display a more "authoritative" parenting style, as opposed to an "authoritarian" or "permissive" style. An authoritative style is characterized by responsiveness and warmth, and a careful monitoring of children's behaviour, whereas authoritarian parents tend to be over-demanding, less flexible, and lacking responsiveness and warmth. Permissive parents tend to be overly indulgent and set few limits on children's behaviours. Chapter 8 examines whether the relationship between children's outcomes and SES is mediated by differences in parenting styles. The analysis goes beyond previous work in this area by examining how different dimensions of SES are related to schooling outcomes and parenting styles.

A substantial proportion of Canadian children display behavioural, emotional, or psychological disturbances which are sufficiently serious to warrant concern for their present functioning and future developmental health. In order to guide policy and practice intended to address these problems, it is important to gain a better understanding of the sources of these developmental disturbances. Chapter 9 uses data describing the sample of 2- and 3-year-olds and 8- and 9-year-olds to investigate the role of parenting, especially as it relates to the effects of SES on behavioural disorders during childhood.

A cliché of modern life is "spending quality time" with one's children. Do some children succeed, despite social and economic difficulties, mainly because their parents are more engaged in their lives? Is there really such a thing as "quality time," or is it simply a question of the amount of time parents are engaged in play or school activities with their children? Chapter 10 addresses questions concerning parental involvement as a mediating factor between SES and child outcomes, and takes on some of the thorny issues involved in balancing work and family life. This chapter is likely to be of particular interest to parents as well as the policy community, as the findings confront some of our perceptions about the way in which family income and social class influence children's outcomes.

The manner in which family members relate to one another clearly has an effect on children's behaviour. As part of the interview with the children's parents, the NLSCY included an extensive set of questions pertaining to "family functioning," with questions about communication, approaches to problem-solving, role conflicts, affective involvement, and alcohol use. Chapter 11 examines parents' responses to these questions and determines the relationship between family functioning and children's behaviour problems. It provides estimates of the extent to which family dysfunction influences behaviour and examines whether it is a key mediator of the relationship between child behaviour problems and SES.

As many as five percent of the Canadian adult population suffers from depression at any given time. One of the most consistent findings in the literature on depression internationally is that women are twice as likely as men to be affected by clinical depression. Clinically depressed parents experience greater difficulty in nurturing their children, which in turn affects the children's outcomes. The analyses in Chapter 12 estimate the prevalence of depressed mothers in Canada and examine the extent to which SES increases the likelihood of experiencing a depressive disorder. The analyses determine the relationship between maternal depression and parenting styles, and examine the effects of maternal depression on child outcomes.

Chapter 13 is concerned with the effects of growing up in a single-parent family. One in ten Canadian families with children are headed by single mothers, and we know that on average these families are of lower SES. We also know that children from single-mother families are at increased risk of emotional and behavioural problems, but the interpretation of this finding and its implications for policy are far from obvious. Most previous analyses of the effects of single-parenthood have treated single-parenthood as a separate entity. But single parents differ in their employment status, income, and levels of education. The analyses in this chapter establish a typology for single-parent families, based on their socioeconomic characteristics. It uses this typology to examine the effects on children's outcomes associated with growing up in a single-parent family.

A significant number of Canadian mothers had their first child during their teen years. Research in the US has shown that the children of teenage mothers are more prone to experiencing emotional and behavioural disorders and falling behind in academic achievement. Yet we know relatively little about the children of teenage mothers in Canada. Chapter 14 examines the socioeconomic circumstances of teen mothers in Canada and compares them to older mothers in their parenting styles, engagement, family functioning, and levels of depression. The analyses then examine whether the children of teen mothers are especially prone to behavioural disorders or low academic achievement.

Life at school

Changes in family structure and employment patterns have led to an increased use of different types of child-care arrangements for preschool-aged children. The last decade has seen particularly sharp growth in the employment rates of women with children and in the number of dual-earner families. In 1994, 63 percent of Canadian women with children were employed, and in the last 25 years the number of dual-earner families has almost doubled. These changes in work patterns have implications for child care; however, little is known about the characteristics or circumstances of parents that influence families' child-care choices. Chapter 15 examines the types of child-care arrangements used by Canadian parents for their preschool-aged children, the characteristics and circumstances of parents that influence child-care choices, and the impact of different types of child-care arrangements on children's school readiness.

Findings from recent national studies of school achievement indicate that the Canadian provinces differ in their academic achievement. Are these differences also evident in the data describing mathematics achievement in the NLSCY? If so, why do some provinces do better than others? Can we identify aspects of school quality that might explain these differences? Chapter 16 compares the results from the NLSCY with the findings from three other national studies. It then examines the extent of variation within and between schools in each province and determines how much of the variation is attributable to students' family background and various factors describing the students' classrooms and schools.

Early adolescence is a period of important emotional, social, and cognitive transitions. Most striking are the rapid and dramatic biological changes that occur during this period. Pubertal maturation signifies impending fertility and an important milestone in the adolescent's life. Chapter 17 examines the relationship between child and family characteristics and the level of pubertal development of pre-adolescent girls. The analysis furthers our understanding of the environmental and personal characteristics associated with early pubertal maturation.

Chapter 18 examines the role that peer relationships have on adolescents' outcomes. Peers play a central role in the social development of children and adolescents. During early adolescence there are significant changes in the significance and structure of the peer group, and the nature and the quality of adolescent peer groups have long-term consequences. Researchers have linked positive peer relationships to positive mental health outcomes at mid-life, while negative peer interactions, such as peer rejection, are related to both internalizing and externalizing behaviour problems such as drug use and delinquency. Thus, peers play an important role in shaping adolescents' psychological and social development.

Investing in children

Meeting the needs of vulnerable children is high on the federal and provincial government agendas. Local communities have also recognized the need to improve and extend the services offered to families and children. During the past few years, the efforts of provincial governments to monitor the effectiveness of schools have increased pressure on principals and teachers to restructure schools and modify classroom practices in ways that will improve children's academic outcomes. And perhaps more than ever before, parents have been bombarded with information that stresses the importance of good parenting, particularly during the few years of life when the neural capacity of the brain's cortex is being developed. The large community of Canadians who are concerned about the health and well-being of children are continually asking how they can best invest their time and resources to meet their needs and ensure that they have the best possible chances of success.

The aim of the last two chapters is to synthesize what has been learned about childhood vulnerability from this extensive analysis of the first wave of data from the NLSCY and to discuss the implications of the findings for Canadian social policy. Chapter 19 begins with a presentation and discussion of a final set of analyses, which attempt to integrate the several factors that influence childhood vulnerability at the levels of the family, school, neighbourhood, and community. These macro-level analyses provide a backdrop against which to place the more detailed findings presented in the separate chapters. It is used therefore to summarize the main findings of the book. Chapter 20 tackles a fundamental question underlying this research: can socioeconomic gradients be altered through policy and reform, and by the efforts of concerned citizens? This chapter calls for a renewal of Canadian social policy by building an infrastructure for a family-enabling society.

NOTES

1   The NLSCY sample did not include children living in institutions (approximately 0.5% of children newborn to age 11) or children living on First Nations reserves. Children living in the northern territories were surveyed in a different process, and these children are not included in the data file that was used for the analyses in this book.

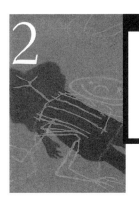

A Gradient Approach to the Study of Childhood Vulnerability

2

ELIZABETH SLOAT &
J. DOUGLAS WILLMS

■ Two Lines of Inquiry Into Childhood Vulnerability

THE DOMINANT APPROACH to the study of childhood vulnerability has aimed to identify risk and protective factors that are related to undesirable life outcomes, including problems associated with illness and disease, behaviour, and cognitive development. The assumption is that if these factors can be identified, then social programs can be designed to reduce risk factors and strengthen protective factors, thereby reducing the prevalence of vulnerable children. For example, smoking is a risk factor for disease, and considerable effort has been directed toward abating the factors that prompt adolescents to start smoking and the frequency of their cigarette use (Bruvold, 1993; Chassin, Presson, Sherman & Edwards, 1992; Johnson & Gerstein, 1998). Similarly, studies have shown that breast-feeding contributes to the emotional well-being of a child and is a protective factor against infectious diseases (Hanson et al., 1985; McIntyre, 1996). Thus, we would expect community-health programs that encouraged mothers to breast-feed and gave them the necessary information and support would reduce childhood vulnerability. We refer to studies that take this approach as *risk and protective factor research*.

Another approach, which we refer to as *social context research*, has attempted to discover whether children's life outcomes are affected by the characteristics of the group to which they belong, independent of their individual social and

23

economic background (Manski, 1993; Willms, 1986). Recent research on teen pregnancy serves as a good example. It suggests that peer groups have strong effects on teenagers' decisions about sexuality and child-bearing, which are independent of the teens' social and economic background (Crane, 1991; Evans, Oates & Schwab, 1992). Social context research is also concerned with whether certain structural features of institutions or communities affect children's and adolescents' outcomes. With respect to breast-feeding, for example, researchers would be concerned with whether mothers working in low-income jobs encountered less flexible work arrangements, making it more difficult to breast-feed their babies.

This chapter has four sections. The first two sections discuss the theoretical underpinnings of risk and protective factor and social context research respectively, identify some of the themes emerging from each type of research, and describe some of the limitations of the two approaches. The third section defines socioeconomic gradients and discusses some of the salient issues concerning their definition. The fourth section indicates how an approach that focusses on socioeconomic gradients within communities can integrate risk and protective factor and social context research in a way that addresses many of the limitations identified in the first two sections.

■ Risk and Protective Factor Research

Most investigations of childhood vulnerability have been based on *investment theory*, an economic theory attributed mainly to Nobel laureate Gary Becker (Becker, 1981; Becker and Tomes, 1986). The model presumes that children receive an endowment from their parents, which includes biological attributes coded in DNA, as well as a cultural endowment determined by their parents' norms, values, and preferences; their income and wealth; and their access to resources. Parents invest time and money in the human capital of their children, primarily through expenditures on education and health care. Although the emphasis of investment theory has been on the transmission of earnings and wealth from one generation to the next, the idea that children's social, emotional, and intellectual development depends on parents' investments is firmly rooted in the child-development literature.

Other theories root the cause of childhood vulnerability in family and parenting practices (McLoyd, 1990; Patterson, DeBarsyshe & Ramsey, 1989). Children are more likely to have behaviour problems or poor cognitive development if their parents are unsupportive, unresponsive, or lacking warmth. When parents are depressed or undergo periods of severe stress, they are more likely to be tense and irritable with their children and become less engaged in activities that contribute to their children's emotional and intellectual development. Marital relations become strained, and the family generally does not function as a cohesive unit. These pressures also affect children's development. According to this theory, low income and periods of unemployment are important not because parents have fewer material resources to invest in their children but because poverty contributes to parents' ability to parent. The most important risk factors associated with this theory pertain to parents' "style" of parenting, the extent to which parents are engaged with their child, the cohesiveness or adaptability of the family, and maternal depression.

A more pessimistic version of this theory is the so-called culture of poverty theory, which holds that poor people have certain values and norms of behaviour that are inconsistent with success in the dominant culture (see the discussion in Lareau, 1989). For example, poor parents may view certain aberrant behaviours as acceptable or place less emphasis on the importance of schooling. They may also be less inclined to become involved in their child's education, as they consider it to be the purview of the school. This theory is particularly controversial, especially when it is used to explain differences among racial or ethnic groups, because it does not incorporate structural features of society such as economic and social segregation, racism, and discrimination, which contribute to the sense of hopelessness and futility felt by families living in poverty.

The task for researchers working in this paradigm, whether they subscribe to investment theory or to one of the theories pertaining to stress and parenting, seems straightforward: to determine which risk (or protective) factors best predict whether a child will experience a particular life outcome.[1] For example, Rumberger (1995) attempted to identify the risk factors associated with whether adolescents were vulnerable to dropping out of school before completing grade ten. His research, based on a large representative sample of American youth, identified a set of 28 factors that might potentially be related to whether children were prone to dropping out. The set included the sex and ethnicity of the children, the child's family background, prior academic achievement, and a comprehensive list of factors describing the child's behaviour and attitudes towards school. The analysis found that nearly all of the 28 factors were predictive of whether a child left school before graduation.

Shortcomings of risk and protective factor research

Although the risk and protective factor approach appears straightforward, it has several shortcomings that make it difficult to draw inferences for informing public policy or influencing the practices of parents and educators. One is that the approach treats all risk factors with equal status, even though some risk factors are more strongly predictive of an outcome than others. For example, in the case of Rumberger's (1995) research on dropping out of school, students who had failed a grade at some point in their school career or who had changed schools for any reason were more likely to drop out. But failing a grade had a much stronger predictive relationship than changing schools; in fact, it was by far the most important risk factor. Most research on risk factors employs some form of multiple regression, a statistical technique used to describe the relationship between an outcome variable and a set of predictor variables. Multiple regression analyses reveal the strength of the predictive relationships; however, in the transfer from research to practice, emphasis is often placed on the list of risk factors without due attention to the strength of the relationships.

A related problem is that most risk factors seem to have relatively weak effects when considered in isolation, but their combined effect can be strong. We also suspect there are periods when the effects of certain risk factors are probably more acute, especially during the critical periods when a child's brain and nervous system are being developed (Cynader & Frost, 1999). Also, some effects appear to be cumulative. For example, several recent studies have shown that children growing up in poor families are more vulnerable to experiencing a broad range of undesirable life outcomes. The degree of vulnerability depends on both the extent and the duration of poverty (e.g., Duncan & Brooks-Gunn, 1997; Mayer, 1997).

Theoretically, for some trait of an individual or a characterization of their behaviour to be considered a risk factor, it must both precede and be predictive of the undesirable life outcome (Kraemer, et al., 1997). For example, having low academic achievement in the early grades is a risk factor for dropping out of school. The trait clearly precedes the undesirable outcome, and numerous studies have shown that children with low academic achievement are more likely than those with average or high achievement to drop out of school (Audas & Willms, 2000). The term *predictive*, however, is normally used to indicate a causal link between the trait or behaviour and the undesirable outcome. A causal link means that if we could alter an individual's trait or behaviour, the likelihood of that person experiencing the undesirable behaviour would also change.

However, this may or may not be so; for example, in the case of drop-outs, some other factor that is correlated with achievement, such as behaviour problems, may be underlying the low academic achievement/dropping out relationship. Researchers tend to use the term *risk factor* rather loosely, without providing a strong theoretical basis or evidence of a causal relationship. This problem is related to two further shortcomings of risk and protective factor research.

Many risk factors are difficult or impossible to manipulate, while others can feasibly be changed through intervention. Rumberger's risk factors for dropping out included factors that cannot be changed, such as a child's sex and ethnicity; factors that would be difficult to change, such as parents' income and education; and factors that could be improved, such as the actions of teachers, the amount and quality of homework that children do, or the extent to which parents participate in school-related activities. Rumberger was careful to distinguish between unalterable factors such as sex and ethnicity, and intervening factors associated with student behaviour and achievement; but many researchers fail to make this distinction. In many cases unalterable factors dominate the list of risk factors related to life outcomes, perhaps because factors such as sex, ethnicity, and family structure are easier to measure than factors that capture the subtle processes associated with policy and practice. This shortcoming of risk and protective factor research may contribute to the pessimistic conclusion, shared by many people, that the life course of vulnerable children is largely predetermined by family background.

Another shortcoming of risk and protective factor research pertains to the clarity with which causal models have been specified. Researchers and practitioners frequently use the term *children at risk* to refer to children who possess one or more risk factors that are predictive of a host of undesirable outcomes. But this term may make us ask, at risk of what? Part of the problem is that the set of relevant risk factors depends upon what outcome is being considered. It also depends upon the age of the child. For example, the risk factors associated with conduct disorders during the pre-school years are quite different from those associated with conduct disorders among teens. Similarly, the risk factors associated with the use of illegal drugs during early adolescence differ from those associated with conduct disorders. The problem is even more complicated, because undesirable outcomes at one developmental stage (such as being hyperactive during elementary school) may be risk factors for undesirable outcomes at a later developmental stage (such as low academic achievement during the intermediate school years). Thus, unless the research is grounded in a theoretical model, it is impossible to distinguish between negative life outcomes and the processes that lead to them.

Some researchers have dealt with these shortcomings by approaching questions about vulnerability from the opposite direction. Rather than focussing on a particular life outcome and striving to identify all relevant risk factors, they have examined the effects of a single risk factor on a wide range of life outcomes. Research on the effects of poverty is the most prominent example (Duncan & Brooks-Gunn, 1997; Mayer, 1997). In many respects this approach is preferable in that it tends to have more immediate implications for public policy. However, it does not help us identify the relative importance of particular risk factors at each developmental stage.

■ Social Context Research

Two prominent sociologists, Pierre Bourdieu and James Coleman, have stressed the importance of the resources inherent in social relationships and how these resources can be used to realize particular goals. Their work provides some useful starting points by distinguishing between different forms of capital. They used the economic term *capital* as a metaphor for the cultural and social assets of a family that lead to better educational and socioeconomic outcomes. Both maintained that economic capital—income and material wealth—is an important part of the equation linking family background to outcomes. With respect to educational outcomes, for example, families with greater economic capital are better able to have one parent remain at home during the child's formative years, afford high-quality daycare and schooling, and provide high-quality learning materials. But for Bourdieu and Coleman, economic capital alone cannot account for the strength of the relationship between social class and outcomes or explain why the learning outcomes of children with similar economic capital varied across social settings. They maintained that other forms of capital contributed directly and interacted with economic capital to strengthen the relationship between social class and outcomes.

Bourdieu's (1977) concept of cultural capital has to do with the values, forms of communication, and organizational patterns possessed by the dominant class. It is a familiarity and knowledge of high-status culture and a disposition—which he calls *habitus*—toward certain linguistic and social competencies. With respect to children's learning outcomes, for example, schools are middle-class institutions that value middle-class language patterns, authority relations, and organizational structures (Lamont & Lareau, 1988). Thus, children raised in middle-class environments possess the "cultural capital" that enables them to appreciate the curriculum and adapt to school life. Their parents feel comfortable relating to school staff and being involved in school activities. They possess a wide range of strategies for achieving what they perceive to be best for their child (Lareau, 1987).

Economists have used the term *human capital* to embody the skills and cumulative learning essential to economic growth (Becker, 1964; Schultz, 1963). Coleman (1988) distinguished between human capital and *social capital*, which "comes about through changes in the relations among persons that facilitate action" (Coleman, 1988, p. 100). He elaborated on the concept by identifying three forms in which social relations become an asset that brings about action. The first form—obligations, expectations, and trustworthiness of structures— relies on the notion of social exchange: when one individual does something for another, an expectation is established in the giver and an obligation in the receiver. The number of these expectation-obligation relationships present in a social structure will vary depending on how trusting people are of one another in the particular environment. The second form entails the informal networks that people use to obtain information. For example, within a neighbourhood, parents discuss matters such as when and how to enroll in certain programs for their children, who they consider to be the best teachers, and how best to manage problems they encounter with their school (Echols & Willms, 1995). The third form of social capital is norms and effective sanctions. Coleman argued that when these are effective, they constitute an especially potent form of social capital. For example, norms for high academic achievement established by rewards from the community outside the school reinforce and strengthen the mission of the school. More generally, effective norms lead people to work for the public good.

Limitations of social context research

Researchers studying the effects of social context have a particularly difficult task. First, they must define and operationalize the relevant group or community, thereby setting boundaries on who is considered in the set of social relationships. For example, the relationships among children and adults within a neighbourhood arguably affect children's development, but does the neighbourhood include people on the same street, people within a two- or three-block radius, or people in some larger geographical entity made up of several hundred families (e.g., Sampson, Morenoff & Earls, 1999)? Next, researchers must attempt to understand the subtle processes associated with the "culture" of the group that affect individuals' behaviours. But even if these problems can be adequately addressed, they must consider the many complex interactions that can occur between individuals and groups: for example, the effects of the social relationships inherent in groups may have positive effects on some types of individuals and negative effects on others.

There are many ways that the term *community* can be defined. Indeed, most people are members of several overlapping communities. For example, school-age children are usually members of their immediate family, their extended family, their neighbourhood, their classroom, and their school. They can also be members of sports teams, church groups, or hobby clubs, just to name a few. The values and norms of these communities, and the actions of the people in them, all exert some influence on children's behaviours. Geographic communities, such as neighbourhoods, are difficult to define and operationalize, in that this entails somewhat arbitrary decisions about boundaries. But even when community membership can be relatively well defined, its effects can vary as new leaders emerge and group dynamics change. The problems associated with defining community have probably caused many researchers to steer clear of this line of inquiry or to conclude that the effects of community are inextricably tied to their history and local context, such that generalizations about the effects of social context are impossible.

② The second major shortcoming of social context research is that the constructs associated with "culture" are usually difficult to define and measure. For example, most educators would agree that the "disciplinary climate" of a classroom or school has important effects on children's learning. But disciplinary climate is a multi-faceted construct: it includes dimensions associated with the norms and values of the school, the extent to which rules and expectations are understood and accepted, and perceptions about whether disciplinary measures are fair and consistent (Willms, 1992a). Therefore, understanding the disciplinary climate of a school requires an understanding of the wider culture of the school and its historical context. Attempts to measure disciplinary climate in quantitative studies have shown that there is usually considerable variation among students' and teachers' assessments within the same school (Pallas, 1988; Ma & Willms, 1995). Measuring constructs such as "social support" is probably even more difficult, because the construct is less tangible and because people's perceptions of what constitutes support probably vary a great deal among individuals, and even from day to day for the same person.

A number of researchers have recently tried to operationalize the concept of social capital as elaborated by Coleman (e.g., Furstenberg & Hughes, 1995; McLanahan & Sandefur, 1994; Morgan & Sörensen, 1999; Sampson et al., 1999). Coleman suggested that intergenerational closure—the extent to which parents in a community know each other and, in particular, know the parents of their children's friends—is an important element in generating social capital. When social networks are closed, parents are better able to discuss their child's behaviour and academic achievement with other parents, monitor their child's actions, and establish norms (Furstenburg et al., 1995). They are also better able to share information, lobby for institutional change, and generally provide greater social support. The second critical element generating social capital is reciprocal exchange, which refers to the extent to which parents interact by sharing information and resources, especially in ways that reinforce child-rearing. Thus, it is not enough for parents to know the parents of their child's friends; they must interact with them in ways that facilitate action. Sampson et al. (1999) expand the concept to include informal social control and mutual support of children: social capital is more abundant when neighbours are willing to intervene on behalf of other children and take responsibility for all children in their community. Recent research on social context has been concerned mainly with the degree of social closure, the frequency of social exchanges, and whether these interactions are purposeful, such as sharing information or enforcing norms.

③ The third shortcoming of social context research is that it has generally failed to capture interactions between factors at the micro and macro level. For example, schools with a high degree of closure may have more parents volunteering to assist in classroom activities. But if parent volunteers are used mainly for assisting less-able pupils, their effect may be much stronger for some children than for others. In addition, some aspects of social context can have strong effects at the individual level but relatively weak effects at the group or community levels (e.g., Ho & Willms, 1996; Carbonaro, 1999).

■ A Definition of Socioeconomic Gradients

In our study, the term "socioeconomic gradient" is used to refer to the relationship between a social outcome and socioeconomic status for the individuals of a specific community. The social outcome can include any measurable trait describing an individual's well-being. It can be a continuous measure, such as children's test scores on an academic achievement test, or a dichotomous outcome, such as whether or not a child has a specific disease. The term *socioeconomic status* (SES) refers to the relative position of a family or individual in an hierarchical social structure, based on their access to, or control over, wealth, prestige, and power (Mueller & Parcel, 1981). SES is usually operationalized as a composite measure of income, level of education, and occupational prestige (Dutton & Levine, 1989; Mueller & Parcel, 1981). Our interest in this study is primarily on outcomes describing children's behaviour and cognitive development, and how these are related to family SES. Therefore, our measure of SES is a statistical composite of the income, level of education, and occupational prestige of the child's parents (Willms & Shields, 1996). Factors such as family structure (e.g., single- vs. two-parent family), immigration status, or whether the mother was a teenager when the child was born are not considered a dimension of SES, even though they are usually correlated with SES in most populations.

The meaning of SES and its constituent components are central to understanding socioeconomic gradients. The notion of a variable is that it attributes the variable possession of a phenomenon to each member at a particular level of analysis. For example, family income is variably attributed to each family in the National Longitudinal Survey of Children and Youth (NLSCY). When researchers make comparisons across jurisdictions (e.g., neighbourhoods, communities, provinces, countries) or over time, they normally assume that the attributed phenomenon has an invariant hermeneutic status across all families. This is what McPherson and Willms (1986) called the *atomistic assumption*. This assumption is easily challenged, because part of the causal and hermeneutic significance of one person's status depends on that of others in their neighbourhood, community, or country. For example, a family income of $50,000 likely has a much different meaning for a family living in rural Newfoundland than for a family living in downtown Toronto. This is not simply a matter of taking into account the cost of living or calculating disposable income, but concerns the actual meaning of family income as part of what we call SES. The same criticism applies to other components of SES. Indeed, it applies to all variables in any statistical analysis: even a straightforward variable such as family size can differ in its meaning across groups and over time (e.g., Willms, 1992b). Consequently, we can argue that the attributes that identify one person's SES are purely relational and cannot be defined except in relation to other individuals. A researcher adopting this stance must specify the relevant community, yet there is no logical reason to presume this should be the local neighbourhood, the municipality, or the province. In the extreme, one could argue that the relational aspect of SES, or any variable, depends on many different sets of relationships, which can only be understood through intensive ethnographic study.

There are examples of these two approaches in the recent work of the Canadian Institute of Advanced Research (Keating & Hertzman, 1999). Case, Griffin and Kelly (1999) defined father's education relationally in describing the socioeconomic gradients for some of the countries that participated in the Third International Mathematics and Science Study, whereas Willms (1999) used an atomistic approach to depict socioeconomic gradients for the IALS. A case can be made for either approach, and each has its limitations. In this volume, variables are treated atomistically. We prefer this approach because it allows us to gauge the effects of variables in their absolute terms, such as discerning the effects associated with an increase in income of $10,000. If such an effect does exist, and varies among units, we can attempt to model that variation. This approach also allows us to make comparisons across small units, such as enumeration areas or schools.

The definition above states that a socioeconomic gradient is the relationship between an outcome measure and SES; like the relationship between any two variables, it can be weak or strong. We would like to have some means of assessing the relative strength of a relationship, so we could make comparisons across populations and over time, or perhaps compare the relative strength of gradients across outcomes. Strength is not straightforward. The problem is that a relationship may be strong in relative terms; for example, we might observe large differences in an outcome measure for children from families of low and high SES. But within either group, there could be considerable variation among children in their outcomes; that is, there may be many other factors contributing to children's scores on the outcome, such that SES has a fairly small effect in absolute terms. Thus, we really require two measures to assess the strength of a gradient. The two approaches are described in Sidebar 2.1.

The strength of socioeconomic gradients is also sometimes confused with the degree of inequality. Socioeconomic gradients refer to the relationship between an outcome and some measure of SES, whereas inequality refers to the extent to which wealth or income are distributed across members of a society. Although countries with relatively steep gradients may tend to have greater income inequality and those with gradual gradients may have relatively less income inequality, this is not necessarily the case.

The gradients depicted in Figure 2-1 are linear (i.e., a straight line); however, we do not presume this to be the case. A number of population health studies

The most common measure of association used in the social sciences is the correlation coefficient, also known, when regression analysis is used, as R-squared. R-squared denotes the proportion of variation in the outcome measure that is explained by the explanatory variable. Some analysts report the *unstandardized regression coefficient*, which is the expected change in the outcome measure for a one-unit change in the explanatory variable. The unstandardized regression coefficient is also a useful measure. In discussing this issue, we use a simple example of the relationship between children's vocabulary scores and family income.

Figure 2.1 displays two gradients based on hypothetical data, one which is relatively weak, the other which is fairly strong. The relationship between the two variables is modelled as a linear relationship: individuals' vocabulary scores are equal to some constant, plus some factor times family income, plus a residual unique to each individual. In this example, the constant for both gradients is 90, and the factor associated with family income is 0.2. This factor (0.2) is the unstandardized regression coefficient. In the case of a simple linear regression describing the

Figure 2.1A

The strength of a socioeconomic gradient

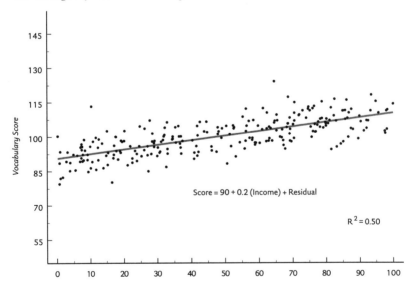

Score = 90 + 0.2 (Income) + Residual

$R^2 = 0.50$

relationship between two variables, the regression coefficient indicates the expected change in the outcome (Y) for a one-unit change in the explanatory variable (X). It expresses the strength of a gradient. For example, it indicates that for each $1000 increase in income, vocabulary scores will increase by 0.2 points. For someone interested in the potential effect of an income transfer payment, this is much more useful than a correlation coefficient or R-squared.

However, even though the regression relationships are identical for the two gradients, one relationship could be considered weak and the other strong, as the R-squared values are 0.10 and 0.50 respectively. In the case of the first gradient, the individuals' vocabulary scores are not tightly clustered around the regression line; but for the second gradient they are. Thus, R-squared is also an important indicator of the nature of the gradient.

In this example, the reason that the unstandardized regression coefficients are identical but the R-squared values differ is because the variation in vocabulary scores differs considerably. One could construct another example with the same coefficients and R-squared values, but with the variation in family income differing between the two cases and the variation in vocabulary scores being the same. Researchers often recalibrate either the outcome

Figure 2.1B

The strength of a socioeconomic gradient

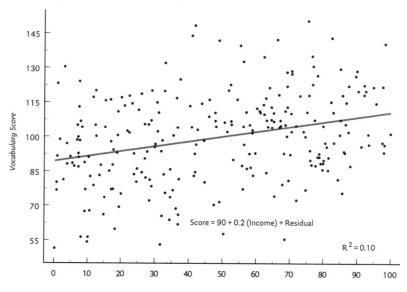

Score = 90 + 0.2 (Income) + Residual

$R^2 = 0.10$

measure or the measure of SES, or both, so that these measures are on the same scale across populations or studies. One strategy is to *standardize* the measures, so that they have a mean of zero and a standard deviation of one. When this is done, the regression coefficient (called the standardized regression coefficient) is equivalent to the correlation between the two variables, and its squared value is R-squared.

This seems to solve the problem, but it presents a new one. Suppose that the two gradients above depicted results for children in two Canadian provinces. The regression coefficient is the expected change in the outcome measure for a one-unit change in the explanatory variable. If both vocabulary scores and income were standardized, the regression coefficient would indicate the expected change in the vocabulary scores—expressed in standard deviation units for that province— for an increase in family income of one standard deviation. This is difficult to interpret, because the scale for vocabulary scores now differs for the two provinces, and the explanatory variable is no longer in dollars but in some other unit that also differs for the two provinces. Consequently, we maintain that an analysis of gradients should report both the unstandardized regression coefficient and R-squared. The unstandardized coefficient provides an indication of the *relative* importance of an explanatory variable, and the R-squared provides an indication of the overall (or *absolute*) strength of the relationship. These two statistics are analogous to the two statistics commonly used by epidemiologists to denote *relative risk* and *absolute risk,* which are appropriate when the variables are dichotomous.

have shown that the strength of the relationship between mortality and income, and between health status and income, diminishes with higher levels of income (Epelbaum, 1990; House et al., 1990; Mirowsky & Hu, 1996; Wolfson, et al., 1999; Wolfson, Rowe, Gentleman & Tomiak, 1993). The principal hypothesis is that after people have met their basic needs for food, clothing, and housing, further increases in income contribute only marginally to their health. Health status is also related to levels of education, and some researchers have argued that education and literacy may serve as alternative resources for income in affecting health status (Mosley & Cowley, 1991). Education and literacy may be especially important in low-income countries, in that levels of maternal literacy affect life expectancy at birth and the health of newborns (Sen, 1993). Within the US, socioeconomic factors are related to amount of physical exercise, nutrition, and smoking (Ross & Wu, 1995; Jacobsen & Thele, 1988; Winkleby, Jatulis, Frank & Fortman, 1992). The research has not examined in detail whether income and education interact in their effects on health, or the extent to which aspects of lifestyle mediate these relationships. It has also not considered the possibility of a dynamic relationship whereby low income causes poor health and poor health causes low income (Mirowsky & Hu, 1996).

This study is concerned with whether socioeconomic gradients for children's outcomes are linear or curvilinear. Unlike the growing body of research on health outcomes, there is little evidence that gradients are curvilinear for developmental outcomes; however, we want to test this hypothesis for two reasons. First, if the gradients for health status during infancy are curvilinear and if poor initial health status affects developmental outcomes such as temperament and language acquisition, then we would expect to observe a curvilinear gradient for these outcomes as well. Second, some of the processes that lead to curvilinear gradients for health may also apply to developmental outcomes. In families where parents are struggling to meet the basic needs of food, clothing, and shelter while trying to invest in the human capital of their children, small increases in income may have important effects on their children's development; whereas in families that have their basic needs met and are able to provide educational toys, reading materials, recreational programs, and so on, additional income may have relatively little effect on their children's outcomes. If the gradient is curvilinear, we want to know where it begins to level off, as this point has important implications for how we define poverty and how we attempt to abate it.

Two other aspects of the definition require elaboration. In the discussion of the limitations of social context research we noted that the term *community* is difficult—or in some sense impossible—to define, yet we cannot escape defining it operationally for the purpose of estimating gradients. If we can momentarily set theoretical definitions aside, we can invoke a means that is practical from an empirical perspective. The statistical modelling underlying this research typically entails some form of multiple regression analysis, whereby a dependent variable (e.g., children's mathematics achievement) is regressed on one or more independent variables (e.g., SES and other family background factors). An important assumption underlying traditional multiple regression is that the observations are independent; that is, the observations of one individual are not in any way systematically related to the observations of another individual. If two children come from the same family, the same classroom, or next door to each other, then their observations are not independent and the assumption of independence is violated. From this perspective, we could think of a community as a set of individuals whose social outcomes are inter-correlated but independent of individuals in other communities. This is not inconsistent with the definition offered in Chapter 1: a group of citizens who are collectively concerned about the health and well-being of their children. It also allows us to think of children as being nested hierarchically within communities, such that a child is a member of one and only one community. This notion does not fit well with the possibility of overlapping communities, but it provides a starting point from which we can make progress. Statisticians are developing complex statistical models that can handle data nested in a non-hierarchical structure (Goldstein, 1995), which would be appropriate for modelling data describing overlapping communities. However, these techniques are in their early stages of development.

Finally, the definition indicates that the gradient describes the outcome-SES relationship for individuals within a society. However, we are also interested in the strength and functional form of gradients within communities in a society, and how they are related to the overall socioeconomic gradient. For example, we could estimate the overall socioeconomic gradient for mathematics for a province, but each school within the province also has its own socioeconomic gradient. We could examine the relationships among these gradients and determine the average within-school gradient. Some of the most important educational policy issues, such as how students are allocated to schools within a community and to various school programs within a school, require an understanding of gradients at these levels of analysis (Willms, 1999). This statement also holds true with respect to socioeconomic gradients for provinces, cities, and communities defined in other ways.

■ Socioeconomic Gradients as an Integrating Framework

The study of socioeconomic gradients is not novel. Indeed, the relationships between health and SES and between educational/occupational attainment and SES have been a primary concern of researchers for decades (e.g., Bielby, 1981; Sewell, Hauser & Featherman, 1976). Some of the important features that distinguish this work from previous work are that (1) it focusses on outcomes rather than risk factors and encompasses a broad set of outcomes; (2) it systematically examines the strength and functional form of socioeconomic gradients; (3) it determines whether levels of outcomes and gradients differ among communities; and (4) it discerns whether particular aspects of family or community life explain why gradients exist. That is, it aims to further our understanding of the causal mechanisms and developmental pathways that lead to desirable social outcomes.

Our analytic approach integrates social context with risk and protective factor research in two stages. The first stage entails the estimation of socioeconomic gradients for all of Canada and separately within each province and community. These estimates allow us to examine the strength and functional form of socioeconomic gradients for each outcome and discern the extent to which gradients differ among communities. Knowing the extent to which communities vary in their outcomes and at what level (e.g., provinces, cities, neighbourhoods) is fundamental to social context research. If the cultural and social capital of a community affect children's outcomes, then we would expect to observe differences among communities in outcomes that are independent of the socioeconomic backgrounds of the families within them. Finding these differences entails the use of a statistical technique called hierarchical linear modelling (HLM), which is introduced in Chapter 4 and used there to examine variation among provinces, cities, and neighbourhoods. HLM is used again in Chapter 16 to examine variation among schools. The technique allows us to test the three specific hypotheses pertaining to variation among schools in their gradients. These are discussed in Sidebar 2.2.

The second stage involves identifying the important risk and protective factors that mediate SES. Mediating variables describe processes that explain why certain relationships hold (Baron & Kenny, 1986). For example, the time parents spend engaged with their children is a potential mediator of the relationship between SES and children's outcomes. One of the primary aims of this study is to determine the extent to which various aspects of community and family life mediate the relationship between SES and childhood outcomes.

The role of mediators is depicted in Figure 2.3. The SES gradient is the large arrow in the middle of the diagram between SES and outcomes (path A). The potential mediating factors are classified into two groups. One emphasizes family life and includes family functioning, parenting styles, maternal depression, and the extent to which parents are engaged with their children in learning and play activities. The second group includes factors associated with the institutions and wider contexts that affect children's development. The aim of our analyses is to determine whether SES is related to aspects of community and family life (paths B and C), and whether these factors affect children's outcomes (paths D and E). If these relationships are evident, then the

Sidebar 2.2

Three hypotheses about differences among communities

Researchers have tended to refer to socioeconomic gradients without much attention to the unit of analysis or whether the gradients depict the relationship for a country, a province or state, or a specific community. Indeed, much of the literature on income gradients in health has been based on data aggregated to the national or state level. However, the estimates of gradients depend on the unit of analysis and the population considered. Here we attempt to bring some clarity to this issue by testing three specific hypotheses.

HYPOTHESIS OF DIFFERENCES AMONG COMMUNITIES IN THEIR OUTCOMES: This hypothesis holds that communities differ in their childhood outcomes. We expect this hypothesis to hold, because we know there is wide variation among Canadian communities in their socioeconomic characteristics and, given the relationship between many childhood outcomes and SES, childhood outcomes probably also vary among communities. However, we are less certain that communities vary in their outcomes after we take account of children's family background. For example, if we ask "How do children with average socioeconomic background fare in

Figure 2.2A

Diverging socioeconomic gradients

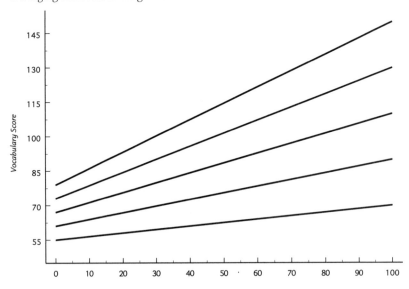

 Vocabulary Score (y-axis)

each community?", the answer may be that the variation among communities is relatively small. Thus, we wish to test the hypothesis that communities differ in their childhood outcomes, even after taking into account the socio-economic characteristics of the families in those communities.

HYPOTHESIS OF CONVERGING GRADIENTS: This hypothesis is concerned with whether the slopes of the socioeconomic gradients vary significantly among communities and, if so, whether the gradients diverge or converge at higher levels of socioeconomic status (see Figure 2.2). If gradients converge, it suggests that communities do not vary substantially in their outcomes for children from high-SES families, whereas they vary considerably for children from low-SES families. The reverse is true if gradients diverge at higher levels of SES. We state the hypothesis as the hypothesis of converging gradients, because the findings for socioeconomic gradients pertaining to youth literacy indicate a strong pattern of converging gradients among countries and among states and provinces (Willms, 1999).

HYPOTHESIS OF DOUBLE JEOPARDY: This hypothesis holds that children in low-SES families are more likely to be vulnerable, but

Figure 2.2B

Converging socioeconomic gradients

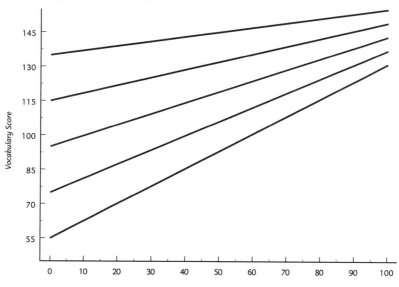

children from low-SES families who also live in low-SES communities are especially vulnerable. The hypothesis stems from research pertaining to the effectiveness of schools. A number of studies have found that children with average SES tend to have better schooling outcomes if they attend a school with high average SES, rather than a school with low average SES (e.g., Brookover et al., 1978; Rumberger & Willms, 1992; Shavit & Williams, 1985; Summers & Wolfe, 1977; Willms, 1985, 1986). Thus, the "context" of the school has an effect on a child's outcomes, over and above the effects associated with the child's individual family background. The contextual effect—the benefit associated with attending a high-SES school—is generally attributed to positive peer interactions, parental involvement, high expectations of school staff and parents, and a positive disciplinary climate in the school. Moreover, there is some indication that this effect is particularly pronounced for children from low-SES families (Willms, 1985), and therefore we refer to this as the hypothesis of double jeopardy.

community and family factors are considered mediators of the socioeconomic gradient. Technically, for a variable to be considered a mediator of a socioeconomic gradient, the variable must be significantly related to SES (e.g., parenting styles would need to be significantly related to SES—path C), the outcome of interest would need to be related to the variable (e.g., children's early vocabulary skills would need to be related to parenting style—path E), and the strength of the relationship between SES and the outcome (path A) must be reduced (or even eliminated) when the mediating factor is taken into account.

The integration of social context and risk factor research addresses many of the limitations of the two approaches, as described above. First, it forces us to define "community" in operational terms. Even though any single definition can be easily challenged, the analytic approach provides a means for systematically examining whether outcomes vary among geographic or institutional entities. Thus, we can estimate the extent of variation among communities defined in various ways and discern whether this variation can be explained by various features of the communities. Second, the gradient provides a succinct description of the relationship between childhood outcomes and SES. A nation's social policy is mainly concerned with the social outcomes of its most vulnerable citizens, and most governmental policies involve the redistribution

Figure 2.3

Mediators of socioeconomic gradients

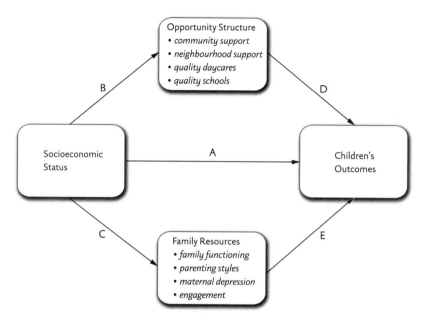

of income to targeted groups or the provision of services and in-kind benefits (see Chapter 19). Thus, an analysis of gradients can provide a simple test of whether social policies or specific interventions are successful: do they raise and flatten socioeconomic gradients?

Third, the approach explicitly separates socioeconomic factors from other risk factors and provides a means for judging the relative importance of various risk factors. Instead of asking only whether a potential risk factor is statistically significant, we can ask, "What is the magnitude of the effect of the risk factor on childhood outcomes for children of varying socioeconomic backgrounds?". From the perspective of interventions, we could ask, "If we could eliminate the risk factor, what effect would that have in raising and flattening socioeconomic gradients?". Fourth, the approach combines micro-level analyses at the individual level with macro-level analyses at the levels of neighbourhood, school, and larger community. We can ask, for example, whether some communities are successful because they have higher levels of social support or whether some schools are successful because they have better qualified teachers. One can also construct models that incorporate interactions between the micro and the macro; for example, whether the relationship between behaviour disorders and SES within a community is affected by the availability of recreational facilities, or whether the gap in academic achievement among children with differing family backgrounds is attributable to the practice of streaming students according to their ability.

The gradient approach does not address the difficult issues concerning the measurement of culture. The NLSCY includes a measure of neighbourhood social support and a number of variables describing school and classroom climate. However, these data are rather thin compared to the detailed information at the levels of the child and family. Although most researchers studying childhood development recognize the importance of community context and local culture, the research in this vein is in its early stages. Human Resources Development Canada has recently embarked on a large-scale study of community factors affecting children's development during the pre-school years. This study—called *Understanding the Early Years*—will collect detailed community-level data in at least fifteen Canadian communities. These data will be linked to the NLSCY so that researchers will soon be able to assess the effects of community-level variables on children's development. The analyses in this volume confirm the importance of integrating risk factor and social context research, as children's healthy development and well-being depends on both the families and communities in which they live.

NOTES

1   In this discussion, we use the term "risk factors" as a shorthand for "risk and protective factors," because from a methodological perspective, the absence of a protective factor, such as a baby not being breast-fed, can be treated in analysis as a risk factor.

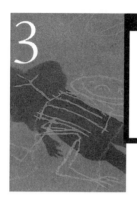

The Prevalence
of Vulnerable
Children

J. DOUGLAS WILLMS

WE USE THE TERM *VULNERABLE CHILDREN* in this volume instead of *children at risk* because our focus is on outcomes rather than on factors that predict outcomes. The term *at risk* carries with it the concept of risk factor, which can be *any* factor that precedes and is predictive of an undesirable life outcome. Thus, children at risk could include children living in poverty, children of particular racial or ethnic origins, or boys or girls, depending on the outcome being considered. One can estimate the prevalence of children at risk of experiencing certain outcomes, but it is impossible to estimate the prevalence of children at risk in a general sense.

Vulnerable also connotes susceptibility—that is, that one is *exposed* or liable to experience some undesirable life outcome in the future. We would have been on safer ground simply to refer to children who have low scores on assessments of cognitive development and behaviour. However, the term *vulnerable* fits in many respects because children who display poor cognitive and behavioural outcomes during their early years *are* vulnerable to unemployment and poor physical and mental health as young adults. In fact, poor cognitive or behavioural outcomes as a child are a much better predictor of most future life outcomes than low socioeconomic status (SES) or other prominent risk factors (Power, Manor, & Fox, 1991; Pulkkinen & Tremblay, 1992; Rodgers, 1990). Thus, poor cognitive and behavioural outcomes as a child can be considered the most important risk factor. We also prefer "vulnerable" because it implies that circumstances can improve through children's own efforts and with the support of their families and others in their community. Indeed, most children with poor cognitive and behavioural outcomes during their early years prove to be remarkably resilient and are not destined to lives of poverty or poor health (e.g., Werner & Smith, 1992). Instead, we think of these children as vulnerable in the sense that, unless there is a concerted and prolonged effort to intervene on their behalf, their chances of leading healthy and productive lives are reduced.

One of the strengths of the National Longitudinal Survey of Children and Youth (NLSCY) is that it includes a comprehensive set of measures that describe children's cognitive and behavioural outcomes for a nationally representative sample. Most school-based studies of children, such as the National Educational Longitudinal Study of US high school students (National Center for Education Statistics, 1989), emphasize schooling outcomes, especially academic achievement, factors pertaining to family background, and the organizational and instructional features of schooling. By contrast, longitudinal studies of children's behaviour typically aim to assess the effects of an intervention and therefore emphasize the collection of detailed data at specific sites. Thus, the samples tend to be small and not nationally representative; the Montreal Longitudinal Experimental Study (Tremblay, Mâsse, Pagani, & Vitaro, 1995) is a good example. In a national survey, however, the data covering both outcomes and processes are broad, but not as deep as is possible in a small study. National surveys provide a set of basic indicators, which often need to be supplemented with data from other sources.

Thus, although coverage of cognitive and behavioural outcomes can be viewed as a strength of the NLSCY, the survey also has important limitations. For example, the only measure of cognitive outcomes for children aged six to eleven in the first year of the study is a short test of children's computational skills in mathematics. This measure covers only a small area of the domain of cognitive ability. The second and subsequent cycles of the study include a test of reading ability and a more extensive test of mathematics skills, but even with these we cannot claim to have adequately covered the domain of cognitive skills. The measures of children's behaviour are arguably more comprehensive but also subject to the same criticism. (These limitations are discussed further at the conclusion of this chapter.)

Our definition of vulnerability does not include physical or mental handicaps, learning disabilities, or health problems. We consider these to be potential risk factors but not outcomes *per se*. For example, children with a physical handicap face many challenges every day, and having a physical handicap is certainly predictive of particular life outcomes. But as such, like gender or ethnicity, a handicap is a risk factor for particular outcomes, not an outcome in itself. Therefore, unless a handicapping condition or health problem resulted in a behaviour problem or poor cognitive development, the child would not be considered vulnerable in this study.

■ Measures of Development and Markers of Vulnerability

A critical issue for this study was whether to use continuous or categorical measures to describe children's outcomes. For example, we could describe children's receptive vocabulary using the scaled scores on the Peabody Picture Vocabulary Test (PPVT) or decide upon a threshold score and denote with a dichotomous variable (i.e., zero or one) whether or not a child had a PPVT score below the threshold. From an analytical perspective, continuous measures are preferable when the measurement instruments are adequate to furnish scores that can be ordered and have equal intervals. Information is lost if we perform any manipulation that transforms the scores into a dichotomous variable or into a variable with multiple categories.

However, a strong case can be made for using categorical variables in a study concerned with social policy and childhood vulnerability. Social policy is concerned mainly with achieving particular outcomes for society as a whole, but especially for targeted groups. The policy community is interested in whether certain policies or interventions reduce the percentage of people who score below some critical cut-off score. For example, policy discussions focus on issues such as reducing the incidence of newborns with low birth weight or providing programs for illiterate citizens, even though birth weight is certainly a continuous measure and most researchers treat literacy skills as a construct with an underlying continuous distribution (e.g., Organization for Economic Co-operation and Development and Statistics Canada, 1995). Categorical results are generally easier to understand. For example, a graph displaying the percentage of children with low vocabulary scores in each province can be easily understood by a broad policy audience, but a presentation of mean or median vocabulary scores requires an explanation of how to interpret the magnitude of the observed differences. Dichotomous variables also allow the researcher to use the concepts of *relative risk* and *attributable risk*, which are becoming increasingly familiar to the policy community.

Moreover, many constructs, especially those pertaining to children's behaviour, have been treated as dichotomous for diagnosis: that is, a person either does or does not have a particular disorder. *The Diagnostic and Statistical Manual of the American Psychiatric Association* (1980) (DSM-III) provides specific diagnostic criteria for disorders such as hyperactivity, physical aggression, and anxiety. The criteria include a set of relevant clinical features (e.g., signs, symptoms, clinical tests) and decision-making rules relating clinical features to the diagnosis (Young, 1982/83). The task of the clinician or researcher, then, is to collect adequate data to make correct diagnoses or classifications. From this perspective, it makes sense to consider a child either hyperactive or not hyperactive, for example, rather than placing a child on some continuum ranging from not at all hyperactive to extremely hyperactive.

In the analyses throughout this volume, we opted to use both continuous and dichotomous measures, with the exception of behavioural measures. We refer to them respectively as *measures of development* and *markers of vulnerability*. In the case of PPVT scores, for example, we examine relationships with SES using the scaled PPVT scores—a measure of development—and a variable indicating whether or not a child scored below 85—a marker of vulnerability. We took this approach because it is feasible that some risk factors may predict whether a child has a particularly low score but be only weakly related to their position on a continuum, and vice versa. Both approaches are informative.

In the case of measures of behaviour, we employed latent class analysis (see Sidebar 3.1) to assign children to clusters (Baillergeon, Tremblay, & Willms, 2000). Analysts have recently advocated latent class analysis and other "person-oriented" approaches to discern the extent to which individuals fit into two or more groups based on some set of indicators or clinical features (Achenbach, 1991; Bergman & Magnusson, 1997; Rindskopf & Rindskopf, 1986; Young, 1982/83). For most behaviour problems, we found that children fit consistently into three categories rather than two (e.g., hyperactive, somewhat hyperactive, not hyperactive). We use the descriptive term *behaviour problems* rather than the diagnostic term *behaviour disorders* to suggest that we have classified children based on reports of their behaviour but do not presume to have achieved a clinical diagnosis. The set of outcomes also includes a measure of pro-social behaviour, which we treat as a continuous measure.

Figure 3.1 presents the measures of development and markers of vulnerability. These are the principal outcome measures used throughout the study. A detailed description of the measures is provided in Appendix A at the end of the volume (pp. 381–87).

Sidebar 3.1
Latent class analysis

Latent class analysis (LCA) is a technique that can be used to classify individuals into a set of mutually exclusive classes, based on the distribution of responses to a set of questions (Clogg, 1979; Clogg & Goodman, 1986). We use LCA in this study to determine which children could be considered to have particular behaviour disorders, based on their parents' responses to a set of questions pertaining to their behaviour. For example, the NLSCY scale on hyperactivity contains seven questions, such as, "How often would you say that your child *can't sit still, is restless, or hyperactive?*" The possible responses include "never," "sometimes," and "often." LCA was used to classify children based on the pattern of responses to the seven questions.

The common approach to classifying children with scales is to assign a score to each item (e.g., Never = 0; Sometimes = 1; Often = 2), add the scores for the set of items, and decide on some cut-off score to classify those with and without the particular trait. This method assumes that all items have the same weight and that a classification of "often" is twice as important as a classification of "sometimes." With this approach, the decision regarding the cut-off score is arbitrary, and therefore the estimated prevalence of the behaviour problem is also arbitrary. (In many cases, these assumptions may be reasonable, and if a particular scale has been used extensively, the cut-off score is less arbitrary because it derives its validity from accepted standards among researchers and clinicians.)

In using LCA, we do not assume that all items are equally good indicators of a particular behaviour problem, because a number of researchers have argued that this is probably not the case (Anastasi, 1988; Hambleton & Swaminathan, 1985; Traub, 1983). We also apply the procedure separately for boys and girls, and for each age cohort. This separation allows for the possibility that the weight accorded to a particular item can vary, depending on the age and sex of the child (Baillergeon, Tremblay, & Willms, 2000). Thus, if a certain behaviour, such as not sitting still, is relatively normal at a young age or more normal for boys than for girls, this fact is taken into consideration in the classification.

Finally, LCA allows for the possibility that there may be more than two classes. Indeed, the analysis reveals that, for most behaviour problems, the responses yield three classes, such as hyperactive, mildly hyperactive, and not hyperactive.

Figure 3.1

Developmental outcomes and markers of vulnerability

	Infants	Babies	Toddlers	Preschoolers	Primary Years	Intermediate Years
	0	1	2 3	4 5	6 7 8	9 10 11
Measures of Development						
Motor and social development (MSD) (Standardized, mean = 100, SD = 15)	○	○	○ ○			
Receptive vocabulary (PPVT-R) (Standardized, mean = 100, SD = 15)				○ ○		
Mathematics (Age equivalent, months)					○○○	○○○
Temperament						
• Good-natured (0–10)	○	○	○ ○			
• Independent (0–10)	○	○	○ ○			
• Consistent (0–10)	○	○	○			
• Adaptable (0–10)		○	○ ○			
• Obedient (0–10)			○ ○			
Pro-social behaviour			○ ○	○ ○	○○○	○○○
Markers of Vulnerability						
Low motor and social development	●	●	● ●			
Low receptive vocabulary (below 85)				● ●		
Low mathematics (at least 1.5 years behind)					●●●	●●●
Difficult temperament (any score less than 3)	■	■	○ ○			
Behaviour problems						
• Anxiety			■ ■	■ ■	■■■	■■■
• Emotional disorder			○ ○	○ ○	○○○	○○○
• Hyperactivity			○ ○	○ ○	○○○	○○○
• Inattention			○ ○	○ ○	○○○	○○○
• Physical aggression			○ ○	○ ○	○○○	○○○
• Indirect aggression				○ ○	○○○	○○○

The vulnerability indices

Children were considered vulnerable in the cognitive domain if they were identified as having low MSD scores at ages zero through three, low PPVT-R scores at ages four and five, or low mathematics scores at ages six through eleven (see the solid circles in Figure 3.1). We refer to the prevalence of children with low cognitive scores as the *cognitive index*. Children were considered to be vulnerable in the behavioural domain if they had a difficult temperament at ages zero and one, or had any one of the six behaviour problems at ages two through eleven (see the solid squares in Figure 3.1). We refer to the prevalence of behaviour problems as the *behaviour index*. Children were then coded as vulnerable if they were identified as being vulnerable in either the cognitive or behavioural domains. The index of vulnerability is the prevalence of children who were considered vulnerable.

■ National Results

Measures of development

Table 3.1 displays the mean scores and standard deviations for the measures of motor, social, and cognitive development. The estimates were derived using the design weight for the study, which takes into account non-response bias and the sample design (e.g., children in smaller provinces were over-sampled, and therefore have a smaller design weight). Thus, the figure portrays national estimates.

The MSD scores have a mean of 100 and a standard deviation of 15 for infants (0 to 12 months), babies (12 to 24 months), and toddlers (ages 2 and 3). This is to be expected because the scores were scaled to have a mean of 100 and a standard deviation of 15 in one-month intervals. Similarly, the PPVT-R scores have a mean close to 100 and a standard deviation close to 15. The estimates can vary slightly from being exactly the scaled values because of missing data.

The mathematics computation score indicates whether a child scored above or below his or her same-age peers, measured in months of schooling. Thus, the mean score on this variable is close to zero months. What is more interesting is that the standard deviation is 13.55 months for children aged 6 through 8, and 15.99 months for children aged 9 through 11. A rough rule on most standardized tests is that one standard deviation is equivalent to one grade level during the primary years and about two years of schooling during the secondary

Table 3.1

Means and standard deviations for measures of motor, social, and cognitive development

	Infants (n=1703)	Babies (n=1752)	Toddlers (n=3635)	Preschoolers (n=3673)	Primary pupils (n=5318)	Intermediate pupils (n=5374)
	Mean (SD)	Mean (SD)	Mean (SD)	Mean (SD)	Mean (SD)	Mean (SD)
Motor and social development	100.00 (14.99)	100.18 (15.11)	100.07 (15.05)			
Pre-school vocabulary				99.32 (15.60)		
Mathematics computation					-1.47 (13.55)	0.76 (15.99)
Temperament						
• Good-natured	7.66 (1.44)	7.05 (1.56)	6.60 (1.55)			
• Independent	5.64 (1.98)	6.14 (2.22)	6.36 (2.10)			
• Consistent	8.21 (1.76)	7.52 (1.95)	7.10 (2.12)			
• Adaptable		7.42 (1.68)	7.65 (1.57)			
• Obedient			4.92 (1.90)			
Pro-social behaviour			5.28 (2.85)	5.60 (2.04)	6.24 (1.93)	6.45 (1.82)

school years (Willms & Jacobsen, 1990). The results for this test are slightly more variable but generally consistent with this rule. In practical terms, this means that in a typical grade-three classroom of twenty-four pupils, only about two-thirds—sixteen pupils—would score within one grade level of the average child. There are likely to be four pupils who score more than a full grade level above their peers and four who have scores comparable to grade-one students. In higher grades, children's skill levels tend to be even more heterogeneous, which is evident in the NLSCY data.

The mean scores of the temperament scales tend to be quite high. On the ten-point scales of good-natured, independent, consistent, and adaptable, the average ratings were in the range 5.64 to 8.21, with a median of 7.1. The mean score on the obedient scale, which pertains only to toddlers, was 4.92; this score is comparable to the mean score on the pro-social behaviour scale for that age group. The data reveal an interesting trend: scores on the good-natured and consistent scale appear to decrease with the age of the child, whereas the scores on the independent and adaptable scales increase. This trend raises some interesting questions concerning temperament and what is meant by the term *obedient* as children enter the so-called terrible twos: on the one hand, parents find their children more fussy and irritable and less consistent in their behaviour, yet also more independent and adaptable to new situations. Tremblay et al. (1992; Tremblay, 1999) also noted that children's physical aggression tends to peak around the age of 28 months. These data indicate also that parents' ratings of pro-social behaviour are relatively low at ages 2 and 3, but increase steadily from 5.29 to 6.45 as children get older.

Markers of vulnerability

Table 3.2 summarizes the results pertaining to the prevalence of vulnerable children. The results for the overall composite vulnerability index suggest that 28.6 percent of Canadian children were vulnerable; this figure also means that more than 70 percent are not experiencing either cognitive difficulties or behaviour problems. Of the children considered vulnerable, 12.1 percent were vulnerable in the cognitive domain and 19.1 percent had behaviour problems. The prevalence of children with both low cognitive scores and behaviour problems was relatively small—only three percent. ~ both

In the cognitive domain, approximately fourteen to sixteen percent of children had low MSD or PPVT-R scores. These results stem from the level at which the cut-off score for vulnerability was set. However, 8.31 percent of the children aged 6 to 8 had low mathematics scores, indicating that they were about one and a half years behind their peers in computation skills. The prevalence increased slightly, to 9.55 percent, for children aged 9 through 11.

The prevalence of behaviour problems ranges from 17.39 to 21.67 percent and does not display a clear trend with age. There are, however, some clear trends in the results for the specific types of behaviour problems. First, among the six types of behaviour problems, hyperactivity has the highest prevalence at all ages and therefore dominates the behaviour index. Inattention, which is somewhat related to hyperactivity (and even shares one item in the scale: "can't concentrate, can't pay attention for long"), has the second highest prevalence.

Table 3.2

Prevalence of vulnerable children

	Infants (n=1703)	Babies (n=1752)	Toddlers (n=3635)	Preschoolers (n=3673)	Primary pupils (n=5318)	Intermediate pupils (n=5374)
	Percent	Percent	Percent	Percent	Percent	Percent
Low motor and social development	14.61	14.88	13.58			
Low receptive vocabulary				16.22		
Low mathematics score					8.31	9.55
Difficult temperament	16.12	14.11	14.66			
Behaviour disorder			20.79	17.39	18.79	21.67
• Anxiety			1.72	1.94	5.19	7.25
• Emotional disorder			0.85	1.33	4.64	6.01
• Hyperactivity			14.41	12.85	11.46	13.30
• Inattention			6.62	4.54	6.31	8.68
• Physical aggression			4.10	2.08	3.30	2.33
• Indirect aggression				0.98	2.28	2.01
Vulnerability index	27.76	26.06	30.98	29.54	26.34	28.80

Note: Overall, 28.61 percent of Canadian children were vulnerable. Of these, 12.05 percent had low cognitive scores, 19.06 percent had behaviour problems, and 3.00 percent had both low cognitive scores and behaviour problems.

For both of these behaviour problems, the prevalence is high at ages two and three but decreases when children reach preschool age. There is also an increase from the primary to intermediate school years. The prevalence of children with emotional problems or anxiety increases steadily with the children's age. These emotional problems are referred to as "internalizing behaviours" and tend to be more prevalent among girls. Finally, the prevalence of behaviour problems associated with physical or indirect aggression tends to be relatively low, ranging from two to three percent, except for toddlers, where it is about four percent.

These trends need to be interpreted with attention to the latent class scaling technique used to classify children. For example, with respect to anxiety, the absolute rating levels on the anxiety items were not used to determine which children were considered to have anxiety problems. Rather, the latent class scaling assesses whether there are clusters of children whose pattern of ratings is similar; this assessment was done separately by age and gender. The average ratings on the anxiety items could increase or decrease with age and could differ by sex, and this would not necessarily affect the size of the clusters with similarly low scores at each age-by-sex group.

■ Differences Between Boys and Girls

Table 3.3 displays differences between the sexes in the prevalence of vulnerability as gauged by the cognitive index, the behaviour index, and the overall vulnerability index. Statistically significant differences between means are indicated with bold text.

On average, boys tend to be more vulnerable than girls, due to both cognitive difficulties and behaviour problems. For the cognitive index, the prevalence of vulnerable boys was 13.67 percent, compared with 10.38 percent for girls. The sex differences were especially pronounced for toddlers, with more than twice as many boys as girls having low scores in motor and social development. As well, more boys than girls had low scores on the PPVT-R at ages four and five. On the mathematics test, the prevalence of boys with low scores did not differ significantly from that of girls, but among children at the intermediate school age, more boys than girls had low scores.

A higher prevalence of boys with behaviour problems is evident among infants and babies: nearly seventeen percent of boys had very low scores on the temperament scale, compared with just over thirteen percent of girls. However, among toddlers and preschool children, the differences between the sexes were less than one percent and were not statistically significant. The large differences between boys and girls in behaviour problems appear when they enter school. For primary school children, the prevalence of behaviour problems among boys was more than one and a half times that of girls. The differences at the intermediate level were smaller, but at this age the prevalence of behaviour problems for boys was still considerably higher than the prevalence for girls.

Figure 3.2 is a bar chart with standard error bars (see Sidebar 3.2) that displays sex differences for each age group for the six different types of behaviour problems. For the two internalizing behaviour problems, anxiety and emotional problems, the prevalence varies considerably after children reach

Table 3.3

Prevalence of vulnerable children by sex

	Infants and babies (n=3455)	Toddlers (n=3635)	Preschoolers (n=3673)	Primary pupils (n=5318)	Intermediate pupils (n=5374)	All children (n=21,455)
	Percent	Percent	Percent	Percent	Percent	Percent
Cognitive index						
Boys	**15.63**	**18.26**	**16.87**	7.79	**11.40**	**13.67**
Girls	**13.77**	**8.66**	**15.56**	8.73	**7.61**	**10.38**
Behavioral index						
Boys	**16.76**	20.99	16.90	**23.29**	**24.08**	**21.02**
Girls	**13.21**	20.58	17.92	**14.12**	**19.14**	**17.02**
Vulnerability index						
Boys	**28.64**	**34.36**	29.60	**29.69**	**32.12**	**31.13**
Girls	**25.17**	**27.41**	29.49	**23.06**	**25.32**	**26.00**

Note: *Differences between means that are statistically significant (p < 0.05) appear in boldface.*

school age. Girls have a higher prevalence of anxiety-related problems than boys at all ages except ages two and three. The pattern is less clear for emotional problems, and overall the sex differences are statistically insignificant. The prevalence of hyperactivity for boys is on average about sixteen percent and fairly constant across ages two through eleven. This score is higher than that of girls at all ages, which is relatively high during the toddler and preschool ages and then falls to about eight percent. Inattention among boys is very low during the toddler years and then increases steadily as they get older, reaching its highest level of about eleven percent during the intermediate years. The pattern for girls is opposite: very high during the toddler years—about eleven percent—and then declining to less than four percent by primary school. The prevalence is slightly higher during the intermediate years, about six percent, but still much lower than that of boys.

The prevalence of physical aggression is highest for boys at ages 2 and 3, at about 6.6 percent; thereafter, it ranges from 3 to 5 percent. The prevalence of physical aggression is lower for girls across the age range, ranging from one to two percent. The prevalence of indirect aggression is only about one percent for both sexes at ages four and five, and does not exceed three percent for any age group. (The NLSCY did not include data on indirect aggression for toddlers.) The prevalence is higher for girls than for boys at both the primary and secondary school years, but the differences are relatively small.

The results in Figure 3.2 make it clear that the behaviour index, which is the prevalence of any of these behaviour problems, is strongly affected by the prevalence of hyperactivity and inattention. Moreover, the higher prevalence for boys of any type of behaviour problem is affected mainly by the higher prevalence of hyperactivity and inattention during the primary and secondary school years. Anxiety and emotional problems weigh into the index more heavily after children enter school. By the time girls reach the intermediate school years, these internalizing problems become as prominent as hyperactivity and inattention.

■ Variation Among Provinces

The prevalence estimates for each of the ten provinces are displayed in Figure 3.3. The prevalence rates on the cognitive index for seven of the provinces do not differ significantly from the national average. Manitoba and New Brunswick both have a prevalence that is about two percent higher than the national average; Quebec has a slightly lower prevalence than the national average. The provinces differ considerably more on the behavioural index. The prevalence of children with behaviour problems in Quebec is almost five percent higher than the national average, whereas the prevalence in British Columbia, Alberta, Saskatchewan, Ontario, New Brunswick, Prince Edward Island, and Newfoundland is lower than the national average. The results for Quebec and New Brunswick raise a number of questions, as Quebec has a lower than average prevalence of cognitive problems, but a higher than average prevalence of behaviour problems, whereas the reverse holds for New Brunswick. Thus, the observed variation in these indices is not simply due to provincial variation in SES.

The last graph in Figure 3.3 displays variation in the overall vulnerability index. Manitoba and Quebec have higher than average rates of vulnerability, while British Columbia, Alberta, Ontario, Prince Edward Island, and Newfoundland have lower than average rates. However, the differences are relatively small; in most provinces, the prevalence does not differ by more than 2 percent from the national average of 28.6 percent.

Figure 3.2

Differences between boys and girls in the prevalence of behaviour problems

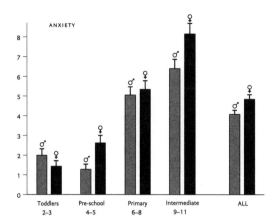

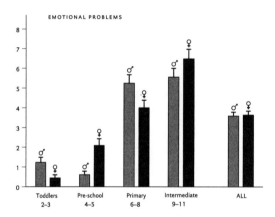

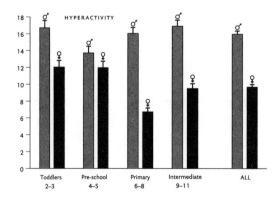

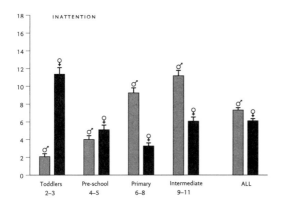

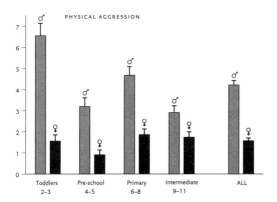

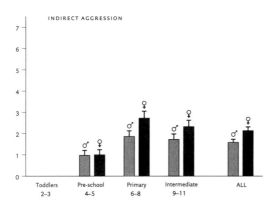

■ Variation Among Neighbourhoods

The aim of this analysis was to identify areas where there is likely to be a particularly high percentage of vulnerable children and display these areas on maps of each province. In the next chapter, the analysis is extended in an attempt to discern whether particular characteristics of neighbourhoods have an effect on children's outcomes, over and above the effects associated with children's individual family backgrounds. This analysis identifies "neighbourhood types," using enumeration areas as an operational definition of "neighbourhoods." Enumeration areas (EAs) are small geographic areas, which on average comprise about 400 families. There are about 40,000 EAs in Canada. We appreciate that EA boundaries do not accurately capture the boundaries of neighbourhoods as they would be defined by local residents, and thus we are likely to underestimate neighbourhood effects. However, the use of EAs is a practical and inexpensive means to determine whether research in this vein may be productive.

Sidebar 3.2
Bar charts with error bars

In a bar chart, the height of the bars displays the prevalence for a particular group. The thin line at the top of each bar indicates how accurately the prevalence was estimated. These thin lines, called error bars, encompass one standard error above and below the estimate and represent the 68-percent confidence interval for the estimate. (If the lines were doubled in length, they would represent the 95-percent confidence interval.) The confidence level means that if repeated samples were selected from the population under similar conditions and 68-percent confidence intervals were drawn, they would contain the true estimate about 2 times out of 3 (or 19 times out of 20 for 95-percent confidence intervals). The error bars can also be used to determine approximately whether the difference in prevalence estimates for two groups is statistically significant: if the bottom of the standard error line for the group with the higher prevalence is above the top of the standard error line for the group with the lower prevalence, then we can infer that the difference is statistically significant (with about 95-percent confidence).

Figure 3.3

Variation among provinces in the prevalence of vulnerable children

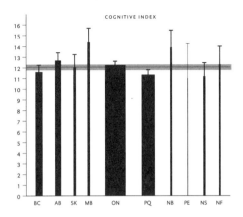

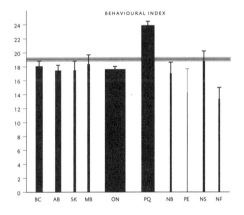

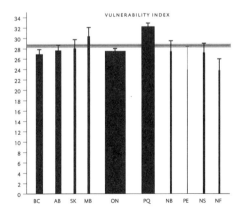

Sidebar 3.3
Cluster analysis

Cluster analysis is in many ways similar to latent class analysis. It is used to form clusters of objects or individuals, based on how similar they are with respect to a number of defining characteristics. The researcher decides which characteristics are most relevant.

Cluster analysis is used in biology to classify animals and plants, and in medicine to identify diseases and their stages. For example, if 100 objects were being considered, the analysis would examine their characteristics and in the first step form a cluster comprising the two objects that were most similar. The next step would examine the characteristics of the 99 objects (the newly formed cluster and the 98 single objects) to find the two that were most similar. It would join them into a new cluster. The process would continue in this way, step by step, until a small number of clusters were formed which had relatively dissimilar characteristics. The researcher decides when to stop the process of joining clusters, based on how dissimilar the clusters are at each step.

Table 3.4
Mean scores of defining characteristics of neighbourhood "types" (EAs)

	N	Median income	Years of education	Percent youth employed	Percent adults employed	Percent non-immigrants	Percent two-parent families	Mean SES
1	1249	24.28	10.13	93.19	63.16	97.81	78.07	-1.74
2	2479	34.83	10.87	43.91	79.56	97.76	79.53	-1.27
3	3341	29.58	11.40	70.66	84.12	90.45	56.40	-1.15
4	5493	37.11	11.97	95.90	90.00	92.60	58.55	-0.31
5	9013	43.65	11.66	76.17	90.81	96.49	80.78	-0.10
6	8072	40.80	11.20	98.28	92.86	98.05	85.40	0.08
7	8142	59.86	12.64	93.38	94.73	95.99	87.84	0.98
8	1577	37.86	13.83	87.44	96.17	94.83	88.92	1.99
All	39366	44.92	11.78	85.51	89.98	95.71	78.21	0.00

Sidebar 3.4
Factor analysis

Factor analysis is a longstanding technique used in the social sciences to represent a set of *observed* or measured variables in terms of a smaller set of *latent* or theoretical variables. For example, the NLSCY interviews of the "person most knowledgeable" (PMK) included a series of 25 questions pertaining to parenting practices. The responses to each question could be treated as a separate variable; however, it would be impractical to display all of the possible relationships among the 25 parenting variables and the other variables of interest. Factor analysis was used to reduce the set of 25 variables into 4 theoretically meaningful latent variables, or factors. These factors are referred to as "responsive parenting," "consistent parenting," "firm approach," and "rational parenting," and are used as separate variables in the analysis.

Factor analysis generally entails four steps (Kim & Mueller, 1978). The first step involves collecting the data and determining the means and standard deviations of the variables as well as the correlations among them. The second step involves determining the number of theoretical variables or factors that can adequately explain the relationships among the set of observed variables. Sometimes the researcher has an hypothesis about the number of factors and the observed variables that correspond to them; the goal is to discern how well the data conform to the hypothesized relationships. This is called *confirmatory* factor analysis. In most cases, researchers conduct *exploratory* factor analysis and use the data to determine how many factors are appropriate.

At the third step, called factor rotation, the analysis determines the best correspondence between the observed and theoretical variables, and the weight that should be assigned to each observed variable. At this step, the analysis reveals whether some of the observed variables do not fit well with any of the theoretical variables. The fourth step computes, for every individual (or unit), a scaled score for each of the factors. These factors are used as either outcome or predictor variables in the main analyses.

We used cluster analysis (see Sidebar 3.3) to classify all Canadian EAs into "neighbourhood types," based on demographic data from the public file of the 1991 Canadian Census. The clustering was based on six characteristics of the EAs: median income, percentage of non-immigrants, percentage of two-parent families, average number of years of education, percentage of employed youth, and percentage of employed adults. We chose this set of characteristics because we knew from analyses of the NLSCY data that income, levels of education, and parents' employment were significantly related to children's developmental outcomes. We also included immigrant status and family structure in the analysis, as these variables tend to be related to a family's socioeconomic status.

The cluster analysis sorted the EAs into eight types.[2] The average scores on the six defining characteristics for each of the eight types are displayed in Table 3.4. The last column of Table 3.4 provides the mean socioeconomic status score, which is the first principal component of a factor analysis (see Sidebar 3.4) of the six variables for the full sample, excluding those with no children.

Appendix B (pp. 389–406) provides a description of the eight neighbourhood types, a table of the distribution of EA types by province, and sixteen colour maps. The eight neighbourhood types were ordered, based on their average SES, as derived from the six variables, and were assigned a colour which is used on the maps. The set of maps includes a map of Canada, a map for each province, and separate maps for each of Vancouver, Winnipeg, Toronto, Ottawa, Montreal, and Halifax.

Figure 3.4 displays the amount of variation among neighbourhood types in the prevalence of vulnerable children. The prevalence estimates vary from a high of 34.2 percent for Type 1 to 18.3 percent for Type 8. The high prevalence for Type 1 neighbourhoods is not surprising, as these neighbourhoods have very low income and education levels and high unemployment. Similarly, the low prevalence of vulnerable children in Type 8 neighbourhoods is expected; these neighbourhoods have very high levels of income and education and low levels of unemployment.

A somewhat surprising finding is that the prevalence of vulnerable children in Types 3, 4, 5, and 6 are all close to 30 percent, only slightly above the national average. These four neighbourhood types comprise about two-thirds (65.8 percent) of all EAs. The prevalence for Type 2 neighbourhoods, 26.7 percent, is somewhat anomalous. The low prevalence in this type of neighbourhoods stems from a low prevalence of behaviour problems; the prevalence of children with cognitive problems does not differ from the national average. The main

Figure 3.3

Variation among provinces in the prevalence of vulnerable children

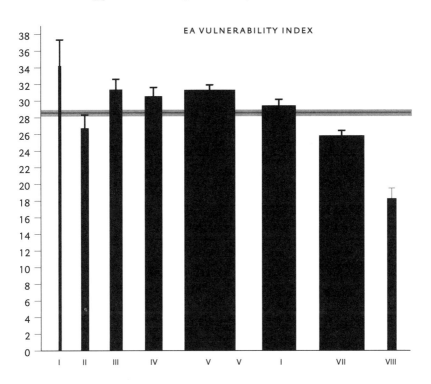

distinguishing features of Type 2 neighbourhoods are their relatively low levels of education and youth employment. The median family income is nearly $35,000, which is close to that of Type 4 neighbourhoods. Disproportionate numbers of Type 2 neighbourhoods are in the four Atlantic provinces, and the prevalence of behaviour problems in these provinces is below the national average (see Figure 3.3). Type 7 EAs have a median family income of nearly $60,000 and an average level of education of 12.6 years, and thus one might expect a very low prevalence of vulnerable children. However, the prevalence in Type 7 EAs is 25.8 percent, which is only about three percent below the national average.

When we embarked on this analysis, we expected to identify one or two neighbourhood types where the majority of vulnerable children resided. If this had been the case, we could then locate specific geographic areas within each province and present a case for targeting resources in those areas. However, the analysis clearly shows that vulnerable children are much more evenly dispersed across the country. It is only in the Type 1 and Type 8 neighbourhoods, those with the very lowest and very highest SES, where the prevalence of vulnerable children differs dramatically from the national average. Type 1 neighbourhoods comprise only about three percent of all neighbourhoods, and thus the vast majority of neighbourhoods are relatively good places to raise children. Over one-quarter (26.5 percent) of these neighbourhoods are in the Atlantic provinces; another 28 percent are in Quebec. Type 8 neighbourhoods make up about 4 percent of all neighbourhoods, and the majority of these— 56.4 percent—are in Ontario. An informal inspection of the maps suggests that although there is a disproportionate number of Type 1 neighbourhoods in the Atlantic provinces, they do not appear to be concentrated in particular areas of the major cities. This is not the case for Type 8 neighbourhoods, however, which are clearly concentrated in particular areas of Canada's major cities. To some extent, therefore, we could say that Canada is gated but not ghettoed.

■

THE PRINCIPAL AIMS OF THIS CHAPTER were to describe the outcome measures used in this study and to estimate the prevalence of vulnerable children in Canada. The approach differs from most previous research in that it examines children's cognitive and behavioural outcomes rather than risk factors. A number of important findings emerged from the analysis.

1. *Of Canadian children, 28.6 percent are vulnerable.* This figure may be higher than many people expect. The estimate of prevalence depends on the criteria established for defining vulnerability; and indeed, if we had more stringent criteria, the estimate would be lower. However, we have maintained the criteria presented in this chapter for three reasons.

    First, the criteria are consistent with those used in other research and with practice in the field. For example, a cut-off score of 85 on the PPVT-R, which is one standard deviation below the mean, is often used to identify children who are likely to require special-educational services. Similarly, primary or intermediate school children who score one and a half grade levels below their peers in reading or mathematics arguably require remedial assistance if they are to progress successfully. Recall that our measure of vulnerability is intended to identify children whose chances of leading healthy and productive lives are reduced unless there is a concerted and prolonged effort to remedy their problems.

Second, our estimates of prevalence are consistent with estimates derived from other research. Our estimated prevalence of behaviour problems for Canada is 19.1 percent and for Ontario, 17.6 percent. The estimated prevalence of behaviour problems among children aged 4 to 16 in Ontario in the mid 1980s was 18.1 percent (Offord et al., 1987). This is remarkably close to our estimate, given that Offord's team used considerably different methods to define behaviour problems.

Third, indicators of secondary school completion and levels of literacy are consistent with our estimated prevalence of childhood vulnerability. In 1993, 29.2 percent of Canadian youth failed to graduate from secondary school at the typical age (OECD, 1996; see Table R11.1). Analyses of the International Adult Literacy Study (IALS; Organization for Economic Cooperation and Development & Statistics Canada, 1995) revealed that about ten percent of youth aged sixteen to twenty-five scored at Level I, the lowest level on the IALS tests, and a further twenty-five percent scored at Level II. We do not know whether these youth would have met our criteria for vulnerability as children, but the IALS results found that adults with scores at Levels I and II were more likely to be unemployed or in lower-paying jobs.

2. *The prevalence of children with low cognitive scores is 12.8 percent, and 19.1 percent have 1 or more behaviour problems; only 3.0 percent have both cognitive and behaviour problems.* We had expected a much stronger association between cognitive and behavioural problems; however, the results suggest that the majority of children in this age range with cognitive problems do not have behaviour problems, and vice versa. It may be that children with low cognitive ability have milder forms of behaviour problems, especially anxiety or emotional problems, than those who are considered vulnerable in this study, or that children with poor cognitive skills are prone to developing behaviour problems at a later age. Similarly, children with behavioural problems probably do not achieve their full potential in the cognitive domain, even though their scores do not fall below the criteria established for vulnerability. These children may also be prone to low academic achievement at the secondary level.

An immediate implication of this finding is that interventions aimed at addressing cognitive problems are not likely to also reduce the prevalence of behaviour problems and vice versa. These issues need to be tackled separately.

3. *The prevalence of childhood vulnerability is higher among boys than girls.* The results suggest that about 31.1 percent of boys are vulnerable, compared to only 26 percent of girls. These differences are apparent in both the cognitive and behavioural domains. Within the behavioural domain, the differences stem primarily from the higher prevalence of hyperactivity, inattention, and physical aggression among boys. However, the prevalence of internalizing problems—anxiety and emotional problems—is higher among girls at the intermediate level. These problems are usually not as apparent to parents and teachers as hyperactivity or physical aggression, but they can also have important long-term implications for children's health and well-being.

4. *Provinces differ considerably in the proportions of children deemed vulnerable.* The variation is especially pronounced on the behaviour index. A puzzling finding is the relatively high percentage of children in Ontario with low cognitive scores compared with Quebec, whereas Quebec has a substantially higher percentage of children with behaviour problems. The differences in cognitive scores are due primarily to the higher mathematics achievement in Quebec, which has been observed in previous studies (Willms, 1996). The analyses in Chapter 16 of this volume attempt to explain some of the interprovincial variation in mathematics achievement. We do not have a good explanation for the variation in the behaviour index, which needs to be investigated further.

5. *The prevalence of vulnerable children differs among neighbourhoods.* One can identify areas with a particularly high or low prevalence, but the vast majority of vulnerable children are distributed fairly evenly within each province. One of the goals of this analysis was to locate communities where there is an especially high prevalence of vulnerable children. The analysis shows that this is difficult, because the vast majority of vulnerable children are fairly evenly dispersed across the country in middle-class neighbourhoods.

■

THE VULNERABILITY INDEX PROVIDES a means for monitoring children's outcomes, understanding socioeconomic gradients, and determining the pathways of positive child development. In these analyses, it provides a means for making comparisons among jurisdictions, including provinces, cities, and other communities. In the next chapter, it is used to examine socioeconomic gradients.

When longitudinal data become available, it will be possible to depict trends in vulnerability based on the index and examine trajectories for different subgroups of population. We will be especially interested in examining changes in the socioeconomic gradients for vulnerability over time. One can be critical of the index because it does not cover all aspects of children's development. However, the index will be refined as the study matures and as better outcome measures become available. Such refinements will require some effort to standardize the index to ensure its usefulness for monitoring trends, much in the same way that major economic indices are altered from year to year.

The policy community is not only interested in monitoring children's developmental outcomes, but also in identifying the family, school, and community factors that lead to positive childhood development. Because the NLSCY is comprehensive and longitudinal, and can be responsive to research findings emanating from earlier cycles of the survey, it will serve not only to help us understand how well we are doing, but also to support the capacity for research on child development.

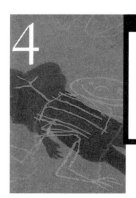

Socioeconomic Gradients for Childhood Vulnerability

J. DOUGLAS WILLMS

THIS CHAPTER PROVIDES ESTIMATES of the socioeconomic gradients for Canada for the range of cognitive and behavioural outcomes described in Chapter 3. It also examines the extent to which socioeconomic gradients vary among provinces, cities, and neighbourhoods. The strategy is to present the gradients associated with family income first, because they provide a simple introduction to the concept of gradients and their statistical features. Income gradients are also of special interest because many social policies are concerned with the transfer of income to poor families or with targeted programs for economically disadvantaged groups.

The gradients associated with socioeconomic status are presented next. Socioeconomic status (SES) refers to the relative position of an individual or family on a hierarchical social structure, based on their access to or control over wealth, prestige, and power (see Chapter 2). In this study, SES is operationalized as a composite measure of the parents' levels of education, the prestige of their occupations, and family income. The analysis then examines the relationships between developmental outcomes and the full set of socioeconomic indicators, alongside other demographic characteristics. Finally, this analysis examines the variation among provinces, cities, and neighbourhoods in their average levels of outcomes and their gradients. These analyses address eight of the ten research questions set out in Chapter 1 and provide tests for

p. 85- Maternal ed.
statistically significant

Multiple linear regression is used to express the relationship between an outcome (or dependent) variable, such as children's mathematics achievement scores, and a set of predictor (or independent) variables, such as family income, parents' education, and the sex of the child. In general, the researcher posits a "model" of the relationship between the dependent and independent variables, based on theory and prior research, and by particular beliefs and values. Data are collected from a sample of the target population, and the model is "fit" to the data to determine whether it is a reasonable portrayal of the observed relationships. The analysis yields a set of weights called "regression coefficients." These indicate the effect that each variable has on the independent variable.

More precisely, the regression coefficients denote the expected change in Y (the dependent variable) for a one-unit change in X (the independent variable), given all other variables in the model are held constant. This is a powerful tool for policy purposes, as it can estimate, for example, the difference in mathematics scores for two hypothetical children who are similar in all respects except family income, where one has a family income of $30,000 and the other has a family income of $40,000. Similarly, the regression coefficient for a dichotomous variable (e.g., sex is coded with males = 0 and females = 1) denotes the average difference in outcome scores

the hypotheses pertaining to differences among communities, converging gradients, and double jeopardy.

The analyses in this chapter, and in most chapters of the book, employ some form of multiple regression to examine the relationships among variables describing children's outcomes, family background, and mediating processes. These techniques are somewhat more complicated than frequency tables or cross-tabulations, which are normally used to portray univariate or bivariate relationships among variables. Multiple regression techniques are used to describe relationships among sets of three or more variables; they often reveal important aspects of relationships that would not otherwise be evident. Although we strive to portray the findings in ways that are accessible to the non-statistical reader, an understanding of the general purposes of these techniques—and a few of the key concepts underlying them—is likely to further the reader's appreciation of the results. This chapter includes three sidebars, between those with and without the characteristic, given that the effects of other variables in the model are held constant. This makes it possible to ask questions such as, What is the difference between immigrant and non-immigrant children, before and after taking account of parents' family income and level of education?

Statistical programs used for regression analyses provide estimates of the coefficients and their standard errors. The standard error is an indicator of how accurately a coefficient was estimated. Researchers in the social sciences normally consider a "confidence interval" in which they are reasonably certain the "true value" of a coefficient lies. A 95-percent confidence interval is determined by adding two times the standard error to the regression coefficient to obtain the upper bound, and subtracting two times the standard error to obtain the lower bound. Theoretically, if repeated samples were selected from the population under similar conditions and 95-percent confidence intervals were constructed, they would contain the true value of the coefficient 19 times out of 20. If the 95-percent confidence interval does not encompass zero, the researcher concludes that the true value of the coefficient is not likely to be zero and states that the relationship is statistically significant at the 0.05 level. Throughout this book, we use bold text to indicate coefficients that are significant at the 0.05 level, which means that the probability that the observed relationships could have happened by chance is only 5 percent.

similar to those in Chapter 3, which describe the purposes and underlying concepts of these statistical techniques. These should be sufficient for the reader who does not wish to delve into the statistical details.

■ Gradients Associated with Family Income

Measures of development

Table 4.1 presents the gradients associated with family income,[1] which were estimated using multiple linear regression (see Sidebar 4.1). Each outcome variable was regressed on income and income-squared. Coefficients which are statistically significant ($p < 0.05$) are indicated with bold text. For motor and social development (MSD), family income explains less than one percent of the variance. Although the estimated coefficients are statistically significant, they

Table 4.1

The relationship between measures of development and family income (unstandardized regression coefficients)

	Infants and babies		Toddlers		Preschoolers		Primary pupils		Intermediate pupils	
	Beta	R²	Beta	R²	Beta	R²	Beta	R²	Beta	R²
Motor and social development										
• Income	**-0.396**	0.7	**0.368**	0.4						
• Income squared	**0.152**		-0.024							
Pro-social behaviour										
• Income			**-0.071**	0.4	-0.003	0.0	0.012	0.0	**0.052**	0.6
• Income squared			0.011		0.007		0.001		0.004	
Preschool vocabulary										
• Income					**1.212**	3.4				
• Income squared					**-0.128**					
Mathematics computation										
• Income							**0.719**	2.2	**1.165**	2.5
• Income squared							**-0.125**		-0.051	

Note: Coefficients that are statistically significant (p < 0.05) appear in boldface.

are trivial in substantive terms: the results indicate that an increase of $10,000 in family income is associated with a change of less than one half of one point in a child's MSD score. Similarly, the relationships between pro-social behaviour and family income are extremely weak across the age range two through eleven: in all cases, income explained less than one percent of the variance.

The relationship between children's receptive vocabulary at ages 4 and 5 is somewhat stronger, but even in this case, family income accounts for only 3.4 percent of the variance. The coefficient indicates that an increase of $10,000 in family income is associated with an increase in PPVT-R scores of about 1.2 points. The negative coefficient for "income-squared" indicates that the relationship is weaker at higher levels of income. Figure 4.1 displays the income gradient for PPVT-R. The gradient line is drawn to cover incomes in the range of about $12,400 to $93,800, which are estimates of the fifth and ninety-fifth percentiles respectively of family income for the Canadian population with

Figure 4.1

A curvilinear income gradient for receptive vocabulary, children aged 4 and 5

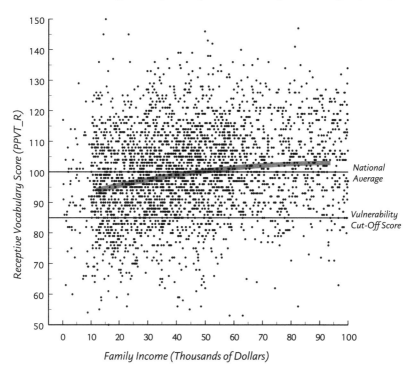

children in this age range. The figure shows that the slope of the income gradient is slightly steeper at lower levels of income, and begins to level off at incomes above around $60,000.

The figure also includes a scatterplot of children's receptive vocabulary scores against family income, as well as lines denoting the national average (a score of 100) and the criteria for defining vulnerability (a score of 85). The figure shows that at every level of family income there is a wide range of PPVT-R scores. As one would expect, there is a greater number of children from poor families—say, for example, families with incomes below $20,000—who are considered vulnerable than among those from more affluent families. However, even among poor children, many children score well above the national average. Moreover, the majority of children whose scores fall below 85 on this test were not from poor families, but from families with average or above-average incomes.

Sidebar 4.2

Logistic regression

In many instances, the outcome variable for a regression analysis is dichotomous. For example, it can denote whether a child *has* or *does not have* a particular trait, such as being hyperactive or not being hyperactive, or whether a child has or has not experienced a particular event, such as failing a grade in school. If so, we are usually interested in the probability or likelihood of the child having the trait or experiencing the event at a particular time and how various characteristics of the child, such as age, sex, or family income, affect that probability. The logic underlying logistic regression is similar to multiple regression, except that the regression coefficients are more difficult to interpret. However, the coefficients can be converted to odds ratios with a simple mathematical transformation, and odds ratios are more easily interpreted.

The odds of an event occurring are the likelihood of the event occurring divided by the likelihood of the event not occurring. For example, if an event has a 75-percent probability of occurring, then the odds would be $[0.75/(1-0.75)]$, which is 3.0. An event with an odds of 1.0 has an equal chance of occurring or not occurring. An odds *ratio* is simply the ratio of the odds for two different sets of circumstances. For example, one could assess the odds of

an event occurring for girls and for boys, and calculate the ratio of the odds. Regression coefficients for logistic regression can be converted to odds ratios by estimating *e* raised to the power of the coefficient. Odds ratios are interpreted in a fashion similar to multiple regression coefficients: they denote the ratio of the odds of an event occurring after a one-unit change in the independent variable, compared to what it was previously, given all other independent variables in the model are held constant.

For example, suppose the outcome variable in a logistic regression was whether or not a child repeated grade one. If the odds ratio for mother's education were 0.95, it would indicate that the odds of a child repeating a grade for a mother with 13 years of education was only 95 percent as large as the odds of a child whose mother had 12 years of education (or 12 years compared with 11 years, etc.). Thus, increasing levels of maternal education reduce the odds of a child repeating grade one. Coefficients for dichotomous independent variables express the odds ratios for the two groups denoted by the variable. For example, if the odds ratio for "female" (i.e., sex coded with males = 0 and females = 1) were 0.90, it would indicate that the odds of repeating grade 1 for females was only 90 percent that of males. For a simple introduction to logistic regression, see Norusis/SOSS Inc. (1992).

The relationships between mathematics computation scores and family income is slightly weaker than for PPVT-R scores. The coefficient for family income for primary-age children indicates that an increase of $10,000 in income is associated with a difference in mathematics scores equivalent to about 0.7 of a month of schooling. At the intermediate level, the relationship is slightly stronger—equivalent to about 1.2 months of schooling. For both primary- and intermediate-level children, the relationship is slightly curvilinear, similar to PPVT-R, but the curvilinearity is statistically significant only for primary-age children.

Markers of vulnerability

Table 4.2 displays the odds ratios associated with family income for the markers of vulnerability. These are based on results from logistic regressions of the dichotomous (zero–one) vulnerability variable regressed on family income and the square of family income (see Sidebar 4.2). With the exception of MSD for infants and babies, the odds ratios for family income range from 0.82 to 0.95. In all cases, the income-squared coefficient is close to 1.0, which indicates that there is no significant bend in the gradient. Thus, the logistic model with a linear income coefficient fits the data reasonably well.

For behaviour problems, the odds ratio is on average about 0.90. This indicates that the odds of a child having a behaviour problem decrease by about 10 percent for every $10,000 increase in income. For preschool vocabulary, the odds ratio is 0.82. Figure 4.2 displays the gradient for low PPVT-R scores associated with family income. It shows that the likelihood of a child having a low PPVT-R score declines steadily with rising income. There is a slight bend in the gradient at about $50,000 or $60,000, but it is not possible to identify a well-defined income threshold. The odds ratios for mathematics computation range from 0.82 to 0.85. Thus, the income gradient for the likelihood of a child having a low mathematics score would be similar to the income gradient for low PPVT-R scores displayed in Figure 4.2.

■ Gradients Associated with Socioeconomic Status

Measures of development

The socioeconomic gradients for the measures of childhood development are displayed in Table 4.3. The relationships between MSD and SES and between

Table 4.2

The relationship between markers of vulnerability and family income (odds ratios)

	Infants and babies		Toddlers		Preschoolers		Primary pupils		Intermediate pupils	
	Odds Ratio	R^2	Odds Ratio	R^2	Odds Ratio	R^2	Odds Ratio	R^2	Odds Ratio	R^2
Low motor and social development										
• Income	1.025	0.4	**0.953**	0.3						
• Income squared	**0.980**		1.006							
Difficult temperament										
• Income	**0.954**	0.3	0.988	0.0						
• Income squared	1.005		1.000							
Behaviour disorder										
• Income			**0.875**	2.9	**0.933**	0.7	**0.918**	1.1	**0.898**	1.9
• Income squared			0.998		1.013		1.015		**1.028**	
Preschool vocabulary										
• Income					**0.822**	4.9				
• Income squared					1.008					
Mathematics computation										
• Income							**0.850**	3.3	**0.817**	4.2
• Income squared							**1.043**		0.991	

Note: Odds ratios that differ significantly from 1.0 (p < 0.05) appear in boldface.

pro-social behaviour and SES are quite weak, similar to the case for family income. For each of these outcomes, less than two percent of the variance can be explained by SES. The relationships between PPVT-R scores and SES are considerably stronger, with about six percent of the variance attributable to SES. The coefficient indicates that an increase of one standard deviation in SES is associated with a gain in PPVT-R scores of about 3.9 points. Thus, on average, there is about an eight-point difference in the PPVT-R scores of families with low SES (for example, one standard deviation below the national average) and those with a relatively high SES (for example, one standard deviation above the national average). Differences in mathematics scores for children in low- and high-SES families range from about four to six months of

Figure 4.2

*The income gradient for low receptive vocabulary scores,
children aged 4 and 5*

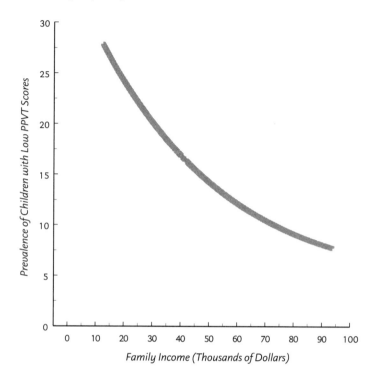

Family Income (Thousands of Dollars)

schooling. Generally, the coefficients for SES-squared were not statistically significant, indicating that the relationships are linear.

Markers of vulnerability

The odds ratios associated with SES for the various markers of vulnerability are displayed in Table 4.4. They indicate the change in odds associated with an increase of one standard deviation in SES. With the exception of MSD scores for infants and babies, the odds ratios are less than 1.0, as we might expect. The odds ratio for MSD for toddlers is 0.73. Thus, the likelihood of a toddler in a relatively high-SES family (e.g., one standard deviation above the

Table 4.3

The relationship between measures of development and socioeconomic status (SES) (unstandardized regression coefficients)

	Infants and babies (n=3737)		Toddlers (n=3868)		Preschoolers (n=3909)		Primary pupils (n=5659)		Intermediate pupils (n=5719)	
	Beta	R²	Beta	R²	Beta	R²	Beta	R²	Beta	R²
Motor and social development										
• Socioeconomic status	**-0.930**	0.5	**2.103**	1.7						
• SES-squared	-0.348		**-0.587**							
Pro-social behaviour										
• Socioeconomic status			-0.037	0.0	0.030	0.1	**0.128**	0.4	**0.150**	0.7
• SES-squared			-0.012		-0.056		**-0.040**		-0.017	
Preschool vocabulary										
• Socioeconomic status					**3.858**	6.0				
• SES-squared					-0.093					
Mathematics computation										
• Socioeconomic status							**2.180**	4.4	**3.067**	3.2
• SES-squared							0.222		-0.080	

Note: Coefficients that are statistically significant (p < 0.05) appear in boldface.

national average) having a low MSD score is about 73 percent that of a child in a family with nationally average SES. The odds ratios for behaviour disorders range from 0.67 for toddlers to 0.81 for preschoolers. The odds ratios for low PPVT-R scores and for low mathematics scores range from 0.58 to 0.60. Thus, children in high-SES families are much less likely to be vulnerable than those in low-SES families.

■ **Gradients Associated with SES and Family and Child Characteristics**

Measures of development

The aim of the next sets of analyses is to unpack the SES gradient into its constituent components and to expand the set of potential explanatory variables

Table 4.4

The relationship between markers of vulnerability and socioeconomic status (SES) (odds ratios)

	Infants and babies Odds Ratio	R^2	Toddlers Odds Ratio	R^2	Preschoolers Odds Ratio	R^2	Primary pupils Odds Ratio	R^2	Intermediate pupils Odds Ratio	R^2
Low motor and social development										
• Socioeconomic status	1.041	0.4	**0.726**	2.3						
• SES-squared	**1.073**		**1.095**							
Difficult temperament										
• Socioeconomic status	**0.905**	0.2	0.974	0.0						
• SES-squared	1.023		0.994							
Behaviour disorder										
• Socioeconomic status			**0.672**	3.6	**0.809**	1.1	**0.804**	1.2	**0.769**	1.8
• SES-squared			0.981		1.023		0.949		1.038	
Preschool vocabulary										
• Socioeconomic status					**0.580**	6.6				
• SES-squared					1.048					
Mathematics computation										
• Socioeconomic status							**0.585**	4.1	**0.599**	4.4
• SES-squared							0.918		0.983	

Note: Odds ratios that differ significantly from 1.0 (p < 0.05) appear in boldface.

to include various family and child characteristics. The multiple regression results for the measures of development are shown in Table 4.5. The intercepts are estimates of the expected scores for a group of children that was nationally representative; that is, of nationally average income, mother's education, etc., and with a representative mix of single parents, teen mothers, and immigrant families.[2]

The set of coefficients has relatively little explanatory power for MSD for infants and babies; it explains less than three percent of the variance. For toddlers, the most important explanatory variables are the parents' level of education and whether the mother was at home rather than working full-time outside the home. MSD scores increased with higher levels of education— each additional year of either the mother's or the father's level of education was associated with an increase of about 0.4 of a point. MSD scores were about

Table 4.5

The relationship between measures of development and family and child characteristics (unstandardized regression coefficients)

	Infants and babies	Toddlers	Preschoolers	Primary children	Intermediate children
	Motor and social development	Motor and social development	PPVT-R	Mathematics computation	Mathematics computation
Intercept	**99.321**	**99.991**	**100.250**	**-0.926**	**1.096**
Socioeconomic status					
• Income	-0.296	-0.031	**0.498**	-0.053	**0.948**
• Income-squared	**0.131**	0.005	**-0.100**	-0.069	-0.069
• Mother's education	-0.258	**0.437**	**1.106**	**0.663**	**0.481**
• Mother works part-time	-0.348	-1.198	**1.559**	0.393	0.195
• Mother at home	-1.094	**-3.443**	0.721	-0.133	**2.006**
• Father's education	0.080	**0.369**	**0.278**	**0.404**	**0.696**
• Father's occupation	-0.560	0.413	**0.687**	0.360	**-0.969**
Family and child characteristics					
• Single parent	0.712	1.636	-0.843	-1.946	0.736
• Teenage mother	1.150	1.693	**-3.580**	-0.051	-2.048
• Number of siblings	**-1.776**	-0.383	**-1.543**	0.059	-0.177
• Immigrant					
- Within last 4 years	-2.466	-1.028	**-10.781**	3.037	-0.386
- 5 to 9 years ago	**-3.944**	**-8.015**	**-11.382**	**-3.306**	-0.998
- More than 10 years ago	0.997	**-3.915**	**-8.917**	0.720	1.259
• Female	**1.766**	**7.042**	0.385	-0.736	**2.195**
R-squared	2.8	9.3	13.2	5.7	4.3

Note: Coefficients that are statistically significant (p < 0.05) appear in boldface.

3.4 points lower for mothers who were at home, compared with those working full-time. MSD scores were also somewhat lower for children whose parents were immigrants: the differences ranged from one to eight points. Finally, girls' MSD scores were about seven points higher than boys'.

Nearly all factors in the model were significantly related to children's receptive vocabulary at ages four and five. The effect of family income was about

0.50, indicating that PPVT-R scores increase by about half a point for each increase in income of $10,000. Note that this estimate is less than half the effect associated with income in Table 4.1. This difference is because the estimate is the expected change in PPVT-R scores associated with an increase in income of $10,000, after taking account of the other variables in the model. There was a relatively large effect on vocabulary scores associated with the mother's level of education—about 1.1 points for each additional year of education. This is about four times as large as the effect associated with the father's level of education. The PPVT-R scores are also, on average, about 1.6 points higher for mothers who are working part-time. (They are also higher for mothers who are not working outside the home, but the difference is not statistically significant.) The father's occupation is also a significant predictor of early vocabulary skills, but the effect is relatively small.

There are also important effects associated with family structure. Children with more siblings, on average, have lower scores: each additional sibling is associated with a decrease of about 1.5 points. Children whose mothers were teenagers when the children were born have considerably lower scores, on average about 3.6 points lower. There were no statistically significant differences associated with single-parent families or with the sex of the child. The average scores of children whose parents were recent immigrants is lower, which is to be expected because the test language (either English or French) is a second language for most of these children.

For mathematics scores, the most important predictors were the mother's and father's levels of education. Taken together, they amount to an increase of one month of schooling for each additional year of education for the mother and father. Thus, children whose parents have four years of post-secondary education would, on average, have scores that are about four months of schooling higher than children whose parents had completed high school but had no post-secondary education. There was an effect of about two months of schooling for intermediate-age children associated with mothers being at home, but this was not consistent across the age range. There was an anomalous negative effect associated with father's occupation, but it is relatively small. The effects associated with family and child characteristics were in nearly all cases small and not statistically significant. The only significant effects were a negative effect for children in families that immigrated within the past five to nine years, but this was evident only for primary-age children. Girls scored about two months of schooling higher than boys at the intermediate level.

Table 4.6A

The relationship between markers of vulnerability and family and child characteristics (odds ratios)

	Infants and babies	Toddlers	Preschoolers	Primary children	Intermediate children
	Motor and social development	Motor and social development	PPVT-R	Mathematics computation	Mathematics computation
Socioeconomic status					
• Income	1.050	1.028	**0.886**	0.928	**0.873**
• Income-squared	**0.973**	1.008	1.005	**1.044**	0.982
• Mother's education	0.980	**0.916**	0.857	**0.864**	0.935
• Mother works part-time	0.999	1.069	0.841	0.936	1.061
• Mother at home	1.239	**1.810**	1.103	0.841	1.098
• Father's education	0.994	**0.919**	0.985	0.954	0.950
• Father's occupation	**1.147**	0.963	0.918	0.876	1.008
Family and child characteristics					
• Single parent	1.492	0.729	1.051	1.082	1.147
• Teenage mother	**0.573**	0.797	**1.475**	0.735	0.937
• Number of siblings	**1.267**	1.003	**1.169**	0.953	1.009
• Immigrant					
- Within last 4 years	1.031	1.394	**2.943**	1.486	**2.103**
- 5 to 9 years ago	**2.164**	**2.561**	**8.641**	0.686	1.380
- More than 10 years ago	1.152	**1.828**	**3.628**	0.947	0.719
• Female	0.866	**0.408**	1.005	1.211	**0.113**
R-squared	3.7	9.3	17.1	6.1	8.2

Note: Odds ratios that differ significantly from 1.0 (p < 0.05) appear in boldface.

Markers of vulnerability

COGNITIVE DIFFICULTIES: The odds ratios associated with the full set of explanatory variables are displayed in Tables 4.6a and 4.6b. In Table 4.6a, the results pertain to the likelihood of a child having a low score in either MSD, PPVT-R, or mathematics. These markers were used to construct the vulnerability index for cognitive difficulties.

The results suggest that family income is related to PPVT-R at ages four and five, and mathematics at ages nine to eleven. The odds ratio for mother's education is on average about 0.91 across the age range. This is a large effect:

Table 4.6B

The relationship between markers of vulnerability and family and child characteristics (odds ratios)

	Infants and babies	Toddlers	Preschoolers	Primary children	Intermediate children
	Difficult temperament	Behaviour disorder	Behaviour disorder	Behaviour disorder	Behaviour disorder
Socioeconomic status					
• Income	0.956	0.995	0.973	1.010	0.959
• Income-squared	1.008	**0.977**	1.007	0.997	**1.018**
• Mother's education	1.034	0.970	**0.933**	**0.940**	**0.925**
• Mother works part-time	1.179	1.031	**1.252**	0.975	1.089
• Mother at home	1.072	1.145	0.801	0.883	**1.246**
• Father's education	0.970	0.962	1.040	0.979	1.018
• Father's occupation	0.964	**0.891**	**0.874**	0.959	0.938
Family and child characteristics					
• Single parent	0.823	**2.095**	**1.402**	**1.965**	**1.492**
• Teenage mother	**1.471**	**1.899**	0.941	**2.014**	1.306
• Number of siblings	0.962	1.011	0.937	0.935	**0.887**
• Immigrant					
- Within last 4 years	0.811	**0.448**	0.799	**0.184**	**0.072**
- 5 to 9 years ago	0.794	**2.086**	1.222	**0.424**	**0.429**
- More than 10 years ago	1.163	1.216	0.856	1.023	**0.637**
• Female	**0.765**	0.985	1.115	**0.502**	**0.691**
R-squared	1.3	7.0	2.5	7.8	6.6

Note: Odds ratios that differ significantly from 1.0 (p < 0.05) appear in boldface.

it means that the odds of a child being vulnerable in the cognitive domain decreases by about ten percent for each additional year of maternal education. In contrast, the odds ratio for father's education is on average about 0.96, and is only statistically significant for MSD at ages 2 and 3. The effects of the other SES variables are not significant across the age range. This is also the case for the variables describing other family and child characteristics. Children whose parents have recently immigrated tend to be more vulnerable to low MSD and PPVT-R scores, but this is not the case for mathematics for children whose families have been in the country for at least five years.

Perhaps the results of greatest interest are those for PPVT-R. The set of background variables explains about seventeen percent of the variance. The results suggest that a child is more likely to have a low PPVT-R score if the family is relatively poor, if the mother has a low level of education and was a teen when the child was born, and if the child has several siblings. The increased vulnerability associated with low maternal education and number of siblings suggests that early language development may be related to the quality and quantity of a child's exposure to language (Willms, 1999). I repeated the logistic regression in Table 4.6a for PPVT-R, substituting the number of siblings variable with three dummy variables denoting birth order. The odds ratios for low PPVT-R scores associated with being second-born, third-born, and fourth-born, compared with first born, were 1.45, 1.98, and 1.49 respectively. (Only the odds ratios for second- and third-born were statistically significant, however.) These results provide strong evidence that the first-born child is much less likely to have exceedingly poor verbal skills upon entry to school. They also suggest that exposure to adult language has a strong effect on verbal skills.

BEHAVIOUR PROBLEMS: The first four columns of Table 4.6b display the results pertaining to the likelihood of a child having a behaviour problem. The results indicate that income has a very minor role: the odds ratios range from 0.96 to 1.01, and only the odds ratio for intermediate school children is significant. Maternal education, however, is significant at all ages, except for toddlers. For children aged 4 to 11, the odds ratio is about 0.93, indicating that for each additional year of maternal education, the odds of a child having a behaviour problem decrease by about 7 percent. This effect is not evident for the father's level of education. Children whose fathers have a high-status occupation are less vulnerable: the odds ratios range from 0.87 to 0.96. The most significant finding, however, pertains to the increased vulnerability associated with single parenthood: here the odds ratios range from 1.40 to 2.10, which indicates that children living in single-parent families are much more likely to display behaviour problems. Children living with teenage mothers are also more likely to display behaviour problems, but the odds ratios are not as strong as for single parents. (These differences are examined in detail in Chapters 13 and 14.)

The results pertaining to number of siblings suggest that children are *less* likely to have behaviour problems if they have more siblings. As with the model for early receptive vocabulary, I repeated the logistic regression analysis with

Table 4.6c

The relationship between vulnerability indices and family and child characteristics (odds ratios)

	Cognitive index	Behavioural index	Vulnerability index
Socioeconomic status			
• Income	**0.958**	0.986	**0.961**
• Income-squared	1.001	1.001	1.001
• Mother's education	**0.936**	**0.949**	**0.947**
• Mother works part-time	1.011	1.089	1.073
• Mother at home	**1.301**	0.996	1.137
• Father's education	**0.961**	0.996	0.992
• Father's occupation	0.992	**0.934**	**0.940**
Family and child characteristics			
• Single parent	0.915	**1.602**	1.247
• Teenage mother	1.015	**1.404**	**1.231**
• Number of siblings	1.018	**0.961**	**0.967**
• Immigrant			
- Within last 4 years	**1.367**	**0.373**	**0.626**
- 5 to 9 years ago	**1.856**	**0.820**	1.123
- More than 10 years ago	**1.467**	0.896	1.115
• Female	**0.732**	**0.757**	**0.771**
R-squared	3.5	3.6	3.3

Note: Odds ratios that differ significantly from 1.0 (p < 0.05) appear in boldface.

dummy variables denoting birth order. The odds ratios associated with being second-born, third-born, and fourth-born, compared with first-born, were 0.96, 0.69, and 0.94 respectively; however, only the odds ratio associated with third-born was significant. Nevertheless, these results suggest that children may be less vulnerable to behaviour problems if they have more brothers and sisters. ✳

The odds ratios for the variables denoting immigrant status vary considerably, from 0.07 to 2.09, but generally the ratios are less than 1.0. For school-age children especially, the likelihood of a child having a behaviour problem is much lower for children whose parents are recent immigrants than for non-immigrant children.

The findings also show that girls are much less prone to displaying behaviour problems during the school-age years.

OVERALL VULNERABILITY: Table 4.6c displays the odds ratios for the vulnerability indices. For the cognitive index, the results indicate that children are less likely to be vulnerable if they are living in a family with a relatively high level of income, with a father who has a prestigious occupation, and with a mother who has a high level of education and is working at least part-time outside of the home. Males are more likely to be vulnerable than females, and children whose parents have recently immigrated are also more likely to be vulnerable in the cognitive domain.

The pattern is somewhat different for the behavioural index. The mother's level of education continues to play an important role, as does the sex of the child, but family income and the mother's working status were not significant predictors of whether a child was vulnerable. However, the results indicate that children from single-parent families and children whose mothers were in their teen years when the child was born are much more likely to have behaviour problems. Contrary to the results for cognitive difficulties, children whose parents have recently immigrated are less likely to be vulnerable. Children with more brothers and sisters are less prone to behaviour problems.

For the composite vulnerability index, the results indicate that the most important aspects of family background and child characteristics are the mother's level of education, the father's occupation, whether the mother was a teen when the child was born, and the sex of the child. The effect of family income, although statistically significant, is relatively small. The results for immigrant status is less certain, because its effects differ for cognitive difficulties and behaviour problems. Overall, however, the models account for less than four percent of the variance, suggesting that family background is not a strong predictor of childhood vulnerability.

■ Relative Risk Versus Attributable Risk

Multiple regression and logistic regression are powerful tools for assessing the multivariate relationship between an outcome and a set of variables. However, from a policy perspective, it is difficult to discern the relative importance of regression coefficients or odds ratios, especially when the overall relationship, as gauged by R-squared, is weak. For example, the odds ratio for teen mothers for most outcomes is fairly large, but there are relatively few teen mothers in Canada, and therefore programs aimed to reduce the incidence of teen births would not dramatically reduce the prevalence of vulnerable children. Two useful statistics, commonly used by epidemiologists, are *relative risk* and

Table 4.7

Relative risk (RR) and attributable risk (AR) associated with family background and child characteristics

	Cognitive difficulties		Behaviour problems		Vulnerable	
	RR	AR (%)	RR	AR (%)	RR	AR (%)
Family income less than $25,000	1.47	10.8	1.45	10.5	1.41	9.5
Mother's education less than secondary	1.61	13.2	1.51	11.3	1.47	10.4
Mother not working outside the home	1.47	12.8	1.08	2.4	1.19	5.7
Father has low-status job	1.17	2.6	1.23	3.5	1.23	3.6
Single parent	1.16	2.3	1.61	8.7	1.36	5.2
Teenage parent	1.18	0.7	1.66	2.4	1.43	1.6
Recent immigrant	1.43	7.2	0.79	-4.1	0.99	-0.2
More than one sibling	1.14	4.4	0.88	-4.2	0.95	-1.6
Male	1.32	13.8	1.24	10.7	1.20	9.1

attributable risk. Relative risk is the ratio of the proportion of people who are vulnerable among those who have been exposed to a particular risk factor, to the proportion of people who are vulnerable among those who have *not* been exposed to the risk factor. As a multiplier, it indicates the degree to which the likelihood of a person being vulnerable might increase if the person changed from being *unexposed* to the risk factor to being *exposed* to the risk factor. Attributable risk expresses the proportion of the total occurrence of vulnerability that could be attributed to a particular risk factor. These two statistics are based on bivariate relationships and are limited in that respect. However, they do provide a means for assessing the relative and absolute effects of a particular variable.[3]

Table 4.7 displays the relative risk and attributable risk for the set of variables most strongly related to childhood vulnerability in the previous analyses. For each family background variable or child characteristic, it is necessary to dichotomize the variable based on some arbitrary cut point. For example, for family income, I have taken $25,000 as the cut point and considered incomes below this level to constitute risk.

For cognitive difficulties, the risk factors with the highest relative risk are low family income, low maternal education, a mother who does not work outside the home, and a family that has recently immigrated. The attributable risk associated with low family income is 10.8 percent, which suggests that if we could boost everyone's income above that level, the prevalence of vulnerability would only be reduced by about 10 percent. The attributable risk associated with maternal education and the mother's employment status is slightly higher, but still only about thirteen percent. Only a small fraction of cognitive difficulty in children is attributable to children who are recent immigrants.

The risk factors for behaviour problems with the highest relative risk are living in a single parent family and having a teenage mother. However, the attributable risk associated with these factors is rather low: for single parents it is 8.7 percent, and for teenage parents it is only 2.4 percent. As with cognitive difficulties, low family income and low maternal education have a relative risk of about 1.5, and an attributable risk of over 10 percent. The attributable risk associated with males is also over ten percent.

The estimates of relative risk for overall childhood vulnerability indicate that the five most important factors are low maternal education, teenage motherhood, low family income, single parenthood, and low paternal occupational status, in that order. Only one factor—low maternal education—has an attributable risk of over ten percent.

Many children, however, have more than one risk factor. In fact, only about half (51.5 percent) of all children in the sample had none of the five risk factors. Figure 4.3 displays the relative risk associated with having one or more of the above risk factors. As one would expect, the relative risk increases as the number of risk factors increases. The maximum relative risk is 2.13, for children with 4 risk factors. (The decline for five risk factors is due to the small sample size.) The graph also displays the "cumulative" attributable risk associated with one or more risk factors; for example, the cumulative attributable risk for three risk factors is the attributable risk associated with having either one, two, or three risk factors. At 5 risk factors, the cumulative attributable risk levels off at 19.2 percent. This is instructive: it indicates that even if we could eliminate all the risk factors associated with family background, we would reduce childhood vulnerability by less than twenty percent.

Sidebar 4.3
Hierarchical linear modelling

Data in the social sciences are often structured hierarchically. For example, students are typically nested within classes, which are nested within schools, which are nested within school districts. In the case of the NLSCY data, children are nested within families, and we consider families to be nested within neighbourhoods and larger communities. Researchers often select their sample in a way that explicitly takes account of a hierarchical structure. For example, a researcher might sample schools from the population of all elementary schools in a province and then sample ten students from each school.

Hierarchical linear modelling (HLM) is a specialized regression technique that is designed to analyze hierarchically structured data (Goldstein, 1995; Raudenbush & Bryk, 2002). With traditional regression approaches, (e.g., multiple regression and logistic regression), one of the underlying assumptions is that the observations are independent; that is, the observations of any one individual are not in any way systematically related to the observations of any other individual. This assumption is violated, for example, if some of the observed children are from the same family or attending the same school. The consequences of violating the assumption of independent observations are that the estimates of the regression coefficients can be biased and the estimates of standard errors are too small. Therefore, there is a risk of inferring that a relationship is statistically significant when it may have occurred by chance alone.

Moreover, the interest both theoretically and with respect to policy is often in the within-unit relationships, whether these relationship vary among units, and, if so, whether the variation is related to characteristics of those units. For example, the average level of academic achievement and the relationship of academic achievement to family income may vary among schools within a schooling system. The researcher and policy-maker may be interested in whether schools with high average achievement and more equitable achievement have smaller class sizes, different kinds of instructional techniques, or differing forms of school organization (Lee, Bryk, & Smith, 1990; Raudenbush & Willms, 1995). The basic idea underlying HLM is that there are separate analyses for each unit at the lowest level of a hierarchical structure, and the results of these analyses (usually the regression coefficients) become the dependent variables for analyses at the next level of the hierarchy. There are numerous applications of hierarchical linear models, including models for examining the effects of schools on student achievement (Raudenbush & Willms, 1995; Raudenbush & Bryk, 2002), changes in children's outcomes over time (e.g., Bryk & Raudenbush, 1987; Willms & Jacobsen, 1990), the stability of institutional effects (Willms & Raudenbush, 1989), and the extent to which communities are segregated along ethnic or social-class lines (Willms & Paterson, 1995).

In this study, the explicit hierarchical structure is children nested within families. For most of the analysis, however, we examine the relationships for specific age cohorts, such as the subsample of children aged four and five. For these cohorts, there is relatively little nesting within families, because among those families with more than one child, nearly all of them have only one child in the narrow age range. Our preliminary analyses found that traditional approaches yielded estimate that were very close to estimates based on HLM, and thus in most cases we use traditional approaches.

Our primary interest in the use of HLM is in examining the variation in children's outcomes within and between communities. We want to determine whether there are community "effects" that are not associated with children's individual-level background characteristics. In other words, are some communities more effective than others in reducing childhood vulnerability, and, if so, why? The HLM analysis estimates a separate regression model for each community. These provide an estimate for each community of the expected score of a child with nationally average background characteristics. The analysis allows us to examine how much variation exists between communities and to identify particularly effective and ineffective communities. The second stage of the HLM analysis asks whether these community effects are related to features of the community. Our community-level data include demographic variables derived from the 1996 Canadian census and a measure of social support based on the aggregate of the responses of the "person most knowledgeable" (PMK) to a set of questions pertaining to the level of social support they experience.

Figure 4.3

Relative risk and cumulative risk versus number of risk factors

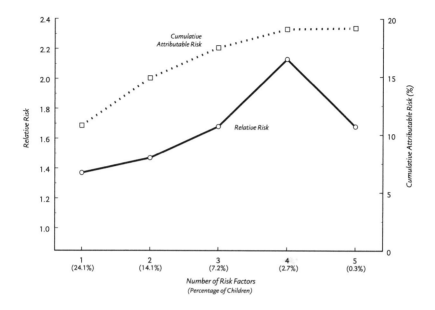

■ Variation Among Neighbourhoods, Cities, and Provinces in Childhood Vulnerability

The final set of analyses in this chapter examines whether the prevalence of childhood vulnerability varies among neighbourhoods, cities, and provinces within Canada. The aim of the analyses is to test the hypotheses of differences among communities, converging gradients, and double jeopardy for these spatial units of analysis: neighbourhoods, cities, and provinces.

The analyses employ a relatively complex statistical technique called hierarchical linear modelling (HLM), which takes account of the hierarchical structure of the data (see Sidebar 4.3). In these analyses, the outcome measure is whether or not a child is vulnerable, as defined by the vulnerability index.[4] Therefore, the hierarchical models in these analyses fit a logistic regression model for each spatial unit (neighbourhoods, cities, and provinces). The intercepts from these models can be converted to estimates of the prevalence for

Table 4.8

Variation among neighbourhoods, cities, and provinces in the prevalence of childhood vulnerability

	Neighbourhoods (1247 enumeration areas)			Cities (64 census metropolitan areas)			Provinces (10 provinces)		
	I	II	III	I	II	III	I	I	III
Average likelihood (%)	28.3	26.7	27.5	28.6	28.5	28.7	27.8	26.5	26.2
Child-level (odds ratios)									
• Socioeconomic status		**0.74**	**0.75**		**0.76**	**0.76**		**0.76**	**0.75**
• Female		**0.77**	**0.78**		**0.77**	**0.77**		**0.77**	**0.77**
Variation among units									
• Low prevalence (%)	21.2	20.1	21.0	25.5	25.4	25.5	26.0	24.4	24.0
• High prevalence (%)	36.6	34.6	35.2	31.9	31.8	32.1	29.6	28.7	28.6
• Gradual gradient (odds ratio)		0.58			0.75			0.75	
• Steep gradient (odds ratio)		0.95			0.77			0.77	
Unit-level (odds ratios)									
• Median income			1.04			1.08			1.05
• Two-parent families			**0.99**			1.00			0.99
• Years of education			0.99			0.93			0.97
• Social support			0.97			0.97			1.37

Note: Odds ratios that differ significantly from 1.0 (p < 0.05) appear in boldface.

each spatial unit, and the other coefficients from these models can be converted to odds ratios (see Sidebar 4.2). The hierarchical analysis also provides estimates of the variation among spatial units in the estimated logistic regression coefficients, and a chi-square test of whether these regression coefficients vary statistically among spatial units. Thus, it can discern whether the observed variation in estimates of prevalence is likely to be "true" variation, rather than variation due to sampling or measurement error. The estimates of the variance in intercepts are difficult to interpret. Therefore, to facilitate interpretation, I estimated the prevalence for a unit which was one standard deviation below the average for all units, and the prevalence for a unit which was one standard deviation above the average for all units. The results are presented in Table 4.8.

Neighbourhoods

The first column of Table 4.8 is a "null model" for neighbourhoods. It is called a null model because it does not include any covariates, such as socioeconomic status; it is simply concerned with whether the likelihood of a child being vulnerable varies among neighbourhoods. The analysis includes all children in the National Longitudinal Survey of Children and Youth (NLSCY) sample who were in enumeration areas that had a sample size of at least five children. The sample was made up of 7,555 children in 1247 enumeration areas. The analysis provides an estimate of the likelihood of vulnerability for each neighbourhood, an estimate of the variance of these estimates among neighbourhoods, and an estimate of the average level of vulnerability for all neighbourhoods.

The analysis indicates that neighbourhoods vary in their prevalence of vulnerable children. The estimate of the average prevalence of vulnerability for Canadian neighbourhoods is 28.3 percent, but the prevalence ranged from 21.2 percent to 36.6 percent. About two-thirds of all neighbourhoods would have a prevalence within that range.

The second model fit a separate logistic regression for each neighbourhood, which includes, at the child level, the composite SES variable and the dummy variable for sex. The model provides an estimate for each neighbourhood of the expected prevalence of childhood vulnerability, after taking account of the socioeconomic status and sex of the children sampled for that neighbourhood. The average of the adjusted prevalence for the 1247 neighbourhoods was 26.7 percent. One would expect that some of the variation among neighbourhoods is attributable to the SES of the families who live there and therefore would be smaller after adjusting for SES. The range of prevalence for the adjusted model is 20.1 percent to 34.6 percent, which is smaller than for the unadjusted model, but the reduction is not substantial. Thus, the wide range in prevalence among neighbourhoods is only partially explained by family SES.

The model also provides an estimate of the odds ratio associated with SES for each neighbourhood. The average of these odds ratios is 0.74, which is consistent with the estimates provided earlier in this chapter. The odds ratios range among neighbourhoods from 0.58 to 0.95, which is a substantial variation; however, because of the small sample size within neighbourhoods (on average only about six children), it was not statistically significant. Consequently, the data do not provide a strong test as to whether the gradients within neighbourhoods converge. I also tested whether the odds ratios for sex varied significantly among neighbourhoods, and this variation was also not statistically significant.

The third model asks whether some of the variation among neighbourhoods can be explained by the demographic characteristics of the neighbourhoods or the measure of social support. The hypothesis of double jeopardy holds that children are more likely to be vulnerable if they live in neighbourhoods with lower SES. The model includes three indicators of the socio-economic characteristics of the neighbourhoods: median income, percentage of two-parent families, and average number of years of education. The odds ratios for two-parent families and years of education are less than 1.0, which is consistent with the hypothesis of double jeopardy, but the coefficients are close to 1 and significant only for two-parent families. The odds ratio for median income, although not statistically significant, is above 1.0, contrary to the hypothesis. The odds ratio for social support is 0.97. Although not statistically significant, this figure suggests that having a supportive neighbourhood reduces vulnerability.

Cities

The second set of models examines the variation in vulnerability among 64 Canadian cities. The estimates are based on data for 9,097 children sampled in these cities. The average prevalence across cities was 28.6 percent, which is identical to the estimate for all Canadian children. Prevalence varies significantly among cities, ranging from 25.5 percent to 31.9 percent.

The second model in this set includes the measures for SES and sex. The average odds ratio for SES is 0.76 and does not vary significantly among cities— the range is from 0.75 to 0.77. Thus, although the analysis indicates that the prevalence of vulnerable children varies from city to city, the gradients are quite similar across cities. We can also conclude, therefore, that the hypothesis of converging gradients does not hold.

Finally, the model is extended to include the city-level demographic variables and mean levels of social support. The results suggest that children living in cities with a high level of parental education and a high level of social support are less likely to be vulnerable. This is consistent with the hypothesis of double jeopardy. However, as with the neighbourhood results, the effects are not statistically significant, and the effect for median family income is in the opposite direction. Thus, there is not strong evidence of double jeopardy.

Provinces

The prevalence estimates for each province are discussed in Chapter 3 and displayed in Figure 3.3. The hierarchical analysis presented in Table 4.8 indicates that this inter-provincial variation is statistically significant. Moreover, the variation among provinces does not diminish after we take account of SES at the individual level—in fact, it increases slightly. This increase is because some of the provinces with lower levels of income and parental education have a relatively low prevalence of vulnerable children (e.g., Saskatchewan and the Atlantic provinces). As with the analyses for neighbourhoods and cities, the inter-provincial variation could not be explained by the aggregate measures of SES or the mean level of social support.

■

This chapter attempts to address eight of the ten questions regarding socioeconomic gradients set out in Chapter 1. It examines the role of income and a composite index of SES separately before identifying the specific components of SES with the strongest relationships to the childhood outcomes measured in this study. In presenting the gradients, the emphasis is not on whether particular socioeconomic factors are statistically significant, but whether the relationships are strong in substantive terms. Thus, the emphasis is on the magnitude of the particular regression coefficients and the proportion of variance explained by SES and demographic characteristics. These two statistics—regression coefficients and proportion of variance explained—are similar in meaning to relative risk and attributable risk as used in epidemiology. As part of this analysis, I established cut-off scores on the prominent explanatory factors and estimated the relative risk and attributable risk associated with childhood vulnerability. Finally, this chapter presents the findings of an extensive multilevel analysis aimed at understanding variation among neighbourhoods, cities, and provinces.

The main findings of these analyses are presented below, following the order of the research questions set out in the first chapter.

1. *Socioeconomic gradients are evident in children's temperament during the first two years of infancy.* The results indicate that a $10,000-increase in family income is associated with a decrease of about 5 percent in the likelihood of an infant or baby being identified by the mother as having a difficult temperament (see Table 4.2). Similarly, children whose family SES that is

one standard deviation above the national average are ten percent less likely to have a difficult temperament (see Table 4.4). However, this relationship is weaker at ages two and three, and is not statistically significant. Overall, the model explains less than one-half of one percent of the variance. Chapter 6 examines babies' temperament in greater detail and finds that certain aspects of temperament are more strongly related to socioeconomic factors.

2. *Socioeconomic gradients appear to get steeper as children get older.* On the measures of motor and social development, pro-social behaviour, and mathematics computation, the magnitude of the regression coefficients for both family income and SES increase with the age of the child (see Tables 4.1 and 4.3). Similarly, the likelihood of a child having low motor and social development or low mathematics skills tends to be more strongly related to family income and SES for older children (see Tables 4.2 and 4.4). There are two exceptions, however. One is the marker of difficult temperament, which has a stronger relationship with income and socioeconomic status for infants than for toddlers. The other is the marker of behaviour disorders, which has a relatively strong relationship with income and SES during the toddler years, but then fits the general pattern for children aged four through eleven.

3. *Socioeconomic gradients are especially strong for children's early vocabulary skills.* The gradients for PPVT-R scores associated with both family income and SES are steeper than all other observed gradients (see Table 4.1 and 4.3). This is the case also for the results pertaining to the likelihood of a child having a low PPVT-R score. This result may be due to the quality of the PPVT-R instrument, as it has a reliability of about 0.94 for this age group, whereas motor and social development and pro-social behaviour have a reliability of about 0.80. An equally plausible explanation, though, is that children's early vocabulary development is directly influenced by the quality and quantity of language spoken by the parents and the extent to which parents engage their child in language-related activities during the preschool years, whereas the measures pertaining to behaviour are more closely related to less tangible factors such as parenting style, and mathematics computation is more closely related to factors associated with the quality of schooling.

4. *Children are less likely to be vulnerable if they are female and if their mothers have a high level of education.* These are the only two factors that have a strong relationship with both the cognitive and behavioural indices (see Tables 4.5, 4.6a, 4.6b, and 4.6c). The effects of other factors tend to vary depending on the outcome considered. Cognitive difficulties tend to be more closely related to low family income, fathers who have a low level of education, and mothers who are not employed outside the home. In contrast, behaviour problems tend to be associated strongly with whether the mother is a single parent or had the child when she was a teen. Children with more siblings tend to have more cognitive difficulties but fewer behaviour problems. The same applies for recent immigrants.

5. *Gradients associated with family income and socioeconomic status tend to be linear.* For some outcomes, the gradient associated with family income is curvilinear, levelling off at higher level of income (see Table 4.1). But the degree of curvilinearity is quite small and only discernible at incomes above $60,000 (see Figures 4.1, 4.2, and 4.3). There is also no discernable non-linearity in the gradients for SES. These findings provide strong evidence that we cannot identify an income threshold below which there is a much higher prevalence of childhood vulnerability.

6. *Single parents and young mothers are two groups within our society whose children are particularly vulnerable to behaviour problems.* Children in single-parent families and children whose mothers were teens when the children were born are about 1.6 times as likely to have behaviour problems (see Table 4.7). Although the attributable risk associated with these two groups is relatively small, especially for teen mothers, the findings suggest that if there is a case for targeted interventions, it would be for programs that provide these parents strategies to encourage positive behaviour and deal with problem behaviour. The results also stress the importance of universal programs aimed at preventing early pregnancies.

7. *Socioeconomic gradients for most childhood outcomes are fairly weak.* In the models that included a full complement of socioeconomic and demographic factors, the explanatory factors explained less than ten percent of the variance (see Sidebar 2.1). The only exception was early receptive vocabulary,

where the model explained about thirteen percent of the variance in children's PPVT-R scores. In analyses of schooling outcomes that employ a similar set of socioeconomic variables, R-squared values of 25 percent or higher are common.

8. *The prevalence of childhood vulnerability varies substantially among neighbourhoods and cities.* The analyses indicate that the prevalence of vulnerable children ranges from about 20 to 35 percent among neighbourhoods and from about 25 to 32 percent among cities. This is substantial variation by any standard, and only a small fraction of this variability is attributable to socioeconomic factors (see Table 4.8). Provinces also vary in their rates of childhood vulnerability.

The modelling was not successful in affording a strong test of the hypothesis of converging gradients. At the neighbourhood level, the analysis suggested considerable variation in the strength of the gradients, but with so few children sampled per neighbourhood, the reliability of the estimated slopes was very low. At the levels of city and province, the analysis suggested relatively little variation among cities or among provinces in the slopes, and therefore it was not possible to determine whether gradients converged.

The evidence of a double-jeopardy effect was weak. Analysis indicated that low-SES children are even more vulnerable if they live in communities with a high percentage of single-parent families, but overall the effects were weak. The analysis also did not provide strong evidence that some neighbourhoods or cities are successful in reducing vulnerability because there is a high level of social support. Again, the effects were in the expected direction but were not statistically significant.

The lack of power in this analysis for testing hypotheses about community-level effects probably stems from at least two sources. First, the NLSCY sample was not explicitly designed to test such hypotheses; rather, it was designed to increase the accuracy of provincial estimates. A study aimed at discerning why communities vary in their outcomes would require a design whereby a number of communities were sampled first, and then large random samples were drawn from each community. Second, the choice of unit may be incorrect. Cities may be too large a unit, and enumeration areas may be too small. Enumeration areas are also probably a poor proxy for neighbourhoods, particularly with respect to the ways in which social and cultural capital affect children's outcomes. An analysis that combined contiguous enumeration areas on the basis of certain criteria may yield geographical units that better reflect how neighbourhoods affect children's outcomes (Konarski & Willms, 2000). Further research in this area would also benefit from analyses that take account of the spatial relationships of one unit to another. For example, one might expect that if one community is particularly effective in reducing vulnerability, many of the adjacent communities would also be effective.

■

In this type of study, one cannot claim a *causal* relationship between explanatory factors and childhood vulnerability. For example, even though family income is related to childhood outcomes, we cannot claim that income supplements to poor families would necessarily reduce childhood vulnerability. However, to some extent, these findings provide an upper limit on the size of the effect one might anticipate. The results suggest that if we could increase the income of all families below $25,000, we would reduce the prevalence of childhood vulnerability by about 10 percent—that is, from 28.6 percent to about 25.7 percent. An intervention that ensured all future mothers completed secondary school would have about the same effect (see Table 4.7). Children who face several risk factors can be more than twice as likely to be vulnerable, but even if we could ameliorate all of the most important risk factors, we would only reduce childhood vulnerability by about 20 percent, from 28.6 percent to about 22.9 percent (see Figure 4.7).

Overall, therefore, these findings present a serious challenge to the "culture of poverty" thesis and to risk-factor research that suggests childhood vulnerability stems predominantly from poverty or low SES. The findings do not suggest that we should give up our efforts to reduce poverty: no child should have to face the many challenges associated with growing up in a poor family. But the findings do present a strong case for universal rather than targeted interventions. Interventions directed predominantly at poor families or poor communities will not substantially reduce childhood vulnerability.

The findings also emphasize our lack of understanding of childhood vulnerability. If low income or other socioeconomic factors are not the culprits, why do we have such a high prevalence of childhood vulnerability? And why is it that we can observe large variation among neighbourhoods and cities across Canada, but not discern why they vary? It seems that the important determinants of vulnerability have more to do with the culture or functioning of families and communities than their economic circumstances. However, research in this vein is more difficult. The constructs are difficult to define and measure; the processes are complex and interactive; and the important aspects of culture probably interact across the units of family, school, and community. The remaining chapters in this volume venture into this domain and take us a little further in our understanding of childhood vulnerability.

NOTES

1   The NLSCY collected data describing household income from the "Person Most Knowledgeable" (PMK). These data were provided in the database as categorical data to ensure confidentiality. The categorical responses were recoded to a single interval-level measure, with $1,000 units, by using the mid-value of each category (e.g., $10,000 to $14,999 was recoded to 12.5). Those with incomes below $10,000 were coded as 7.5, and those with incomes above 80,000 were coded as 90. In the regression analyses, the income variable was transformed to $10,000 units and centred on the national mean of $48,464. Therefore, a one-unit increase in an estimated regression coefficient represents the expected change in the outcome measure associated with a $10,000-change in income.

2   This average is achieved by "centring" the explanatory variables by subtracting the national mean from each child's score. For example, the national mean level of maternal education is 12.45 years. Thus, 12.45 is subtracted from the years-of-education variable for each child. This has no affect on the estimates of the coefficients, with the exception of the intercept (and any non-linear terms, such as income-squared).

3   There are multivariate variants of relative and attributable risk (see Rothman & Greenland, 1998), but these were not presented here as they are redundant to the results presented in Table 4.6a.

4   The same analyses were also conducted for the cognitive and behavioural indices. For the cognitive index, the variation among units in the first model was not statistically significant and thus it was not practical to carry the modelling further. For the behaviour index, the variation among neighbourhoods was statistically significant, but after SES was included in the model, the variation was not statistically significant. The variation among cities and among provinces was also statistically significant, but the findings were largely similar to those for the overall vulnerability index, and therefore these results are not presented separately.

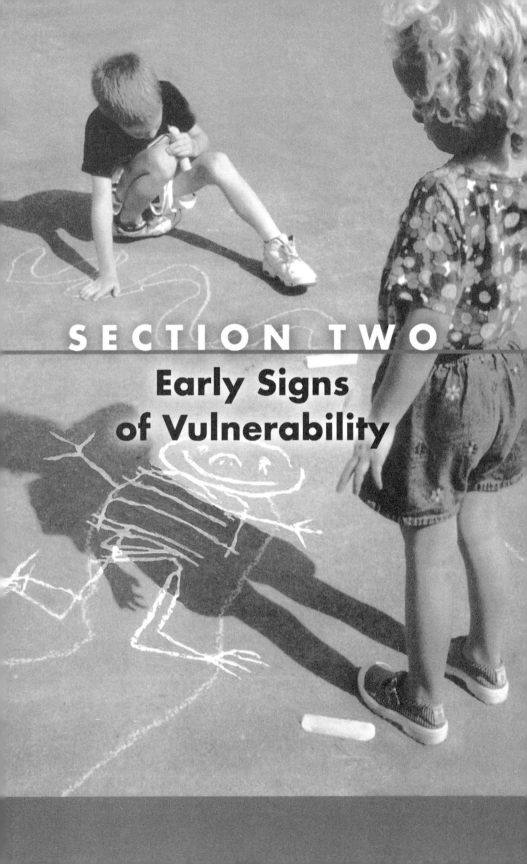

SECTION TWO
Early Signs
of Vulnerability

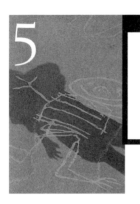

Identifying Vulnerable Children at an Early Age

CHRISTA JAPEL, CLAUDE NORMAND,

RICHARD TREMBLAY, & J. DOUGLAS WILLMS

TEMPERAMENT MAY BEST BE VIEWED as a general term referring to the _how_ of behaviour. Temperament differs from ability and motivation, which can be viewed as the _what_ and _why_ of behaviour, in that temperament refers to a behavioural style (Thomas & Chess, 1977). Two children, for example, may be equally skilful in riding a bicycle, playing an instrument, or assembling a difficult puzzle, and they may share the same motives for engaging in these activities. Yet these two children may differ significantly with regard to the speed with which they move, the ease with which they approach a new person or environment, the intensity and character of their moods, and the effort required to distract them when they are absorbed in an activity.

These individual differences in behaviour and temperament can play significant roles in the genesis and evolution of behaviour problems in children. Results from the seminal New York Longitudinal Study, conducted during the 1960s, indicated that children with difficult temperament—characterized by irregular eating and sleeping patterns, intense reactions to stimuli, initial aversion and slow adaptation to changes in their environment, and frequent negative affect—were at greater risk for later behaviour problems (Thomas, Chess, & Birch, 1968). Since then, evidence of an association between difficult temperament during infancy and later social and emotional functioning has been mounting (e.g., Bates, Bayles, Bennett, Ridge, & Brown,

1991; Bates, Maslin, & Frankel, 1985; Guerin, Thomas, Olivier, & Gottfried, 1999). But empirical evidence of the predictive validity of temperament measures during early childhood is the subject of considerable debate, partly because measures of temperament appear to be only moderately stable during the first few years of life (Finegan, Niccols, Zacher, & Hood, 1989). For example, Thomas and Chess (1982) found that only measures of temperament after age three were predictive of later adjustment. Their work is supported by findings from a longitudinal study of a large cohort of children in New Zealand, which indicate that temperament assessed at age three is associated with behaviour problems at age fifteen (Caspi, Henry, McGee, Moffitt, & Silva, 1995), personality traits in young adulthood (Caspi & Silva, 1995), and psychiatric disorders in older adults (Caspi, Moffitt, Newman, & Silva, 1996).

Despite this controversy, recent evidence suggests individual differences in neuro-behavioural functioning can be detected even before birth. For example, some researchers have found more active fetuses to be more temperamentally difficult infants at ages three and six months (DiPietro, Hodgson, Costigan, and Johnson, 1996). The characteristics associated with difficult temperament are generally considered to be constitutionally based (or in a sense, "hard-wired") and associated with reactivity and self-regulation (Rothbart & Bates, 1998).

Infants do not develop in a vacuum, however; they grow up in an environmental system (Wachs, 1992). The manner in which their innate behavioural characteristics interact with features of their environment affects the course of their development. For example, Werner and Smith (1992) noted that easy infant temperament represented an important protective factor in a high-risk environment of poverty and poor family functioning. Temperamentally difficult infants appeared to be at greater risk for later maladjustment, partially because they elicited more negative responses from caregivers in a low socioeconomic context. Temperamental traits may therefore be moderated or amplified by environmental conditions. This *goodness of fit* (Lerner & Lerner, 1983) between the child's temperament and the demands and characteristics of the environment may account for a variety of positive and negative outcomes: a good fit would lead to favourable mental health outcomes, whereas a poor fit would be predictive of impaired function and maladjustment.

The measures of temperament used in most of this research rely on parents' descriptions of their child's behaviour. Some researchers have criticized parents' ratings as overly subjective and claim that they say more about the personality of the parents than the temperament of the child. Bates, Freeland,

and Lounsbury (1979), for example, noted that the mothers' personality and family background were major predictors of the mothers' ratings of infant temperament. Sameroff, Seifer, and Elias (1982) also found that temperament ratings could be predicted from the social status, anxiety level, and mental-health status of the mother. Vaughn, Bradley, Joffe, Seifer, and Barglow (1987) found mothers of difficult infants to be more anxious, suspicious, and impulsive. They had lower self-esteem than mothers of easy infants and were somewhat more likely to endorse negative statements about themselves. Earlier analyses of the National Longitudinal Survey of Children and Youth (NLSCY) revealed that early childbearing, poor family functioning, hostility in parenting, and the presence of hyperactive or anxious siblings were associated with maternal perceptions of difficult temperament (Normand et al., 1996). Thus, there is strong support for the view that parents' ratings of children's temperament are affected by their own experiences and characteristics.

But this may not render them invalid as predictors of later social and emotional functioning. Sameroff et al. (1982) suggested that the parents' perceptions of their child may even have a greater impact on their child's development than the child's actual temperament, because perceptions affect mother-and-child interactions. However, even though background and parental personality variables have been shown to be significant predictors of difficult child temperament, they explain only a small proportion of the variance in the temperament measures (Bates, 1994). Like Rothbart and Bates (1998), we view mothers' reports as consisting of both objective and subjective components; as such, they provide a useful perspective on both the personality of their children and the environmental factors that contribute to their children's development.

The Infant Characteristics Questionnaire (ICQ), developed by Bates, Freeland, & Lounsbury (1979), is frequently used to assess infant temperament. It is a short screening device based on mothers' ratings for assessing difficult temperament in four- to six-month-old infants. The ICQ is based on the dimensions of temperament used in the New York Longitudinal Study and contains aspects of temperament that can pose a challenge to the mother. Factor analyses of the items yielded four dimensions, labelled as *fussy–difficult*, *unadaptable*, *dull*, and *unpredictable*. Lee and Bates (1985) developed a slightly longer version of the ICQ for thirteen- and twenty-four-month-olds, which they called the Child Characteristics Questionnaire (CCQ); its scales are similar to the ICQ. Finegan et al. (1989) developed the Preschool Characteristics Questionnaire (PCQ) as an extension of the ICQ and CCQ. Factor analyses of the PCQ revealed four factors labelled *persistent/unstoppable, negative adaptation and affect, difficult,* and *irregular*.

The NLSCY is the first large-scale survey to use the ICQ. In this chapter we present an analysis of the responses of more than 8,000 parents of 3- to 47-month-old children who rated their child's temperament. The chapter has three objectives. First, it seeks to determine whether the factor structure and psychometric properties of the subscales derived from a nationally representative sample of Canadian children are comparable to those of the ICQ and its versions for older children. The ICQ, CCQ, and PCQ were validated with samples of 322, 160, and 121 children respectively, predominantly from middle- and upper middle-class backgrounds. The data from Bates et al. (1979) showed that the most salient and consistent factor up to age two was difficult temperament, which mainly refers to frequent and intense expression of negative affect. On the other hand, Finegan et al. (1989) found that, among three- and four-year-old children, the factor referred to as unstoppable/persistent accounted for the largest proportion of the variance. This suggests that, in older children, behaviours related to compliance appear to be more dominant in the mother's perceptions of temperament.

This chapter also intends to verify whether parental perceptions of temperament are related to other markers of vulnerability, such as low birth weight, delays in motor and social development, and behavioural problems. Low birth weight is an important marker of a baby's health, associated with an increased risk of developmental delays, physical limitations, and social and psychological problems (Cusson & Lee, 1994; Peacock, Bland, & Anderson, 1995; Ross, Scott, & Kelly, 1996; Saigal et al., 1994). Delays in motor, social, and cognitive development and behavioural problems during early childhood have been shown to put children at risk for later social and psychological maladjustment (Prior, Smart, Sanson, & Oberklaid, 1993; White, Moffitt, Earls, Robins, & Silva, 1990).

Finally, this chapter examines the relationship between measures of temperament and aspects of socioeconomic status (SES). The relationship between SES and temperament outcomes remains unclear. Sameroff et al. (1982) found socio-demographic variables contribute to maternal ratings of infant temperament, whereas Bates et al. (1979) found mothers' occupational status to be only weakly related to children's temperament. Some studies have shown parent and family characteristics other than SES to be significant predictors of difficult child temperament (e.g., Maziade, Boudreault, Thivierge, Capéraà, & Côté, 1984; Normand et al., 1996; Wolk, Zeanah, Garcia-Coll, & Carr, 1992). Differences with respect to the size of the samples and their composition, the nature and number of predictors, and the outcome measures may explain the divergence of these results. Nevertheless, they raise the question why SES is less consistently related to temperament outcomes, although it is consistently associated with the prevalence of behavioural maladjustment among older children, even after controlling for a range of intermediate variables known to be associated with child behaviour problems (Bor et al., 1997; Oberklaid, Sanson, Pedlow, & Prior, 1993; Offord & Lipman, 1996; Wasserman, DiBlasio, Bond, Young, & Colletti, 1990). Since difficult temperament appears to be related to later adjustment problems and SES is a better predictor of behavioural adjustment in later life than it is of difficult temperament during infancy and early childhood, the relationship between SES and temperament outcomes needs to be explored further.

■ Method

Temperament was assessed in the NLSCY by administering the ICQ and its versions for older children to the "person most knowledgeable" (PMK) about the child. The PMKs of 8,605 children aged 3 to 47 months provided information about their child's temperament. In 89 percent of cases, the PMK was the biological mother; in 9.2 percent, it was the biological father; and in the remaining 1.8 percent, it was step-parents, adoptive parents, or other careproviders.

In the ICQ, parents are asked to compare their child to others in response to questions such as *How easy or difficult is it for you to calm or soothe your baby when he or she is upset?*. The response scale for all items ranges from one (easy) to seven (difficult), with four representing "about average." The item content and the number of items vary with the age of the child. Parents of 3- to 5-month-old children are presented 21 items, whereas parents of 36- to 47-month-old children rate their child on 32 items. High scores on the ICQ indicate difficult temperament. However, we preferred to focus on positive aspects of temperament and therefore recoded scores so that high scores corresponded to easy or agreeable temperament. To achieve consistency with other scales in this book, we also scaled the scores to have a range of one to ten, rather than one to seven.

We then used principal component analysis with varimax rotation to extract temperament factors for four age groups: 3 to 11 months, 12 to 23 months, 24 to 35 months, and 36 to 47 months. The factor analysis yielded 4 temperament factors for 3- to 11-month-old and 12- to 23-month-old children, and 5 tempera-

Table 5.1

ICQ items of the various temperament dimensions by age group

Temperament dimensions	3–11 months	12–23 months
Good-natured	• easy or difficult to calm or soothe when upset • how many times per day fussy and irritable • how much crying and fuss in general • how easily upset • when upset, how vigorously crying and fussing • what kind of mood generally • how changeable mood • overall degree of difficulty	• easy or difficult to calm or soothe when upset • how many times per day fussy and irritable • how much crying and fuss in general • how easily upset • when upset, how vigorously crying and fussing • what kind of mood generally • how changeable mood • overall degree of difficulty
Independent	• wants to be held • how much attention other than for caregiving • when left alone, plays well	• how much attention other than for caregiving • when left alone, plays well
Consistent	• easy or difficult to predict sleep and wake-up • easy or difficult to predict when hungry • easy or difficult to know what is bothering when cries	• consistent in sticking with sleeping routine • consistent in sticking with eating routine • response to new foods
Adaptable	• reaction when being dressed • response to changes in everyday routine • response to first bath	• response to changes in everyda routine • response to new playthings • response to new person • response to new place • how well adapts to new experiences
Obedient		

24–35 months	36–47 months
• easy or difficult to calm or soothe when upset • how many times per day fussy and irritable • how much crying and fuss in general • how easily upset • when upset, how vigorously crying and fussing • what kind of mood generally • how changeable mood • overall degree of difficulty	• easy or difficult to calm or soothe when upset • how many times per day fussy and irritable • how much crying and fuss in general • how easily upset • when upset, how vigorously crying and fussing • what kind of mood generally • how changeable mood • overall degree of difficulty
• how much attention other than for caregiving • when left alone, plays well	• how much attention other than for caregiving • when left alone, plays well
• consistent in sticking with sleeping routine • consistent in sticking with eating routine • response to new foods	• consistent in sticking with sleeping routine • consistent in sticking with eating routine
• response to changes in everyday routine • response to new playthings • response to new person • response to new place • how well adapts to new experiences	• response to changes in everyday routine • response to new playthings • response to new person • response to new place • how well adapts to new experiences
• how easy or difficult to take places • persists in playing with objects when told to stop • continues to go someplace when told to stop • gets upset when removed from activity he/she should not do • persistent in trying to get attention when adult is busy	• how easy or difficult to take places • persists in playing with objects when told to stop • continues to go someplace when told to stop • gets upset when removed from activity he/she should not do • persistent in trying to get attention when adult is busy

ment factors for 24- to 35-month-old and 36- to 47- month-old children. Based on the item loadings of the factor analysis we constructed five scales—good-natured, independent, consistent, adaptable, and obedient—based on the mean scores for the items with high loadings on each factor.

Using these scales, we estimated the correlations between the various aspects of temperament and low birth weight (LBW), motor and social development (MSD), and behaviour problems. We used the conventional definition of LBW, which is a newborn who weighs less than 2500 grams (the other measures are described in Chapter 3). To determine whether the different temperament dimensions were associated with particular behavioural problems reported for two- and three-year-olds, we also estimated correlations between the temperament factors and whether the child was classified as being in the extreme category of hyperactivity, anxiety, emotional disorder, inattention, physical aggression, opposition, and separation anxiety. Finally, we used multiple regression to determine the relationships between the various aspects of temperament and sex, SES, and family structure. The scaling of these family background measures is also described in Chapter 4.

■ Results

Table 5.1 presents the ICQ items that loaded on our five temperament scales for each age group. Table 5.2 presents the means, standard deviations, and reliability coefficients (Cronbach's alpha) for the five temperament scales. Across all age groups, the *good-natured* dimension of child temperament emerged as the strongest factor with the highest internal consistency. Cronbach's alpha ranged from 0.77 to 0.79. This factor is identical to the *fussy–difficult* dimension of the ICQ, which had similar internal consistency and emerged as the most important factor in the three age-adjusted forms (Bates & Bayles, 1984). The other dimensions arising from our factor analyses largely reproduce the factor structure of the ICQ (Bates et al., 1979). The factor we called *consistent* corresponds to the ICQ factor called *unpredictable; adaptable* corresponds to the ICQ's *unadaptable;* and *obedient* resembles the ICQ's *resistant to control* and the PCQ's *persistent/unstoppable.* However, our scale labelled *independent* comprised items which were part of a factor in the longer version of the ICQ called *fussy–difficult–demanding* for one-year-old children and *dependent* for two-year-old children. In our analyses, *independent* constituted a separate and consistent factor across the four age groups.

Table 5.2

Measures of infants' and babies' temperament

	Reliability (Cronbach's alpha)				Mean	Standard Deviation
	Age 0	Age 1	Age 2	Age 3		
Good-natured (8 items)	0.77	0.79	0.78	0.79	6.94	1.58
Independent (2 or 3 items)	0.51	0.55	0.52	0.51	6.15	2.13
Consistent (3 items)	0.63	0.50	0.52	(0.40)	7.56	2.01
Adaptable (6 items)	(0.24)	0.65	0.65	0.62	7.55	1.61
Obedient (5 items)			0.74	0.70	4.91	1.91

Note: Scales with reliabilities below 0.50 (in parentheses) were not used in subsequent analyses.

Table 5.3

Correlations of measures of temperament with low birth weight, motor and social development, and behaviour, by age

	Low birth weight				Motor and social development				Behaviour problems	
	0	1	2	3	0	1	2	3	2	3
Good-natured	**-0.08**	-0.04	-0.01	-0.01	-0.03	0.04	**0.09**	**0.10**	**-0.27**	**-0.33**
Independent	**-0.10**	**-0.05**	0.02	**-0.05**	-0.00	-0.05	**0.05**	0.04	**-0.15**	**-0.21**
Consistent	-0.05	**-0.09**	**-0.06**		**0.05**	0.02	**0.09**		**-0.12**	
Adaptable		**-0.05**	**-0.09**	-0.03		**0.07**	**0.14**	**0.15**	0.00	**-0.11**
Obedient			-0.01	0.01			**0.12**	**0.08**	**-0.29**	**-0.34**

Note: Correlations that differ significantly from 0 (p<0.05) appear in boldface.

Table 5.3 presents the correlations between the five temperament subscales and LBW, MSD, and behaviour problems (correlations significant at a level of p < 0.05 are presented in bold text). Although a number of associations between temperament and markers of vulnerability are statistically significant, the correlation coefficients are generally very low, suggesting weak relationships. This was particularly the case for LBW, for which all correlations were -0.10 or weaker. For MSD, the correlations were considerably stronger for two- and three-year-old children than for younger children. The strongest relationships were for *adaptable* and *obedient*. Overall, however, the strongest correlations were observed for behaviour problems. Children aged two and three considered by their parents to be good-natured and obedient were less likely to have a behaviour problem.

Table 5.4 presents the correlations between the five temperament factors and the seven dichotomous behavioural variables. Overall, the temperament scales had the strongest relationships with hyperactivity and opposition. Among the five measures, *good-natured* and *obedient* were the best predictors of these two behaviour problems. The temperament measures were also related to emotional disorder and separation anxiety; for these behaviour problems, the strength of the relationships was fairly consistent across the temperament measures, with correlations ranging from -0.09 to -0.20. Although most of the correlation coefficients are fairly small—less than 0.15—some could be considered fairly substantial given that the measures of behavioural problems are dichotomous, indicating whether or not a child was classified in the most extreme category.

Table 5.5 shows the results of regression analyses for each of the five temperament measures regressed on sex and the full set of variables describing socioeconomic status and family structure. The samples for these analyses comprised all children aged zero to three years for the first four temperament measures, and ages two and three for *obedient*. None of the SES variables were consistently significant across the set of temperament measures. However, mothers who worked part-time reported their children as being less good-natured, adaptable, and obedient, compared with mothers who were working full-time, either at home or outside the home. Among the family-structure variables, the effects associated with being a teenage mother were most predominant: mothers who were teens when their children were born rated them lower on all five temperament scales. The ratings by single parents also tended to be lower than those of parents in two-parent families; however, the differences are not as large as those associated with being a teen mother and

Table 5.4

Correlations of measures of temperament with behaviour problems

	Hyper-activity	Anxiety	Emotional disorder	Inatten-tion	Physical	Opposition aggression	Separation anxiety
Good-natured	**-0.27**	**-0.14**	**-0.19**	**-0.15**	**-0.19**	**-0.35**	**-0.16**
Independent	**-0.18**	**-0.09**	**-0.12**	**-0.08**	**-0.08**	**-0.13**	**-0.17**
Consistent	**-0.10**	**-0.15**	**-0.20**	-0.02	-0.03	**-0.09**	**-0.09**
Adaptable	-0.04	**-0.05**	**-0.09**	**-0.06**	**-0.06**	-0.02	**-0.10**
Obedient	**-0.30**	**-0.12**	**-0.11**	**-0.13**	**-0.19**	**-0.33**	**-0.15**

Note: Correlations that differ significantly from 0 (p<0.05) appear in boldface.

Table 5.5

The relationship between measures of temperament and family and child characteristics (unstandardized regression coefficients)

	Good-natured	Independent	Consistent	Adaptable	Obedient
Intercept	**6.887**	**6.152**	**7.434**	**7.516**	**4.861**
Socioeconomic status					
• Income	-0.009	0.005	-0.006	0.013	0.009
• Income-squared	0.005	0.000	**0.020**	0.002	0.007
• Mother's education	**-0.029**	-0.015	**0.044**	-0.025	-0.019
• Mother works part-time	**-0.202**	-0.116	-0.028	**-0.367**	**-0.177**
• Mother at home	-0.043	-0.091	0.009	0.074	**-0.166**
• Father's education	0.005	0.001	-0.010	0.025	-0.026
• Father's occupation	**0.056**	-0.042	0.005	-0.026	0.043
Family and child characteristics					
• Single parent	**-0.193**	-0.035	**-0.225**	0.087	-0.134
• Teenage mother	**-0.426**	**-0.301**	**-0.265**	**-1.081**	**-0.758**
• Number of siblings	**-0.070**	**0.136**	**-0.085**	0.022	0.039
• Immigrant					
- Within last 4 years	**0.330**	0.159	-0.008	**0.562**	**1.283**
- 5 to 9 years ago	-0.023	-0.122	**-0.537**	0.083	0.165
- More than 10 years ago	0.068	**-0.222**	0.022	-0.098	0.051
• Female	0.071	0.089	-0.018	**0.155**	**0.295**
R-squared	0.012	0.007	0.019	0.023	0.029

Note: Coefficients that are statistically significant (p<0.05) appear in boldface.

were significant only for the *good-natured* and *consistent* ratings. Parents who were recent immigrants rated their children higher on three of the five temperament scales, but this finding does not appear to be supported by the findings associated with immigrants who had been in the country for five years or longer. Finally, females tended to have more positive temperament ratings, but the differences between the sexes were relatively small and significant only for the *adaptable* and *obedient* ratings. Overall, we conclude, with the exception of the differences associated with being a teen mother (and to a limited extent with being a single parent), the relationship between temperament and family background is very weak. Indeed, the proportion of variance explained by the full set of background variables was in all cases less than three percent.

■ Discussion

The focus of this study was the validation of a widely used instrument of infant and child temperament with a large nationally representative sample of Canadian children. We also assessed whether parents' perceptions of their children's temperament were related to SES or family structure. Four important findings emerged from the study.

1. *Children's temperament can be assessed reliably as early as the first year of life.* The analyses show that a stable factor structure can be extracted from the NLSCY data describing children's temperament. (See Tables 5.1 and 5.2.) Across all age groups, the good-natured scale emerged as the most salient factor, with a reliability of about 0.78. Four secondary factors—independent, consistent, adaptable, and obedient—which were based on fewer items, had lower levels of internal consistency, ranging from 0.50 to 0.74. There was relatively little variation across the age groups in the types of items that loaded on each of the factors. The factors emerging from this study are remarkably similar to those identified for the ICQ by Bates et al. (1979). Although difficult temperament also emerged as the most important factor in each of the age-adjusted versions of the ICQ, Bates (1996, personnel communication) found secondary factors vary across versions. Thus, our analysis, which was based on a much larger and more heterogeneous sample than those used in previous studies using the ICQ, provided a factor structure which was more stable from birth to age three. The relatively low reliability of two of the subscales, Independent and Consistent, was undoubtedly due to having only two to three items for each subscale.

We believe the full scale could be improved by increasing the length of each subscale to 7 or 8 items, such that the overall scale comprises about 35 to 40 items.

2. *Measures of children's temperament are only weakly related to markers of vulnerability at the individual level.* The temperament scales had low to moderate correlations with our markers of vulnerability. The relationships between temperament and low birth weight, and between temperament and motor and social development, were statistically significant but weak for all age groups (see Table 5.3.) This finding suggests that mothers of children with low birth weight or delayed motor and social development do not necessarily perceive their child as temperamentally difficult. A few moderate correlations emerged between temperament and behaviour, suggesting that good-natured and obedient children were less likely to manifest behaviour problems, particularly hyperactivity, physical aggression, and oppositional behaviour (see Table 5.4). This finding is not surprising, as temperament and behaviour were assessed concurrently and the information was collected from the same person. The conceptual bases of these constructs also probably overlap.

   Perhaps what is more interesting is that, although the temperament measures were less strongly related to internalizing disorders, there were significant relationships with each of the five temperament subscales. It may be, therefore, if researchers developed better subscales pertaining to independence, consistency, and adaptability, the temperament measures would provide a better indication of internalizing disorders. When the second and subsequent waves of NLSCY data become available, we will be able to determine whether measures of children's temperament are predictive of later life outcomes. An important point, though, is that even if concurrent or longitudinal relationships between temperament and vulnerability are fairly weak, the measures can be useful as part of a set of indicators of health and well-being for assessing population health at the community, provincial, or national levels.

3. *Measures of children's temperament are weakly related to family structure and SES.* Factors associated with family structure and SES did not explain much of the variance in the temperament measures (see table 5.5). There are several possible explanations for this finding. One is that parents may be biased in their ratings, because typically they have no previous experience

or experience with only one or two other children. Thus, it is difficult for them to assess whether their child is easier or more difficult than other children. Weak relationships could also arise if the measures of family background were unreliable, but we do not suspect this to be the case in this study. Finally, it could be that children's temperament is relatively independent of family background and that families of every socioeconomic group are vulnerable to having a child with a difficult temperament. We prefer this explanation and suspect that other factors, not included in our analysis, may have a stronger relationship with parents' perceptions of temperament. Maternal depression, for example, increases the risk of a mother perceiving her infant as difficult (Japel, McDuff, & Tremblay, 1997). Mothers in dysfunctional families, characterized by low family cohesion and inadequate parenting, also may tend to view their child as being difficult (Normand et al., 1996).

Overall, these results should help to dispel the myth that low income by itself is a risk factor for child maladjustment. In this study, children from low-income families were not more likely to be perceived as temperamentally difficult. It may be, however, that income interacts with other factors, such as maternal depression or family dysfunction, and subsequently leads to difficult child temperament. Multiple risk factors have previously been associated with a greater likelihood that the parent perceives the child as difficult (Rothbart & Ahadi, 1994).

4. *Teen mothers are more likely than any other group to report that their child has a difficult temperament.* We found that teenage mothers rated their child lower on each of the five temperament subscales (see Table 5.5). Teenage mothers are at greater risk for giving birth to children with low birth weight; poverty is also more prevalent among teenage mothers. Under conditions of poverty, an infant is significantly more likely to be born constitutionally vulnerable and to be difficult to care for (Halpern, 1993). A low-birth-weight infant that is also fussy is likely to overtax the limited physical and emotional resources of an already stressed mother. One study that successfully reduced the risk of unfavorable outcomes for children in multi-risk environments is the Elmira Prenatal/Early Childhood Project (Olds *et al.*, 1997). It provided families with home visits from nurses who started their interventions during pregnancy and continued until the children were two years of age. The nurses informed parents about fetal and infant development,

and helped families to improve their social-support system and their use of other health and human services. The study demonstrated that when home-visitors establish a rapport with families, not only does the quality of care-giving improve but also the quality of the mother's psycho-social adjustment. This study and other research suggest that home-visitation programs are likely to be successful if they improve family functioning by teaching parents communication skills and effective problem solving (Dunst, Trivette, & Thompson, 1991); widen parents' social networks (McDonough, 1993); and provide information that will increase parents' access to community resources and improve their parenting skills (van den Boom, 1994).

■

This study has several implications for further research. First, we need to revise our measures of temperament to include more items relevant to adaptability, consistency, independence, and obedience. This revision will involve more conceptual work, because the distinction between the constructs of independence and obedience is subtle, especially as it applies to toddlers. Second, we require longitudinal analyses to determine whether early measures of temperament predict subsequent child outcomes. Such analyses can also examine the interactions between temperament and SES. Third, we need to assess whether measures of temperament assessed at the macro-level are amenable to change. For example, could a community provide the needed education and social support required to effect a significant improvement in temperament and other early indicators of children's health and well-being? This question points to the fourth implication for further research: we need a number of small, action-oriented research studies to assess the efficacy of community-based interventions that are designed to improve family functioning, develop parents' skills, and increase social support.

Physical Aggression Among Toddlers

Does It Run in Families?

RAYMOND BAILLARGEON, RICHARD TREMBLAY,

& J. DOUGLAS WILLMS

A UNIQUE FEATURE of the National Longitudinal Survey of Children and Youth (NLSCY) is that up to four children from each family studied were selected and assessed on a number of different behavioural and emotional characteristics. Most studies of children's behaviour, except for twin studies, have included only one child per family. This limitation has prevented researchers from addressing the important issue of family membership on the development of children's behaviour problems. One would expect that children brought up in the same family would tend to be more alike in their behavioural characteristics than are children from other families. In a previous analysis of NLSCY data, Tremblay et al. (1996) found that family membership accounted for 38 percent of the observed variation in physically aggressive behaviour, after controlling for age, sex, socioeconomic status, and family structure. The variation attributable to family membership for other behavioural and emotional problems, such as emotional disorder, inattention, and hyperactivity, was also shown to be important, but less so than for physical aggression.

These findings suggest that childhood behavioural problems, such as physical aggression, may run in families. It is an important policy issue because a number of studies have indicated that interventions during early childhood are more likely to be successful than interventions during early adolescence, when behaviour problems become chronic (Durlack, 1997; Karoly et al., 1998; Tremblay & Craig, 1995). If behaviour problems are concentrated in families, siblings of children diagnosed with behaviour problems—especially younger siblings—should be the target of preventive interventions. The planning of successful preventive interventions also requires an understanding of why behaviour problems run in families. Some parents may lack parenting skills or experience highly stressful events during the key developmental periods of one or more of their children. Siblings may also have a negative impact on each other. It is easy to imagine that a physically aggressive first-born child might teach aggressive behaviour to younger siblings or evoke other kinds of emotional difficulties. However, because most survey studies of children's development have targeted only one child per family, this question has not been extensively studied.

This chapter aims to describe how concentrated the behavioural problems among siblings in Canadian families are and to evaluate whether the likelihood of a younger sibling manifesting physically aggressive behaviour depends on the older siblings' having been physically aggressive. More specifically, we addressed the following questions. Is the youngest child's level of physical aggression related to the level of physical aggression manifested by an older child in the family? Is this association still present after taking into account the effect of other environmental factors that are known to be associated with an increased likelihood of observing physically aggressive behaviour in children? We chose physical aggression because our analyses revealed that physical and indirect aggression were most concentrated in families and because physical aggression tends to be one of the most troublesome problems to parents and other children.

■ Background

Youth violence is a major concern in most industrialized countries. A recent survey by Statistics Canada reported that one in four Canadians felt unsafe walking at night in their neighbourhood (Sacco, 1995). In an effort to respond to public fears, Canada has recently changed its Young Offenders Act to enable courts to impose more severe sentences on violent young offenders.

Most studies of serious delinquency have shown that a small number of youths commit the majority of offenses (Farrington, 1987). The Cambridge Study in Delinquent Development found that a relatively small proportion of families accounted for a large proportion of all juvenile and adult court convictions. Farrington, Barnes, and Lambert (1996) followed 411 males coming from 397 different south London families from age 8 to age 40. They carried out searches of the criminal records of the sample of males and their wives, and of all biologically related members of the birth family. The results suggest that offending is strongly concentrated in families: half of the convictions were accounted for by only 6 percent of the families. Further, "convictions of one family member were strongly related to convictions of every other family member" (p. 47): 53 percent of males with a convicted family member (either a parent or sibling) were themselves convicted, compared with only 24 percent of those without a convicted family member. Robins et al. (1975) obtained similar results in a study of black urban families in the United States: children were more likely to be delinquent when their mothers had a history of delinquency.

Such results indicate that delinquent behaviour during adolescence and adulthood runs in families, but they do not explain the mechanisms by which the inter-generational transmission of delinquency occurs. Twin studies have been used to identify the extent to which genetic and environmental effects are involved. By comparing same-age siblings who share the same genes and environment (monozygotic twins) to same-age siblings who share only half their genes but share the same environment (dizygotic twins), it is possible to contrast genetic effects and environmental effects. In these studies, environmental effects are also divided into those which are common to both twins, and those which are unique (Plomin et al., 1997). In a review of twin studies from 6 different countries over a 60-year period, Gottesman and Goldsmith (1994) reported that 51.5 percent of monozygotic twins were similar in terms of criminal behaviour, compared with 23.1 percent of dizygotic twins.

A recent study of twins in the US indicated that the difference in concordance of anti-social traits between monozygotic and dizygotic twins was much greater during adulthood than during adolescence (Lyons et al., 1995). The results suggested there were no genetic effects on anti-social traits during adolescence, but important genetic effects on anti-social traits during adulthood. The authors concluded that the similarity of anti-social behaviour during adolescence was mainly due to family environments, while the similarity during adulthood, once siblings have left the common family environment, was due to genetic similarity.

Using data from six longitudinal studies from Canada, New Zealand, and the United States, Nagin and Tremblay (1999) and Broidy et al. (1999) showed that chronic physical aggression during the elementary school years is the best behavioural predictor of violent behaviour during adolescence. These results, and those of the twin studies described above, would suggest strong familial similarities in physical aggression among siblings during childhood.

The literature provides convincing evidence that physical aggression runs in families. However, what remains unclear is whether, on a population basis, there is a sufficient concentration of physical aggression to warrant targeting interventions to particular families. The methods used in previous research also do not provide estimates of the likelihood of a second-born child being aggressive, given that the first-born child was aggressive; or similarly, whether a third-born child is likely to be aggressive, given that either one or both of the first two children were aggressive. The NLSCY allow us to directly estimate these effects, before and after controlling for socioeconomic status.

■ Method

The sample for this analysis was made up of all children aged two through eleven. In the first analysis, we examined the extent to which the six types of behaviour problems—hyperactivity, anxiety, emotional disorder, inattention, physical aggression, and indirect aggression—were concentrated in families. The analysis pertained only to children who were classified in the extreme categories of these behaviour problems (see Chapter 3). We also examined the degree to which children with any of the six behaviour problems were concentrated within families. The most comprehensive way to display concentration is with a Lorenz curve, which is often used to show the extent to which minority children are concentrated within particular schools or neighbourhoods (Zoloth, 1976). The Lorenz curve displays the percentage of children with a particular trait, in this case a behaviour problem, included in a certain percentage of families. For example, if children with hyperactivity were heavily concentrated in families, we might expect to see 25 percent of all hyperactive children concentrated in only 10 percent of all families. We estimated the Lorenz curves for each disorder, but display only a few summary statistics for each disorder. For physical aggression and anxiety, we display the Lorenz curve results up to a level of 50 percent of all aggressive children. (At levels above 50 percent, these particular curves converge slowly to the diagonal line, meeting it at the 100-percent level.)

In the second analysis, we used the classification information pertaining to the extreme and moderate categories of physical aggression. For second- and third-born children, we attached information to each child's record that described the older siblings' level of aggression; that is, highly aggressive, moderately aggressive, or non-aggressive. We then estimated five logistic regression models. The first model selected only first-born children, including children who were in families with only one child, and twins and triplets with no older siblings. (Note that for all models, we included multiple-birth children, but did not treat their twin or triplet as an older sibling. We did, however, consider their older siblings, if any.) The regression analysis estimated the likelihood of a child being aggressive as a function of the set of socioeconomic and demographic characteristics used in Chapter 4. The second and third models used data for second-born children. These models estimated the effects of having an older sibling that was either highly or moderately aggressive, before and after controlling for socioeconomic and demographic factors. Similarly, the fourth and fifth models used data for third-born children. For this group, there were nine possible combinations among siblings of highly aggressive (H), moderately aggressive (M), and non-aggressive (non-agg). After some preliminary analyses, we found we could collapse some of the categories (e.g., HH, HM, and MH), and improve the accuracy of the estimates.

■ Results

Table 6.1 displays the concentration of children with behaviour disorders in Canadian families.[1] It presents the percentage of families in which 10, 25, and 50 percent of all children with a particular disorder are concentrated. For example, 10 percent of children with hyperactivity are concentrated within only 5.2 percent of all families; 25 percent of children with hyperactivity are concentrated within 21.2 percent of all families; and one half of all children with hyperactivity are concentrated in 47.1 percent of all families. The table provides sufficient evidence to make two points: first, the degree of concentration is similar for hyperactivity, anxiety, emotional disorder, and inattention, with approximately 5.2 to 5.4 percent of families accounting for 10 percent of all children with these problems; second, the degree of concentration is greatest for physical aggression and indirect aggression, with about 3.7 to 4.6 percent of families accounting for 10 percent of children with problems related to aggression. Figure 6.1 displays the Lorenz curve for physical aggression, which has a relatively high concentration, and for anxiety, which has a relatively low concentration.

Table 6.2 displays the odds ratios associated with physical aggression for first-, second-, and third-born children. The results for first-born children are similar to what one would expect for the full population. They indicate that children are more prone to physically aggressive behaviour if they are in low-

Table 6.1

Concentration of children with behaviour disorders in families

	Hyper-activity	Anxiety	Emotional disorder	Inattention	Physical aggression	Indirect aggression	All disorders
Pct–10	5.2	5.2	5.4	5.2	4.6	3.7	4.9
Pct–25	20.7	21.2	19.8	20.9	18.4	17.1	15.5
Pct–50	47.1	47.6	46.5	47.3	45.6	44.4	43.7

Note: Pct–10 is the percentage of families in which ten percent of children with a particular behaviour disorder are concentrated. Pct-25 and Pct-50 are interpreted similarly.

Figure 6.1

The concentration of children with behaviour problems

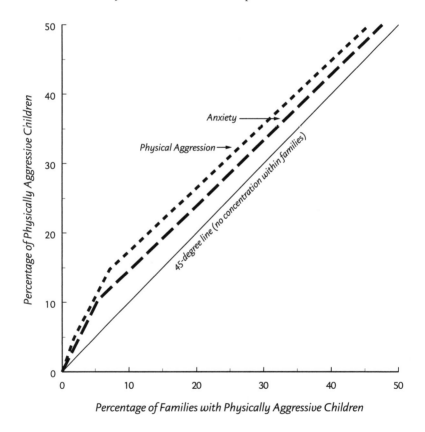

Table 6.2

Likelihood of the second- and third-born child being physically aggressive (odds ratios)

	First-born	Second-born I	Second-born II	Third-born I	Third-born II
Socioeconomic Status					
• Income	**0.91**		1.01		0.88
• Income-squared	1.01		**0.96**		1.05
• Mother's education	**0.89**		0.94		0.84
• Mother works part-time	**1.58**		1.03		0.90
• Mother at home	0.98		0.98		0.88
• Father's education	1.00		0.99		1.15
• Father's occupation	**0.85**		0.90		0.90
Family and child characteristics					
• Single parent	**2.35**		2.15		1.05
• Teenage mother	1.36		1.57		**3.50**
• Number of siblings	**1.29**		0.92		0.95
• Immigrant					
- Within last 4 years	**0.20**		0.01		0.00
- 5 to 9 years ago	**0.41**		0.71		0.00
- More than 10 years ago	**0.44**		0.64		0.92
• Female	**0.39**		**0.28**		**0.26**
Older sibling was physically aggressive					
• First child was:					
- highly aggressive (H)		**4.33**	**3.37**		
- moderately aggressive (M)		**2.84**	**2.42**		
• First and second child were:					
- HH, HM, or MH				**13.35**	**11.81**
- H(non-agg) or (non-agg)H				**33.20**	**24.29**
- MM				**05.85**	**05.44**
- M(non-agg) or (non-agg)M				**04.91**	**03.95**

Note: Odds ratios that differ significantly from 1.0 ($p<0.05$) appear in boldface.

income or single-parent families, if their mothers have low levels of education or are working part-time, or if their fathers are in low-status occupations. Immigrant families have considerably lower levels of physical aggression. Children who have at least one sibling are more prone to being aggressive.

The second column of Table 6.2 provides the odds ratios for a second-born child being aggressive, given that the first-born child is aggressive. If the first-born child was highly aggressive, the odds of the second-born child being highly aggressive were 4.33 to 1; and if the first-born child was moderately physically aggressive, the odds of the second-born child being aggressive were 2.84 to 1. The odds ratios are only slightly lower, 3.37 and 2.42 respectively, when the full complement of socioeconomic and family background variables are added to the model. A striking finding is that socioeconomic status is virtually unrelated to whether the second-born child is aggressive, given that the first child is either moderately or highly aggressive.

The fourth and fifth columns display the results for third-born children. The pattern is similar except that the odds ratios are even stronger. For example, if one of the first two children was highly aggressive and the second was either highly aggressive or moderately aggressive, the third-born child would be more than ten times as likely to be aggressive as a third-born child whose older siblings were non-aggressive. Even if one or both of the older siblings was moderately aggressive, the odds of the third child being highly aggressive is about four or five to one. The odds ratios associated with having only one sibling that was highly aggressive are very high, and we do not have a good explanation for this. It may be a statistical aberration, stemming from small sample sizes, but in some cases it could also be related to a genetic disorder that occurs in a somewhat predicable manner.

■

This study examined the extent to which children with behaviour problems are concentrated in families. It found that, of the main types of behaviour problems, concentration within families is greatest for physical and indirect aggression. The analysis also examined the likelihood that a second- or third-born child would be aggressive, given that one of the first two children was also aggressive. Two important findings emerge for this analysis.

1. *Ten percent of children with behaviour problems are concentrated in about five percent of all families with children who have behaviour problems.* The concentration is even stronger for behaviour problems related to aggression (see Table 6.1). In this study, the information about children's behaviour came from the same informant, in most cases the child's mother; this may account for some of the observed concentration. But it may also stem from other factors, including genetic factors, and features of the home and community environment, including parenting behaviours, family functioning, and social support. The importance of siblings' interactions should not be overlooked, especially the influence that an older child may exert on a younger sister or brother.

   In many respects, the extent of concentration does not appear to be important. It is certainly much weaker than the concentration of adult convictions found by Farrington, Barnes, and Lambert in their study. But if we compare these results to those in Chapter 4, which suggested that if we could eradicate poverty, we would reduce behaviour problems and overall vulnerability by about ten percent, then these findings take on greater significance. They suggest that if we could provide effective interventions for only about four to five percent of the families who have children with behaviour problems, we would have a comparable decrease in childhood vulnerability.

2. *The odds of a second child being highly physically aggressive if the first child was aggressive is about three to four times higher than if the first child was non-aggressive.* The odds ratios associated with a third child being aggressive are even greater if one or more of the first two children were aggressive. These results may have implications for family planning. We do not suggest that they should discourage parents of an aggressive child from having a second or third child, especially given that physical aggression peaks in young children around 28 months (Tremblay et al., 1996), just at the time when many parents may consider their options. But parents should be aware of the risks and not naïvely think they are less likely to have a second child with similar problems. Indeed, this may be an important time for parents of a child with behaviour problems to seek professional help and additional support. This suggestion also makes sense from a social policy perspective, as interventions during early childhood are more likely to be successful than later interventions, once behaviour problems have become chronic (Durlack, 1997; Tremblay & Craig, 1995).

NOTES

1 The weighted number of children with behaviour problems and the number of families (in parentheses) were as follows: hyperactivity: 2378 (2246); anxiety: 828 (792); emotional disorder: 661 (614); inattention: 1270 (1208); physical aggression: 559 (260); indirect aggression: 260 (233); all disorders: 3706 (3291).

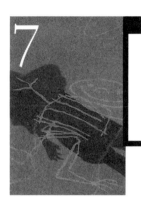

The Effects of Smoking and Drinking During Pregnancy

SARAH K. CONNOR &
LYNN MCINTYRE

RECENT RESEARCH HAS DEMONSTRATED that there is a relationship between the socioeconomic characteristics of families and their children's peri- and post-natal outcomes. Two important markers of vulnerability at birth are low birth weight (LBW) and prematurity. Conventional definitions consider LBW as a weight of less than 2500 grams and prematurity as a birth before 37 weeks of gestation. Babies born prematurely, or of low birth weight, are at increased risk of early infant and childhood morbidity and mortality (Schulsinger et al., 1993). In Canada, LBW is responsible for approximately 75 percent of early infant deaths (Levitt et al., 1993). These children may also suffer from long-term physical and developmental disabilities, which can profoundly affect them for the rest of their lives. Undergoing a caesarean or a mid-forceps delivery also increases the risk of morbidity for the mother and her infant (Bofill et al., 1996; Turcot et al., 1997).

While findings relating to the effects of some factors, such as maternal age, are conflicting (Ng & Wilkins, 1994; Peipert & Bracken, 1993), several social and demographic characteristics have consistently been shown to be associated with adverse outcomes. Poverty, for instance, is related to LBW and prematurity. Levitt et al. (1993) report that the risk of LBW is higher among "educationally, socially, and economically deprived women" (p. 768). Other studies have shown that the risk of poor outcomes is higher for single parents and for those having their first child (Ng and Wilkins, 1994; Parker and

Schoendorf, 1992). Soliman and Burrows (1993) found that women giving birth to their first child were also more likely to undergo caesarean section.

In trying to understand why there is a strong link between socioeconomic status (SES) and adverse outcomes at birth, researchers have attempted to determine the factors that may contribute to an unhealthy pregnancy. Two of the most important factors are inadequate nutrition and the use of tobacco, alcohol, and other drugs. This chapter is concerned with the effects of using tobacco and alcohol during pregnancy. One of our aims is to provide a profile of Canadian women who smoke or drink during pregnancy. We do this by determining the extent to which these behaviours are related to SES, family structure, and the age of the mother. Our second aim is to determine the strength of the relationships between adverse outcomes and various aspects of SES and family structure. The analysis includes four markers of vulnerability: LBW, prematurity, whether specialized medical care was required after delivery, and whether the delivery was complicated. Finally, we attempt to determine the effects of smoking and alcohol use on these peri- and post-natal outcomes. In doing so, we ask whether these behaviours mediate the relationship between SES and adverse outcomes at birth

■ Cigarette Use During Pregnancy

The relationship between smoking during pregnancy and poor birth outcomes has been well documented. Pregnancy complications, such as spontaneous abortion and ectopic pregnancy, are more common when mothers smoke. Babies born to smokers are often reported to be premature and underweight, and suffer from a variety of health problems (Dejin-Karlsson et al., 1996; Ershoff, Quinn, & Mullen, 1995). Furthermore, there is evidence that, after birth, these children continue to feel the effects of their pre-natal exposure to cigarette smoke and may suffer from long-term problems. For instance, Weitzman, Gortmaker, and Sobol (1992) found an increase in behavioural disorders such as hyperactivity and anti-social behaviours in children with mothers who smoked either during or after pregnancy. Sexton, Fox, and Hebel (1990) found that children whose mothers smoked during pregnancy scored lower on cognitive and developmental tests than children of mothers who quit during pregnancy. More recently, maternal smoking has been linked to an increased incidence of idiopathic mental retardation (Drews, Murphy, Yeargin-Allsopp, & Decoufle, 1996).

Despite the risks associated with smoking during pregnancy, cigarette use continues to be a serious problem among Canadian women. Studies have found that when smoking women become pregnant, a significant number of them continue to smoke even though they are aware of the harmful effects that cigarettes can have on their unborn children (Macleod-Clark & Maclaine, 1992). The data for the National Longitudinal Survey of Chidren and Youth (NLSCY) indicate that 23.7 percent of the mothers smoked during pregnancy.[1] This number is somewhat lower than previous figures for Canada, which estimated that 30 to 40 percent of Canadian women smoked throughout their entire pregnancy (Gupton, Thompson, Arnason, Dalke, & Ashcroft, 1995).

Previous studies have found that certain socioeconomic factors are associated with smoking during pregnancy. Dejin-Karlsson et al. (1996) noted that mothers who smoke during pregnancy tend to be unmarried, younger, and less educated than mothers who did not smoke. Having more than one child, not living with the child's father, and being exposed to passive smoke in the household are also associated with woman continuing to smoke during pregnancy (Cnattingius, Lindmark, & Meirik, 1992).

■ Alcohol Use During Pregnancy

Children exposed to the effects of alcohol *in utero* are more likely to suffer from a class of disorders known as fetal alcohol syndrome (FAS) and fetal alcohol effects (FAE). Symptoms of FAS include facial abnormalities, pre- and post-natal growth deficiencies, and damage to the central nervous system, which can be manifest through learning disabilities, behavioural problems, and delayed development. Over 100 infants affected by FAS are born in Canada each year. Although these infants represent a small fraction of the total number of babies born each year, FAS is the third leading cause of mental retardation (Remkes, 1993) and has been classified as "one of the leading causes of preventable birth defects and developmental delay" (Health Canada, 1996). Children suffering from FAE have a milder form of the disorder and exhibit these symptoms in varying degrees (Dedam, McFarlane, & Hennessy, 1993; Loney, Green, & Nanson, 1994). FAS and FAE stem from excessive alcohol consumption or "binge" drinking during pregnancy (Loney, Green, & Nanson, 1994; Nanson 1997). A few studies have found a relationship between FAS and low SES (Abel, 1995), but relatively little is known about the social or demographic characteristics of women whose children are affected by FAS or FAE (Nanson, 1997).

Evidence of the harmful effects of exposure to large quantities of alcohol on the fetus is unequivocal. However, there is some controversy about whether small to moderate amounts of alcohol can be safely consumed during pregnancy (Koren, 1996; Pereira, Olsen, & Ogston, 1993). Studies from the Centers for Disease Control and Prevention indicate that about 21 percent of women in the US drink some alcohol during pregnancy, and that on average, alcohol consumption increases with the mother's age, education, and income (Morbidity and Mortality Weekly Report, 1995). In this study, we find that 17.5 percent of Canadian women drink some alcohol during pregnancy.

Because of the social stigma associated with smoking and drinking during pregnancy, some women may under-report their consumption in a social survey. Bruce, Adams, and Shulman (1993) found, for example, that rates of disclosure were lower when data were collected through face-to-face interviews than through mail questionnaires. Therefore, the actual number of women who smoke or drink during pregnancy, and the level of their consumption, may be higher than the estimates obtained in this study. Nevertheless, the NLSCY affords a unique opportunity to study the characteristics of Canadian women who smoke or drink during pregnancy and to determine whether these behaviours are related to early markers of vulnerability. As subsequent cycles of the NLSCY become available, we will be able to gauge the long-term effects of *in utero* exposure to these substances on children's social and cognitive development.

■ Method

The analysis in this study is limited to the NLSCY sample of respondents who were the biological mothers of infants and babies (newborn to 23 months). Data were provided by 4188 mothers. The interviewers asked them whether they smoked during their pregnancy; for those who reported that they had smoked, the interviewer asked how many cigarettes per day they had smoked and whether they had smoked that amount during the first, second, and third trimesters of their pregnancy. Following these questions, the interviewers asked them how frequently they consumed alcohol during their pregnancy; for those who reported that they had drunk, the interviewers asked how many drinks they consumed when they drank. The interviewers also asked questions about the stage of pregnancy at which the women consumed alcohol. We constructed two dichotomous variables denoting whether the mothers had smoked or drunk alcohol during their pregnancy and two variables denoting the amount they smoked or drank. The smoking variable estimates the average number of cigarettes smoked per day, and the drinking variable denotes the average number of drinks consumed per month. Only 5.3 percent of the mothers both smoked and drank during pregnancy, and therefore we did not create a separate category for these mothers.

The analyses first examined the prevalence of drinking and smoking during pregnancy. Logistic regression was used to assess the relationship between drinking and smoking, and the age of the biological mother. In the model for smoking versus non-smoking, a quadratic term was required to capture a statistically significant non-linear effect. The model was then extended to include the full set of variables describing socioeconomic status and family structure (these variables are described in Chapter 3). The model also includes a variable denoting whether the baby was the mother's first child.

The analyses then examined the effects of smoking and drinking on the four early markers of vulnerability.[2] The dichotomous outcome variables were regressed on the set of variables describing SES and family structure. The variables denoting whether the mother was a smoker or drinker were then added to the model. We also examined models that included the variables denoting the amount of cigarettes and alcohol consumed, but these were not statistically significant when entered alongside the dichotomous variables identifying smokers and drinkers. Finally, we tested a mediation model in which the only independent variables were the mother's age, whether the baby was the first child, SES, and the two dichotomous variables identifying smokers and drinkers.

■ Who Are the Smoking and Drinking Mothers?

Table 7.1 shows the percentages of women who smoked or drank alcohol during their pregnancy. It indicates that 23.7 percent of the mothers smoked at some point during their pregnancy; of these women, only 15.8 percent managed to quit, leaving 84.2 percent of them smoking throughout their entire pregnancy. On average, they smoked about ten cigarettes per day. In contrast, only 17.5 percent of mothers drank during pregnancy; and among these women, 61 percent drank during the first or second trimesters, and 70 percent drank during the third trimester. Only 41 percent drank throughout the entire pregnancy. The average amount of alcohol consumed by women who drank was 2.1 drinks per month; we have used the term *moderate drinking* to describe this behaviour. Among women who drank, 2.5 percent were classified as "binge" drinkers. On the occasions that these women drank alcohol, they had at least five drinks.

Sample design

Table 7.1

The prevalence of smoking and drinking during pregnancy

	Percentage	Number
Women who smoked during pregnancy	23.7	
Among smokers		
• smoked during first trimester	90.0	
• smoked during second trimester	92.1	
• smoked during third trimester	91.7	
• smoked throughout pregnancy	84.2	
Average number of cigarettes per day		10.1
Women who drank during pregnancy	17.5	
Among drinkers		
• drank during first trimester	60.5	
• drank during second trimester	61.4	
• drank during third trimester	69.6	
• drank throughout pregnancy	41.0	
• "binge" drinkers	2.5	
Average number of drinks per month		2.1

Figure 7.1

Percentage of mothers who smoked or drank moderately during pregnancy

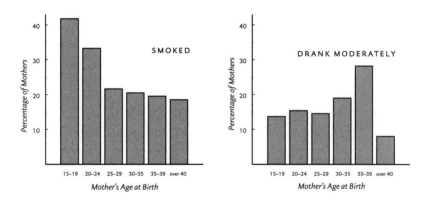

Table 7.2

Factors related to smoking and moderate drinking during pregnancy (odds ratios)

	Smoker		Drinker	
	I	II	I	II
Socioeconomic status				
• Income		**0.91**		1.05
• Income-squared		1.01		1.01
• Mother's education		**0.86**		**1.09**
• Mother works part-time		0.88		**1.30**
• Mother at home		1.10		1.19
• Father's education		**0.93**		1.08
• Father's occupation		**0.84**		**0.90**
Family structure				
• Single-parent		**1.57**		1.35
• Age of biological mother	**0.94**	1.00	**1.05**	**1.04**
• Age-squared	**1.003**	0.997		
R-squared	1.9	9.3	0.9	2.4

Note: Odds ratios that differ significantly from 1.0 (p<0.05) appear in boldface.

The relationship between smoking and moderate drinking with the age of the mother when the child was born is displayed in Figure 7.1. Younger mothers were much more likely to smoke than older mothers. Among teen mothers, 42 percent smoked during pregnancy, whereas only 33 percent of mothers aged 20 to 24 smoked and about 20 percent of mothers above age 25 smoked. The opposite pattern is evident with respect to moderate drinking: among mothers under 30, about 15 percent consumed some alcohol during pregnancy, but 19 percent of the 30–34 age group and 28 percent of the 35–40 age group were moderate drinkers. However, mothers over 40 seem to be much more cautious: only about 8 percent were moderate drinkers.

The odds ratios for smoking and moderate drinking associated with SES and family structure are displayed in Table 7.2. The first model shows the odds ratios for smoking and drinking associated with increasing age. In the case of smoking, the ratio is less than 1.0, indicating that older mothers are less likely to smoke. The quadratic term, which is statistically significant, indicates a curvilinear relationship, as is shown in Figure 7.1. The odds ratio for drinking is greater than 1.00, indicating that the likelihood of moderate drinking increases with the age of the mother (the curvilinear effect for mother's age was not statistically significant).

In the second model, income, the level of education of the mother, and the level of education and occupation of both the mother and father are predictive of whether a mother smokes during pregnancy. For example, an increase in family income of $10,000 is associated with approximately a nine-percent decrease in the likelihood of a mother smoking. Each additional year of maternal education is associated with a fourteen-percent decrease in the likelihood of a mother smoking. Single mothers were more than 1.5 times as likely to smoke during pregnancy than mothers who were living with their husbands. The effects of maternal age on smoking were trivial and non-significant. Therefore, the analysis shows that younger mothers have a greater propensity to smoke during pregnancy, but their behaviour is consistent with older mothers who have similar levels of income, education, and family structure.

The pattern for drinking shows that mothers with higher SES are more likely to drink moderately. The dominant factors include the mother's and father's level of education and whether the mother was working part-time. Income had a relatively weak relationship, and the relationship with father's occupation was in the opposite direction, with mothers less likely to drink when their husbands were in higher-status jobs. The relationship between drinking and age was not mediated by SES.

■ The Effects of Smoking and Moderate Drinking on Early Markers of Vulnerability

The logistic regression results for adverse outcomes on SES, family structure, and whether the mother smoked or drank during pregnancy are shown in Table 7.3. Mother's education and whether it was the mother's first child are the most significant predictors of whether the child had LBW. The odds ratios indicate that for each additional year of education of the mother, the likelihood of a LBW baby is reduced by about ten percent. Similarly, the odds of a first child having LBW are about 1.43 times (i.e., 1.00/0.70) that of a subsequent child. The coefficients for the other SES factors generally indicate that families with higher SES are less likely to have a LBW child, but these effects were not statistically significant. Smoking had a significant adverse effect on the likelihood of a LBW baby: the odds of a smoker's child being LBW was 1.5 times that of a non-smoker's child.

The relationships between having a premature baby and SES factors were not as strong as those for LBW. The only significant factor was whether the mother was working part-time outside the home; such mothers were less likely

Table 7.3

Effects of smoking and moderate drinking during pregnancy on early markers of vulnerability (odds ratios)

| | Markers of Vulnerability | | | | | | | |
| | Low birth weight | | Premature | | Special care required | | Complicated delivery | |
	I	II	I	II	I	II	I	II
Socioeconomic status								
• Income	0.97	0.98	0.97	0.97	0.97	0.97	1.02	1.02
• Income-squared	0.99	0.99	1.00	1.00	1.00	0.99	1.00	1.00
• Mother's education	**0.89**	**0.90**	0.97	0.97	**1.06**	**1.06**	1.01	1.01
• Mother works part-time	0.73	0.75	**0.64**	**0.63**	0.86	0.87	0.88	0.90
• Mother at home	0.79	0.78	0.83	0.83	**0.71**	**0.72**	0.84	0.86
• Father's education	0.96	0.97	0.95	0.95	0.97	0.97	**0.94**	**0.94**
• Father's occupation	0.91	0.91	0.99	1.00	0.98	0.98	0.90	0.89
Family structure								
• Single parent	0.86	0.83	1.09	1.07	1.24	1.26	0.73	0.75
• Not the first child	**0.70**	**0.68**	0.80	0.80	**0.74**	**0.74**	**0.39**	**0.39**
• Age of biological mother	1.02	1.02	1.00	1.00	0.99	0.99	**1.06**	**1.06**
• Smoked		**1.51**		1.13		0.98		0.94
• Drank moderately		0.75		1.21		**0.72**		**0.65**
R-squared	2.4	2.9	0.7	0.8	0.6	0.6	1.3	1.5

Note: Odds ratios that differ significantly from 1.0 (p<0.10) appear in boldface.

to have a premature child than mothers who were working full-time either at home or outside the home. Smoking and moderate drinking were not significantly related to premature delivery.

Mother's level of education was significantly related to whether special care was required after delivery, but the effect was in the opposite direction from the expected result: mothers with higher levels of education were *more* likely to require special care for their baby immediately after delivery. Mothers who were at home were also more likely to require special care for their baby, but this variable is difficult to interpret as the category includes mothers who were on maternity leave. Results for the other variables suggested that mothers with higher SES were less likely to require special care, but the coefficients were not statistically significant. First-born children were also significantly more at

Table 7.4

Mediation effects associated with smoking and moderate drinking during pregnancy (odds ratios)

| | Markers of Vulnerability | | | | | | | |
| | Low birth weight | | Premature | | Special care required | | Complicated delivery | |
	I	II	I	II	I	II	I	II
Socioeconomic status	**0.71**	**0.75**	**0.82**	**0.83**	0.99	0.99	**0.88**	**0.88**
Not the first child	**0.69**	**0.67**	**0.77**	**0.77**	**0.69**	**0.69**	**0.38**	**0.38**
Age of biological mother	1.02	1.03	1.00	1.00	0.99	0.99	**1.07**	**1.08**
Smoked		**1.50**		1.13		0.96		0.90
Drank moderately		0.72		1.19		**0.71**		**0.64**
R-squared	1.9	2.4	0.5	0.6	0.4	0.4	0.7	0.9

Note: Odds ratios that differ significantly from 1.0 (p<0.10) appear in boldface.

risk. Smoking did not have a significant effect on this marker of vulnerability, but moderate drinking had a significant *positive* effect; that is, mothers who drank moderately during pregnancy were about 28 percent less likely to have a child needing special care. This anomaly is discussed in the concluding section.

The pattern of results is similar for complicated deliveries. The only significant SES factor was father's education: mothers married to men with more education were less likely have a complicated delivery. First-born children were also more vulnerable. Mother's age was significantly related to this adverse outcome: older mothers were more likely to have a complicated delivery. As with special care, smoking did not have a significant effect, whereas moderate drinking had a statistically significant positive effect.

Table 7.4 displays the overall relationship between the four markers of vulnerability and SES, before and after, including the variables identifying smokers and moderate drinkers. Age of the mother and whether it was a first child are also included in these models. The results indicate that smoking partially mediates the relationship between SES and LBW: the likelihood ratio associated with a higher SES increases from 0.71 to 0.75 when smoking and drinking are included in the model. There was no evidence of a mediating effect for the other three markers of vulnerability.

■ Policy Implications

Four of the most salient markers of vulnerability in infancy include low birth weight, prematurity, medical conditions requiring special care after delivery, and complications during delivery. Several studies have found that mothers with relatively low SES are more likely to experience these unfavourable peri- and post-natal outcomes (Moore et al., 1994; Ng and Wilkins, 1994; Parker & Schoendorf, 1992). The research is less certain, however, about the mechanisms that lead to socioeconomic gradients at birth: they could be attributable to factors such as access to quality health care; the health and nutrition of the mother during pregnancy; the use of tobacco, alcohol, and other substances during pregnancy; or a wide range of other factors associated with living conditions and family life.

This study examines the effects of the use of tobacco and alcohol. Six of the most important findings are discussed below.

1. *Approximately 23.7 percent of Canadian mothers smoked during pregnancy, and of these, nearly 85 percent smoked throughout the entire pregnancy.* Even today, with the concerted effort directed toward helping people quit smoking, many pregnant Canadian women continue to smoke. With more teenage girls than teenage boys starting to smoke and more men than women quitting smoking (Canadian Council on Smoking and Health, 1993), smoking presents a serious problem for Canadian women. Our analyses found that more than 40 percent of teen mothers smoked during pregnancy, more than twice the rate for mothers age 25 and older (see Table 7.1 and Figure 7.1). We expect that the family and social context of the mother is an important contributing factor to whether a mother is willing and able to quit. At least one study has found that women are more likely to smoke during pregnancy, and to relapse after their child is born, if their co-habiting partner is also a smoker (Nafstad, Botten, & Hagen, 1996). We expect that peers also play an important role (e.g., Evans, Oates, & Schwab, 1992; Price, Cioci, Penner, & Trautlein, 1993). Thus, future research needs to examine the role that peers and family play in determining whether mothers smoke during pregnancy.

2. *About 17.5 percent of Canadian mothers consumed some alcohol during pregnancy, but on average those who drank consumed only about two drinks per month.* Very few women—only 2.5 percent of those who drank—reported

that they drank at least five drinks on the occasions that they drank. Canadian women appear to be more prudent in their use of alcohol during pregnancy than they are with cigarettes (see Table 7.1 and Figure 7.1). The vast majority of women reported that they did not drink during pregnancy, and among those who did, very few had more than one or two drinks on a single occasion. Only seven percent of all mothers reported drinking throughout the entire pregnancy. The profile of women who drink also differs from that of smokers: those who drink tend to be older and of higher SES than non-drinkers (see Table 7.2).

3. *Smoking during pregnancy has a harmful effect on an unborn child.* The infants of mothers who smoked during pregnancy were one and a half times more likely to have LBW than infants of non-smokers (see Tables 7.3 and 7.4). This finding is consistent with a large body of research that documents the increased likelihood of prematurity, LBW, and a host of other problems attributable to *in utero* exposure to smoke. But our study shows that these effects are apparent in a large nationally representative sample of women, even after taking into account the SES and family structure of the mother. The estimates derived from our analysis probably undervalue the harmful effects of smoking. One reason is that the classification of smoker includes mothers who occasionally smoked one or two cigarettes, and the data were not sufficiently strong to determine the effects of the amount smoked. Some women may also have under-reported the amount they smoked. Despite these limitations, the analysis found a strong effect on the likelihood of a child being of low birth weight.

4. *Infrequent drinking of small amounts of alcohol during pregnancy (on average about two drinks per month) does not appear to have harmful effects on an unborn child.* There is no dispute among researchers or health professionals that consuming excessive amounts of alcohol can have devastating effects on children's outcomes at birth and on their long-term health and well-being. The research is less clear, however, on the effects of mild or moderate drinking. This study found that women who drank were equally likely to have a premature or LBW baby as non-drinkers, and *less* likely to have complications during delivery or require special care for their baby after delivery (see Table 7.3).

We offer this finding with some cautionary remarks. First, the effects of exposure to alcohol *in utero* may not be evident at birth but may lead to cognitive, behavioural, and developmental deficiencies that only become apparent as children grow older (see Dedam, McFarlane, & Hennessy, 1993; Health Canada, 1996; Remkes, 1993). Second, the observed positive effects of alcohol use may be an artifact of a mis-specified statistical model. For example, it could be that the women who report occasional drinking tend to be those who also have the economic and social resources to eat well and exercise regularly during their pregnancy. Alcohol use during pregnancy was related to age and SES in our sample, and therefore the accuracy of our estimates depends on how well our measures of SES capture differences between drinkers and non-drinkers in their social and economic resources.

Nevertheless, it is possible that drinking small amounts of alcohol during pregnancy does not have any deleterious effects. This may be comforting for women who suffer anxiety or guilt for having had the occasional drink during their pregnancy. It is not possible with this type of study to establish a "safe limit" for alcohol consumption during pregnancy, and for ethical reasons it is difficult, perhaps impossible, to design and carry out such a study. Health Canada (1996) recommends that in the absence of strong evidence that moderate drinking is not harmful, "the prudent choice for women who are or may become pregnant is to abstain from alcohol."

5. *The first-born child is significantly more prone to adverse outcomes at birth.* Mothers are most likely to have problems with their first birth than with subsequent children, even after taking into account their SES and family structure (see Tables 7.3 and 7.4). First-born children are nearly one and a half times more likely to be LBW and to require special care after delivery. The mothers are about two and a half times more likely to have complications during delivery. These findings stress the importance of first-time mothers receiving prenatal care, which can counteract some of the risks associated with the first delivery. The Canadian Council on Children and Youth estimated that in Canada, "for every dollar spent on prenatal care, the government could save $3.38 in caring for low-birth-weight infants" (Levitt et al., 1993, p. 769).

6. *Neither young mothers nor single mothers were particularly at risk of having a child with adverse outcomes at birth, once account is taken of their socioeconomic status.* The level of education of the mother was associated with the likelihood of a LBW baby, and the overall measure of SES was associated with three of the adverse outcomes (see Tables 7.3 and 7.4). But single

parenthood and maternal age were not related to any of the markers of vulnerability once socioeconomic factors were taken into account. Teen mothers who smoke and have low levels of education are more likely to have a vulnerable child, but no more so than older mothers who smoke and have comparable levels of education.

Michielutte et al. (1992) found that very young mothers—those under sixteen—were more likely to give birth to a pre-term, LBW infant. Due to insufficient sample size, our results do not pertain to very young mothers. Others studies have reported an increased risk of poor outcomes associated with being a single parent (e.g., Moore et al., 1994). We found that the children of single mothers seemed to fare worse on three of the markers of vulnerability, but these effects were not statistically significant and were smaller after we took account of SES. Ng and Wilkins (1994) noted that, on average, Canadian women are waiting until they are older to have their first child and that the number of LBW babies born to unmarried mothers has been decreasing in Canada since the 1960s.

■

The two most revealing findings of this research is the high rate of smoking among mothers in their teens and early twenties, and the strong relationship between smoking and the likelihood of having a LBW baby. A significant challenge for our society is to help pregnant women quit smoking, and more generally, to reduce the prevalence of smoking among our young people.

One kind of intervention that may help us meet that challenge is cessation programs for young mothers trying to quit smoking. All mothers want the best for their children. Therefore, if women understand the inherent dangers of smoking, their motivation to quit when they discover they are pregnant is extremely high. Cessation programs typically involve training in how to quit, usually given by health professionals, and social support, usually through phone calls, visits, and regular mailings. The cost-effectiveness of cessation programs has been well established with randomized experiments (Dolan-Mullen, Ramirez, & Groff, 1994). In a recent study conducted in four clinics in Alabama, the support component of the intervention involved assigning each smoking mother to a "buddy" who reinforced her efforts to quit. The researchers found that 31 percent of the experimental group quit smoking, compared with only 20.8 percent in the control group. (Windsor et al., 1994).

An earlier study by Sexton and Hebel (1984) found that not only were women who had participated in a cessation program more likely to quit smoking, but also their babies were on average 92 grams heavier than those of the mothers in a control group.

Although this kind of intervention is likely to reduce the prevalence of vulnerable children in the short term, it does not address the larger issue concerning the prevalence of smoking among our youth. This issue calls for large-scale programs aimed at educating our youth about the costs of smoking to their own health and to the health and well-being of their children.

NOTES

1   Questions about to smoking were asked of the mothers of infants and one-year-old babies; these mothers gave birth in 1993 or 1994.

2   The sample sizes for these analyses ranged from 3938 to 3952 for the first 3 markers of vulnerability. However, the questions pertaining to a complicated delivery were asked only of the mothers of infants (0 to 11 months), and therefore the sample size for that analysis was only 1880.

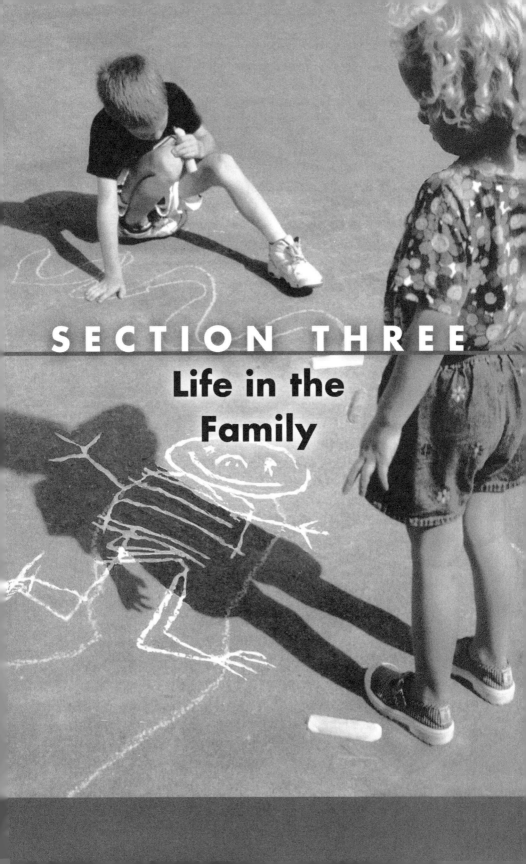

SECTION THREE
Life in the Family

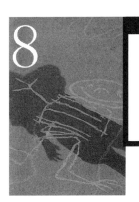

The Effects of Parenting Practices on Children's Outcomes

RUTH K. CHAO &

J. DOUGLAS WILLMS

RESEARCH HAS CONSISTENTLY SHOWN that children do better in school when parents monitor their behaviour, are responsive to their needs, and encourage independence with a democratic approach. This combination of monitoring, responsiveness, and encouragement was conceptualized by Baumrind (1967) as an authoritative style of parenting, in contrast to authoritarian and permissive styles. *Authoritative* parents establish a warm and nurturing relationship with their children but set firm limits for their behaviour. Within those limits, they present options to them, discuss alternate ways of behaving, and allow them to participate in family decisions. Authoritarian parents are characterized as being highly controlling, requiring their children to meet an absolute set of standards. They are less flexible and lack responsiveness and warmth. Permissive parents are typified as overly nurturing: they provide few standards for behaviour and are extremely tolerant of misbehaviour. In addition to these traits, consistency in parenting is considered by some theorists to be an equally important component of positive parenting.

The authoritative parenting style has been found to be positively related to a number of schooling outcomes, including academic achievement, school grades, time spent on homework, positive school behaviour, and completion of secondary school (Lamborn, Dornbusch, & Steinberg, 1996; Beyer, 1995; Taylor, Hinton, & Wilson, 1995; Steinberg, Lamborn, Dornbusch, & Darling, 1992; McLaughlin & Vacha, 1992; Lamborn, Mounts, Steinberg, & Dornbusch,

1991; Rumberger, 1990; Dornbusch et. al, 1987; Wadsworth, 1986). Children of authoritarian and permissive parents tend to have relatively poor schooling outcomes, and researchers have found deleterious effects associated with inconsistent, rejection-oriented parenting (Conger, Conger, Elder, Lorenz, Simons & Whitbeck, 1992).

One of the assumptions underling the "culture of poverty" thesis is that children of poor parents have negative schooling outcomes because of the way they are raised. With respect to the literature on parenting styles, the argument is that parents with fewer resources tend to be authoritarian or permissive, and their style of parenting contributes to the difficulties their children often experience. But this argument is problematic for several reasons. One is that "parenting styles" are conceptual categories; it is likely that many parents have average scores on traits such as responsiveness, control, and the encouragement of independence, and therefore do not fit neatly into any one of the three categories. Second, relatively few studies have examined the relationship of parenting practices to particular aspects of socioeconomic status (SES), and research has not adequately determined the extent to which positive practices mediate the effects of SES on children's outcomes. It may well be that these practices have positive effects for nearly all parents, independent of their socioeconomic background. A third reason is that most of the studies have examined the effects of parenting practices on adolescents' outcomes, and therefore relatively little is known about their effects on the social and cognitive outcomes of younger children. Finally, studies in the US that have compared the effects of parenting practices among ethnic groups have found that authoritarian practices do not have the strong negative effects on schooling outcomes for minority children that they do for European American children (Baldwin, Baldwin, & Cole, 1990; Chao, 1994; Lamborn, Dornbusch, & Steinberg, 1996; Steinburg, Dornbusch & Brown, 1992). This finding has raised questions about whether more authoritarian practices may be preferable in certain contexts, such as impoverished and dangerous neighbourhoods (Lamborn et al., 1996), or within certain cultures (Chao, 1994).

This chapter analyses the responses to twenty-five questions pertaining to parents' practices. A factor analysis of these responses revealed four dimensions of parenting, which capture a range of practices. We asked whether these practices vary across the age range two through eleven and whether parents can be classified into homogeneous categories that correspond to authoritative, permissive, and authoritarian styles. We then examined the relationship between parenting practices and the full range of SES factors used earlier in this book.

Our aim was to determine whether certain aspects of parents' educational and economic resources have a particularly strong relationship with parenting practices. Finally, we determined whether our measures of parenting approaches are related to child outcomes, and if so, whether they mediate the effects of SES. In testing the parenting-as-mediator model, we also examined whether the effects of parenting approaches on child outcomes vary depending on the child's age.

■ The Relationship Between Parenting Practices and SES

Although a substantial body of research demonstrates the effects of SES on parenting practices, most studies have equated SES with parental education, particularly the mother's education, or have treated SES as a composite variable and have not tried to discern whether particular aspects of SES are related to positive parenting (Hoff-Ginsberg and Tardiff, 1995; Ross & Willigen, 1997). Most studies have ignored effects associated with income and occupational status.

In their review of income effects on parenting, Hoff-Ginsberg and Tardiff (1995) claim that income does not account for differences in parenting. However, they distinguished studies based on family income from those that focussed on economic hardship, which they further differentiated according to whether the hardship was due to economic loss or change, or to more chronic and persistent poverty. Economic loss has been found to be related to a decrease in parental warmth and an increase in inconsistent, rejection-oriented discipline (Conger, Conger, Elder, Lorenz, Simons & Whitbeck, 1992; Elder, Conger, Foster, & Ardelt, 1992; Lempers, Clark-Lempers, & Simons, 1989; Elder, Nguyen, & Caspi, 1985). Poverty, or chronic deprivation, is associated with an overall diminished capacity for supportive, consistent, and involved parenting (McLeod, Kruttschnitt, & Dornfeld, 1994; McLeod & Shanahan, 1993; McLoyd, 1990).

Studies that have examined the relationships between parenting practices and parents' education have found that more-educated parents tend to be more authoritative and less authoritarian, as well as more democratic and child-centred, in comparison to less-educated parents. In their discipline strategies, more-educated parents have been found to be less punitive and more rational in their approach. For example, they are more likely than less-educated parents to discuss rules with their children and explain the reasons behind the rules (Parke & Buriel, 1998). Most of these studies have emphasized the relationship with the mother's level of education, however, even though the term "parents' education" is used.

In contrast, studies that have examined the effects of occupational roles on parenting behaviour have dealt primarily with the occupational roles of the fathers. These date back to early studies by Kohn and Schooler (1978; Kohn, 1977) that concentrated on the qualities of men's work, especially occupational autonomy. The argument is that men who experience a high degree of occupational autonomy value independence in their children, whereas men who are in highly supervised jobs with little autonomy value conformity. More recent work by Greenberger, O'Neil, and Nagel (1994) included mothers, but concluded that their occupational status was less predictive of parenting practices than that of fathers.

The relationships between parenting practices and employment status are somewhat more complex, because unemployment usually entails economic hardship and its effects probably differ for mothers and fathers. Researchers have been primarily concerned with whether mothers' full-time employment has a detrimental effect on children's development. However, mothers' employment seems to have both positive and negative consequences on parenting. Hoffman (1989) found that mothers who work outside the home tended to teach their children to be self-sufficient and assume responsibility for household tasks at an early age. The independence of the children was associated with greater motivation to succeed in school. But Dornbusch et al. (1985) found maternal employment to be negatively related to monitoring and supervision, which led to earlier dating and an overall increase in peer involvement. Studies focussing on the work status of fathers have been concerned mainly with the effects of being unemployed. These studies have also yielded mixed results: unemployed fathers increase their involvement in child care but decrease their nurturing behaviours in comparison to employed fathers (Harold-Goldsmith, Radin, & Eccles, 1988).

Parenting practices as a mediator of SES

A number of studies suggest, either explicitly or implicitly, that parenting practices constitute one of the most important factors contributing to the relationship between socioeconomic background and children's outcomes. However, most studies that have attempted to test a parenting-as-mediator model have not included a wide range of SES indicators. Instead, they have been primarily concerned with the effects of severe economic deprivation and hardship. One set of studies, discussed above, focused on economic loss or change. This research demonstrated that some of the effects of economic loss on children's psychosocial adjustment were attributable to a decrease in nurturing behaviour and an increase in inconsistent, rejection-oriented discipline (Conger et. al, 1992; Elder et. al, 1992; Lempers et. al, 1989; Elder et. al, 1985). The other set of studies, which focussed on more chronic deprivation and poverty, found that economic hardship adversely effects children's adjustment by diminishing parents' capacities for supportive, consistent, and involved parenting (McLeod et al., 1994; McLeod & Shanahan, 1993; McLoyd, 1990).

Almost all the studies examined the effects of parenting on psychosocial outcomes, such as adolescent distress, depression, loneliness, anti-social behaviour, hyperactivity, and self-competency. Only one study (Hanson et al., 1997), which considered the effects of household economic resources, included schooling outcomes (i.e., school grades or class ranking for children in the earlier grades, and behaviour problems at school).

■ Method

Our analyses proceeded in four stages. The first stage involved the use of factor analysis to discern the structure underlying the 25 items used in the National Longitudinal Survey of Children and Youth (NLSCY). These items asked parents how often they respond to their child in certain ways, such as *How often do you get angry when you punish [your child]?*. Every item has five possible responses. Data for the negatively worded items were recoded such that high scores denote positive parenting practices. We employed principal components factor analysis with varimax rotation. We examined whether the factor structure varied with the age of the child, by conducting separate analyses for the two- to five-year-old cohort and the six- to eleven-year-old cohort. We found that the factor structure was remarkably similar for the two cohorts, and therefore based our decisions regarding scaling on results for the full age range two through eleven. The factor analysis identified four separate factors, which we labelled *Rational, Responsive, Firm Approach*, and *Reasons with Child*. Three of the twenty-five items were not used in the analysis because they loaded too heavily on more than one factor and did not contribute to the reliability of the scale. The scaled scores for each parent was the average score for the set of items that loaded on each factor, and therefore have a potential range from one to five. As with other scales in the volume, we rescaled the parenting scales to range from zero to ten.

Rational parenting had a reliability of 0.75 and included 9 items. Parents who scored high on this scale were those who reported that they did not have problems managing their child's behaviour, and when they did punish their child, the punishment did not depend on their mood, nor did they get angry. *Responsive* parenting, with a reliability of 0.80, included 6 items. Responsive parents praised their child frequently and were more often engaged with them in activities that interested the child. The *Firm Approach* parenting scale had a reliability of 0.66 and contained 5 items. Parents who scored high reported that when they asked their child to do something, they made sure that he or she did it. These parents seldom ignored bad behaviour and were more consistent in punishing their children when they did not do as they were told. The scale *Reasons with Child*, made up of only 2 items, had a reliability of 0.64. Parents scoring high on this scale reported that when their children broke the rules or did something that they were not supposed to, they calmly discussed the problem and described alternate ways of behaving that were more acceptable.

Our *Responsive* scale is similar to that used in other studies and corresponds fairly well to Baumrind's description of a responsive parent. Similarly, our *Firm Approach* scale includes items that correspond to the description of a controlling parent, in that it describes the parent who is sure to enforce the rules, but it does not include items describing whether there is a rigid set of rules. The *Reasons with Child* scale probably measures the dimension of parenting described as a democratic approach. Although the scale is not as extensive as we would like, we feel it is a nice addition to the three traditional constructs, as it captures a different dimension than control. It serves to identify parents who are more erratic in their parenting practices and prone to lapse into rejection-oriented discipline.

The second stage of our analyses used cluster analysis to determine whether parents could be categorized easily into distinct groups based on their scores on the four parenting scales. We used k-means clustering, based on nearest centroid sorting (Anderberg, 1973), and examined solutions based on two, three, four, and five clusters. We found that a four-cluster solution achieved convergence most readily and was easiest to interpret. As with the factor analysis, we examined results separately for the cohorts of two- to five-year-old children and six- to eleven-year-old children. Although a four-cluster solution was preferable for both cohorts, the patterns of scores differed between the cohorts, and therefore we present the results separately for each cohort.

The third stage of our analysis fitted an ordinary least-squares regression of the parenting-practice scores on the full set of variables describing SES, family structure, sex, and age.

The final stage of our analysis regressed the primary set of childhood outcome variables (see Chapter 3) on the set of variables describing SES, family structure, sex, and age (see Chapter 4), and the set of four parenting-practice variables. Ordinary least-squares regression was used for the continuous dependent variables, and logistic regression was used for the dichotomous dependent variables. The results for the regression model without the parenting-practice variables are presented alongside the results of the full model, so that the mediating effects of parenting practices can be more easily discerned. Finally, to achieve a single measure of the mediating effects of parenting practices, we repeated the analysis using only the SES variable and the four parenting-practice variables.

■ Parenting Practices and Age of the Child

The average scores for each of the parenting variables, by age of the child, are displayed in Figure 8.1. The scores for the *Rational* and *Firm Approach* scales did not vary significantly with the age of the child. The overall mean of the *Rational* scale was 7.27 and the standard deviation was 1.49. The mean score for *Firm Approach* was also 7.27, but the scores were somewhat more variable; the standard deviation was 1.68. The scores on the scale *Reasons with Child* increased by about 0.8 points between the ages of 2 and 4, and thereafter were consistent with age, following the pattern of the *Rational* and *Firm Approach* scales. The mean score on the *Reasons with Child* scale was 7.01, and the standard deviation was 1.80. The most dramatic results pertain to the *Responsive* scale. The average scores on this scale declined steadily with age, starting at a mean of 8.23 for 2-year-old children and dropping to a mean of 5.79 for 11-year-old children. The overall mean score on this scale was 7.04, with a standard deviation of 1.68.

■ Classifying Parents According to Style

Table 8.1 provides the results of the cluster analyses. It gives the percentage of parents in each cluster and shows the means and standard deviations for each of the four scales of parenting practices. The means are expressed as differences from mean scores for that cohort. The table also displays the mean SES score for each cluster.

Among the parents of preschool children, a large cluster comprised about three-eighths of the sample. These parents scored considerably higher than

Figure 8.1

Parenting practices and child's age

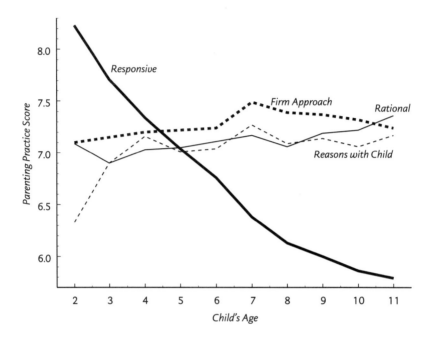

average on all four parenting scales. We characterized them as *Authoritative*. This cluster was also the most homogeneous group; the standard deviations across the four scales ranged from 0.96 to 1.16. Another cluster, which we labelled *Authoritarian*, scored high on *Firm Approach* but not as high as the authoritative cluster. These parents tended to be less rational in their approach and were less likely to reason with their child. About a quarter of parents fell into this category. The third cluster, which we labelled *Permissive*, scored very low on *Firm Approach* but relatively high on the scales associated with responsiveness and a democratic approach. They were slightly more erratic in their approach than the average parent. Permissive parents also constituted about a quarter of parents. The fourth cluster, which we refer to as *Permissive–Irrational*, contained about fourteen percent of the sample. Like the permissive parents, this group scored low on *Firm Approach*, but unlike permissive parents, they seldom discussed problems in a calm way or provided alternatives. Their practices also tended to be more erratic.

Table 8.1

Characteristics of parent clusters based on parenting practices

PRESCHOOL CHILDREN *(ages two to five)*

Cluster label	Authoritative		Authoritarian		Permissive		Permissive–Irrational	
Percentage cases (n=7002)	37.6		24.8		23.7		13.9	
	Mean	(SD)	Mean	(SD)	Mean	(SD)	Mean	(SD)
Parenting practice								
• Rational	0.64	(0.96)	-0.67	(1.22)	-1.2	(1.20)	-0.34	(1.45)
• Responsive	0.55	(1.06)	-0.97	(1.28)	0.14	(1.13)	0.01	(1.41)
• Firm approach	1.18	(0.96)	0.62	(1.01)	-1.64	(1.11)	-1.50	(1.54)
• Reasons with child	1.45	(1.16)	-1.17	(1.09)	0.65	(1.00)	-2.94	(1.50)
Socioeconomic status	0.26	(1.00)	-0.00	(0.97)	-0.17	(0.97)	-0.14	(0.96)

SCHOOL-AGE CHILDREN *(ages six to eleven)*

Cluster label	Authoritative		Authoritarian		Permissive		Irresponsible	
Percentage cases (n=9635)	32.3		28.8		23.8		14.9	
	Mean	(SD)	Mean	(SD)	Mean	(SD)	Mean	(SD)
Parenting practice								
• Rational	0.69	(1.01)	-0.39	(1.10)	0.21	(1.00)	-1.07	(1.34)
• Responsive	0.68	(1.14)	-0.58	(1.16)	0.46	(1.18)	-1.08	(1.24)
• Firm approach	1.33	(0.92)	0.78	(0.86)	-1.49	(1.03)	-2.01	(1.22)
• Reasons with child	1.38	(1.07)	-1.10	(1.20)	0.57	(1.08)	-1.78	(1.24)
Socioeconomic status	0.21	(1.00)	0.07	(0.98)	-0.12	(0.99)	-0.22	(0.97)

For the parents of school-age children, there are also three clusters which we labelled *Authoritative*, *Authoritarian*, and *Permissive*. These clusters, which made up 32.2, 28.8, and 23.8 percent of the sample respectively, have similar profiles to those of the parents of preschool children. The fourth cluster differs. We labelled it *Irresponsible* because the parents in this group score uniformly low on all four parenting scales. This group comprises nearly fifteen percent of the sample.

The pattern of SES scores is similar for both cohorts. The parents considered authoritative have the highest average SES, which is approximately one-quarter of a standard deviation above the national average. The average SES of authoritarian parents is close to the national average, whereas permissive parents have below-average SES. The permissive-irrational and irresponsible parents both have low SES, about one-fifth of a standard deviation below the national average. One should note, however, that although the clusters differ in their mean SES, the standard deviations of SES are close to 1.00 in all cases. Thus, these clusters are not homogeneous with respect to their SES, and we conclude that the differences within clusters in their SES far outweigh the differences between them.

■ **The Relationship Between Parenting Practices and Family Background**

Table 8.2 displays the results for the regression of parenting-practice scores on SES factors, family structure, sex, and age. For three of the scales—*Rational, Firm Approach*, and *Reasons with Child*—the overall relationships are very weak. In these regressions, the independent variables account for less than five percent of the variance. For responsive parenting, the independent variables account for 38.0 percent of the variance. However, the effects of age account for most of the explanatory power of this model; SES factors, family structure, and sex by themselves account for only 6.4 percent of the variance. Mothers who were not working outside the home tended to be slightly more responsive to their children, compared with mothers who were working either part-time or full-time outside of the home. Single parents had lower scores on this scale also, as did mothers of larger families. Mothers who were in their teens when their children were born reported being slightly more responsive. In all cases, however, the effects are weak: the differences are less than 0.30 on the 10-point scale. We conclude from this analysis that positive parenting practices are *not* strongly related to SES or family structure.

■ **The Effects of Parenting Practices on Children's Outcomes**

Table 8.3 displays the effects of parenting practices on children's outcomes. The effects associated with a rational approach are generally positive: this factor is significantly related to mathematics test results and the likelihood of a child having a behaviour problem or repeating a grade at school. The effects

Table 8.2

Relationships between parenting practices and family background
(unstandardized regression coefficients)

	Parenting practice			
	Rational	Responsive	Firm approach	Reasons with child
Socioeconomic status				
• Income	0.000	-0.004	**0.061**	-0.005
• Income-squared	-0.016	**0.004**	**-0.005**	-0.003
• Mother's education	-0.003	**0.015**	**0.084**	**0.058**
• Mother works part-time	**-0.169**	**-0.150**	**0.242**	0.012
• Mother at home	0.000	**0.253**	**0.065**	**0.066**
• Father's education	**0.018**	**0.035**	**0.043**	**0.019**
• Father's occupation	**0.030**	0.017	**-0.039**	-0.005
Family structure, sex, and age				
• Single parent	**-0.235**	**-0.162**	**0.098**	-0.022
• Teenage mother	-0.077	**0.101**	0.083	-0.114
• Number of siblings	0.020	**-0.233**	**0.085**	**-0.095**
• Female	**0.221**	0.031	-0.022	**0.056**
• Age	**-0.055**	**-0.274**	0.022	**0.064**
R-squared	2.9	38.0	4.6	2.0

Note: Coefficients that are statistically significant (p<0.05) appear in boldface.

associated with high rational scores are considerable. Consider the case of two parents, one who scored 7.0 on the 10-point scale, and another who scored 8.0. (This is less than the difference between typical authoritative and authoritarian parents.) The odds of the parent with the higher score having a child with a behaviour problem would be only 0.55 times that of the parent with the lower score. The odds of the more-rational parent's child having repeated a grade would only be 0.77 that of the less-rational parent. Although one needs to be cautious about inferring causation, it is important to note that these effects far outweigh the effects of family income or maternal education.

The effects of responsive parenting are mixed. The children of highly responsive parents are more likely to display pro-social behaviours and are less likely to have a behaviour problem than children of less-responsive parents. These effects are consistent with the literature. But children of highly responsive parents have lower average scores in mathematics than their same-age

Table 8.3

Effects of parenting practices on children's outcomes
(unstandardized regression coefficients)

	Social and cognitive skills					
	Pro-social behaviour		Preschool vocabulary		Mathematics computation	
	I	II	I	II	I	II
Socioeconomic status						
• Income	**-0.03**	**-0.03**	**0.74**	**0.70**	**0.64**	**0.62**
• Income-squared	**0.01**	**0.01**	**-0.14**	**-0.14**	**-0.09**	-0.08
• Mother's education	**0.04**	0.01	**1.12**	**1.05**	**0.53**	**0.48**
• Mother works part-time	**0.17**	**0.10**	**1.68**	**1.47**	0.29	0.26
• Mother at home	0.07	-0.03	0.34	0.31	1.16	1.23
• Father's education	0.02	-0.00	0.11	0.08	**0.60**	**0.62**
• Father's occupation	0.00	0.01	0.56	0.57	-0.45	-0.40
Family structure, sex, and age						
• Single parent	**-0.13**	-0.09	0.24	0.26	0.16	0.05
• Teenage mother	0.04	0.02	**-2.72**	**-2.88**	-1.23	-1.15
• Number of siblings	-0.11	-0.02	-1.44	-1.47	-0.15	-0.31
• Female	**0.76**	**0.74**	0.56	0.62	**1.01**	0.91
• Age	**0.18**	**0.25**			**0.38**	0.25
Parenting practice						
• Rational		-0.01		-0.14		**0.41**
• Responsive		0.32		0.13		**-0.88**
• Firm approach		**0.09**		**0.82**		0.18
• Reasons with child		**0.20**		0.00		**0.40**
R-squared	8.7	17.6	8.1	8.9	4.3	5.0

Note: Coefficients that are statistically significant (p<0.05) appear in boldface.

peers and are more likely to be one full grade level behind. The effect was in the same direction for repeating a grade, but was not statistically significant.

Maintaining a firm approach was positively associated with pro-social behaviour and preschool vocabulary scores, and decreased the likelihood of a behaviour problem or a low vocabulary score. The results were in the same direction for the two outcomes pertaining to mathematics, but were not statistically significant. This aspect of parenting was unrelated to whether a child had repeated a grade.

Finally, children whose parents more often discussed behaviour problems with them tended to be more pro-social, have better scores in mathematics,

Table 8.3 *(cont.)*

Effects of parenting practices on children's outcomes (odds ratios)

	Markers of vulnerability							
	Behaviour problem		Low vocabulary		Low mathematics		Repeated a grade	
	I	II	I	II	I	II	I	II
Socioeconomic status								
• Income	0.99	0.99	**0.86**	**0.86**	**0.88**	**0.88**	**0.90**	**0.90**
• Income-squared	1.00	1.00	1.01	1.01	1.01	1.01	1.01	1.01
• Mother's education	**0.94**	**0.93**	**0.86**	**0.87**	**0.90**	**0.89**	**0.91**	**0.91**
• Mother works part-time	**1.12**	1.07	0.83	0.83	0.96	0.96	1.05	1.00
• Mother at home	1.01	1.04	1.18	1.16	0.98	0.95	**1.37**	**1.36**
• Father's education	1.00	1.01	1.02	1.03	0.97	0.96	0.96	0.96
• Father's occupation	**0.93**	**0.94**	0.94	0.95	0.99	1.00	0.91	0.91
Family structure, sex, and age								
• Single parent	**1.72**	**1.59**	0.89	0.89	0.93	0.91	**1.72**	**1.64**
• Teenage mother	**1.50**	**1.47**	1.17	1.17	1.00	0.94	1.33	1.30
• Number of siblings	**0.93**	**0.90**	**1.14**	**1.14**	1.00	1.02	1.00	1.02
• Female	**0.76**	**0.88**	0.96	0.95	**0.68**	**0.67**	**0.60**	**0.64**
• Age	**1.03**	**1.04**			**1.36**	**1.37**	**1.39**	**1.43**
Parenting practice								
• Rational		**0.55**		1.05		1.00		**0.77**
• Responsive		**0.96**		1.04		1.08		**1.08**
• Firm approach		**0.97**		**0.90**		0.97		1.01
• Reasons with child		**1.03**		**0.89**		1.06		1.03
R-squared	2.4	10.5	5.0	5.9	3.3	3.5	3.8	4.3

Note: Odds ratios that differ significantly from 1.0 (p<0.05) appear in boldface.

and be less vulnerable to being more than one grade level behind in mathematics. However, reasoning with the child was not significantly related to the other outcome variables.

The analyses reported in Table 8.3 assume that the effects of parenting practices do not vary with the child's age. We extended the regression model to test whether any of the four parenting style variables had more important effects at certain ages. The analyses revealed significant age-by-parenting-practice interactions for pro-social behaviour and for the likelihood of a behaviour problem. For pro-social behaviour, the interaction term indicated that the effects of rational parenting ranged from -0.18 at age 2, to 0.18 at age 11 (an

Table 8.4

Mediation effects associated with parenting practices
(unstandardized regression coefficients)

	Social and cognitive skills					
	Pro-social behaviour		Preschool vocabulary		Mathematics computation	
	I	II	I	II	I	II
Socioeconomic status	**0.07**	-0.01	**3.83**	**3.56**	**2.77**	**2.71**
Parenting practice						
• Rational		**0.10**		-0.24		**0.48**
• Responsive		**0.06**		0.29		**-0.87**
• Firm approach		**0.10**		**0.81**		0.23
• Reasons with child		**0.26**		0.11		**0.40**
R-squared	0.1	7.9	6.0	6.8	3.4	4.2

Note: Coefficients that are statistically significant (p<0.05) appear in boldface.

average effect of -0.01, reported in Table 8.3). Similarly, the effects of responsive parenting on pro-social behaviour ranged from 0.24 at age 2 to 0.40 at age 11. In contrast, the effect of maintaining a firm approach did not vary with the child's age, and the effect of providing reasons declined from 0.28 at age 2 to 0.10 at age 11. The same pattern was apparent for the likelihood of a child having a behaviour problem: the odds ratios declined with age for rational and responsive parenting, and increased with age for providing reasons. These age-related findings, taken together with those reported in Figure 8.1, are especially important with respect to responsive parenting. They suggest that parents tend to become less responsive as their child matures, when responsive parenting has its most important effects on behaviour.

■ Parenting Practices as a Mediator of the Effects of SES

Table 8.3 provides estimates of the effects of the components of SES on children's outcomes, before and after controlling for parenting practices (i.e., Model I compared with Model II). Generally, the impact of SES factors that significantly affect children's outcomes declines slightly after parenting-practice variables are included in the model. For example, the effect on preschool vocabulary scores associated with a 1-year increase in mother's education is

Table 8.4 *(cont.)*

Mediation effects associated with parenting practices (odds ratios)

	Markers of vulnerability							
	Behaviour problem		Low vocabulary		Low mathematics		Repeated a grade	
	I	II	I	II	I	II	I	II
Socioeconomic status	0.77	0.80	**0.57**	**0.59**	**0.62**	**0.62**	**0.56**	**0.57**
Parenting practice								
• Rational		**0.55**		1.05		1.05		**0.80**
• Responsive		**0.94**		1.04		1.03		0.96
• Firm approach		**0.96**		**0.90**		0.94		0.98
• Reasons with child		**1.04**		**0.89**		1.07		1.06
R-squared	1.1	9.7	3.8	4.7	1.7	1.9	1.6	2.1

Note: Odds ratios that differ significantly from 1.0 (p<0.05) appear in boldface.

1.12 points; but this effect is *mediated* by parenting practices and declines to
1.05 after parenting practices are taken into account. The effect of mother's
education remains significant, but is not as strong. Similar results are evident
for the effects of mother's education on mathematics scores, where the effect
declines from 0.53 to 0.48 months of schooling. These findings suggest that at
least some of the effect on cognitive outcomes associated with the level of the
mother's education is attributable to parenting practices.

Table 8.4 shows the mediating effects of parenting practices on the
summary measure of SES. The parenting-practice variables mediate the effects
associated with SES for every outcome variable, but the mediating effects are
not strong. In the case of pro-social behaviour, SES has a very weak relationship even before considering parenting practices: average scores on the
10-point scale increase by only 0.07 points with an increase of 1 standard deviation in SES. Parenting practices mediate this effect, but unimportantly, given
the weak relationship between pro-social behaviour and SES. Parenting practices mediated the effect associated with SES on preschool vocabulary scores;
the coefficient decreases by about 7.0 percent, from 3.83 to 3.56. The SES
effect on mathematics scores decreases by 2.2 percent with the inclusion of
the parenting-practice variables. The mediating effects for the markers of
vulnerability appear to be even weaker. For example, the likelihood of a child
having a behaviour problem decreases by 23 percent (the odds ratio is 0.77)

with an increase of 1 standard deviation in SES; after taking parenting practices into account, the decrease in the likelihood associated with SES is 20 percent. The mediating effects are similar for low vocabulary scores, and even weaker for low mathematics scores or repeating a grade.

■ Policy Implications

The literature on the effects of parenting suggests that monitoring a child's behaviour carefully, providing a warm and caring environment, and encouraging independence lead to superior schooling outcomes. This chapter analyzes data derived from questions asked of the parents of more than 19,000 children 2 to 11 years old. An analysis of their responses identified four important dimensions of parenting, which could be viewed as rational, responsive, firm, and reasoning. Five important findings emerged from this analysis.

1. *The extent to which parents are responsive to their children declines steadily as children get older.* This relationship stands in sharp contrast to rational parenting, which increases considerably from ages two to for, and the use of a firm approach and reasoning, which do not vary substantially with the child's age (see Figure 8.1).

2. *Only about a third of parents can be considered to have an authoritative parenting style, in the sense this term is used in the literature.* About a quarter of parents were characterized as authoritarian, and a further quarter as permissive. The analysis identified a fourth category of parents, made up of slightly less than fifteen percent of parents. These parents scored low on all aspects of positive parenting and were characterized as permissive–irrational or irresponsible (see Table 8.1).

3. *Parenting practices were not strongly related to SES or family structure.* When parents were categorized according to their style, the groups were not homogeneous with respect to SES. Moreover, a full range of variables describing family structure and SES accounted for only about two to six percent of the variation in parents' practices. Thus, both positive and negative parenting practices are apparent in all types of families (see Table 8.2).

4. *Parenting practices have important effects on a child's social and cognitive outcomes and on the likelihood that a child is vulnerable in some way.* Generally,

there were strong positive effects on children's outcomes associated with positive parenting practices. These effects seemed to be particularly strong for pro-social behaviour and the likelihood that a child would have a behaviour problem. The effect of responsive parenting is particularly interesting, because the effects increase with the child's age. This is important, given that levels of responsive parenting decline as the child gets older. There was one anomalous finding: children of more responsive parents had slightly lower mathematics scores and were more likely to be at least one year behind their peers in mathematics. Our conjecture is that children's results during the early years of schooling may induce parents to praise their children more often and spend more time with them (see Table 8.3).

5. *Parenting practices do not account for the relationship between children's outcomes and SES.* Mediating effects of parenting practices on SES gradients were apparent for all of the outcome measures, but the effects are small. The largest mediating effect was associated with children's early vocabulary scores, parenting approaches reduced the SES effect by about seven percent (see Table 8.4).

These findings present a serious challenge to the "culture of poverty" thesis and the widespread belief that the children of poor families do not fare well because of the way they are raised. These findings, based on a large representative sample of Canadian families, show that positive parenting practices have important effects on childhood outcomes, but that both positive and negative ✓ parenting practices are found in rich and poor families alike. Thus, good parenting is a concern for all parents.

The results also imply that universal programs aimed at improving parents' practices would be preferable to targeted programs. Because positive practices are only weakly associated with SES, it is not feasible to identify parents with relatively poor skills on the basis of socioeconomic factors. And given that only about a third of parents might be characterized as authoritative, most parents could benefit from training programs that improved their skills. A short course on positive parenting practices, delivered to parents in a fashion similar to prenatal classes, might be helpful. The aim would be to provide parents with practical ways to monitor their children's behaviour, engage with them positively, and encourage their independence.

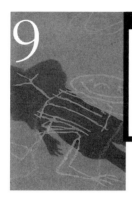

Parenting and Children's Behaviour Problems

FIONA MILLER, JENNY JENKINS,

& DAN KEATING

A SUBSTANTIAL PROPORTION of Canadian children display behavioural problems, including emotional disorders and psychological disturbances, which are serious enough to warrant concern for their present functioning and future development. The results cited in Chapter 3 of this volume indicate that the prevalence of one or more behavioural problems among Canadian children aged 4 to 11 was about 19.1 percent. Using a much different methodology, Offord and Lipman (1996) estimated the prevalence for this age range to be 20.7 percent. This represents not only a substantial proportion of children and families who need to cope with these difficulties, but also represents a substantial risk of lifelong consequences for many children (Offord & Lipman, 1996).

We need to better understand the source of these behavioural problems to guide the policies and practices intended to address them. Researchers have identified a number of factors that contribute to the development of behavioural problems during childhood. Socioeconomic status (SES) is usually considered foremost as a source of vulnerability, and indeed the prevalence of a number of behavioural problems has been found to be higher at lower levels of SES, both in the National Longitudinal Survey of Children and Youth (NLSCY) (see Chapter 4) and in other samples, including the Ontario Child Health Study (Offord et al., 1992; Offord & Lipman, 1996). However, SES itself is not the primary causal factor; rather, it can be seen as a proxy for a number of factors that influence the child's development, including social and community support, familial relationships, and parenting style (Coulton, Korbin, Su, & Chow, 1995; Deater-Deckard, Dodge, Bates, & Pettit, 1994; Jenkins & Smith, 1990; Wakschlag, Chase-Lansdale, & Brooks-Gunn, 1996).

Chapter 8 showed that children's behaviour problems were associated with their parents' style of parenting. Parents who were firm but rational in their approach and who were responsive to their children's needs were less likely to have a child with a behaviour problem. This finding is consistent with literature that has examined the causes of anti-social or aggressive behaviour, especially among boys. The two most critical aspects of parenting are parental warmth, as opposed to hostility or harshness, and consistency (Deater-Deckard et al., 1996; Olweus, 1980; Patterson, 1982; Pettit & Bates, 1989; Lefkowitz, Eron, Walder, & Huesmann, 1977; West & Farrington, 1973). Mothers with relatively low SES tend to face higher levels of familial stressors and experience low social support (Dodge, Pettit, & Bates, 1994). When they interact with their children, they tend to show less warmth and higher levels of controlling, disapproving, and restrictive behaviours than mothers with relatively high SES (Dodge et al., 1994; Hoff-Ginsberg & Tardif, 1995). Thus, there is some evidence that these aspects of parenting are associated with SES (Dodge et al., 1994; Hoff-Ginsberg & Tardif, 1995) and are therefore potential mediators of the relationship between SES and behavioural outcomes. This chapter extends the analyses in Chapter 8 by examining the potential mediating effects of parenting practices on the relationship between childhood behaviour and SES for particular types of behaviour problems. These analyses focus particularly on "harsh," or ineffective, parenting and consistency.

There are two major types of behaviour problems, often referred to as internalizing and externalizing disorders. Internalizing disorders involve disturbances of affect; they include emotional disorders (feelings of sadness, depression, and dysphoria), anxiety (feelings of fearfulness, worry, or nervousness), and separation anxiety (clinging, dependent, and distressed when separated from parents). In contrast, externalizing disorders typically involve negative behaviours that are problematic for the child and disturbing to others. They include conduct disorders (cruelty and threatening or physically attacking people), physical aggression (getting into many fights, hitting, kicking, biting), and hyperactivity (fidgety, impulsive, and acting without thinking). The results in Chapter 3 show that the prevalence of these behaviour problems vary according to a child's age and gender. Adolescents, for example, are more likely to have conduct disorders, while preschoolers are more likely to experience separation anxiety. The analyses in Chapter 8 also revealed that the effects of responsive parenting and maintaining a rational approach varied with the child's age. Accordingly, we are interested in whether the effects of harshness and consistency on particular behavioural problems also vary with a child's age.

This chapter investigates the relationships among SES, parenting practices, and internalizing and externalizing childhood disorders in a nationally representative sample of Canadian children. To explore whether the patterns of relationships differ by the age of the child, we examined the NLSCY sample of two- and three-year-olds and eight- and nine-year-olds. The internalizing disorders included emotional problems and anxiety. For younger children, separation anxiety was also included. The externalizing disorders included hyperactivity and physical aggression. For older children, conduct disorder was also included. For each type of childhood problem, we asked four questions:

- Is harshness and consistency in parenting related to SES?
- Is the prevalence of childhood behaviour problems related to SES?
- Do parenting practices mediate the relationships between SES and childhood behaviour problems? (See Chapter 2 for a discussion of mediating variables.)
- Does the relationship between parenting practices and behaviour problems differ at varying levels of SES; or in statistical terms, is there an SES-by-parenting practice interaction?

Our study builds on previous work in several ways. It examines the role of parenting practices as a mediator and a moderator of the relationship between SES and childhood behaviour problems, including both externalizing and internalizing disorders. It looks at children in two different age groups, thereby permitting comparison of the sources of childhood behaviour problems at different points in the developmental pathways.

Hostile and harsh parenting

Hostility and power assertion in the parent–child relationship have consistently been identified as important predictors of psychopathology in childhood, particularly the onset of externalizing behaviour disorders (Olweus, 1980; Patterson, 1982). Dodge, Bates, and Pettit (1990) investigated the relationship between harsh discipline and childhood aggression among children entering elementary school. Six months before the children entered school, their parents were interviewed about the frequency and severity with which they gave physical punishment to their children. On entering school, the children's aggression with peers was assessed by interviews in which all children in the class were asked to nominate children who were mean or got into many fights. The children were also presented neutral stimuli depicting other children's actions and were asked to assess their intentions. The findings indicated that frequent and severe physical punishment in the home was associated with more aggression towards peers in school, and that children who had been subjected to high levels of physical punishment were more likely to attribute hostile intent to other children's neutral actions.

Richman, Stevenson, and Graham (1982) found that children with behaviour problems were four times more likely to have a parent who spoke critically about them and three times more likely to have a parent who lost control with them physically than were children who did not display behaviour problems. Harsh parenting has also been found to be associated with increases in externalizing disorders and aggression (Simons, Whitbeck, Conger, & Chyi-In, 1991), as well as some internalizing disorders, particularly depression (Sternberg, Lamb, Greenbaum, Cicchetti, Dawud, Cortes, et al., 1993).

Positive interactions and consistency in parenting

A lack of positive interactions and affection in parent–child relationships is also associated with childhood behaviour problems. Pettit and Bates (1989) carried out home observations of parent–child interactions when babies were six, thirteen, and twenty-four months old. Mothers were rated on the positive affect they showed towards their children, including affectionate contact (six months), affectionate teaching (thirteen months), and verbal stimulation (twenty-four months). When the children were four years old, their mothers rated their behaviour. Lower levels of positive maternal affection in the first two years predicted internalizing and externalizing disorders when the children were four years old.

The roles of supportive and harsh parenting were explored further in a longitudinal study examining their joint and independent contributions to child adjustment between kindergarten and grade six. Pettit, Bates, & Dodge (1997) measured four aspects of supportive parenting prior to children's entry to kindergarten, including mother–child warmth, positive maternal involvement, inductive discipline, and pro-active teaching. Measures of harsh parenting (physical punishment) and family vulnerability (low SES, single parenthood, and familial stress) were also administered at this time. Measures pertaining to behavioural, social, and academic adjustment were also completed by teachers in both kindergarten and grade six. The findings indicated that supportive and harsh parenting played significant roles in adjustment, both concurrently and longitudinally. When levels of harsh parenting and kindergarten adjustment were controlled for, supportive parenting predicted children's level of adjustment in grade six. Moreover, supportive parenting acted as a buffer, reducing the negative effects of family adversity and socioeconomic disadvantage on measures of adjustment in grade six.

The association between inconsistent and ineffective discipline and externalizing behaviour disorders has been documented since the earliest studies of the antecedents of anti-social behaviour in children (Lefkowitz et al., 1977; West & Farrington, 1973). Consistency and effective disciplinary strategies are also associated with child adjustment. Patterson et al. (1993) defined this construct as an interrelated set of skills that entails accurately tracking and classifying a child's behaviour, ignoring trivial coercive events, and using effective consequences when punishment is necessary.

■ Method

The analyses in this chapter were based on data reported by parents for 3,669 children 2 and 3 years old and 3,298 children 8 and 9 years old. The variables pertaining to family background include the composite measure of SES, mother's employment status (working part-time or working at home versus working full-time), family structure (single- versus two-parent family), whether or not the mother was a teen parent, and the number of children in the family. Sex was coded "o" for males, "1" for females. The measures of behavioural problems included separation anxiety (for two- and three-year-old children only), emotional disorder, anxiety, hyperactivity, physical aggression, and conduct disorders (for eight- and nine-year-old children only). The construction of these variables is described in Chapter 3.

The measure of *harshness* was derived from parents responses to eight items pertaining to their parenting practices:

- How often do you get annoyed with <child's name> for saying or doing something (he/she) is not supposed to?
- How often do you tell (him/her) that (he/she) is bad or not as good as others?

- How often do you get angry when you punish <child's name>?
- How often do you have to discipline (him/her) for the same thing?
- Of all the times you talk to <child's name> about (his/her) behaviour, what proportion is praise?
- Of all the times you talk to <child's name> about (his/her) behaviour, what proportion is disapproval?
- When <child's name> breaks the rules or does things that (he/she) is not supposed to, how often do you raise your voice, scold, or yell at (him/her)?
- When <child's name> breaks the rules or does things that (he/she) is not supposed to, how often do you use physical punishment?

The possible answers for the first four questions were *never, about once a week, a few times a week, one or two times each day*, and *many times each day*. The possible answers for questions five and six were *never, less than half the time, about half the time, more than half the time*, and *all the time*; and the possible answers for questions seven and eight were *always, often, sometimes, rarely*, and *never*. Responses were scaled on a ten-point scale. For the full population of children aged 2 to 11, the scale had a mean of 3.09, a standard deviation of 1.20, and a reliability of 0.71.

The measure of *consistency* was derived from parents' responses to five items:

- When you give <child's name> a command or order to do something, what proportion of the time do you make sure that (he/she) does it?
- If you tell (him/her) (he/she) will get punished if (he/she) doesn't stop doing something, and (he/she) keeps doing it, how often will you punish (him/her)?
- How often does (he/she) get away with things that you feel should have been punished?
- How often is (he/she) able to get out of punishment when (he/she) really sets (his/her) mind to it?
- How often, when you discipline (him/her), does (he/she) ignore the punishment?

The possible answers for these questions were *never, less than half the time, about half the time, more than half the time*, and *all the time*. These responses were also scaled on a ten-point scale. For the full population of children aged 2 to 11, the scale had a mean of 7.38, a standard deviation of 1.73, and a reliability of 0.66.

Three sets of regression models were fit to the data, corresponding to the strategy recommended by Baron and Kenny (1986) for examining mediating and moderating effects. The first set was ordinary least-squares regressions of the continuous measures, harshness and consistency, on sex and the full set of family background measures. These models aimed to address the research question about patterns of parenting practices related to SES. The second set of regression models fit logistic regressions of the dichotomous measures of internalizing and externalizing behaviour measures on sex and the full set of family background measures. This analysis determines whether the prevalence of behaviour problems is related to family background. The last set of regression models extends the logistic regressions to include harshness and consistency. These regression models were extended further to include interaction terms for SES-by-harshness and SES-by-consistency. However, with the exception of the model for hyperactivity among toddlers, the interaction terms were not statistically significant, and thus we do not report the findings for the fourth set of regressions in a separate table.

■ Family Background, SES, and Parenting Behaviour

The relationships between the two measures of parenting with sex and family background are displayed in Table 9.1. The relationships with SES are consistent with earlier literature: parents with higher levels of SES tend to be less harsh and more consistent in their parenting practices. The relationship was somewhat stronger for consistency than harshness. These findings were evident for both age groups. Similarly, mothers who were teen parents when the child was born reported higher levels of harshness and less consistency. This relationship was significant for two- and three-year-old children, but slightly weaker and not statistically significant for eight- and nine-year-old children. The findings for mothers' employment status were somewhat anomalous: mothers who worked part-time reported higher levels of harshness and more consistency than those who worked full-time. Mothers of two- and three-year-old children who were not working outside the home had significantly lower levels of consistency. Parents reported they were less harsh with their daughters than with their sons. Although the relationships between parenting practices and family background are statistically significant, they are rather weak, accounting for five percent or less of the variance in the two measures.

Table 9.1

Relationship between harshness, consistency, and family background (unstandardized regression coefficients)

	Ages 2 and 3		Ages 8 and 9	
	Harsh	Consistent	Harsh	Consistent
Mean score	3.185	7.104	3.112	7.433
Socioeconomic status	-0.089	0.317	-0.067	0.327
Mother works part-time	0.228	0.103	0.097	0.302
Mother at home	0.092	-0.184	0.012	0.044
Single Parent	0.114	0.044	0.058	-0.024
Teenage mother	0.214	-0.369	0.178	-0.159
Number of siblings	0.014	0.050	-0.018	0.101
Female	-0.194	0.086	-0.317	-0.065
R-squared	0.023	0.050	0.025	0.048

Note: Coefficients that are statistically significant (p<0.05) appear in boldface.

■ Prevalence of Childhood Disorders and Family Background

The relationships between the measures of childhood disorders with sex and family background are shown in Table 9.2, denoted as Model I. The results indicate a significantly reduced risk of childhood disorders associated with increases in SES for both age groups. Children aged two and three years in high-SES families were less likely to experience separation anxiety or to be hyperactive or physically aggressive. Similarly, children aged eight and nine years from higher-SES households had a significantly reduced risk of experiencing any of the five behavioural problems. The relationships tended to be slightly stronger for eight- and nine-year-old children than for two- and three-year-old children. The odds ratio for conduct disorders among the older children was 0.18, and for the other four disorders ranged from 0.65 to 0.78. These ratios represent considerable effects. Consider two groups of children. One group has an average family SES half a standard deviation below the mean; the other has an average family SES half a standard deviation above the mean. Using an odds ratio of 0.66 for example, the odds for the high-SES group experiencing a disorder are only two-thirds those of the low-SES group.

The reduced risk of behaviour problems associated with low SES is uniformly stronger for externalizing disorders than it is for internalizing disorders, especially for the two- and three-year-old children. Recall, however, that the data were based on parents' assessments and therefore require cautious interpretation. It may be that symptoms associated with externalizing disorders, such as hyperactivity or physical aggression, are easier to identify than symptoms of internalizing disorders, such as anxiety or emotional disorders.

■ The Effects of Parenting Behaviour and Their Role as a Mediator of SES

Model II in Table 9.2 extends Model I by including the two measures of parenting behaviours. Harshness significantly increases the likelihood that a child will experience a childhood behaviour disorder. For younger children in this study, the odds ratios associated with a one-point increase in harshness ranged from 1.16 to 1.96; for older children, they ranged from 1.92 to 3.98. On average across the two cohorts, for emotional disorder, anxiety, hyperactivity, and physical aggression, the odds ratio is nearly 2.0, which indicates that the odds of experiencing a disorder nearly doubles with each one-point increase on the harshness scale.

Positive effects for consistency are also evident but are not as pronounced. The effects were significant for separation anxiety in the younger cohort and for conduct disorders, hyperactivity, and physical aggression in the older cohort. The effects were not statistically significant for emotional disorder or anxiety in either cohort.

Taken together, these findings suggest that parenting behaviours have a much stronger effect on childhood behaviours than SES. The odds of experiencing a behaviour disorder for a child from a low-SES family (e.g., one standard deviation below the national average) are on average about twenty percent greater than for a child in an average-SES family. This effect could be compensated for by a two-point increase on the consistency scale or a very small decrease on harshness scale.

To test whether parenting practices mediated the effects of SES, the contribution of SES to behaviour problems alone was compared to its contribution in the presence of the parenting practice variables (i.e., Model I compared with Model II in Table 9.2). The inclusion of parenting variables did not significantly reduce the contribution of SES to behaviour problems. We conclude that parenting behaviours, as assessed in the NLSCY, are not a significant mediator of the effects of SES on behaviour problems for either younger or older children, regardless of the type of problem. Both SES and parenting practices contribute significantly to behaviour problems, but they appear to have independent effects.

Table 9.2

The relationship between behaviour markers of vulnerability and parental harshness and consistency (unstandardized regression coefficients)

CHILDREN AGES TWO AND THREE

	Separation anxiety		Emotional disorder	
	I	II	I	II
Socioeconomic status	**0.85**	0.89	1.27	1.28
Mother works part-time	1.16	1.13	4.15	3.21
Mother at home	**1.72**	**1.67**	**8.51**	**7.92**
Single Parent	0.95	0.91	**3.93**	**3.24**
Teenage mother	**2.12**	**1.98**	**4.72**	**3.85**
Number of siblings	0.93	0.93	0.84	0.78
Female	**0.19**	0.20	**0.39**	0.47
Harsh		**1.16**		**1.88**
Consistent		**0.89**		1.05
R-squared	0.059	0.066	0.012	0.023

CHILDREN AGES EIGHT AND NINE

	Conduct disorder		Emotional disorder	
	I	II	I	II
Socioeconomic status	**0.18**	**0.23**	**0.68**	**0.71**
Mother works part-time	0.30	0.22	1.05	1.04
Mother at home	0.32	0.24	**0.47**	**0.44**
Single Parent	6.06	3.53	**2.11**	**2.16**
Teenage mother	2.01	2.74	0.70	0.64
Number of siblings	1.10	1.42	0.97	1.00
Female	1.01	2.23	1.17	**1.48**
Harsh		**3.98**		**1.96**
Consistent		**0.49**		0.98
R-squared	0.006	0.011	0.016	0.047

Note: Coefficients that are statistically significant (p<0.05) appear in boldface.

Table 9.2 (*cont.*)

The relationship between behaviour markers of vulnerability and parental harshness and consistency (unstandardized regression coefficients)

CHILDREN AGES TWO AND THREE

	Anxiety		Hyperactivity		Physical aggression	
	I	II	I	II	I	II
Socioeconomic status	1.30	**1.38**	**0.68**	**0.73**	**0.72**	**0.77**
Mother works part-time	0.66	0.52	0.92	0.83	0.94	0.75
Mother at home	1.41	1.28	0.90	0.84	0.67	**0.59**
Single Parent	1.95	1.72	**1.54**	**1.50**	1.43	1.30
Teenage mother	**5.29**	**4.22**	**1.86**	**1.64**	**2.65**	**2.28**
Number of siblings	1.04	1.02	1.00	0.99	**1.31**	**1.36**
Female	0.88	1.05	**0.67**	**0.76**	**0.20**	**0.22**
Harsh		**1.96**		**1.70**		**1.92**
Consistent		0.99		0.87		0.93
R-squared	0.010	0.023	0.038	0.097	0.034	0.064

CHILDREN AGES EIGHT AND NINE

	Anxiety		Hyperactivity		Physical aggression	
	I	II	I	II	I	II
Socioeconomic status	**0.78**	**0.80**	**0.65**	**0.68**	**0.67**	**0.77**
Mother works part-time	1.04	1.00	1.12	1.13	1.31	1.33
Mother at home	**0.62**	**0.58**	0.93	0.92	0.97	0.99
Single Parent	**1.93**	**1.96**	0.94	0.90	**2.98**	**3.24**
Teenage mother	1.26	1.20	1.35	1.25	1.27	1.12
Number of siblings	0.92	0.94	**0.76**	**0.76**	1.05	1.11
Female	1.04	1.27	**0.41**	**0.46**	**0.24**	**0.28**
Harsh		**1.85**		**1.92**		**2.44**
Consistent		1.05		**0.92**		**0.84**
R-squared	0.009	0.031	0.048	0.111	0.031	0.070

Note: Coefficients that are statistically significant (p<0.05) appear in boldface.

Figure 9.1

The relationship between behavioural markers of vulnerability and parental harshness and consistency

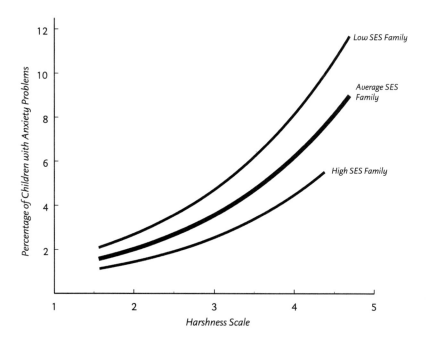

■ Parenting Effects on Behaviour Problems at Different Levels of SES

Even though we did not find parenting behaviours to be a mediator of the relationship between SES and childhood disorders, parenting may moderate the effects of SES. If so, the effects of parenting on behaviour would be stronger or weaker at differing levels of SES. This was tested by extending Model II to include SES-by-harshness and SES-by-consistency interaction terms. For both two- and three-year-olds and eight- and nine-year-olds, SES was not a significant moderator of any of the parenting effects on behaviour problems. Taken together with the absence of mediating effects, the results imply that SES and parenting are largely independent sources of influence on behaviour problems for both age groups.

Our hypothesis was that the effects of positive parenting would be less substantial among high-SES families; that is, SES would serve as a buffer against harsh and inconsistent parenting. For the older cohort, the direction of the interaction terms (negative for SES-by-harshness and positive for SES-by-consistency) supported this hypothesis, and in the case of harshness, the interactions approached statistical significance for conduct disorders and anxiety. The effects were trivial for the other three disorders. These results do not provide strong evidence in support of the buffering hypothesis, but they do not countermand it.

Figure 9.1 shows the relationships among anxiety disorders and harshness for three subgroups of children: low SES (less than one standard deviation below the mean), average SES, and high SES (more than one standard deviation above the mean). The lines depict the likelihood that a child would experience an anxiety problem, at varying levels of harshness. These results were derived from the extended regression model described above. The lines are drawn such that they include the range of harshness scores (from the tenth to ninetieth percentiles) observed in the data for each subgroup.

The figure displays all the main findings discussed above. First, the range of harshness scores is similar across the three subgroups; that is, parenting behaviours are only weakly related to SES. Second, there is a significant gap between the three lines at all levels of SES. In the middle of the range on the harshness scale, the gap between low and high SES families is about two percent. In other words, SES has an effect on behaviour disorders, but the effect is quite small. Third, all three lines rise dramatically with increasing levels of harshness; that is, harsh parenting increases the likelihood of a child experiencing an anxiety problem. The effects are statistically significant and large in substantive terms. Fourth, the slope of the line for high-SES parents is not as steep as the slope for low-SES parents. Although the differences in the slopes of the lines (i.e., the SES-by-harshness interaction) was not statistically significant, the effects of parenting appear to be slightly more pronounced for children in low-SES families.

■ **Summary and Policy Implications**

Previous research has indicated that behaviour disorders in children, particularly externalizing disorders, are associated with harsh parenting. Frequent, severe punishment in the home is associated with greater hostility and aggression towards peers and a higher prevalence of externalizing disorders. Parents who are supportive and consistent in their approach to parenting are also less likely to observe behaviour problems in their children. Much of the previous work has been based on selected samples of high-risk children. Our study examined the effects associated with harsh and consistent parenting for two samples representing all two- and three-year-old and eight- and nine-year-old children in Canada. In addition to broadening the set of behavioural measures to include internalizing disorders, this study also examined whether parenting practices mediated the relationship between SES and behaviour problems or served to buffer some of the adverse effects associated with living in a low SES family. Several significant finding emerged.

1. *There are substantial effects of both SES and parenting on behaviour problems among both older (eight- and nine-year-old) and younger (two- and three-year-old) children.* The consistency of these patterns is striking and is reinforced by their coherence with previous research. Lower SES and problematic parenting are each a substantial factor associated with the presence of behaviour problems. This conclusion was evident for internalizing as well as externalizing disorders, which have been studied more often. SES appeared to be more strongly associated with externalizing disorders than with internalizing disorders in both age groups, although we are cautious in our interpretation because the data were obtained from a single respondent— the person most knowledgeable about the child—and because externalizing behaviours are by definition easier to observe than internalizing disorders.

2. *Harsh parenting dominated the predictions of behaviour problems for both age groups.* This finding was not expected based on prior research. But the magnitude of the effects is striking: a one-point decrease on the ten-point scale of harsh parenting yields a decreased risk of about fifty percent at both ages. The contribution of consistent parenting was less uniform, although for externalizing disorders in the older age group the effect was statistically significant, with a reduced risk associated with more consistent parenting of eight to fifty-one percent.

3. *Children in low-SES families and children of teenage mothers were more likely to be subjected to problematic parenting.* This relationship was somewhat stronger for consistent parenting than harshness. However, most of the variance in parenting behaviours was not accounted for by SES and other family background variables.

The effects on children's behaviours associated with SES or other aspects of family background are not attributable to poor parenting practices. These findings suggest the developmental factors that might explain why children in low-SES families are somewhat more prone to behavioural disorders do not seem to include parenting practices, at least as they are measured in the NLSCY. The benefits of positive parenting practices also seem to be equally strong across poor and affluent families alike.

4. *A comprehensive understanding of the complex relationships affecting children's behaviour requires consideration of a range of factors in a longitudinal analysis.* The impact of SES on behaviour problems is substantial and is not explained by parenting practices. Parenting practices seem to have an even greater impact and are important at all levels of SES. This is particularly so when the full promise of the NLSCY can be realized with the exploration of longitudinal relationships when subsequent observations of these children have been completed and analyzed (Keating and Mustard, 1996).

From a practical perspective, these results emphasize the significant vulnerabilities that attend growing up in lower-SES circumstances or in homes where parenting is problematic. The challenges facing parents in lower-SES households are substantial, and not only with respect to raising their children. To support healthy development, a range of supports are needed, including a blend of universal, targeted, and clinical services (Offord et al. 1999), as well as a generally higher social investment in healthy child development (Keating & Hertzman, 1999). Because these results highlight the impact of parenting at all SES levels, the value of universal programs should be noted. These could range from a greater emphasis on parenting, family studies, and human development in the high-school curriculum to the creation of early childhood development and parenting centres (McCain & Mustard, 1999).

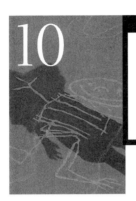

10 Balancing Work and Family Life

CYNTHIA COOK &
J. DOUGLAS WILLMS

FEW PEOPLE WOULD DENY that parents' involvement in their child's life affects the child's cognitive development, and emotional and physical well-being. Yet some commentators suspect that, as a society, we are becoming less engaged in our children's lives. A survey of 20,000 teens and families in the US estimated that 25 percent of parents were "disengaged" in that they did not know how their children were doing in school, had no idea who their friends were, and were not aware of how they spent their free time. These parents rarely spent time doing things with their children or talking with them about their day's activities (Steinburg, 1996). If we are, in fact, becoming less engaged, is engagement largely associated with family socioeconomic status (SES)? If so, is it an important buffering mechanism that mediates the relationship between SES and childhood vulnerability? Is the reduction in engagement mainly attributable to the increase in the number of dual-earner families, which in Canada has more than doubled over the past 25 years (Statistics Canada, 1998)? Can parents compensate for less time by spending "quality time," and if so, what exactly is quality time? The answers to these questions are relevant to policies regarding maternity leave, the flexibility of work arrangements, and parents' involvement in schools. They are also of great concern to parents striving to strike the right balance between work and family life. Many parents, especially mothers, feel inadequate if they do not work and guilty if they do.

Research on engagement is complicated for several reasons. Defining *engagement* is difficult in that it necessarily entails subjective judgements about what it means to be engaged and about the quality of the interaction. Even with a clear operational definition of engagement, it is difficult to obtain detailed data on how much time parents are engaged with their children. Some researchers approach the problem by comparing the outcomes of children in families with both parents working to those of children with at least one parent at home. But employment status is probably a poor proxy for engagement, because parents who stay at home may vary in their engagement depending on the cultural and social resources available to them; and for those who work, the amount and quality of their engagement likely depends on the nature of their employment.

This chapter aims to examine the relationship between parental engagement and family SES and to determine whether engagement is an important mediating factor between SES and children's developmental outcomes.

■ Dimensions of Engagement and Their Effects on Outcomes

In 1997, the cover story on *Newsweek* was "The Myth of Quality Time: How We're Cheating Our Kids and What You Can Do." The lead-in to the story read, "Kids don't do meetings. You can't raise them in short, scheduled bursts. They need lots of attention and experts warn that working parents may be short-changing them" (Shapiro, 1997). Researchers have attempted to measure parental engagement and its effects on children in a number of ways. One strand of research has studied parents' involvement in school-related activities, while another has emphasized parents' participation in activities at home, especially reading, and the nature of their relationships with their children. While involvement in school activities is important, and certainly related to engagement at home, our emphasis is on engagement with the child at home.

Generally, parental involvement in school activities through volunteering and participating in parent–teacher organizations is related to children's academic success (Stevenson and Baker, 1987). But Ho and Willms (1996) found that in a large nationally representative sample of US middle-school students, direct involvement in the school had relatively small effects on reading and mathematics achievement, compared with the effects associated with parents helping children with their schoolwork at home and monitoring the time they spent watching television and going out on school nights. The strongest effects on achievement were associated with a more general level of involvement: children had better levels of achievement when their parents regularly displayed an interest in their school program and discussed their day at school. Other researchers have also emphasized the importance of parents establishing a warm and affectionate relationship with their child. They have found that affective measures tend to be associated not only with academic achievement, but also with positive behaviour, both in and out of school (Grolnick and Ryan, 1989; Wenk, Hardesty, Morgan, & Blair, 1994).

Simons, Johnson, and Conger (1994) noted that parents who were less engaged with their child tended to be harsher when they punished misbehaviour, and these practices were related to childhood aggression, delinquency, and a poor sense of well-being. Moreover, there is support for the hypothesis that increased engagement in a child's life during the early years is related to classroom behaviour later in childhood (Bradley, Caldwell, & Rock, 1988). Wenk et al. (1994) suggested that the effects of a loving and involved relationship on children's well-being can offset some of the negative effects of not having a father in the home. Researchers concerned with the development of language and literacy have emphasized the importance of reading to the child every day, as it stimulates children's imagination and helps them to understand words long before recognizing them in text (Greaney, 1986). Regular reading during the early years probably also contributes to positive affective relationships, because it is an enjoyable activity focussed on the child, and it nearly always involves physical closeness.

■ Engagement and Socioeconomic Status

Research on school effectiveness has provided considerable evidence that parents with higher SES tend to be more involved in their children's schooling. Lareau (1989) conducted extensive interviews with the parents and teachers of children attending two schools, one in a predominantly white, working-class community, the other serving a white, upper-middle-class suburb. She concluded that working-class parents were less likely than middle-class parents to attend parent–teacher conferences, promote verbal development, read to their children, take children to the library, attend school events, enroll children in summer school, and make complaints to the principal. Large-scale quantitative studies generally support Lareau's findings and indicate that the level of the mother's education is particularly important. Stevenson and Baker (1987) found that more-educated mothers tended to have more contact with teachers and know more about their children's school performance. They were also more likely to take actions that would lead to better academic achievement, such as ensuring that their child enrolled in college preparatory courses, regardless of the child's previous academic attainment. Harris and Marmer (1996) found that parents who received welfare were on average less involved with their children than those who had never received welfare, but income generally tends to have a relatively weak relationship with parental involvement (Duncan and Brooks-Gunn, 1997). Ho and Willms (1996) claimed that overall the relationship between involvement and SES is statistically significant, but relatively weak. Their study of parental involvement of US eighth-grade students found that SES was unrelated to levels of involvement at home and only weakly related to involvement at school.

Generally, the literature suggests that mothers who work full-time outside the home tend to be less involved with their children (Goldberg, Greenberger and Nagel, 1996; Milne, Myers, Rosenthal, & Ginsburg, 1986). But the relationship is complicated, as it seems to depend on the type of activity considered and the time of day. Richards and Duckett (1994) found that the mother's employment status had little effect on the amount of time she spent with her child in the evening and on weekends, and that mothers who work full-time outside the home tended to spend less time engaged in their children's sports activities but more time helping their children with homework. Grolnick and Ryan (1989) suggest that it may not be the number of hours parents spend with their child that matters most, but instead their availability to discuss school issues and help them with their homework. Muller (1995) found that unsupervised time after school was a significant factor in the negative relationship between maternal employment and children's outcomes. The relationship between involvement and employment also depends on the sex of the child, and this relationship depends on the type of activity considered (Goldberg, Greenberger and Nagel, 1996; Stevenson & Baker, 1987).

■ Parental Involvement as a Mediator Between SES and Children's Outcomes

The studies discussed above generally indicate that involvement is related to SES and that increased involvement is associated with better cognitive outcomes and behaviour. Thus, involvement could be an important mediator of socioeconomic gradients. Although Ho and Willms (1996) claimed the relationship between parental involvement and SES was weak, their work pertained to pre-adolescents in the US. Other researchers have claimed that differences in involvement account for most of the effects of SES (Hess, Holloway, Dickson, & Price, 1994; Crane, 1996). But these studies did not have the kind of detailed data on income, parents' education, and employment which are available in the National Longitudinal Survey of Children and Youth (NLSCY). These data make it possible to examine the mediating effects of involvement for various components of SES. The NLSCY also affords the opportunity to examine the effects of different aspects of involvement on both cognitive and behavioural outcomes across a wide age range.

This study used data pertaining to the full sample of children aged two through eleven. The analyses employ the set of socioeconomic and family-structure variables described in Chapter 4. Parents who participated in the NLSCY were asked six questions about their engagement with their child. Three of these questions pertained to affective engagement; that is, activities regarding the closeness of the parent-child relationship:

1. How often do you praise <child's name>, by saying something like 'Good for you!' or 'What a nice thing you did!' or 'That's good going'?
2. How often do you and he (or she) talk or play with each other, focussing attention on each other for five minutes or more, just for fun?
3. How often do you and he (or she) laugh together?

Three questions pertained to what could be called activity-based engagement:

1. How often do you do something special with her (or him) that she (or he) enjoys?
2. How often do you play sports, hobbies, or games with him (or her)?[1]
3. How often do you read with the child?

The response categories for the first five of these questions were (a) Never; (b) About once a week or less; (c) A few times a week; (d) One or two times a day; and (e) Many times each day. These categories were assigned values of 0, 1, 3, 10, and 20 for (a) to (e) respectively, in order to approximately estimate the "number of incidents per week" for each activity. The sixth variable, concerning frequency of reading, had eight response categories, ranging from "never or rarely" to "many times each day." The response values were recoded to yield a scale indicating the number of times the child was read to each week.

A factor analysis indicated that one underlying factor accounted for 53.6 percent of the variance in the set of items. When we forced the factor analysis to identify two factors, it yielded a (rotated) solution with the three affective items loading heavily on the first factor, the reading item loading heavily on the second factor, and the special activities and play items loading about equally on both factors. For this reason, and because the literature emphasizes the importance of reading to the child, we examined reading separately from the other aspects of engagement. Our main analyses therefore use two variables, which we call *engagement* and *frequency of reading*. Engagement is the number of activities per week averaged across the five items, and frequency of reading is the number of times the child was read to each week.

Our analysis first examined the extent to which engagement and frequency of reading varied with the child's age. We then used ordinary least-squares regression to determine the relationship between engagement and the full set of variables describing SES and family structure. The relationships between engagement and income, and engagement and mothers' employment status, are particularly interesting and are therefore displayed graphically. The regression model also was estimated with the frequency of reading as the dependent variable.

Finally, we estimated regression analyses for the primary sets of dependent and independent variables described in Chapters 3 and 4. The dependent variables include the three measures of social and cognitive skills (pro-social behaviour, preschool vocabulary, and mathematics computation) and the four markers of vulnerability (behaviour problems, low vocabulary score, low mathematics score, and repeating a grade). The independent variables describe SES, family structure, and the child's sex and age. Engagement was then added to the models to determine whether it had an effect independent of family background and whether it mediated particular aspects of SES. We repeated these analyses for pro-social behaviour and preschool vocabulary with frequency of reading as the primary independent variable. Because the frequency of reading was very low after age six, we did not present the effects of reading on mathematics computation scores.

■ Results

Figure 10.1 shows how engagement and frequency of reading vary with the child's age. The results indicate a strong, declining relationship with age. The parents of toddlers reported that they were engaged about two and a half times per day (about seventeen or eighteen times per week) in talking or playing with their child or in doing special activities, hobbies, games, and sports. For

Figure 10.1
Parental engagement and child's age

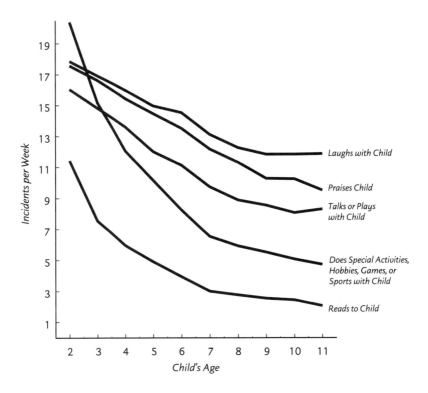

preschoolers, the levels of engagement were about twice per day, and for children in primary school, parents reported being engaged only about once per
day. Reported levels of affective engagement—laughing with the child or
praising the child—were similar to activity-based engagement for toddlers, but
declined less with age and levelled off at about one and a half times per day
for older children. The frequency of reading was considerably lower than other
forms of engagement: it was on average about one and a half times per day for
toddlers, once a day for preschoolers, and less than every other day for children in elementary school.

The relationship between engagement and frequency of reading with SES
and family structure is displayed in Table 10.1. On average, the level of engagement is higher for children in two-parent families, in families with fewer
siblings, and in families in which the parents have relatively high levels of

Table 10.1

Relationship between engagement and family background (unstandardized regression coefficients)

	Engagement score	Frequency of reading
Mean (centred at age six)	**11.20**	**5.24**
Socioeconomic status		
• Income	**-0.05**	0.02
• Income-squared	**0.02**	0.00
• Mother's education	**0.05**	**0.10**
• Mother works part-time	**0.45**	**0.19**
• Mother at home	**0.80**	**0.43**
• Father's education	**0.13**	**0.09**
• Father's occupation	0.02	**0.09**
Family structure, sex, and age		
• Single parent	**-0.58**	**-0.29**
• Number of siblings	**-0.64**	**-0.20**
• Female	0.06	**0.30**
• Age	**-0.92**	**-0.54**
R-squared		
• (without age in model)	0.06	0.04
• (with age in model)	0.32	0.21

Note: Coefficients that are statistically significant ($p < 0.05$) appear in boldface.

education. Mothers who are not working outside the home are also, on average, more engaged with their children than mothers working full-time: the difference is about four-fifths of a point, which means that mothers staying at home indicated they were involved in nearly one extra incident per week on each of the five aspects of engagement. The coefficients for income and income-squared suggest that engagement declines with rising income, but levels off at higher levels of income.

The relationship of engagement with income and mother's employment status is complicated, because income and employment status interact in their effect on engagement. Thus, we estimated separately a model which included the interaction term. Figure 10.2 displays the level of engagement for mothers who stay at home and for mothers who work either part-time or full-time outside the home, by family income. These estimates have been adjusted for the other variables included in the model described in Table 10.1. The results indicate that for mothers staying at home, and for those working part-time outside the home, the extent of engagement decreases slightly with income

Figure 10.2

Parental engagement by family income and mother's employment status

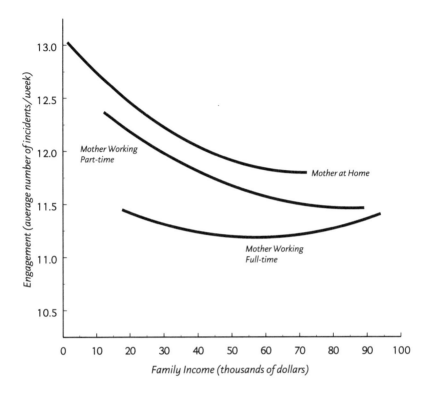

and levels off at a family income of about $50,000. The difference in engagement between mothers at home and those working part-time outside the home is only about one quarter of a point on the scale. In contrast, mothers working full-time outside the home have consistently lower levels of engagement, which does not vary significantly with family income. For mothers in families with incomes of $25,000, the difference in engagement for mothers working full-time outside the home, compared with those at home, is nearly one full point on the scale.

The final analysis examines the effects of engagement on children's outcomes, while controlling for SES and family structure; the results are displayed in Table 10.2. Engagement was significantly related to children's pro-social behaviour and to the likelihood that a child had a behaviour problem. For a 6-year-old child, an increase of 1 point on the engagement scale (i.e., 1 extra activity per

Table 10.2

Effects of parental engagement on children's outcomes (unstandardized regression coefficients)

| | Social and cognitive skills | | | | | |
| | Pro-social behaviour | | Preschool vocabulary | | Mathematics computation | |
	I	II	I	II	I	II
Socioeconomic status						
• Income	**-0.03**	**-0.03**	**0.73**	**0.72**	**0.66**	**0.65**
• Income-squared	**0.01**	**0.01**	-0.10	-0.10	-0.08	-0.08
• Mother's education	**0.04**	**0.04**	**1.10**	**1.09**	**0.58**	**0.58**
• Mother works part-time	**0.21**	**0.16**	**2.16**	**2.01**	0.47	0.50
• Mother at home	0.06	-0.04	0.49	0.28	0.84	0.99
• Father's education	**0.03**	0.01	0.15	0.13	0.18	0.23
• Father's occupation	0.02	0.02	**1.08**	**1.11**	0.13	0.13
Family structure, sex, and age						
• Single parent	-0.13	-0.06	-0.36	-0.28	0.05	0.03
• Number of siblings	**-0.11**	-0.03	**-1.36**	**-1.29**	-0.26	-0.44
• Female	**0.76**	**0.75**	0.85	0.87	0.15	0.18
• Age	**0.17**	**0.34**	-0.10	-0.31	1.03	0.97
Engagement						
• (Adjusted effect)		**0.08**		0.13		-0.17
• (Increment for age)		**0.01**				-0.04
R-squared	0.09	0.14	0.08	0.08	0.04	0.05

Note: Coefficients that are statistically significant (p<0.05) appear in boldface.

week) is associated with an increase of 0.08 on the 10-point pro-social behaviour scale and a 3-percent decrease in the likelihood of a behaviour problem. The results vary somewhat with age: the positive effect of engagement on behaviour is slightly greater for older children than it is for younger children. The effects associated with engagement for the other outcome variables were not statistically significant.

Engagement had the strongest mediating effects on the relationships between childhood outcomes and the mother's employment status and family structure. For example, the positive effect on pro-social behaviour associated with working part-time instead of full-time was reduced from 0.21 to 0.16 when engagement was added to the model. Similarly, introducing engagement changed the negative effect associated with number of siblings from -0.11 to -0.03. The effect of living in a single-parent family, although not statistically significant, was reduced from 0.13 to 0.06. In contrast, the mediating effects

Table 10.2 (cont.)

Effects of parental engagement on children's outcomes (odds ratios)

	Markers of vulnerability							
	Behaviour problem		Low vocabulary		Low mathematics		Repeated a grade	
	I	II	I	II	I	II	I	II
Socioeconomic status								
• Income	0.98	0.98	**0.86**	**0.86**	**0.89**	**0.90**	**0.88**	**0.88**
• Income-squared	1.00	1.00	1.01	1.01	**1.02**	**1.02**	1.01	1.01
• Mother's education	**0.95**	**0.95**	**0.87**	**0.87**	**0.93**	**0.93**	0.97	0.97
• Mother works part-time	1.07	1.10	0.78	0.79	0.88	0.88	1.12	1.12
• Mother at home	1.02	1.06	1.14	1.16	0.94	0.92	**1.45**	**1.45**
• Father's education	1.02	1.02	1.04	1.04	0.97	0.96	**0.93**	**0.93**
• Father's occupation	**0.90**	**0.90**	**0.87**	**0.87**	0.99	0.99	**0.82**	**0.82**
Family structure, sex, and age								
• Single parent	**1.68**	**1.65**	0.99	0.99	0.91	0.92	**1.80**	**1.80**
• Number of siblings	**0.89**	**0.86**	**1.17**	**1.17**	1.06	1.09	1.03	1.04
• Female	**0.75**	**0.75**	0.92	0.91	1.05	1.04	**0.60**	**0.60**
• Age	**1.03**	0.97			**0.91**	**0.95**	**1.41**	**1.40**
Engagement								
• (Adjusted effect)		**0.97**		0.99		1.00		1.01
• (Increment for age)		**0.996**				1.01		1.00
R-squared								

Note: Odds ratios that differ significantly from 1.0 (p<0.05) appear in boldface.

on family income, and on mothers' and fathers' levels of education, were negligible. Although the overall effects are relatively small, these results provide evidence that the amount of time parents have available is related to the extent of parents' engagement, which explains some of the differences in outcomes associated with family structure and working outside the home.

We repeated the analyses described above with frequency of reading as the mediating independent variable; the results are presented in Table 10.3. Reading had a significant effect on both behaviour and preschool vocabulary. The estimated effect of reading on pro-social behaviour is 0.10, which is comparable to the effect of engagement. The effect of reading on early vocabulary scores is very large: 0.46. To place this effect in context, the estimated effect of reading to a child two additional times per week is roughly comparable to the effect associated with one additional year of mother's education, or half the effect associated with the mother staying at home rather than

Table 10.3

Effects of reading to the child on children's outcomes

	Social and cognitive skills (regression coefficients)		Markers of vulnerability (odds ratios)	
	Pro-social behaviour	Preschool vocabulary	Behaviour disorder	Low vocabulary
Socioeconomic status				
• Income	**-0.04**	**0.62**	0.98	**0.89**
• Income-squared	**0.01**	-0.09	1.00	1.00
• Mother's education	**0.03**	**0.99**	**0.95**	**0.87**
• Mother works part-time	**0.13**	**1.92**	1.12	0.74
• Mother at home	0.00	-0.08	1.06	1.21
• Father's education	0.02	0.04	1.02	1.06
• Father's occupation	0.01	**1.19**	**0.91**	**0.85**
Family structure				
• Single parent	-0.09	0.09	**1.63**	0.94
• Number of siblings	**-0.08**	**-1.18**	**0.88**	**1.14**
• Female	**0.70**	0.61	**0.76**	0.91
• Age	0.22	1.01		
Reading to the child	**0.10**	**0.46**	**0.96**	**0.95**

Note: Regression coefficients that are statistically significant and odds ratios that differ significantly from 1.0 appear in boldface.

working full-time. The results also suggest that reading to the child reduces the likelihood of the child having a behaviour problem or having a low preschool vocabulary score.

■ Summary and Discussion

Studies of parents' engagement have been mainly concerned with the extent to which the parents of adolescents become involved in school-related activities, and whether this affects their child's academic achievement. They have shown that involvement in school activities has a strong positive effect, over and above the effects associated with family SES. The few studies that have examined other types of engagement, such as being regularly engaged in play activities with the child or spending time praising the child and laughing together, suggest that increased engagement not only improves cognitive outcomes but also affects the child's behaviour. This literature generally indicates that parents of higher SES are more engaged in their child's life and that mothers who work outside the home are less engaged than those who stay at home. The message portrayed by this research is not encouraging, especially for parents who feel they need the additional income to provide a secure environment for their children, and for those who find work outside the home fulfilling but feel their careers will suffer if they take too much time off or fail to put in long hours. Mothers are most often caught in this double bind: many feel guilty because they work, while others feel inadequate because they do not have fulfilling careers.

However, the relationships between engagement, SES, family structure, employment status, and children's outcomes are much more complicated than most of the literature suggests. Although the research has found statistically significant relationships between engagement and socioeconomic factors, the magnitude of these relationships has not been determined nor have the opposing effects of income and employment status been untangled. Another problem is that it is difficult to define what constitutes being engaged and to measure the quality of different forms of engagement.

The six questions included in the NLSCY about parents' engagement with their child are sufficient for discerning the nature and magnitude of these relationships at the national level and for providing insight into the kind of data on time use and quality of engagement that could be collected in more intensive observational studies. The survey data are helpful also in that they include detailed data describing SES and family structure, and they cover a wide range of children's outcomes for preschool and school-age children. The analyses in this study have provided four findings which contribute to this literature on parental engagement.

1. *Parents' engagement varies considerably with the child's age.* Parents' engagement with their children declines steadily during the toddler and preschool years, and appears to level off once children are in elementary school. For most observers, this relationship is obvious and uninteresting: as children become more independent and play with other children, parents are less likely to be directly engaged with them in play or special activities; and when children are in school, we might expect engagement to decline further. But these findings show that the decrease in engagement associated with *each year* a child gets older is larger than the decreases in engagement associated with being a single parent, having one more child, or working outside the home. Moreover, levels of affective engagement, such as laughing together or praising the child, decline at almost the same

rate. Reading to the child, which is known to have strong beneficial effects on children's language development, also declines sharply during the early years. Overall, then, this finding suggests that the emphasis in the literature (and of many people's concerns) on the effects on children's development of working *versus* not working is somewhat misdirected; the emphasis should be on maintaining a high level of engagement throughout the preschool and elementary school years.

2. *Engagement is only weakly related to family structure and SES, but is influenced by available time.* The most important factors related to engagement, other than the child's age, were variables that directly affected the time available for each child: the mother's employment status, the number of children in the family, and whether it was a single- or two-parent family. Income and the parents' levels of education were statistically significant, but were only weakly related to engagement. Overall, the full set of SES and family-structure variables accounted for only six percent of the variance in parental engagement.

3. *Engagement has a strong positive effect on pro-social behaviour and decreases the likelihood of a child displaying a behaviour problem.* The measure of engagement available in this study is somewhat limited, in that it does not include detailed information about the length of time parents are engaged in various activities, nor does it capture the intensity of involvement. Nevertheless, the results indicated a strong positive relationship between engagement and behaviour, even after taking account of SES and family structure. An increase of 1 point on the engagement scale, which requires increasing involvement by 1 activity per week on each of the 5 aspects of engagement, was associated with an increase of 0.08 on the 10-point pro-social behaviour scale and a decrease of 3 percent in the likelihood of behaviour problems. We believe this outcome to be a lower bound on the effect of engagement, given the nature of our measure. Increased engagement may also have stronger effects in reducing particular types of behaviour problems, such as hyperactivity.

4. *Reading to a child has a particularly strong positive effect on both behaviour and preschool vocabulary skills.* If we use the term "quality time" for a particular type of engagement, then reading to the child would qualify as a quality interaction. Regular reading during the toddler and preschool years had

even stronger effects on behaviour than the overall measure of engagement, and was also significantly related to the child's preschool vocabulary skills. An increase in reading activity of one session per week was associated with a decrease of five percent in the likelihood of a child having a preschool vocabulary score below eighty-five. The analysis also revealed that while the level of the mother's education was only weakly related to engagement, it was moderately related to the number of times a parent read to the child. Like other forms of engagement, however, reading to the child declines sharply during the toddler and preschool years; during the elementary years the average is less than three sessions per week.

The Canadian Policy Research Network (CPRN) characterizes the Canadian family as being increasingly "stretched," with more dual-earner families and with parents working longer hours and taking fewer holidays. These pressures, which have accompanied recent changes in the workplace, are especially acute for young families (Cheal, Wooley, & Luxton, 1998). Despite such measures, the 1995 Survey of Work Arrangements found that nearly one quarter of Canadian women with children wanted more hours on the job, while less than ten percent desired fewer hours. Job sharing was possible for relatively few working women, and most women who shared their jobs wanted more hours (Reesor, 1997). The findings of our study suggest that parents' engagement with their children is related more closely to the time parents have available than to parents' level of education or family income. The findings also document the importance of engagement to children's development. Thus, the findings support CPRN's call for employers to consider the long-run value of family-friendly workplaces and for governments to develop thoughtful and supportive public policies that reinforce the caring role of the family.

NOTES

1   The wording of this question for children under three was "How often do you play games with him (or her)?".

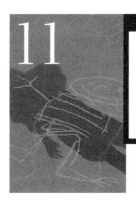

11

Family Functioning
and Children's
Behaviour Problems

YVONNE RACINE &

MICHAEL H. BOYLE

PREVIOUS RESEARCH HAS EMPHASIZED the adverse effects family dysfunction can have on children's behaviour (Brown & Rutter, 1966; Maziade et al., 1985; Smets & Hartup,1988; Byrne, Offord & Boyle, 1992; McFarlane, Bellissimo & Norman, 1995). The concept of family functioning pertains to the viability of the family as an organization or system, and not just to the relationship between spouses or between parents and their children. It refers to the way in which families work together on tasks that are necessary for the family unit to survive. The family is seen as an interactional system, whose structure, organization, and transactional patterns determine the behaviour of the various family members.

If family dysfunction influences children's behaviour, is it a key mediator of the relationship between behaviour problems and family socioeconomic status? Previous literature has indicated that family dysfunction is strongly related to disruptive or acting-out behaviours (Byrne et al., 1992), both on its own and in combination with other childhood behaviour problems. In this chapter, we investigate the effect of family functioning on specific childhood problem behaviours. Our approach is similar to those used in the two previous chapters: we first examine the relationship between family functioning and socioeconomic status (SES), as well as other factors describing family background, and then examine the relationship between behaviour problems and family background, with and without family functioning in the model.

■ Issues Regarding Family Functioning

Olson et al. (1985) conducted an extensive review of the literature regarding family processes and their effects on childhood behaviour. They identified 50 factors, but concluded that most of them represented some aspect of family cohesion or adaptability. Perosa and Perosa (1990) also contend that cohesion and adaptability are critical factors but that they do not adequately cover the domain. Bloom (1985) analyzed four of the most widely used measures of family functioning and identified fifteen factors. Thus, the question of what the concept should include is still being debated (Touliatos, Perlmutter, & Straus, 1990; Tutty, 1995).

Researchers also debate whether family functioning can be validly measured by asking family members themselves—the "insider's perspective"—or whether it requires the observation of an "outsider" to achieve an objective assessment. Perhaps not surprisingly, there is relatively low agreement between ratings based on the two approaches (Green, Kolevson & Vosler, 1985; Sigafoos, Reiss, Rich, & Douglas, 1985). Studies have also shown that assessments of family functioning differ among family members (Sawyer, Sarris, Baghurst, Cross, & Kalucy, 1988; Hampson, Beavers, & Hulgus, 1988; Olson, Russell, & Sprenkle, 1983), and thus there is debate about how best to arrive at an overall family score.

Family functioning and socioeconomic status

Relatively few studies have documented the relationship between family functioning and SES. An analysis of data from the Ontario Child Health Survey for 1822 families indicated that family functioning was significantly correlated with family income, but the correlation was only -0.17 (Byles, Byrne, Boyle, & Offord, 1988). Maziade, Bernier, Thivierge, and Coté (1987) examined the relationship between the "behaviour control" and "communication" subscales of the Family Assessment Device (FAD; Epstein, Bishop, & Levin, 1978) and SES for a sample of 118 families from Quebec City and found no significant correlation. Thus, we do not expect a strong correlation between family functioning and SES; however, the National Longitudinal Survey of Children and Youth (NLSCY) affords the opportunity to examine this relationship with a wide range of socioeconomic variables.

Childhood behaviour problems and family functioning

Three studies have reported a significant relationship between family functioning and childhood behaviour problems, based on the McMaster Model of Family Functioning (Epstein et al., 1978). Maziade et al. (1985) found a significant relationship between family functioning and later clinical behaviour problems of children with difficult temperament, based on a sample of 39 families. A study by McFarlane et al. (1995) of grade ten students from eleven high schools in one educational system examined the effects of family functioning alongside parenting style. The authors concluded that parenting style was a more important determinant than family functioning of adolescents' well-being. Byrne, Offord, and Boyle's (1992) study, based on 1280 2-parent families that participated in the Ontario Child Health Study, found a strong association between family functioning and children who exhibited behaviour problems. Their study is important because it included controls for marital disharmony, domestic violence, parental stress, and whether either parent was receiving treatment for conditions related to their mental health. The researchers also uncovered a stronger relationship between family functioning and behaviour disorders at higher levels of income, suggesting that SES may not be a buffer to the adverse effects of dysfunction.

The impact of dysfunction may also vary depending on the age and sex of the child. Smets and Hartup (1988) found a stronger association between family dysfunction and disruptions in child behaviour for children aged six to eleven than for children aged twelve to sixteen. Offord, Boyle, and Jones (1987) studied the effect of living in a family receiving social assistance for six- to sixteen-year-old children in Ontario. They found that six- to eleven-year-old boys living in welfare families displayed rates of psychiatric disorder almost three times higher than boys of the same age in families not receiving social assistance. Girls from welfare families were also at increased risk for psychiatric disorder, but not to the same extent as boys.

■ Method

The analyses in this study pertain to children six to eleven years old and their families. In examining the relationship between family functioning and SES, and between behaviour problems and family functioning, we divided the sample into primary-age children (six to eight) and intermediate-age children (nine to eleven).

The NLSCY included the FAD "general functioning" subscale. The full FAD is a sixty-item self-report measure made up of six subscales—problem-solving, communication, roles, affective responsiveness, affective involvement, and behaviour control—and a general functioning subscale, which includes twelve items that correlate highly with the six subscales (Epstein, Baldwin, & Bishop, 1983; Kabacoff, Miller, Bishop, Epstein, & Keitner,, 1990). The person most knowledgeable (PMK) about the child was asked to indicate on a four-point scale (strongly agree, agree, disagree, and strongly disagree) the extent to which he or she agreed or disagreed with the following statements:

- Planning family activities is difficult because we misunderstand each other.
- In times of crisis we can turn to each other for support.
- We cannot talk to each other about sadness we feel.
- Individuals in the family are accepted for what they are.
- We avoid discussing our fears or concerns.
- We express feelings to each other.
- There are lots of bad feelings in our family.
- We feel accepted for what we are.
- Making decisions is a problem for our family.
- We are able to make decisions about how to solve problems.
- We don't get along well together.
- We confide in each other.

The twelve items were scaled on a ten-point scale, with higher scores indicating positive family functioning. The scale had a reliability (Cronbach's alpha) of 0.88 for the full sample.

Our first set of analyses used ordinary least-squares regression to examine the relationship between family functioning and SES, using the composite measure of SES, the two dummy variables describing the mother's employment status, and the set of variables describing family structure (see Chapter 4). Our second set of analyses used logistic regression analyses to estimate the odds ratios associated with family characteristics and family functioning for six childhood behaviour problems: anxiety, emotional problems, physical aggression, indirect aggression, hyperactivity, and inattention.

Table 11.1

Relationship between family functioning and family background (unstandardized regression coefficients)

	Ages 6 to 8	Ages 9 to 11
Mean score	**7.779**	**7.769**
Socioeconomic status	**0.289**	**0.254**
Mother works part-time	-0.014	-0.077
Mother at home	0.062	0.061
Single parent	**-0.152**	**-0.135**
Teenage mother	-0.159	-0.059
Numbers of siblings	-0.034	-0.013
Female	-0.058	**0.108**
R-squared	0.047	0.036

Note: Coefficients that are statistically significant (p<0.05) appear in boldface.

■ Results

Most families participating in the NLSCY reported high levels of family functioning. The national average was 7.70, with a standard deviation of 1.43. The scores were skewed towards the high end, however, with over half of the sample scoring above 7.5 on the 10-point scale, and only 3 percent scoring below 5. Thus, the vast majority of families reported high levels of family functioning.

Table 11.1 presents the regression results pertaining to the relationship between family functioning and SES and family structure. The coefficients for SES are 0.289 and 0.254 for the families of primary- and intermediate-age children respectively, which indicated that a one-standard-deviation increase in SES is associated with an increase of slightly more than a quarter of one point on the ten-point family functioning scale. Single parents reported slightly lower family functioning scores than two-parent families, but these differences are also very small. In the families of the intermediate-age children, family functioning was slightly higher in the families with females than in those with males, but the difference was only about one-tenth of one item on the ten-point scale. Family functioning did not have a statistically significant relationship with the mother's employment status, the number of siblings, or whether the mother was in her teen years upon birth of the child. Overall, SES and family structure accounted for less than five percent of the variance in family functioning scores for both age groups.

Table 11.2

The relationship between behaviour problems and family functioning (odds ratios)

CHILDREN AGED SIX TO EIGHT

	Anxiety		Emotional problems		Physical aggression	
	I	II	I	II	I	II
Socioeconomic status	0.93	0.96	**0.79**	**0.82**	**0.73**	**0.77**
Mother works part-time	0.78	0.78	1.06	1.05	**1.70**	**1.64**
Mother at home	**0.63**	**0.64**	0.62	0.63	0.74	0.74
Single Parent	**1.66**	**1.64**	**2.00**	**1.95**	**3.22**	**3.08**
Teenage mother	1.25	1.22	1.27	1.24	**2.16**	**2.10**
Number of siblings	0.89	0.89	1.04	1.03	**1.23**	**1.22**
Female	1.03	1.03	**0.75**	**0.74**	**0.33**	**0.32**
Family functioning		0.89		0.85		0.81
R-squared	1.7	2.2	2.9	3.7	10.0	11.2

CHILDREN AGED NINE TO ELEVEN

	Anxiety		Emotional problems		Physical aggression	
	I	II	I	II	I	II
Socioeconomic status	**0.87**	**0.91**	**0.79**	**0.84**	**0.80**	0.86
Mother works part-time	1.21	1.20	1.43	1.41	2.13	2.07
Mother at home	1.19	1.19	**1.36**	1.35	**1.80**	1.74
Single Parent	**1.66**	**1.62**	**2.65**	**2.51**	**3.95**	**3.46**
Teenage mother	**1.08**	**1.07**	**2.51**	**2.51**	**2.19**	**2.13**
Number of siblings	0.96	0.95	1.05	1.04	**1.29**	**1.30**
Female	1.20	1.24	1.08	1.15	**0.55**	**0.59**
Family functioning		0.83		0.74		0.68
R-squared	1.6	2.7	6.2	8.9	9.6	12.9

Note: Odds ratios that differ significantly from 1.0 ($p<0.05$) appear in boldface.

Table 11.2 (cont.)

The relationship between behaviour problems and family functioning (odds ratios)

	Indirect aggression		Hyperactivity		Inattention	
	I	II	I	II	I	II
Socioeconomic status	**0.64**	**0.73**	**0.78**	**0.80**	**0.83**	**0.86**
Mother works part-time	1.28	1.23	0.91	0.91	1.04	1.03
Mother at home	0.71	0.67	0.84	0.84	**0.53**	**0.54**
Single Parent	**2.82**	**2.57**	1.19	1.18	**1.92**	**1.89**
Teenage mother	**5.66**	**2.65**	**1.66**	**1.63**	**1.73**	**1.69**
Number of siblings	**1.36**	**1.35**	0.81	0.81	0.82	0.81
Female	1.40	1.31	**0.34**	**0.33**	**0.29**	**0.29**
Family functioning		**0.65**		0.91		**0.88**
R-squared	9.1	13.5	7.7	8.0	8.7	9.2

	Indirect aggression		Hyperactivity		Inattention	
	I	II	I	II	I	II
Socioeconomic status	**0.63**	**0.67**	**0.75**	**0.78**	**0.71**	**0.75**
Mother works part-time	1.26	1.24	1.18	1.17	**1.47**	**1.47**
Mother at home	1.31	1.26	1.17	1.17	1.17	1.18
Single Parent	**3.16**	**2.82**	**1.43**	**1.40**	**1.80**	**1.76**
Teenage mother	**2.30**	**2.28**	**1.36**	**1.36**	0.96	0.97
Number of siblings	**1.22**	**1.21**	0.81	0.80	0.86	0.86
Female	1.25	1.37	**0.49**	**0.50**	**0.46**	**0.48**
Family functioning		**0.69**		0.86		**0.85**
R-squared	9.4	12.3	3.2	6.9	6.3	7.3

Note: Odds ratios that differ significantly from 1.0 ($p<0.05$) appear in boldface.

Table 11.2 reports the odds ratios for the set of variables describing SES, family structure, and family functioning, with and without family functioning in the model. The purpose of displaying these two models side by side is to discern whether family functioning has a strong mediating effect on the likelihood that a child will display a behaviour disorder. If family functioning plays a mediating role, the coefficients for the SES variables are closer to 1.0 in the second model, indicating that some of the SES effect can be attributed to family functioning.

The odds ratios for family functioning are below 1.0 for all behaviour problems, for both age groups. For children aged 6 to 8, the ratios range from 0.65 to 0.91 (average about 0.83). This indicates that the odds of a child displaying a behaviour disorder decreases by about seventeen percent for each one-point increase on the ten-point family functioning scale. For the older children, the odds ratios range from 0.68 to 0.86 (average about 0.78), which suggests that family functioning plays an even stronger role for older children than for younger children.[1] The results also indicate that the effects of family functioning are somewhat stronger for indirect and physical aggression, for both age groups.

To put these results in context, consider a family that scored 2 points below the national average of 7.7 on the 10-point scale. (Only 5.9 percent of Canadian families scored at or below this level.) If we consider such families "dysfunctional," then our results suggest that the likelihood of a child displaying a behaviour problem is about 40 percent higher in a dysfunctional family than in an average Canadian family.

To some extent, family functioning mediates the relationship between SES and behaviour problems. For each type of behaviour problem, the odds ratio for SES is closer to 1.0 (i.e., no effect) after family functioning is added to the model. On average, the odds ratio increases by about 0.04, indicating that some of the relationship between SES and behaviour problems is attributable to family functioning. For example, the likelihood of a child in a high-SES family (e.g., a family that is half a standard deviation above the national average) having a behaviour problem is only 73 percent that of a child in a low-SES family (e.g., a family that is half a standard deviation below the national average). However, after account is taken of family functioning, the ratio increases to 77 percent; the advantage associated with SES is not as pronounced. The results also indicate that the increased vulnerability for behaviour problems associated with single parenting or teenage motherhood is somewhat reduced after we take account of family functioning.

We also examined whether the effects of family functioning varied with family SES. We estimated the second model with an SES-by-family-functioning interaction term. This interaction was significant only for anxiety for the younger children and indirect aggression for the older children; however, the results for anxiety suggested that family functioning plays a lesser role for high-SES families than for low-SES families, whereas for indirect aggression, family functioning plays a stronger role for high-SES families than for low-SES families. The latter result is consistent with Byrne et al.'s (1992) findings with respect to family income; but given the lack of a significant relationship for most of the behaviour problems we examined, and the inconsistencies in the direction of the interaction term, we do not claim that the effects of family functioning vary with family SES. We also tested whether family functioning varied depending on whether the child considered was male or female, and did not uncover any significant interactions.

■ Summary and Discussion

A number of small studies have indicated a significant relationship between family functioning and children's behaviour problems. Our study examined this relationship in detail for a large nationally representative sample of Canadian children aged six to eleven. The large sample available from the NLSCY makes it possible to examine the effects of family functioning on different types of behaviour problems, and to determine whether the effects of family functioning vary significantly with family SES or with the sex and age of the child. The analyses yielded four findings relevant to the literature on this topic.

1. *The vast majority of Canadian families have high levels of family functioning.* The general family functioning scale used in this study emphasizes family cohesion and adaptability. For example, the majority of the respondents— in most cases the child's mother—felt that family members could turn to each other in times of crisis and could confide in each other. They also felt that family members could express their feelings with one another and discuss their fears and concerns. Only three percent of the sample scored below five on the ten-point scale.

2. *Family functioning is strongly related to the likelihood that a child will display a behaviour problem.* Moreover, the effects of living in a dysfunctional family tend to become more pronounced as children get older. On average,

children living in dysfunctional families are about 40 percent more likely to display a behaviour problem than those living in families with an average level of family functioning. This relationship varies with the age of the child: for younger children, the increased likelihood is about 35 percent, whereas for older children, it is closer to 45 percent. We expect that the effect may be even more pronounced for children in their teen years, which we will be able to determine when future cycles of the NLSCY become available.

3. *Children living in dysfunctional families are much more likely to display both physical and indirect aggressive behaviours than those living in families that are functioning well.* The relationship between family functioning and behaviour problems is particularly strong for aggressive behaviours. These findings suggest that increased aggression may be a reaction to the problems of living in a dysfunctional family, or that children adopt a different set of behavioural norms. Other researchers have noted that there is greater potential for physical abuse in dysfunctional families (Kolko, Kazdin, McCombs Thomas, & Day, 1993). However, we need to be cautious in inferring a causal relationship: it is equally plausible that the presence of one or more aggressive children in a family contributes negatively to the family's ability to solve problems, communicate effectively, and maintain a high degree of affective responsiveness and involvement. The influence of the child on parental behaviour and the family environment, rather than the other way around, has been repeatedly demonstrated (Margolin, 1981; Fauber & Long, 1991; Rothbaum & Weisz, 1994; Donenberg & Baker, 1993).

4. *Family functioning is not strongly related to SES or family structure. Nevertheless, family functioning to some extent mediates the relationship between SES and behaviour problems.* The results suggest that the difference between a relatively high-SES family and a relatively low-SES family was only about a quarter of one point on the ten-point family functioning scale. The respondents in single-parent families, most of whom were the children's mothers, also rated their family functioning slightly lower than the respondents of two-parent families, but the differences were all very small. Nevertheless, family functioning accounts for some of the effects of living in a low-SES family.

These findings demonstrate the importance of family functioning as one of the significant factors affecting childhood vulnerability. Future cycles of the NLSCY will make it possible to determine the extent to which family functioning is a stable trait of families. We suspect that it is a fairly stable trait, and thus we are interested in the prolonged effects of living in a dysfunctional family. Other researchers have shown that the effects of prolonged poverty are much stronger than living in short-term poverty (Brooks-Gunn, Duncan, & Britto, 1999). Such effects may also be the case for family dysfunction, which would be consistent with our finding that family functioning is especially important during adolescence.

NOTES

1   We formally tested for an age-by-family-functioning interaction and found it was statistically significant for emotional problems, physical aggression, and the overall behaviour index.

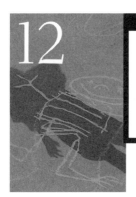

Maternal Depression and Childhood Vulnerability

12

MARIE-ANDRÉE SOMERS &

J. DOUGLAS WILLMS

EVERYONE INEVITABLY EXPERIENCES feelings of discouragement and frustration at some time in their life, often because of financial problems, difficulties in relationships, or thwarted endeavours. For most people, fortunately, these feelings are ephemeral: no one would ever wish to continuously deal with the sadness and lack of concentration that accompany depression. However, about one of every twenty Canadians suffers from depression for prolonged periods (Canadian Mental Health Association, 1995). The effects of depression regrettably reach much further than these five percent, as many sufferers must also cope with the challenges of parenting. Even feelings of mild discouragement experienced in everyday life, which are enough to make a parent absent-minded and irritable, can be sensed by a child. Consequently, the more severe symptoms of depression can have a considerable effect on a child's development.

Depression includes a long list of symptoms, from mild to severe, which can compromise a depressed parent's ability to play an effective role in the life of his or her child. Depression ranges from intense discouragement, which does not seriously affect social functioning, to severe psychosis, which not only drastically impairs a person's ability to participate in social interactions, but is also marked by apathy, restlessness, hostility, hopelessness, inability to concentrate, guilt, suicidal thoughts, and a loss of interest in activities that were once thought pleasant (Brown & Harris, 1978; Canadian Mental Health Association, 1995; Rutter, 1990). Physical symptoms accompanying this state of mind can include an increase or decrease in appetite, weight loss or gain, and sleep disturbances. Full recovery is common, but for some, what was thought recovery is actually only remission, and depression becomes a chronic illness (Canadian Mental Health Association, 1995).

Many factors can trigger depression. Genetics certainly plays a significant role, but only in the case of severe depressive disorders. Environmental factors or life occurrences, on the other hand, are at the root of all types of depression: they include negative episodes in one's life, such as the death of a loved one, poverty, physical illness, marital discord, single parenthood, unemployment, loss of social support, and stressful home and work environments (Brown & Harris, 1978; Webster-Stratton, 1990).

Some striking research findings justify concern for the issue of mothering and depression. One is that married mothers are more likely to fall prey to depression than married fathers (Bebbington, Hurry, Tennant, Sturt, & Wing, 1981; Ross & Mirowsky, 1988); and because mothers are more often the primary caregivers, the repercussions of maternal depression on children are especially far-reaching. Mothers with young children are at greater risk of depressive disorders, and the prevalence increases with the number of children in the family (Brown & Harris, 1978; Canadian Mental Health Association, 1995). This fact is particularly troubling, as early childhood is a critical period, when children are most influenced by their environment.

Earlier chapters in this volume examined the effects of parenting style, engagement, and family functioning as factors affecting child development and as potential mediators of the relationship between childhood outcomes and socioeconomic status (SES). Because these aspects of family life can be influenced by maternal depression, a logical progression of the earlier analyses is to integrate maternal depression into the structure and build a more comprehensive model of family life. Our model is depicted in figure 12.1. In situating maternal depression in this model, our first concern is the extent to which SES is related to depression. If there is a significant relationship, one must also ask whether part of the relationship between SES and the child's outcomes is attributable to the prevalence of maternal depression in low-SES families; that is, whether maternal depression mediates the relationship between SES and childhood outcomes. Finally, we consider the possibility that family functioning and parenting style are affected by maternal depression, which leads us to query whether these factors are mediators of the effect of maternal depression on childhood outcomes. The review of relevant literature that follows, and our statistical analyses, are structured accordingly.

Figure 12.1

The effects of maternal depression on children's outcomes

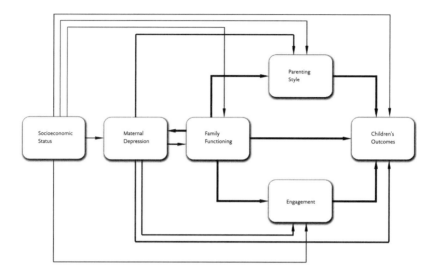

■ Maternal Depression and SES

The reality that mental-health problems are more prevalent among poor adults than among those who are economically advantaged is well supported by research findings (Conger et al., 1992; Rootman, 1988). A debate persists, however, about the causal direction of this relationship: does low SES result in stress and frustration, or do people who are predisposed to mental illness tend to sink to lower levels of SES? Findings from Dohrenwend, Levav, Shrout, and Shwartz (1992) suggest that the direction of causation depends on the mental disorder being considered: for schizophrenia, the disorder seems to lead to low SES, but for depression, it seems that low SES leads in adults becoming depressed.

Among the socioeconomic factors relevant to maternal depression, low family income stands out above all others. Unemployment, through both its frequency and duration, engenders situations where an individual is more likely to be depressed, particularly if the unemployment is involuntary. For example, Turner, Kessler, and House (1991) found that involuntarily unemployed workers have significant levels of depression and anxiety compared with employed workers. In their inquiry, they showed that the relationship between involuntary unemployment and elevated levels of depression is modified by social support, as measured by family functioning, the availability of a confidant, and having a number of close friendships. More specifically, they found this modifying effect operated primarily by buffering the impact of unemployment-related financial strain on mental-health outcomes. Similarly, Walker, Ortiz-Valdes, and Newbrough (1989) found that stay-at-home mothers experience more acute depressive symptoms than mothers who are employed outside the home. Not surprisingly, research in this vein suggests that part of the relationship between unemployment and depression is attributable to financial strain, and thus the ease with which a person can relieve the economic stress of unemployment can greatly affect his or her resilience to depression (Stoppard, 1993; Flynn, 1993). Parents who must endure elevated economic strain are likely to experience anger and frustration, which can affect personal functioning and marital interactions, not to mention family functioning in general (Galambos & Silbereisen, 1987; Sampson & Laub, 1994; Conger et al., 1992).

Although the relationship between depression and SES is well documented, research has not delved very deeply into the measure of SES itself. Most of the literature uses parental income as the sole indicator of SES; relatively little attention has been paid to the level of education of the mother, or, for those who are working outside the home, their occupational status. These factors may also be important determinants of depression. For example, in their study of British civil servants, Stansfeld, Head, and Marmot (1998) found a gradient in emotional well-being by employment grade, with higher depression scores in lower grades. Stressors and support systems were found to explain less than a third of the employment grade differences in depression, while work characteristics explained most of the variation.

■ Maternal Depression and Child Outcomes

Intuition and logic both dictate that maternal depression inevitably affects a child's development, be it because of a debilitated parenting style, a lack of motivation to engage in a child's life, or poor family functioning. Indeed, there is considerable evidence that the children of parents with any major mental disorder are more likely to live with cognitive, social, and academic dysfunctions (Forehand, McCombs, & Brody, 1987). More specifically, Billings and Moos (1983) reported that children of depressed parents experience more physical, psychological, and behavioural problems than children of non-depressed parents.

The effects of maternal depression are apparent early in a child's life. The research indicates that infants of depressed mothers are less attentive and more fussy and irritable, have lower activity levels, and show fewer expressions of satisfaction than infants of non-depressed mothers (Field, 1984; Field et al., 1985). When confronted with indifference or a lack of involvement, infants tend to respond with helpless compliance, whereas infants of depressed mothers react with sounds of protest (Field et al., 1988). Physiological effects of maternal depression on children are also evident: Dawson, Frey, Panagiotides, and Osterling (1997) found that infants of depressed mothers exhibited reduced left frontal lobe activity during play and lacked increased right frontal lobe activity during distress, compared to infants of non-depressed mothers. However, the infants of depressed mothers showed less distress during maternal separation.

Because infancy is the key period in a child's development, postnatal depression also has repercussions in the later years of a child's life. In a study of the effect of maternal depression on the adjustment of five-year-olds to school, Sinclair and Murray (1998) found that both postnatal and recent depression were associated with behaviour problems, particularly among boys and children from lower-SES families. Murray and Cooper (1996) also found that four-year-olds of mothers who have suffered from depression recently or in the past seem to have a significantly compromised cognitive development, as well as behavioural problems.

The effects of maternal depression are also apparent during adolescence and adulthood. It is associated with a three-fold increase in a child's risk of eventually being diagnosed with major depression, substance abuse, or conduct disorder (Schwartz, Dorer, Beardslee, & Lavori, 1990). More generally, as children with depressed parents become young adults, they are at a greater risk of exhibiting feelings of guilt, general difficulties in functioning, and problems in interpersonal relations (Beardslee, Versage, & Gladstone, 1998). Thus, the effects of maternal depression linger on in the lives and behaviour of affected children.

Parenting style and engagement as mediators

Although research has established a link between maternal depression and children's behaviour, there is still debate about whether a child's behavioural problems are the result of maternal depression or the cause of it. A reasonable hypothesis is that depressed mothers are more likely to be harsher in their parenting and less nurturing, increasing the likelihood of behavioural problems (Webster-Stratton, 1990); but at the same time, a child's problematic behaviour surely must contribute to a mother's feeling of helplessness and despair. Nevertheless, most research emphasizes the causal link from maternal depression to children's behaviour problems, with parenting practices as the mediating process.

Several studies, for example, have revealed that diverse forms of maternal depression, such as post-partum depression, affect the face-to-face interactions between infants and their mothers: depressed mothers tend to be less playful and are more often inattentive and irritable while interacting with their children (Cohn, Campbell, Matias, & Hopkins, 1990; Field, Healy, Goldstein, & Guthertz, 1990; Field, 1984; Field et al., 1985; Field et al., 1988). Similar findings have been observed for older children. Longfellow and Szpiro (1983) found that mothers who were depressed and living under stressful conditions had the most difficulty dealing with their children. Although these mothers engaged in interactions with their children as frequently as other mothers, they used more authoritarian and hostile styles when asking something of their children or in responding to their inquiries. There is some evidence that depressed mothers switch from an authoritarian to a permissive parenting style when their attempts to control behaviour with a harsh approach is resisted by the child. Kochanska, Kuczynski, Radke-Yarrow, and Welsh (1987) postulated that depressed mothers often lack the energy for confrontations and are quick to abandon requests for good behaviour to avoid conflict.

Some of the links between maternal depression and parenting style may have more to do with mothers' perceptions of their children than the children's actual conduct. Several researchers have noted that depressed mothers are more likely to see their child's behaviour as disturbed (Forehand, Wells, McMahon, Griest, & Rogers, 1982; Panaccione & Wahler, 1986). Goodman, Adamson, Riniti, and Cole (1994) found that these negative perceptions on the part of the depressed mother can have a devastating impact on her child's self-esteem: depressed mothers made significantly more hostile statements about their children, and consequently, their children had a lower perceived physical appearance, scholastic achievement, and athletic competence, than those of non-depressed mothers.

Family functioning as a mediator

The model in figure 12.1 places maternal depression ahead of family functioning, but the double arrow posits a reciprocal relationship. A substantial body of research indicates that, regardless of the mental illness in question, having a parent in an acute phase of a psychiatric disorder is a predictor of poor family functioning (Friedmann et al., 1997). Nevertheless, there is also evidence that social support and healthy family functioning ease the life of the mentally afflicted parent. For example, D'Arcy and Siddique (1984) investigated the effects of spousal and community support on the mental health of mothers with preschool and school-age children. They reported that spousal support is especially critical to mothers of preschool children who are isolated in their home with their children all day and thereby at greater risk of suffering from depression. Ross and Mirowski (1988) examined these relationships for working mothers with depression, based on a nationally representative study of husbands and wives. They also found that community support, the ease with which child care could be arranged, and the husband's participation in child care had a significant effect on depression. Depressed parents with dysfunctional families are prone to a longer duration of the depressive episode, a lower rate of recovery, and a greater likelihood of relapse (Keitner, Miller, & Ryan, 1994).

Our analysis does not attempt to determine the relative strength of these reciprocal effects, which is difficult even with longitudinal data. For example, Billings and Moos (1985) examined the longitudinal changes in children and family functioning when parental depression either continued or remitted. They found that children of remitted parents functioned better than those of depressed parents, but still fared worse than children with non-depressed parents. The researchers accounted for this finding by introducing family functioning, and found that even though there was an improvement in parents' mental health and the children's social environment due to the remittance, lingering parental symptoms and continued elevated levels of stress partially explained the children's persisting difficulties. This work, and other research (e.g., see McLoyd, 1990), suggests that maternal depression in conjunction with poor family functioning and inadequate parenting may have debilitating effects on a child's development.

■ Method

This study used data from the full sample of National Longitudinal Survey of Children and Youth (NLSCY) children aged zero to eleven. The work builds on the analyses of previous chapters by employing the vulnerability indices for cognitive difficulties and behaviour problems as the primary dependent variables (see Chapter 3), the measures of SES and family background (Chapter 4), parenting styles (Chapter 8), and family functioning (Chapter 11) as explanatory variables.

The measure of depression was based on twelve items from the widely used CES-D scale (Radloff, 1977), which was developed at the Centre for

Epidemiological Studies at the National Institute of Mental Health. It involves asking parents "How often have you felt or behaved this way during the past week?" about the following statements:

- I did not feel like eating; my appetite was poor.
- I felt that I could not shake off the blues even with help from my family or friends.
- I had trouble keeping my mind on what I was doing.
- I felt depressed.
- I felt that everything I did was an effort.
- I felt hopeful about the future. (reversed)
- My sleep was restless.
- I was happy. (reversed)
- I felt lonely.
- I enjoyed life. (reversed)
- I had crying spells.
- I felt that people disliked me.

Parents respond on a four-point Likert scale: Rarely or none of the time (less than 1 day); Some or little of the time (1–2 days); Occasionally or a moderate amount of time (3–4 days); and Most or all of the time (5–7 days). The full CES-D scale is composed of twenty items, with the items scored 0, 1, 2, and 3; the highest possible score is 60. To be consistent with the scales for parenting and family functioning, we scaled the items as 0, 3.33, 6.67, and 10, and averaged them across the 12 items, such that each mother had a score ranging from 0 to 10. The reliability (Cronbach's alpha) of the shortened 12-item scale used in this study was 0.82, which is only slightly lower than the reliability of the 20-item scale (see Radloff, 1977).

For the CES-D scale, people with scores of 16 or higher are classified as depressed, which corresponds to a cut-off of 2.5 on our 10-point scale. In the Radloff (1977) study, the prevalence of depression ranged from 15 to 19 percent for household samples, whereas for the NLSCY the estimated prevalence is 15.6 percent. We find this to be remarkably consistent, given that the samples for the two studies are markedly different and the earlier study was conducted nearly thirty years earlier. However, this figure varies considerably from the prevalence reported by the Canadian Mental Health Association (1995) of only five percent. Given that any cut-off score is arbitrary, the figures here are similar to those used to establish norms for overweight (above the 85th percentile) and obesity (above the 95th percentile). We chose to use the less-stringent criterion, as it yields a more conservative test of the effects of maternal depression on children's outcomes.

Our analyses entailed two sets of logistic regressions. In the first set, we regressed the dichotomous measure of maternal depression on the full set of socioeconomic and family background variables to determine which factors are most strongly related to depression. We then fit a series of models separately to the cognitive and behavioural indices of vulnerability. The first was a baseline model that included only the measures of SES, family background, and the child's sex. The second introduced the dichotomous measure of depression to the model to determine the effects of depression apart from other family background characteristics. The third model introduced the measures of family functioning and parenting style to determine whether some of the negative effects of depression were mediated by these factors. Because the literature indicates the effects of depression are stronger in the early years, we conducted the analyses separately for children aged zero to five, and six to eleven.

■ **Factors Related to Maternal Depression**

Results from the logistic regression of maternal depression on SES and other family background variables are presented in Table 12.1. The first model includes the full set of covariates; the second model includes a reduced set of the most important factors. Among the primary indicators of SES, income, mother's education, and father's occupation are the most important predictors. An increase in family income of $10,000 reduced the odds of being depressed by about nine percent on average. This decrease is comparable to that associated with each additional year of the mother's education, and with an increase of one standard deviation in the father's occupation. Mothers who did not work outside the home were nearly twenty percent more likely to be depressed than those with part-time or full-time jobs.

The most staggering odds ratio pertains to single mothers: they were twice as likely to be depressed than mothers in married relationships. To explore this relationship further, we estimated the odds ratios for single parenthood for each of the items on the CES-D scale, before and after adjusting for the full complement of family background factors. The dependent variable was an item rating in the most frequent category (most or all of the time). Table 12.2 presents the results with the items ordered according to the unadjusted odds ratios. The results clearly indicate that a feeling of loneliness is the strongest factor

Table 12.1

Factors related to maternal depression (odds ratios)

	I	II
Socioeconomic status		
• Income	**0.90**	**0.91**
• Income-squared	1.01	
• Mother's education	**0.92**	**0.92**
• Mother works part-time	0.89	
• Mother at home	**1.12**	**1.18**
• Father's education	1.00	
• Father's occupation	**0.92**	**0.92**
Family structure		
• Single parent	**1.91**	**2.03**
• Teen mother	0.98	
• Number of children	**1.06**	1.05
Immigrant status		
• Within last 5 years	0.98	
• Between 5 and 9 years ago	1.17	
• More than 10 years ago	**1.32**	**1.30**
Sex		
• Female	1.00	
R-squared	8.6	8.5

Note: Odds ratios that differ significantly from 1.0 (p<0.05) appear in boldface.

separating single mothers from those in married or common-law relationships. Single mothers were also most likely to report feeling unhappy and not enjoying life; they had a sense that other people did not like them, and were prone to frequent crying spells.

The number of children in the family was also related to maternal depression, but the effects were relatively small. Each additional child was associated with a five-percent increase in the likelihood of being depressed. In the second model, this factor was not statistically significant but was retained as it was close to statistical significance ($p = 0.057$) and the variable has been found to be significant in other studies. We also attempted to discern whether the age of the children was relevant by fitting models which included either a variable denoting the number of children under three years old or whether the youngest

Table 12.2

Aspects of depression related to being a single parent (odds ratios)

	Unadjusted	SES-adjusted
How often have you felt or behaved this way during the past week?		
I felt lonely	**5.15**	**2.97**
I enjoyed life. (reversed)	**4.33**	**3.00**
I felt that people disliked me.	**3.80**	**2.40**
I had crying spells.	**3.71**	**2.11**
I was happy. (reversed)	**3.68**	**2.17**
I did not feel like eating; my appetite was poor.	**3.06**	**2.11**
I felt that I could not shake off the blues even with help from my family or friends.	**2.77**	**1.92**
I felt depressed.	**2.59**	**1.61**
I had trouble keeping my mind on what I was doing.	**2.25**	**1.50**
I felt that everything I did was an effort.	**2.13**	**1.55**
I felt hopeful about the future. (reversed)	**1.92**	**1.27**
My sleep was restless.	**1.56**	**1.24**

Note: Odds ratios that differ significantly from 1.0 (p<0.05) appear in boldface.

child was an infant. These factors were not statistically significant and thus were not included in our models.

Immigrant mothers who had been in the country for at least 10 years were about 1.3 times as likely to be depressed as other mothers. In contrast, there were no significant differences in the likelihood of being depressed for recent immigrants compared with non-immigrants. One cannot deduce from these findings that the likelihood of an immigrant mother becoming depressed increases with the amount of time spent in the country, as it may have to do with the immigration patterns over the course of the ten years preceding the time of data collection, or the economic and social opportunities afforded immigrants over that period. Untangling such period, cohort, and age effects is not possible with these cross-sectional data.

Table 12.3

The relationship between children's vulnerability and family background, children's characteristics, maternal depression, parenting styles, engagement, and family functioning (odds ratios)

CHILDREN AGED 0 TO 5

	Cognitive index			Behavioural index		
	I	II	III	I	II	III
Family characteristics						
• Income	1.00	1.00	1.00	**0.96**	0.97	0.97
• Mother's education	**0.92**	**0.92**	**0.94**	**0.96**	0.97	0.98
• Mother at home	**1.47**	**1.46**	**1.51**	0.93	0.91	0.95
• Father's education	0.99	0.98	1.00	1.01	1.01	1.03
• Father's occupation	0.97	0.98	0.99	**0.92**	**0.93**	0.94
• Single parent	0.93	0.87	0.85	**1.35**	**1.21**	1.11
• Teenage mother	0.92	0.92	0.88	**1.32**	**1.30**	1.23
• Number of siblings	**1.09**	**1.09**	1.05	0.99	0.98	0.97
• Immigrant						
- within last 5 years	**1.59**	**1.59**	1.38	**0.69**	0.72	**0.63**
- 5 and 9 years ago	**3.22**	**3.16**	**3.00**	1.27	1.22	1.03
- more than 10 years ago	**1.89**	**1.86**	**1.74**	0.95	0.90	0.93
Female	**0.68**	**0.68**	**0.69**	0.97	0.96	1.03
Maternal depression		**1.50**	**1.31**		**2.17**	**1.53**
Family functioning			**0.92**			**0.92**
Parenting style and engagement						
• Rational			**1.10**			**0.73**
• Responsive			**0.91**			0.96
• Firm approach			0.96			**0.92**
• Reasons with child			**0.89**			0.99
• Reads to child			**0.93**			**0.97**
R-squared	5.8	6.2	9.4	1.9	4.0	12.1

Note: Odds ratios that differ significantly from 1.0 (p<0.05) appear in boldface.

Three null findings are worthy of note. First, the father's education was not related to maternal depression—the effects associated with fathers seem to play themselves out through occupation and income. Second, mothers who had their first child when they were teens were not more likely to be depressed than other mothers. This seems to be contrary to findings that will be presented in Chapter 14, which examines results for teenage parents in more detail.

Table 12.3 (cont.)

The relationship between children's vulnerability and family background, children's characteristics, maternal depression, parenting styles, engagement, and family functioning (odds ratios)

CHILDREN AGED 6 TO 11

	Cognitive index			Behavioural index		
	I	II	III	I	II	III
Family characteristics						
• Income	**0.92**	**0.92**	**0.92**	1.00	1.00	1.01
• Mother's education	**0.94**	**0.94**	**0.94**	**0.93**	**0.94**	**0.93**
• Mother at home	0.97	0.97	0.95	1.04	1.02	1.12
• Father's education	**0.93**	**0.93**	**0.93**	1.00	1.00	1.01
• Father's occupation	1.00	1.00	1.01	0.96	0.97	0.98
• Single parent	0.84	0.84	0.83	**1.78**	**1.65**	**1.55**
• Teenage mother	1.05	1.05	1.02	**1.61**	**1.61**	**1.71**
• Number of siblings	1.06	1.06	**1.08**	0.92	0.91	0.88
• Immigrant						
- within last 5 years	1.17	1.17	1.25	**0.12**	**0.12**	**0.15**
- 5 and 9 years ago	**0.43**	**0.43**	**0.44**	**0.44**	**0.42**	**0.37**
- more than 10 years ago	0.89	0.89	0.92	**0.81**	**0.79**	**0.82**
Female	**0.79**	**0.79**	**0.81**	**0.61**	**0.61**	**0.69**
Maternal depression		0.99	0.94		**1.85**	**1.33**
Family functioning			0.96		0.97	
Parenting style and engagement						
• Rational			**0.92**			**0.55**
• Responsive			**1.09**			**0.90**
• Firm approach			1.01			1.00
• Reasons with child			1.03			**1.09**
• Reads to child						
R-squared	3.5	3.5	3.9	6.2	7.5	19.5

Note: Odds ratios that differ significantly from 1.0 (p<0.05) appear in boldface.

Those results indicate that mothers who have their first child when they are in their teen years are more likely to be depressed. Therefore, we estimated a logistic model with only teen mothers in the model, which yielded an odds ratio of 1.75. This is consistent with the findings presented in Chapter 14. We also found that two variables—family income and the level of the mother's education—accounted for nearly all of this effect. The inclusion of these factors reduced the odds ratio from 1.75 to 1.05, and we see from the results in Table 12.1 that the effects on maternal depression associated with teen parenting are fully accounted for by other family-related factors.

■ The Effects of Maternal Depression on Children's Outcomes

Table 12.3 presents the results of the logistic regressions pertaining to the relationships between childhood vulnerability and family background, children's characteristics, maternal depression, and other family processes. The analyses were conducted separately for children aged zero to five and six to eleven.

Children five and under

Model I presents the relationship between the cognitive index and the full set of family background variables and sex of the child. These results are comparable to those of Chapter 4 and are presented here to help discern whether maternal depression is a mediator of family background factors.

Model II includes the measure of maternal depression. It indicates there is a very large, statistically significant effect associated with maternal depression: the children of mothers who are depressed are about 1.5 times as likely to be vulnerable as those whose mothers are not depressed. Note that this estimate is adjusted for all of the family background factors included in the model; the unadjusted odds ratio is 1.69 (not shown in the table). The results also show that maternal depression does not significantly reduce any of the effects associated with family background. Thus, these results provide strong evidence that maternal depression has an effect on children's early cognitive development that is independent of SES.

Model III incorporates the variables describing family functioning, parenting style, and whether the mother reads to the child regularly. These factors account for about 40 percent of the effects of maternal depression, reducing the odds ratio from 1.50 to 1.31. The most important mediators are family functioning, whether the mother is responsive to the child's needs, whether she reasons with the child, and whether the mother reads to the child regularly. Each of these factors were associated with about a ten-percent decrease in the likelihood of a child being vulnerable. There is one anomaly—the effects associated with rational parenting—which is not associated with a reduction in the likelihood of a child being vulnerable (see also Chapter 8).

The results for the behaviour index are similar, except that maternal depression seems to have an even stronger effect on the likelihood of a child being vulnerable. The odds ratio associated with maternal depression, before any statistical adjustment, was 2.43 (not shown in the table). After controlling for the set of family background factors, the odds ratio is 2.17, indicating that children of mothers who are depressed are more than twice as likely to exhibit behaviour problems (at least as the mother perceives them). The inclusion of the family-process variables substantially reduces the effect, from 2.17 to 1.53. The most important mediators pertain to family functioning and two dimensions of parenting style: adopting an approach which is rational and firm. These results also suggest that maternal depression does not substantially mediate the effects on behaviour associated with family socioeconomic background; however, it does mediate the effects associated with being a single parent.

Children over five

The results for the cognitive vulnerability index for children aged six to eleven, which is based on low mathematics scores, suggest that maternal depression is not a determinant of whether a child is vulnerable in this respect. However, this does appear to be the case for behaviour. Children living with depressed mothers were nearly twice as likely to display behaviour problems as those with non-depressed mothers. (The unadjusted odds-ratio was 2.10, not shown in the table.) Similar to the findings for behavioural problems for young children, a substantial amount of this effect is mediated by parenting styles. The most important dimensions of parenting related to a rational approach and responsiveness to the child's needs. As with the results for younger children, maternal depression did not substantially mediate the effects of family background on children's behaviour.

■ Summary and Discussion

This study used the full sample of NLSCY mothers and their children to determine which factors were the most important determinants of maternal depression, and the relationship between maternal depression and childhood vulnerability. The analyses focussed specifically on whether maternal depression was a mediator of the relationship between SES and childhood outcomes, and whether family functioning, engagement, and parenting styles mediated the relationship between maternal depression and childhood outcomes. Four of the most important findings are discussed below.

1. *Mothers were more likely to display signs of depression if they had low income, a low level of education, or a spouse with a less-prestigious occupation. Mothers who were not working outside the home were nearly twenty percent more likely to be depressed, and single mothers were about twice as likely to be depressed as those in married or common-law relationships. Mothers who had immigrated to Canada at least ten years earlier were more likely to be depressed. Depression also increased slightly with the number of children in the family.* Previous studies have pointed to the importance of the relationship between socioeconomic factors and maternal depression; however, they have emphasized the role of low family income (e.g., Conger et al., 1992; Dohrenwend et al., 1992; Rootman, 1988) and involuntary unemployment (e.g., Turner et al., 1991; Walker et al., 1989). This study substantiates the importance of these factors but indicates that the level of the mother's education and the prestige of the father's occupation play an equally important role. Previous research has also stressed the importance of the number of children in the home, especially the number of young children. These results indicate that this is a factor, but the relationship is not especially strong. For example, the increase in the likelihood of being depressed associated with having two additional children is roughly equivalent to a decrease in family income of $10,000 or of the mother having one year less education. When the findings are placed in this context, they suggest that it may not be simply the extra work entailed with having a large family which results in feelings of depression, but also the added economic strain.

   The most important factor associated with maternal depression identified in this study is being a single parent. By itself, the likelihood of a single mother being depressed is about three times that of a mother in a two-parent family (odds ratio is 3.06, not shown in table). Adjusting for the full range of socioeconomic factors reduces the odds ratio to approximately double, which far outweighs any of the other factors. Analyses of the separate items comprising the depression scale indicated that single mothers were much more likely to be lonely and feel that people disliked them. They were also less likely to report that they enjoyed life or that they were happy most of the time.

2. *Children five and under were about one and a half times as likely to have poor cognitive development if their mothers were depressed, even after taking account of other family background characteristics. About two-fifths of this effect could be accounted for by measures of family functioning and parenting*

style. However, this effect was not evident for school-age children. Most of the research on the effects of maternal depression on childhood outcomes has been concerned with children's behaviour rather than their cognitive outcomes (e.g., see Beardslee, Versage, & Gladstone, 1998).

The absence of an effect on cognitive outcomes for older children is an anomaly that calls for further research. The cognitive index for children under five was derived from the measure of motor and social development (MSD) at ages zero to three, and the PPVT-R scores for children aged four and five. We estimated separate models for these variables and found that the odds ratios were somewhat larger for low PPVT-R scores (2.09 for Model II) than for low MSD scores (1.29 for Model II). Thus, we cannot be sure that the relatively small effect for the younger cohort occurs because MSD is a poor proxy for cognitive development. We also expect that the strong effects of maternal depression on early vocabulary development are likely to carry forward into the school years, affecting children's reading and language arts skills. Other research has shown that family SES has stronger effects on reading achievement than on mathematics achievement (Willms, 1992), and this may be the case for maternal depression as well. We will be able to examine this issue when data for the second cycle of NLSCY become available.

3. *Children were about twice as likely to display behavioural problems if their mothers were depressed. Over half of this effect could be accounted for by measures of family functioning and parenting styles.* The effects of maternal depression on behaviour were much stronger than for cognitive development and were more consistent across the measures. Maternal depression did not have a strong mediating effect on the relationship between behaviour and SES; however, it substantially reduced the negative effects associated with being a single parent. In the case of younger children, the likelihood of a child being vulnerable if he or she were living in a single-parent family was 1.35 times that of a child living in a 2-parent family. This ratio reduced to 1.21 after taking maternal depression into account, and to 1.11 (which was not statistically significant) after taking account also of family functioning, parenting style, and engagement. For children aged 6 to 11, there was a comparable reduction: from 1.78 to 1.65 when controlling for maternal depression and to 1.55 when controlling also for family functioning, parenting style, and engagement.

In general, these results suggest that maternal depression is a key determinant of childhood vulnerability, related to and as important as family functioning, parenting style, and engagement. Discussion about depression and childhood vulnerability emphasizes the role of post-partum depression, which to some extent may have engendered a stereotype that maternal depression affects mainly very young children and only for a brief period. Earlier research has also emphasized the relationship between depression and the number of children, especially the number of children of preschool age. Our results indicate that the relationship between the age of the child and the number of children in the family is relatively weak, and pales in comparison to the effects associated with income and unemployment, the level of the mother's education, and the prestige of the father's occupation. Single parents are especially prone to depression. Moreover, our findings emphasize that the effects of depression are more far-reaching, affecting children from birth to age eleven and, we suspect, through adolescence.

Many single parents experience feelings of loneliness and rejection, and that depression accounts for some of the differences in childhood vulnerability associated with growing up in a single-parent family. Research on adults' mental health has emphasized the importance of quality social support (Seeman, 1996) and social integration, especially being married or having close friendships if one is unmarried (House, Williams, & Kessler, 1987). If interventions are to be targeted towards parents in single-parent and low-income families, they need to take into account that many of these parents are probably combatting depression. Support that helps single mothers cope with some of the demands of parenting, and increases their opportunities to interact with others, is likely to yield benefits for the mothers and their children.

NOTES

1   Unfortunately, the measure pertaining to reading with the child and two of the parenting style measures, "firm" and "reasons with child," were not available for children aged zero and one. Thus, for these children, we replaced the missing values on these variables with their overall means, and included in the model a dummy variable denoting whether or not the child was age zero or one versus age two to five. Therefore, the coefficients for these three variables pertain only to children aged two to five (see Cohen & Cohen, 1983).

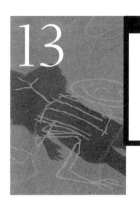

Children's Outcomes in Differing Types of Single-Parent Families

ELLEN L. LIPMAN, DAVID R. OFFORD,

MARTIN D. DOOLEY, & MICHAEL H. BOYLE

MANY CANADIAN FAMILIES are headed by lone parents. According to the 1996 census, more than one million (1,137,505) Canadian families with children were headed by lone parents. Of these families, 83.1 percent were headed by a female parent, while lone fathers accounted for 16.9 percent (Statistics Canada, 1996). Moreover, the proportion of Canadian families led by single mothers has been steadily increasing over the last 25 years (McKie, 1993), and they now account for about 1 in 8 Canadian families. Single mothers are at increased risk for a range of physical and mental health problems (Beatson-Hird, Yuen, & Balarjan, 1989; Lipman, Offord, & Boyle, 1997; Munroe Blum, Boyle, & Offord, 1988; Weissman, Leaf, & Bruce, 1987; Wolfe & Hill, 1992); regrettably, their children also have an increased risk of a range of social, academic, emotional, and behavioural difficulties (Judge & Benezeval, 1993; Kellam, Ensminger, & Turner, 1977; Lipman & Offord, 1997; Lipman, Offord, & Dooley, 1996; Moilanen & Rantakallio, 1988; Munroe Blum et al., 1988).

Single-mother families are often characterized by multiple adversities, such as poverty or low levels of education, but the distribution of such risk variables in single-mother families is by no means uniform. It is conceivable that subgroups of single-mother families, at more extreme risk, account for the increased vulnerability among their children than is evident for single-mother families taken as a group. Identifying subgroups of single mothers with varying levels of risk will have implications for the development of programs and policies for the mothers themselves, as well as for their children.

The outcomes for children from single-mother families are known to vary with the distribution of other risk variables, many of which are associated with being a single parent. For example, single parents are more likely to have low family income, and research has demonstrated repeatedly that poor children have significantly more psychological and social difficulties than non-poor children, including more mental and physical health problems, poor academic results, and social difficulties (Berger, Yule, & Rutter, 1975; Lipman, Offord, & Boyle, 1994; Offord, Boyle, & Jones, 1987; Rutter, Cox, Tupling, Berger, & Yule, 1975). Clearly, discussions about the outcomes of children from single-mother families need to be qualified using characteristics other than family status alone.

Much less research has been undertaken examining the characteristics of children from single-parent families led by fathers, which account for about 2.5 percent of Canadian families. Many studies that contrast the well-being of children from single-parent families with that of children from two-parent families exclude children from single-father families, not only because they comprise such a small proportion of the population but because their income is closer to that of two-parent families than single-mother families (e.g., Dooley, 1994; Lipman, Offord, & Dooley, 1996). It may be that, as is the case for children from single-mother families, the outcomes for children from single-father families depend also on other demographic characteristics.

Our first objective of this chapter is to establish a typology of single-parent families in Canada. We use cluster analysis to identify "types" of single-parent families, based on a number of socioeconomic characteristics, including income and parental education. We then examine the association between the different types of single-parent families and children's outcomes for children aged four to eleven years.

■ A Review of the Literature

Countless studies have examined the differences in childhood outcomes between single- and two-parent families, including studies of academic performance in which variables describing family structure are used as control variables. Our review is limited to research studies of relatively large scale (n > 500) and using probability sampling (such as a random selection from the general population) to achieve a representative sample of children four to eleven years old.

We identified thirteen studies that meet these criteria, which were based on data from ten surveys, including three from Canada, four from the US, and three from elsewhere. The data sets used for the Canadian studies are the 1983 Ontario Child Health Study (OCHS), a cross-sectional community survey with the aim of determining the prevalence and epidemiology of mental and physical health characteristics of 4- to 16-year-old Ontario children using a stratified random sample of over 3,000 children (Boyle et al., 1987); its 1987 follow-up (OCHS-FU) (Boyle, Offord, Racine, & Catlin, 1991); and the National Longitudinal Survey of Children and Youth (NLSCY). The US studies were based on the National Education Longitudinal Survey (NELS; National Centre for Education Statistics, 1989) which included grade-eight students in 1988 and followed them through high school; the Sustaining Effects Study of Title I (Hoepfner, Wellisch, & Zagorski, 1977), which included elementary school children in grades one through six from randomly selected schools; the National Survey of Families and Households 1987-1988 (Sweet, Bumpass, & Call, 1988); and a stratified random sample of children in Baltimore public schools, followed from grade one (Entwisle & Alexander, 1990). The studies from outside of North America include the National Child Development Study, a British birth cohort followed longitudinally since 1958; a Finnish birth cohort followed longitudinally since 1966; and a stratified sample of children in a metropolitan city in Australia (Sawyer, Sarris, Baghurst, Cornish, & Kalucy, 1990).

The results of these studies are somewhat difficult to compare because some studies were cross-sectional while others were longitudinal. They also differ in the types of informants and methods of analysis, and the measures of emotional and behavioural difficulties, and to a lesser extent academic achievement, differ, as do the measures of socioeconomic status (SES) or economic disadvantage, in cases where they were included. Despite these issues, the previous research reveals a number of important patterns.

First, studies that examined the effect of single-parent family status on emotional, behavioural, social, or academic outcomes found a significant independent influence of single-parent family status on at least some, if not most, of the childhood outcomes (Clark, Sawyer, Nguyen, & Baghurst, 1993; Entwisle & Alexander, 1995; Lipman et al., 1996; Mayer, 1997; Milne, Myers, Rosenthal, & Ginsburg, 1986; Moilanen & Rantakallio, 1988; Munroe Blum et al., 1988). In studies where the effect sizes were given as odds ratios (i.e., Lipman et al., 1996; Moilanen & Rantakallio, 1988; Munroe Blum et al., 1988) or where it was possible to estimate relative odds from data presented in the paper (i.e., Clark et al., 1993), the ratios ranged from 1.1 to 4.8. Thus, the odds of a child from a single-parent family having an undesirable outcome were in some cases nearly five times those of a child from a two-parent family. The strength of effects varied by outcome, but most of the outcomes measured in these studies were emotional and behavioural outcomes, or non-standardized academic outcomes such as poor school performance or repeating a grade. In studies where only regression coefficients are provided, the effects vary in magnitude across and within studies, depending on the outcome (Downey, 1994; Essen, 1979; Lipman & Offord, 1997; Thomson, Hanson, & McLanahan, 1994).

Second, the strength of association between single-parent family status and child emotional, behavioural, academic, and social outcomes decreases when the influence of income is taken into account. This suggests that at least some of the negative effect on children's outcomes is associated with having a lower family income, rather than the effect of having only one parent in the family. This finding was evident in all of the studies that examined this relationship (Downey, 1994; Entwisle & Alexander, 1990; Entwisle & Alexander, 1995; Essen, 1979; Ho & Willms, 1996; Lipman & Offord, 1997; Lipman et al., 1996; Milne et al., 1986; Munroe Blum et al., 1988; Thomson et al., 1994), regardless of whether the measure of income was a proxy, such as whether the child was eligible for a free meal subsidy, or was based on parents' reports of income. In a few cases, income was combined with other measures of SES.

Third, the effect of single-parent family status on children's outcomes diminishes further when other indicators of SES, such as parental education and employment, are included in addition to family income (Dooley, Curtis, Lipman, & Feeney, 1998; Downey, 1994; Entwisle & Alexander, 1990; Entwisle & Alexander, 1995; Essen, 1979; Ho & Willms, 1996; Lipman & Offord, 1997; Milne et al., 1986; Moilanen & Rantakallio, 1988; Munroe Blum et al., 1988; Thomson et al., 1994). And finally, the findings are mixed regarding the effects of the length of time a child has spent in a single-parent family (Essen, 1979; Lipman & Offord, 1997; Moilanen & Rantakallio, 1988). Even though this issue is crucial, few studies took it into account. The effect of living in a single-parent family may be non-linear with time; for example, one plausible hypothesis is that when parents separate, the disruption has immediate negative consequences on children's well-being, which diminish as the family adjusts to the changes. An equally plausible hypothesis, though, is that the effects of living in a single-parent family are cumulative and therefore increase over time. These longitudinal trends may be confounded by the age and experience of the mother, but only one study took account of maternal age (Thomson et al., 1994).

Thus, the research indicates that the effects of living in a single-parent family on children's outcomes may vary, depending on the outcome considered, and that at least some of the effects are associated with family SES. The analyses of the first cycle of the NLSCY stand to make an important contribution in that it measures a range of outcomes describing children's behaviour and their cognitive ability, and includes a large number of both single-mother and single-father families. The data also include strong measures of family income, a comprehensive set of other measures of SES, and the age of the mother when the child was born.

■ Method

This study was based on data for the full NLSCY sample of children aged four to eleven and their parents (n = 14,126). The first analysis employed a cluster-analysis procedure for large data sets to identify different "types" of single-parent families.[1] There are several different methods of cluster analysis, and each method requires specification of the criteria used for combining cases into clusters; however, no clustering method is clearly preferred (Blashfield, 1984). The constellation of characteristics we used to form clusters of single-parent families included household income, mother's education, whether the mother works part-time or is at home (vs. working full-time), whether the mother was a teen when the child was born, and whether the single parent was male or female. The construction of these variables is described in Chapter 4.

Two sets of regression analyses were conducted to assess the effects on children's outcomes associated with living in a single-parent family. The first set regressed outcome measures on a set of three dummy variables denoting each type of single parent, which were coded as dichotomous variables with two-parent families as the reference category. These models also included sex, coded one for girls and zero for boys. The second set of regressions included SES and number of siblings. The outcome measures included PPVT-R and mathematics as cognitive measures and the behaviour index as an indicator of behaviour problems (these outcome measures are described in Appendix A, pp. 381–87). We used ordinary least-squares regression for the continuous cognitive measures and logistic regressions for the behaviour index. In the course of our analyses, we found that in some instances the effect on children's outcomes associated with living in a single-parent family varied depending on whether the child was a girl or a boy. In statistical terms, this means there were statistically significant single-parent-by-sex interactions. To simplify the results of these interactions,

Table 13.1

Characteristics of single-parent clusters

	I		II		III		ANOVA(df=2)
Percentage of families	25.0		37.6		37.4		
(n=1764)	Mean	(SD)	Mean	(SD)	Mean	(SD)	F
Income ($1000s)	41.1	(4.9)	21.0	(3.7)	11.2	(2.3)	8904.3
Mother's education (years)	13.6	(2.3)	11.5	(1.9)	11.1	(2.2)	171.1
Mother works part-time (%)	3.4		16.1		19.6		25.7
Mother at home (%)	3.1		36.3		61.1		203.8
Teenage mother (%)	0.5		7.7		11.7		20.6
Single-parent male (%)	18.0		5.5		4.4		39.0

Note: The clusters differed significantly (p<0.05) in their mean scores for all six factors.

we present the bivariate relationships between behavioural outcomes and single-parent status for boys and girls, for each of the specific behavioural problems, for the full sample of children aged four to eleven (n = 13,349).

■ Types of Single-Parent Families

The cluster analysis yielded three distinct types of single-parent families, which are described in Table 13.1. The table also provides the F-statistic for an analysis of variance (ANOVA), which indicates the extent to which the groups are dissimilar in their socioeconomic characteristics. The ANOVA results indicate that family income is by far the most important factor distinguishing the three types of single-parent families. The mother's level of education and whether the mother worked outside the home were also important factors distinguishing family types, but the types were not nearly as homogeneous in these traits as they were in their family income.

The first cluster, labelled Type I, had an average income slightly below the national average for all families with children aged zero to eleven. It comprised one quarter of the single parents. The average family income of this cluster was $41,100, which is about $8,100 less than the national average. However, the average level of education among the single-parent mothers in this group was 13.6 years, which is 1.2 years more than the national average. The majority of the mothers worked full-time outside the home; only 6.5 percent of them were either at home or working part-time outside the home. The majority of single fathers were classified in this cluster, comprising eighteen percent of the Type I families.

The second cluster, labelled Type II, made up about three-eighths of the single-parent population. Its average income was $21,000, only about half that of Type I families. The single mothers, on average, had not completed secondary school. In about a third of these families, the mothers were not working outside the home; close to one in six mothers worked part-time. About one family in eighteen in this cluster was headed by a single father, and about one in thirteen was headed by a mother who gave birth during her teen years.

The third cluster, labelled Type III, also made up about three-eighths of the single-parent population. This cluster is greatly disadvantaged: the average income, $11,200, is less than a quarter of the national average income. The average level of education of the single mothers in this cluster was 11.1 years; most of them had not completed secondary school. More than half of the single mothers did not work outside the home, and only about one in five worked part-time. This cluster included the highest proportion of teenage mothers, and the lowest proportion of single fathers.

■ The Relationship Between Children's Outcomes and Single-Parent Status

Table 13.2 summarizes the relationship between children's outcomes and types of single-parent families. The first model, which does not include adjustment for SES or number of siblings, indicates that children in Type II and Type III single-parent families scored about 4 to 5.6 points lower on the PPVT-R at ages 4 and 5, and were on average about 3 to 5 months of schooling behind in their mathematics, compared with children in two-parent families. Children in these two types of single-parent families were also more likely to manifest a behaviour problem; on average, the odds were more than double those of children in two-parent families.

Children in Type I single-parent families scored slightly lower than children from two-parent families on cognitive measures, but the differences were not statistically significant. The results for behaviour problems for these families were mixed, with relatively fewer children displaying behaviour problems among four- and five-year-olds, and relatively more children displaying behaviour problems among nine- to eleven-year-olds. There may be a trend for children of average SES single-parent families to display more behaviour problems as they get older, and this should be investigated further when longitudinal data are available. These results suggest that the differences in outcomes between children in Type I single-parent families and those in

Table 13.2

Differences in children's outcomes associated with single-parent families

| | Cognitive skills (regression coefficients) | | | | | |
| | PPVT-R Ages 4–5 (n=3279) | | Mathematics Ages 6–8 (n=1556) | | Mathematics Ages 9–11 (n=3594) | |
	I	II	I	II	I	II
Single-parent (vs. two-parent)						
• Type I	-1.20	-2.22	-1.29	-0.71	-0.37	-0.19
• Type II	**-3.95**	**-1.22**	**-5.38**	**-3.68**	**-4.70**	**-2.55**
• Type II	**-5.55**	**-2.19**	**-3.11**	-5.4	**-5.01**	**-1.97**
Female (vs. male)	**1.05**	0.75	-0.42	-0.70	**1.58**	1.72
Socioeconomic status		**3.74**		**2.10**		**2.72**
Number of siblings		**-1.54**		0.11		-0.14
R-squared	0.01	0.07	0.02	0.05	0.01	0.04

Note: Coefficients that are statistically significant (p<0.05) appear in boldface.

two-parent families are quite small compared with the disparities associated with living in Type II and Type III single-parent families.

The second model provides estimates of the differences in outcomes between children in single- and two-parent families, after taking account of SES and number of siblings. These covariates accounted for about half of the disparities in cognitive outcomes associated with living in a Type II or Type III family. They also reduced the odds ratios pertaining to behaviour problems, on average by about 34 percent, but in all cases the children in these types of single-parent families were significantly more likely to have behaviour problems compared with children in two-parent families.[2] Overall, these regression models do not explain a substantial proportion of the variance in the outcome measures—only about two to seven percent—which indicates that much of the variation in these outcomes is attributable to other factors.

Figure 13.1 displays the prevalence among boys and girls of two internalizing behaviour disorders (anxiety and emotional disorders) and two externalizing disorders (hyperactivity and physical aggression), for two-parent families and for each of the three types of single-parent families. As was evident in the results of the regression analyses, children in single-parent families have a higher prevalence of behaviour problems than children in two-parent families.

Table 13.2 *(cont.)*

Differences in children's outcomes associated with single-parent families

	Behaviour problems (odds ratios)					
	Ages 4–5 (n=3499)		Ages 6–8 (n=4992)		Ages 9–11 (n=6522)	
	I	II	I	II	I	II
Single-parent (vs. two-parent)						
• Type I	**0.48**	**0.48**	1.27	1.20	**1.30**	1.22
• Type II	**1.62**	**1.44**	**2.51**	**2.22**	**2.23**	**1.85**
• Type II	**2.08**	**1.74**	**1.93**	**1.57**	**2.09**	**1.52**
Female (vs. male)	1.09	1.09	**0.54**	**0.54**	**0.66**	**0.65**
Socioeconomic status		**0.87**		**0.87**		**0.80**
Number of siblings		0.96		**0.91**		**0.88**
R-squared	0.01	0.02	0.03	0.03	0.02	0.03

Note: Odds ratios that differ significantly from 1.0 (p<0.05) appear in boldface.

However, these analyses indicate that within each of the single-parent family types, including Type I single-parent families, boys have a higher prevalence of behaviour problems for every type of problem. This finding is particularly interesting with respect to internalizing disorders. Considerable research has indicated that internalizing disorders are more prevalent among girls, whereas externalizing behaviours tend to be more prevalent among boys. But these results suggest that this is the case only in two-parent families; in single-parent families boys have a higher prevalence of both internalizing and externalizing disorders.[3]

■

The premise underlying this study is that there is considerable variation in the socioeconomic circumstances of single-parent families, and that treating them as a single entity, as is usually done in analyses pertaining to childhood outcomes, masks some of the important relationships. This study set out to determine whether single-parent families could be grouped into meaningful types based on a number of variables pertaining to SES. It then asked whether children growing up in different types of single-parent families differed in their cognitive and behavioural outcomes from children growing up in two-parent families.

Figure 13.1

Distribution of children aged four to eleven with behaviour problems by child's sex and family type (bar width reflects sample size)

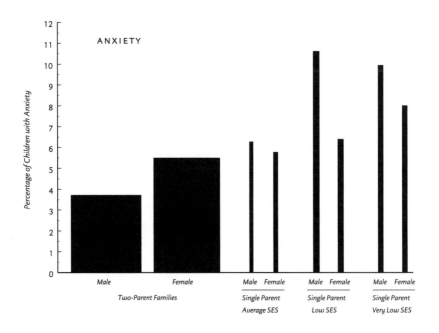

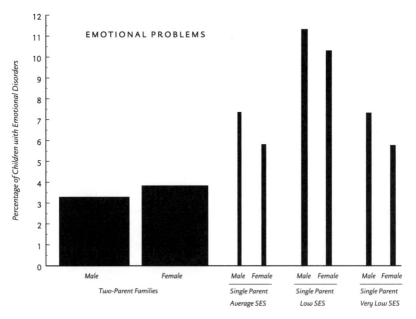

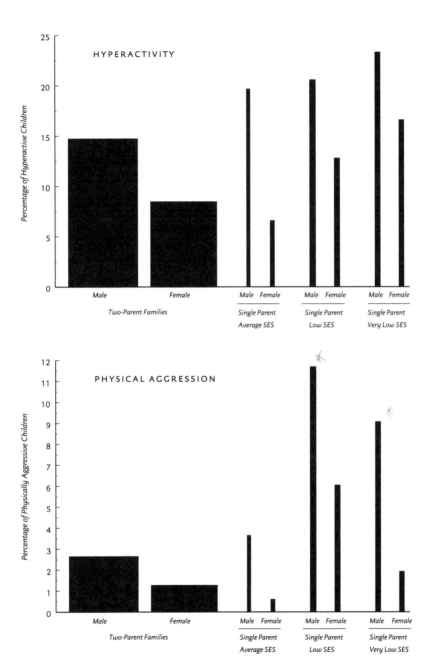

HYPERACTIVITY

Percentage of Hyperactive Children

Male	Female
Two-Parent Families	

Male   Female
Single Parent
Average SES

Male   Female
Single Parent
Low SES

Male   Female
Single Parent
Very Low SES

PHYSICAL AGGRESSION

Percentage of Physically Aggressive Children

Male   Female
Two-Parent Families

Male   Female
Single Parent
Average SES

Male   Female
Single Parent
Low SES

Male   Female
Single Parent
Very Low SES

The analysis then considered whether some of the observed differences could be attributed to the relatively low SES of single parents and whether the effects of single-parent status differed for boys and girls. Four important findings emerged from the study.

1. *There are three fairly distinct "types" of single-parent families, which are characterized mainly by family income and whether or not the mother works outside the home.* The average income of Type I single parents was below the national average, but their level of education was above the national average and over 90 percent of them worked outside the home. The average income of Type II single parents was only $21,000, and slightly less than half of these mothers worked outside the home. Type III single parents were considerably disadvantaged, with an average income of only $11,200; only about one-fifth of these mothers worked full-time outside the home, and a disproportionate number of them were teenagers when their child was born.

2. *Children in Type II and Type III families were more likely to exhibit behaviour problems, have lower scores in receptive vocabulary at ages four and five, and have lower mathematics tests scores at ages six through eleven.* Although the gap in mathematics achievement was only about three to five months of schooling, which may not seem that important, it indicates that many children in single-parent families are also coping with academic challenges. Low achievement may contribute to low self-esteem, and these factors together may lead to both internalizing and externalizing behaviour problems. We do not adequately understand the developmental pathways or the risk and protective factors associated with growing up in a single-parent family. Large-scale longitudinal studies such as the NLSCY can contribute to our understanding, but they must be supplemented with smaller-scale qualitative studies.

3. *The disparities in outcomes between children in single-parent families and those in two-parent families were only partially attributable to differences in family income and other socioeconomic factors.* Our analyses indicate that socioeconomic factors can explain only about a third to a half of the disparities associated with poverty and other socioeconomic factors. This suggests that other factors, such as, for example, the amount of time that parents can engage with their child in play or school-related activities, or the stress

associated with separation or divorce, may also contribute to the differences in outcomes between children in single- and two-parent families.

4. *Boys living in Type II and Type III single-parent families tend to be more prone to exhibiting both internalizing and externalizing behaviour problems than girls.* The results in Chapter 4 indicated that the effects of living in a single-parent family were considerable, especially with regards to behaviour problems. The findings of this analysis indicate that these effects are especially acute for Type II and Type III single-parent families and for boys.

Other studies, based on population surveys, have shown that boys have a higher prevalence of externalizing behaviours than girls (e.g., Ontario Ministry of Community and Social Services, 1986). In this study, boys from single-parent families also demonstrated an increased prevalence of internalizing behaviour problems (i.e., anxiety and emotional disorders). Boys tend to be more vulnerable than girls to stress and upset (Offord, 1989), and thus it may be that boys are less able to cope with the instability presented by separation or divorce of their parents. When the longitudinal data for the NLSCY become available, it will be possible to achieve an even sharper focus on this issue; for example, we will be able to discern whether there is a dramatic increase in behaviour problems immediately following separation or divorce. We will also be able to use hierarchical analyses to examine within-family effects on children of different ages, to determine whether children are especially vulnerable at a particular age.

One of the most important policy issues concerning vulnerable children pertains to income subsidies for the poor. This analysis is based on cross-sectional data, and thus cannot assess the extent to which these family types are permanent states. Certainly many parents with children remarry, and some improve their economic circumstances. Nevertheless, the severity of economic disadvantage that was found among families in the Type II and Type III clusters, which constitute three-quarters of single-parent families, and the consistent, significant association between membership in these two clusters and markers of childhood morbidity is remarkable and alarming. The provision of additional income to very disadvantaged single-parent families may assist in bringing the level of risk of poor childhood outcomes closer to that of children in the Type I single-parent cluster. Employment programs for mothers may also assist with better child development. An initiative to assist with maternal employment for single mothers is currently being undertaken and evaluated in Canada (Mijanovich & Long, 1995). Additional income may be especially helpful if it is used directly to meet children's basic needs (Mayer, 1997).

However, these analyses indicate that low income is not the only factor contributing to the increased vulnerability of children in single-parent families. Moreover, the "attributable risk" associated with low income for children's emotional and behavioural difficulties is quite small (Lipman et al., 1996; see also Chapter 4). Thus, targeting subsidies to single-parent families is not likely to eliminate the prevalence of vulnerable children. If we are to target resources for children in single-parent families, we might achieve better returns from investments in programs that provide counselling and academic support to children following a separation or divorce, or programs such as Big Sisters or Big Brothers, which provide strong role models for children in single-parent families. Investments in more universal programs, particularly sports and recreational programs, may also be more effective in reducing children's emotional and behavioural problems.

NOTES

1   We used k-means cluster analysis, which requires the user to specify the number of clusters desired. To assist with selecting the number of clusters to be formed, 20 random samples of 200 children with replacement from single-parent families (N = 1,764) were generated. The resulting agglomeration schedule for each sample of 200 children, which identifies the cases or clusters being combined at each stage, provides a coefficient indicating the Euclidean distance between clusters for the multivariate set of variables. As the cluster analysis proceeds, the clusters become more dissimilar, and thus the coefficient increases. The point at which the coefficient abruptly increases helps one identify the number of clusters needed to represent the data. We found that a solution based on three clusters adequately represented the data.

2   The percentage decrease for each age group, and for Type II and Type III families was estimated by dividing the decrease in the odds ratios attributable to adjustment by the amount that the unadjusted odds were over 1.0 (i.e., equal odds).

3   The sex-by-single-parent-status interaction terms for anxiety were statistically significant (p < 0.05) for Type II and Type III single-parent families, but not for Type I single-parent families. In the case of emotional disorders, the interactions also suggested that the difference in prevalence rates for boys and girls in single-parent families differed from that of two-parent families, but these were not statistically significant. The results for the two externalizing disorders indicate that the prevalence is greater for boys than for girls in both single- and two-parent families, but the difference between boys and girls did not vary significantly across family types.

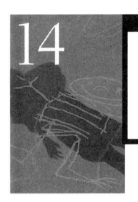

The Effects of Adolescent Child-bearing on Children's Outcomes

14

V. SUSAN DAHINTEN &
J. DOUGLAS WILLMS

ADOLESCENT PARENTING has been perceived as problematic in various ways: as a social and economic disadvantage for the mother, with associated costs to society; as a risk to maternal and infant health; and, more recently, as a risk factor affecting children's cognitive development, academic achievement, and social-emotional functioning. Early correlational studies showed strong evidence of deleterious outcomes for both the mother and child, but this research has since been contested because investigators failed to account for the circumstances that often precede adolescent motherhood, such as poverty and early school-leaving, and often used inappropriate comparison groups. As for obstetrical risk, early findings may have been confounded by inadequate prenatal care. Reviews of recent and more methodologically sophisticated research generally conclude that the effects are considerably smaller than previously thought (Coley & Chase-Lansdale, 1998; Corcoran, 1998; Hoffman, 1998; Maynard, 1997). Some researchers have emphasized the diversity of young mothers' abilities and resources, concluding that only some of their children are vulnerable (e.g., Furstenberg, Brooks-Gunn, & Morgan, 1987).

Although concerns about adolescent parenting have been increasing, the incidence of adolescent child-bearing has actually been decreasing steadily since the late 1950s (Luker, 1996). The rate of adolescent child-bearing among 15- to 19-year-old females, referred to as teen fertility, declined in Canada from

34.8 per 1000 in 1975 to 20.2 per 1000 in 1996 (Statistics Canada, 1995, 1997). The absolute number of teen births similarly decreased by about 50 percent (from 39,212 to 19,920), as did the number of teen births as a proportion of all births in Canada (from 11.3 to 5.6 percent). Although Canada's teen fertility rate is considerably lower than that of the US (54.4 per 1,000 in 1996), it is considerably higher than the rates for Japan, Switzerland, Sweden, and Finland, which ranged from a low of 4 per 1000 in Japan to 11 per 1000 in Finland (Health Canada LCDC, 1999; Ventura & Curtin, 1999). There are also regional variations within Canada, with teen fertility rates ranging from lows of 15.6 and 17.2 per 1000 in Quebec and Ontario, respectively, to a high of 38.0 in Saskatchewan (Statistics Canada, 1997).

In contrast to the declining fertility rate, the rate of non-marital child-bearing among adolescents has risen steadily over the last four decades: 84 percent of adolescent births were to unwed teens in 1997, compared with 37 percent in 1975 and 19 percent in 1960 (Statistics Canada, 1960, 1995, 1997). Some authors have argued that it is this increase in non-marital child-bearing, with its moral undertones and associated economic disadvantages, that has most strongly influenced society's construction of teen child-bearing as a public problem (Coley & Chase-Lansdale, 1998; Corcoran, 1998; Luker, 1996). Nevertheless, a lingering and serious concern is the possible untoward effects of young motherhood on children's outcomes.

The aim of this chapter is to examine the effects of adolescent child-bearing on child development. We separate adolescent mothers into two categories— older and younger teens—in order to discern whether there are differential effects of teen motherhood across the spectrum of adolescence. We also seek to describe the maternal outcomes of teenage child-bearing (e.g., educational attainment, income, and single parenthood) and other maternal characteristics such as depression and parenting practices, and determine whether these factors are important mediators of the relationship between maternal age and child development.

■ Early Child-bearing and Children's Outcomes

There is considerable evidence that children of adolescent mothers perform more poorly, on average, on measures of cognitive development and academic achievement, and are more likely to exhibit behaviour problems than their peers who are born to older mothers. For example, in their 17-year follow-up of more than 300 Baltimore children born to adolescent mothers during the late

1960s, Furstenberg et al. (1987) found excessive rates of grade repetition, high-school failure, delinquency, and other behaviour problems. Similarly unfavourable outcomes for cognitive development and behavioural problems, but not for academic achievement, were found by Dubrow and Luster (1990) in their analysis of 1986 National Longitudinal Survey of Youth (NLSY) data. Maynard's (1997) review of the seven coordinated studies which comprise the *Kids Having Kids* project concluded that substantial differences persist in academic performance, high-school graduation rates, subsequent young teen child-bearing, and incarceration rates, even after taking account of socioeconomic status and other background factors. However, not all studies have been as conclusive. Using 1986–90 data drawn from the NLSY, Geronimus, Korenman, and Hillemeier (1994) were generally unable to distinguish between the children of adolescents and their cousins who were born to older mothers. Furthermore, although Moore, Morrison, and Greene (1997) reported significant deficits in cognitive achievement and academic performance among the four- to fourteen-year-old children of young teen mothers from the NLSY sample when compared to the children of twenty- and twenty-one-year-old mothers, they did not find statistically significant differences in academic performance among the two samples of older offspring drawn from the National Survey of Children.

The developmental outcomes of children born to adolescents also vary across domains and by age of the child. Reviews of the empirical literature suggest that the effects of maternal age are generally absent in infancy; they emerge during the preschool years as small differences and become more pronounced among school children (Brooks-Gunn & Furstenberg, 1986; Coley & Chase-Lansdale, 1998; and Pianta, López-Hernández, & Ferguson, 1997). Moore et al. (1995) found that behaviour problems did not emerge until adolescence, which could not be predicted by the behaviour manifested in younger children. This is consistent with findings from Furstenberg et al.'s longitudinal study and with Pianta et al.'s (1997) failure to demonstrate differences related to maternal age in either retention or behaviour problems among a group of kindergarten students.

Obstetrical risk and adverse birth outcomes may also be related to maternal age. In 1997, 7.1 percent of the babies born to adolescent mothers in Canada were of low birth weight, compared with 5.8 percent of the babies born to all mothers (Statistics Canada, 1997). However, Millar and Chen's (1998) analysis of data from the National Longitudinal Survey of Children and Youth (NLSCY) failed to find an effect for adolescent child-bearing on birth weight after accounting for education, income, and smoking. A study of more than 130,000 mothers in Utah found that young teen mothers were far more likely to deliver a pre-term or low-birth-weight infant than mothers in their early twenties, after controlling for socio-demographic and lifestyle factors (Fraser, Brockert, & Ward, 1995). The children of eighteen- and nineteen-year-old teen mothers were also at significant risk, but less so than those of the younger teens. This and other recent research indicate that biologic immaturity may be related to childhood outcomes (Coley & Chase-Lansdale, 1998; Corcoran, 1998). Most research on early child-bearing, unfortunately, has treated adolescents aged fourteen to nineteen as a homogeneous group. When investigators have examined the effects by maternal age *within* adolescence, they have generally found that younger teen mothers tend to provide poorer home environments than their older teen counterparts, and their children tend to have worse developmental outcomes (Moore et al., 1995, 1997; Dubrow & Luster, 1990; Reis & Herz, 1987).

■ Mediators of the Relationship Between Early Child-bearing and Children's Outcomes

Although the children of adolescent mothers tend to lag behind those of older mothers on measures of cognitive development and social-emotional functioning, there is great variability in outcomes, and not all children of adolescent mothers fare poorly. Some of the risk factors that may explain or exacerbate poor outcomes include living in poverty, low maternal education, and large family size (Furstenberg et al., 1987), whereas having a supportive family has been identified as a protective factor (Birch, 1998). Moreover, these mediating factors may differ in their effects, depending on the age of the child and the developmental domain (Dubrow & Luster, 1990; Furstenberg et al. 1997; Spieker, Larson, Lewis, Keller, & Gilchrist; 1999).

Research indicates that the differences in childhood outcomes associated with teen parenting are independent of socioeconomic disadvantage. Adolescent parents may simply lack the knowledge, skills, and other resources that underpin successful parenting. A number of researchers have found that teen mothers are less verbally and emotionally responsive, and provide a less-stimulating home environment than older mothers who have similar socioeconomic backgrounds (Moore et al., 1995, 1997; Parks & Arndt, 1990; Passino et al., 1993). However, Geronimus et al. (1994) compared the home environments of adolescent mothers with those of their sisters who delayed child-bearing and were unable to distinguish between them. Some reviews conclude that the research results are inconclusive and limited by their focus on early childhood (Coley & Chase-Lansdale, 1998; Pianta et al., 1997).

Maternal depression may underlie findings that suggest adolescent mothers are less verbal and less responsive to their infants. Depressive symptoms are more prevalent among adolescent mothers, which is partially attributable to low income and single parenthood (Deal & Holt, 1998). Maternal depression has been found to be inversely related to maternal confidence and satisfaction (Fowles, 1998; Panzarine, Slater & Sharps, 1995), and associated with a higher prevalence of behaviour problems among children of adolescent mothers (Spieker et al., 1999).

Two other issues related to maternal age are raised in the literature but not resolved. The first is whether the deleterious effects of adolescent child-bearing extend to later-born children, rather than only the child or children born during the mother's adolescence. Surprisingly little is documented on this issue, except for the findings of Moore et al. (1995) that later-born children display outcome patterns similar to the first-born child. The second issue pertains to the most appropriate age-range for the comparison group. Pianta et al. (1997) recommend that mothers aged 20 to 24 years be selected for comparison purposes, whereas Moore et al. (1995) used mothers aged 20 to 21 as a comparison group, arguing that it may be unreasonable to expect efforts to reduce teen pregnancy to delay child-bearing in a high-risk group by much more than one or two years.

■ Method

This study used data relating to children who were born to mothers who were 30 years of age or less at the birth of their first child, and whose primary caregiver was also their biological mother: 15,313 children from 9,750 families. Adolescent parenting is defined as child-bearing at less than 20 years of age, and we differentiate older and younger teen mothers to avoid some of the problems discussed above concerning the heterogeneity of this group. Mothers and their children were categorized into four groups according to the mother's age at child-bearing: fourteen to seventeen, eighteen to nineteen, twenty to twenty-five, and twenty-six to thirty. We chose to break the teen years between seventeen and eighteen, because eighteen is the age when most Canadian youth complete secondary school.

We began by examining the bivariate relationships between the mother's age at the birth of her child and various indicators of child vulnerability from

Table 14.1

Profile of children's outcomes by age of mother

	Age of mother				
	14 to 17	18 or 19	20 to 25	26 to 30	χ^2
Low birth weight	7.0	4.2	5.4	5.2	0.7
Difficult temperament	29.4	26.7	18.7	14.0	**37.5**
Low MSD	9.4	10.4	12.6	13.0	1.6
Low PPVT	25.0	26.7	17.3	14.6	**10.8**
Low mathematics score	13.2	12.6	8.8	8.5	3.4
Behaviour problems	24.3	33.7	23.9	18.7	**91.7**
• Anxiety	4.3	7.2	5.7	4.3	**16.1**
• Emotional disturbance	2.2	10.1	4.7	3.6	**50.9**
• Hyperactivity	18.6	22.4	15.2	12.0	**58.6**
• Inattention	11.5	10.3	8.8	6.4	**30.4**
• Physical aggression	3.6	5.8	3.6	2.9	**14.5**
• Indirect aggression	(0)	6.7	3.1	1.5	**60.7**

Note: Variables were measured at the child level. Age of mother refers to her age when each child was born. Sample size for the four groups were 253, 739, 6248, and 8073; however, these vary for each outcome depending on the age range covered. The difference in the prevalence of low mathematics scores between teen mothers aged fourteen to nineteen and older mothers (twenty to thirty) is statistically significant (χ^2=4.2, p < 0.05). Group differences that are statistically significant (p<0.05) appear in boldface.

the physical, cognitive, and social-emotional domains. The specific measures included low birth weight, difficult temperament, low motor and social development, low receptive vocabulary (PPVT-R), low mathematics scores, and a composite measure of behaviour problems (see Chapter 3). The sample sizes vary by outcome measure, depending on the age range covered by the particular measurement.

We then used analyses of variance (ANOVA) and chi-square analyses to examine differences in maternal and family characteristics by age of the mother at child-bearing. Scheffé tests were performed to identify which specific pairs of means were significantly different. The analyses employed a partial set of the socioeconomic and family structure variables described in Chapter 4, which we refer to as family background, and several variables which we refer to as family processes: parenting practices (see Chapter 8), family functioning (see Chapter 11), and maternal depression (see Chapter 12). Finally, we estimated the effects of the mother's age at child-bearing on two markers of vulnerability—behaviour disorders and low receptive vocabulary—before and after controlling for family background and family processes. Three logistic regression models were estimated for each dependent variable.

■ Children's Outcomes and Mother's Age at Child-bearing

Table 14.1 presents the relationship between children's outcomes and mother's age at childbirth. The table indicates the percentage of children in each maternal age group who received relatively poor scores on measures of health at birth, cognitive development, and behavioural outcomes. Although the overall picture is not easy to comprehend because of inconsistencies related to small sample sizes, in general, the findings are consistent with earlier studies, indicating that older child-bearing is associated with more favourable child outcomes.

Statistically significant differences were found for three of the six measures. The children of adolescent mothers were substantially more likely to demonstrate difficult temperament and have low vocabulary scores than children of the two older groups of mothers. The prevalence of behaviour problems was also significantly higher among the children of eighteen- and nineteen-year-old mothers compared with older mothers, although the children of fourteen- to seventeen-year-old mothers showed no disadvantage when compared with the children of twenty- to twenty-five-year-olds.

The main effects of mother's age on behavioural outcomes could be misleading, however, if there are interaction effects between the mother's age at childbirth and age of the child. Therefore, in Figure 14.1, we display the level of behaviour problems by age of the child for each of the four maternal age groups. The non-parallel results suggest an interaction effect, and the regression analyses reported later indicate that this interaction is statistically significant. Children of older teen mothers show consistently higher levels of behaviour problems, although the level decreases slightly as the child ages, as it does for the children of fourteen- to seventeen-year-olds and twenty- to twenty-five-year-olds. In contrast, behaviour problems increase with age for children of the oldest mothers, so that by eleven or twelve, their behaviour is indistinguishable from that of the younger teen mother group or the twenty- to twenty-five-year-old group and is much closer to the level of the children born to older teen mothers (the gap decreases from about twenty percent at two years to ten percent at eleven years).

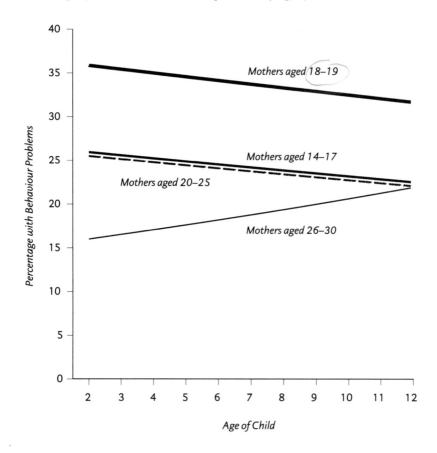

An examination of the findings for the six variables comprising the behaviour index is also instructive. The children of eighteen- and nineteen-year-old mothers demonstrated the highest prevalence of problems for all of the measures except inattention. However, the children of younger teen mothers did not have a high prevalence of behaviour problems: they were rated more favourably than those born to older teens, with the exception of inattention, and more favourably than children born to twenty- to twenty-five-year-old mothers on three of the six measures. A plausible explanation for this anomaly is that mothers' perceptions of their children's behaviour vary by age and type of behaviour. For example, hyperactivity and inattention may be more apparent and disturbing than is anxiety to a young mother. We speculate, later, on other plausible explanations.

Differences among the four parent groups for low birth weight, low motor and social development, and low mathematics scores were not statistically significant. However, the results for mathematics were in the expected direction, with a higher prevalence of low scores among children of adolescent mothers. The differences are also statistically significant when the two teen groups are combined and compared with either of the two older groups. Furthermore, although low birth weight was not significantly different between groups, the incidence of low birth weight among the children of the youngest teen mothers was 30 percent higher than among the children of 20- to 25-year-olds, generally consistent with national data (Statistics Canada, 1997). The lack of statistical significance is probably due to the relatively small sample of fourteen- to seventeen-year-old mothers, combined with the number of children aged zero to three at the time of data collection.

To summarize then, although we found statistically significant differences in both the cognitive and behavioural domains, the findings were not consistent for all indicators in each domain. However, for the measures that did show statistically significant differences (difficult temperament, low receptive vocabulary, and behaviour problems), children of the oldest mothers showed the least vulnerability to poor outcomes.

■ Family Characteristics and Mother's Age at Child-bearing

Table 14.2 displays the results of the second set of analyses, which examined differences in family characteristics by age of the mother at child-bearing. Variables pertaining to socioeconomic status (SES), single parenting, family functioning, and maternal depression were measured at the family level, and are therefore concerned with the age of the mother when her *first* child was born, whereas analyses related to parenting practices are concerned with the mother's age when the *focal* child was born. Therefore, the variables describing SES, family structure, and maternal depression may be considered maternal outcomes of fertility timing, as well as confounding risk factors for child development.

The results clearly show that children born to mothers who began child-bearing during their adolescent years are more likely to be living in families with markedly lower levels of family income and parental education, compared with children of mothers who delayed child-bearing. The between-group

Table 14.2

Profile of mothers' characteristics by age of mother

	Age of mother				ANOVA	
	14 to 17	18 or 19	20 to 25	26 to 30	F	χ^2
Family background						
• Income ($1000s)[1]	24.7 (17.9)	27.1 (18.1)	40.5 (22.9)	52.9 (23.7)	**373.7**	
• Mother's education (years)[1]	10.8 (1.9)	11.0 (2.0)	11.8 (1.8)	12.7 (2.2)	**231.4**	
• Father's education (years)[1]	11.1 (2.7)	11.3 (2.4)	11.9 (2.1)	12.7 (2.5)	**106.9**	
• Mother at home (%)[1]	45.7	52.8	33.9	24.4	**(81.5)**	**239.0**
• Single parent (%)[1]	50.5	39.3	21.8	11.5	**(154.4)**	**438.8**
Family processes						
• Family functioning[1]	7.3 (1.3)	7.3 (1.5)	7.7 (1.5)	7.9 (1.4)	**37.7**	
• Depressed[1]	23.5	24.5	18.5	12.2	**(34.4)**	**102.4**
• Parenting practices						
- Rational[2]	7.1 (1.7)	7.0 (1.6)	7.1 (1.5)	7.3 (1.5)	**15.0**	
- Responsive[2]	7.1 (1.5)	7.1 (1.7)	6.9 (1.6)	7.0 (1.7)	**5.2**	
- Firm approach[2]	6.8 (1.7)	7.1 (1.7)	7.2 (1.7)	7.3 (1.7)	**9.3**	
- Reasons with child[2]	6.96(1.9)	6.9 (1.8)	7.0 (1.8)	7.1 (1.7)	**4.5**	

Note 1: Variables were measured at the family level. Age of mother refers to her age when her first child was born. Sample sizes for the four groups were 237, 659, 4389, and 4465.

Note 2: Variables were measured at the child level. Age of mother refers to her age when each child was born. Sample sizes for the four groups were 253, 739, 6248, and 8073.

Note 3: Group differences that are statistically significant (p<0.05) appear in boldface.

differences in income are substantial; for example, the mean family income for mothers who were 20 to 25 at the birth of their first child was 49 percent higher than the income of mothers who were 18 or 19. Moreover, teen mothers are more uniformly poor: the standard deviation for the two teen groups is about $18,000, compared with about $23,000 for the older mothers. The gap in educational attainment between teen mothers and older mothers is about one year of schooling, which is especially important because of the substantial effects associated with maternal education (see Chapter 4). Moreover, the difference between eleven and twelve years of schooling is critical because it indicates disparities in rates of secondary school graduation, which has implications for success in the labour market. Mothers who were in their teen years at the birth of their first child were less likely to be employed outside the home and more likely to be heading a single-parent family. Moreover, single-parent status was more likely among young teen mothers than among older teen mothers.

Generally, the findings indicate that teen mothers are more likely to be depressed and have lower levels of family functioning than mothers who had their first child after age twenty. Mothers who had their first child after age 25 were the least likely to be depressed and reported the highest level of family functioning. Although not all of the differences among the four groups are statistically significant, mothers who were twenty to twenty-five years old at first childbearing reported significantly higher levels of family functioning than both groups of teen mothers, and lower levels of depression than the eighteen- to nineteen-year-old mothers. The younger teen mothers reported significantly higher levels of depression only when compared with the 26- to 30-year-old mothers.

Although there are statistically significant differences between groups for each of the parenting practices, few substantial differences were found and not all differences were in the expected direction. The observed differences in parenting practices between the 20- to 25-year-old mothers and the mothers who were less than 20 years at the birth of their child were not statistically significant, although the results suggest that younger teen mothers are less firm than 20- to 25-year-old mothers. The differences in parenting practices between the younger and older teen mother groups also were not statistically significant. However, they do suggest a general trend towards improved parenting at older ages, with the oldest group of mothers reporting significantly higher levels of positive parenting behaviours than the 20- to 25-year-old group for all but the category, "reasons with child."

In summary, then, although the findings indicate there are strong bivariate relationships between fertility timing and SES, single-parent status, family functioning, and maternal depression, there is little evidence that parenting practices are substantially associated with maternal age at child-bearing—just as little difference was found, on average, in parenting across the spectrum of SES (see Chapters 8 and 9).

■ The Effects of Maternal Age on Children's Outcomes

Table 14.3 provides estimates of the effects of maternal age at child-bearing on behaviour disorders and low receptive vocabulary, before and after controlling for family background and family processes. Results for the three regression models are presented side by side, so that the mediating effects of each group of factors can be more easily distinguished.

The effects of adolescent child-bearing ranged from being non-significant to strongly disadvantageous. Being born to an older teen mother was associated with a 63-percent increase in the likelihood of a behaviour disorder and a 79-percent increase in the likelihood of low receptive vocabulary. In contrast,

Table 14.3

Relationship between behaviour problems and low receptive vocabulary with maternal age, family background, and family processes

	Behaviour problem			Low receptive vocabulary		
	I	II	III	I	II	III
Age of child	0.99	1.00	1.01			
Age of mother (vs. 20 to 25)						
• 14 to 17	0.92	0.70	0.68	1.54	1.14	1.06
• 18 or 19	**1.63**	**1.37**	**1.34**	**1.79**	1.38	1.38
• 26 to 30	**0.70**	**0.80**	**0.84**	0.78	1.05	1.12
- Child's age by 26–30	**1.06**	**1.04**	**1.04**			
Family background						
• Income		1.00	1.00		**0.99**	**0.99**
• Mother's education		**0.93**	**0.92**		**0.87**	**0.89**
• Mother at home		1.00	1.00		**1.57**	**1.58**
• Father's education		0.98	1.00		0.99	1.00
• Single parent		**1.81**	**1.69**		0.88	0.84
Family processes						
• Family functioning			**0.94**			**0.81**
• Maternal depression			**1.23**			**1.47**
Parenting practices						
• Rational			**0.56**			1.17
• Responsive			0.97			1.05
• Firm approach			**0.96**			**0.89**
• Reasons with child			**1.05**			0.93
R-squared (%)	1.3	3.6	17.1	1.0	7.6	12.3

Note: Odds ratios that differ significantly from 1.0 (p<0.05) appear in boldface.

being born to the oldest group of mothers was associated with decreases in the likelihood of problematic outcomes: compared to children of 20- to 25-year-old mothers, at ages 4 and 5 these children were 22 percent less likely to have poor receptive vocabulary[1] and at age 10, 30 percent less likely to display behaviour problems. Moreover, the effects were significantly larger for younger children than for older children (see Figure 14.1). Contrary to expectations, however, the effects associated with being born to a younger teen mother were not statistically significant. Even the large odds ratio of 1.54 for low receptive vocabulary was not statistically significant, but this is likely due to a lack of statistical power, as data on PPVT-R were collected only for 4- and 5-year-old children.

Family background characteristics were found to substantially mediate the effects of being born to an older teen mother. The increased risk of behaviour problems associated with child-bearing at ages 18 and 19 declined from 63 percent to 37 percent for behaviour problems, and from 79 percent to 38 percent (and non-significance) for low vocabulary scores, when family background variables were added to the model. The addition of family processes in Model III did little to further mediate the effects of maternal age but did increase the amount of total variance explained from 3.6 percent to 17.1 percent for behaviour problems, and from 7.6 percent to 12.3 percent for low receptive vocabulary. These findings suggest that at least some of the disadvantageous outcomes associated with adolescent child-bearing are attributable to SES and family structure, but do not support the hypothesis that parenting practices are the mechanism through which child outcomes are influenced. A final observation is that the independent effects of family characteristics demonstrate a similar pattern to those based on the full sample, which are reported in earlier chapters.

■ Summary and Policy Implications

Adolescent motherhood is generally associated with socioeconomic disadvantages for the mother and poor outcomes for the child. This study used a subset of the NLSCY data to examine the effects of maternal age on various markers of child vulnerability. We compared child outcomes from the physical, cognitive, and social-emotional domains for children born to adolescent mothers with the outcomes of children born to older mothers. We also examined differences in maternal outcomes and family characteristics by age of the mother at child-bearing, and sought to determine the degree to which these factors explained the relationships between maternal age and child development. The study yielded three key findings.

1. *There is a clear pattern of improvement in children's outcomes as mother's age at child-bearing increases.* Children of the oldest mothers (26 to 30 years old) showed the least vulnerability to problematic outcomes in early temperament, preschool vocabulary, behaviour problems, and mathematics. Furthermore, on most measures, children of 18- and 19-year-old mothers showed less-favourable outcomes than children of slightly older mothers. However, the relationship between childhood vulnerability and maternal age was not completely linear, as the children of younger teen mothers did

not show the expected disadvantage compared with older teen mothers, except for a higher incidence of low birth weight (see Table 14.1).

2. *The profile of teen mothers was characterized by disadvantage. The average family income of mothers who had their first child as a teen was about $25,000, approximately half the national average. Their level of education was lower than that of older mothers, and they were much more likely to be single parents and not work outside the home. Although their reported levels of parenting skills did not differ substantially from those of older mothers, teen mothers reported lower levels of family functioning than older mothers. About one in four teen mothers was depressed, which is about twice the prevalence of mothers who had their first child in their late twenties (see Table 14.2).* The findings in this study present a bleak profile for teen mothers, although there is considerable diversity in the socioeconomic outcomes of this group. A study such as the NLSCY cannot identify the underlying causes of teen pregnancy or determine whether teen pregnancy is the main factor leading to poor socioeconomic outcomes or depression. Nevertheless, the cross-sectional findings are strong enough to suggest that that we must continue preventive efforts as well as intervention programs aimed at improving maternal well-being. Efforts to delay the age of child-bearing need to focus less on the individual and choices around sexuality, and more on the larger societal problems underlying adolescent child-bearing. For example, providing a high-school curriculum that is more relevant to the attainment of marketable skills among disadvantaged youth might increase awareness of the perceived costs of a truncated education due to early child-bearing (Corcoran, 1998). These results also provide strong evidence that we need to support efforts that keep teen mothers in school and to address problems associated with maternal depression. The diversity in levels of education and income among teen mothers, and the weak relationships between parenting skills and maternal age, suggest that we need to be cautious not to over-generalize, thereby furthering the negative stereotype of the adolescent mother. The findings also suggest that while there may be many effective interventions programs in place for parenting teens, we should not be complacent about the level or efficacy of current services.

3. *Child-bearing during older adolescence has strong detrimental effects on the likelihood that a child will display a behaviour disorder, especially during the*

preschool years, and have poor receptive vocabulary upon entry to school. These effects are only partly attributable to family background (see Table 14.3 and Figure 14.1). During the preschool years, the prevalence of behaviour problems among the children of mothers who had their first child at age eighteen or nineteen was nearly double that of mothers who had delayed childbearing until their twenties. This has important implications for social policy because most of these mothers will not receive the benefits of programs offered in secondary schools and are unlikely to receive other social services unless their economic or mental health problems become acute. Many of these mothers may require intensive support to develop and maintain educational goals and academic skills, and their children may need additional support in order to develop their full potential during the preschool years.

An interesting finding, however, is that the effects of being born to a younger teen mother were not statistically significant. We speculate that younger teen mothers are more likely to live with their families of origin following the birth of their first child, and therefore may share child-raising responsibilities with their parents and siblings. This explanation is supported by the finding that fewer of the younger teen mothers were married at the time of the study, although we do not know the marital trajectory of either group. Geronimus et al. (1994) suggested that both the adolescent mother and her children may derive advantages from the support of more mature caregivers and that access to such resources may be more readily available within socioeconomically disadvantaged communities. Thus, for adolescent mothers, there could be interaction effects between maternal age, single parent status, and SES on child outcomes.

We anticipate that data from future cycles of NLSCY, and from the Youth in Transition Survey, will advance our understanding of the developmental trajectory for children's outcomes and their relationships with events in the life course of adolescent mothers. We also hope to gain a greater understanding of the effects of early motherhood on later-born children, an analysis that was constrained in this study by the large proportion of adolescent mothers who had borne only one child. This kind of research needs to be supplemented with detailed evaluation research which furthers our understanding of what kinds of programs best meets the needs of teen mothers and their children.

NOTES

1   The p-value associated with the difference was 0.056 and therefore was not significant at p < 0.05. However, the differences in scores for children of the older mothers does differ significantly from those of the two teen groups.

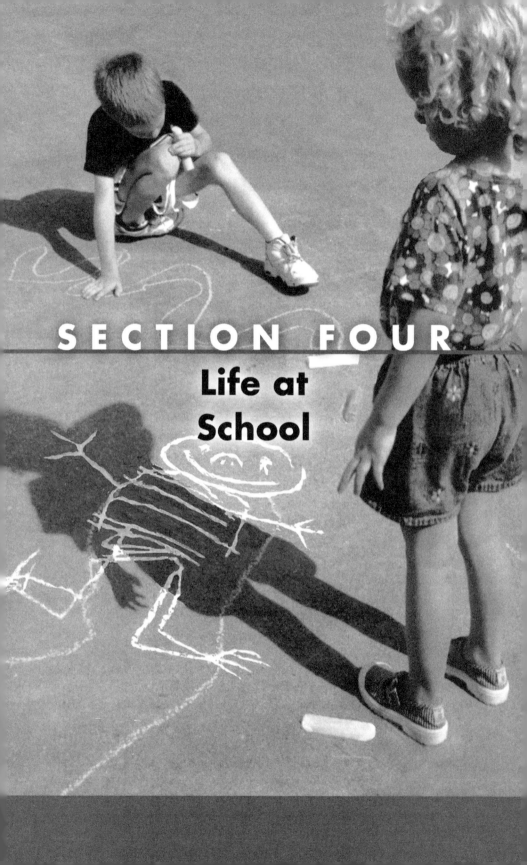

SECTION FOUR

Life at
School

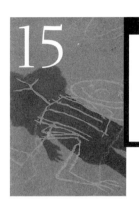

The Importance of Quality Child Care

**DAFNA KOHEN, CLYDE HERTZMAN,
& J. DOUGLAS WILLMS**

FAMILIES ARE INCREASINGLY using daycare centres and making other arrangements to care for their preschool-aged children. The number of dual-earner families has almost doubled in the last 25 years. In 1994, when the data for the National Longitudinal Survey of Children and Youth (NLSCY) were collected, 63 percent of women with children were working outside the home (Statistics Canada, 1995). In most cases, these families require some type of child care. The number of single-parent families in Canada has also increased steadily during the last 25 years, and more than half of the families with incomes below the poverty line are single-parent families headed by women (Ross, Scott, & Kelly, 1996). In most cases, these women do not receive adequate support for child care from their children's fathers. Therefore, if they wish to work outside the home, they must find inexpensive and convenient child care. This increase in single-parent families has also contributed to the increased demand for child care, and especially for less-expensive child-care arrangements. Although these changes in work patterns and family structure have implications for child care, little is known about the factors that influence parents' decisions about child care or the effects these choices have on their children.

This chapter examines the kinds of child-care arrangements used by Canadian parents of preschool children and assesses whether children in different types of child care differ in their social and cognitive skills. The term *daycare* is usually used in a general sense to cover various types of non-parental care, such as care in a licensed daycare centre; care in the home of a care-provider, which is usually called family daycare and may or may not be licensed; care in the child's home by a paid sitter or nanny; and other types of informal arrangements, such as care by a grandparent or other relative. The cost of these care arrangements varies considerably. On average, child care is more expensive in licensed daycare centres than care in family daycare settings, especially for infants. But unregulated arrangements tend to be more flexible and therefore more easily meet the needs of parents who work part-time.

■ Family Characteristics That Influence Child-Care Choices

Two recent large-scale studies have examined the relationships between family background and parents' choices of child-care arrangements. One of these studies, based on data from the American National Household Education Survey, found that for preschoolers aged three to five, families were less likely to choose centre-based care if they had younger children, had a grandparent in the household, or were single parents. Mothers with higher levels of education and mothers who were not working outside the home were more likely to choose centre-based care (Fuller, Holloway, & Liang, 1996). The other study, based on data from a survey of 1,174 mothers of preschool children in Detroit, examined the use of any type of formal care arrangement. It yielded similar findings to the national study with respect to the child's age, the presence of a spouse or relative who could provide care, and the level of education of the mother. The studies differed, however, in their findings pertaining to family income. In the national study, lower-income African-American parents were more likely to use centre-based care than those with higher incomes, whereas in the Detroit study, the opposite effect was observed for the use of a formal child care arrangement. In the US, about 40 percent of all centre-based programs are subsidized by government agencies (Hofferth & Kisker, 1992), and therefore differences in demand may be due to the availability of subsidized programs. Fuller et al. (1996) suggest that the most disadvantaged families, who are eligible for child care subsidies, are more likely to choose centre-based care; but if families are ineligible for subsidies, cost becomes an issue and centre-based care is a less-viable option. Low-income families may also prefer care by family or friends because they are more comfortable leaving their child with someone they know and because the arrangements tend to be more accessible, flexible, and affordable.

■ The Effects of the Quality of Child Care

Researchers examined in depth the effects of child care on children's linguistic, cognitive, and social abilities. The major studies on this issue can be classified into two categories: those aimed at determining the factors associated with quality daycare, as gauged by their effects on the developmental outcomes of *all* children, and those aimed at determining whether compensatory preschool programs benefit *disadvantaged* children. There are relatively few studies in the first category, and most of them have relied on the natural variation in public participation in programs of different types. Studies of compensatory programs have also examined the effects associated with typical daycare programs under normal conditions, but the most celebrated studies have examined the effects of demonstration programs in which researchers and practitioners have tried to design and implement a high-quality program (Barnett, 1995). Studies in both categories have been concerned primarily with licensed daycare centres, as this is the most prevalent form of child care in the US (Hofferth & Kisker, 1992).

The research in both categories has consistently identified three characteristics associated with quality of child care: low child-to-adult ratios, highly educated staff with specialized training, and the availability of facilities and equipment to provide stimulating activities (Arnett, 1989; Berk, 1985; Future of Children, 1995; Howes, Phillips, & Whitebook, 1992; Lazar, Darlington et al., 1982; Phillips, 1987). These dimensions of quality in essence separate "custodial" child care from child care aimed at early childhood development. Indeed, research has linked quality care, defined in these terms, with the linguistic, cognitive, and social competencies of infants (Burchinal, Roberts, & Nabors, 1996), preschoolers (Burchinal, Lee, & Ramey, 1989; Goelman & Pence, 1987; McCartney, 1984; Peterson & Peterson, 1986), and school-aged children (Andersson, 1989; Broberg, Wessels, Lamb, & Hwang, 1997; Rosenthall & Vandell, 1996). These characteristics are emphasized in the licensing requirements of child-care programs in both Canada and the US. Therefore, in many studies, attendance at a licensed daycare is used as a proxy for quality care. However, this assumption may not be valid, especially in Canada, where family daycare serves a larger proportion of children than licensed daycare centres (Pence, Goelman, Lero, & Brockman, 1992).

Two of the most widely cited intervention programs are the Carolina Abecedarian Project (CAP; Campbell & Ramey, 1994) and the High/Scope Perry Preschool Program (H/SPPP; Schweinhart, Barnes, & Weikart, 1993).

Both programs sought to demonstrate the lasting benefits of compensatory preschool programs for disadvantaged children. The CAP provided care and training for forty hours a week, from infancy to age eight. The curriculum was designed to enhance children's cognitive, perceptual motor, and social development, and was delivered in a university setting by highly trained staff. The H/SPPP was less intensive: it entailed a thirty-week program, with two and a half hours of training per day. However, the H/SPPP also included weekly visits to the home, which was considered an important component of the program. Children entered the program at age three and attended for two consecutive years.

The findings of these studies are especially important because they demonstrate that early interventions can have long-lasting effects on children's outcomes. Children who participated in the CAP, compared with children in the control group, had higher test scores in mathematics and reading at age eight and were less likely to have repeated a grade. The H/SPPP children had better school success than their control group counterparts on a number of measures, including achievement test scores, years spent in special education, high-school graduation, and entry into post-secondary schooling. They also had greater success in the labour market, in terms of both employment and earnings. Differences between the control and treatment groups continued to be evident at age 27: those who had received the H/SPPP had higher monthly earnings, were less dependent on social welfare, and had fewer arrests.

The H/SPPP cost $12,356 per child in 1992 constant dollars. Cost-benefit analyses of the returns on this investment estimated that for every (US) dollar spent, 50 cents was saved through decreases in school costs, 72 cents was recovered through increased taxes paid because of higher earnings, and 24 cents was saved because of reduced costs of welfare. But the biggest return— nearly six dollars for every dollar spent in 1992—was through decreases in justice-system and crime-victim costs (Barnett, 1992; Schweinhart et al., 1993).

■ Assessing the Effects of Child-Care Arrangements in Canada

The CAP, H/SPPP, and several other studies have demonstrated the benefits of high-quality preschool "compensatory" programs that have predominantly served disadvantaged children and their families. We do not know whether similar benefits could be realized for disadvantaged children in Canada, and we know relatively little about the effects of child-care attendance on non-disadvantaged children. Many parents face the choice of hiring a babysitter or nanny, making an informal arrangement with a neighbour or relative, or placing their child in a family daycare or daycare centre. Some informal arrangements have even lower child-to-adult ratios than daycare centres, and in many cases the caregivers are well trained and experienced. Thus, we expect that the effects of child-care arrangements probably vary more within types of arrangements than between them (Goelman, Doherty, Lero, LaGrange, & Tougas, 2000).

The NLSCY affords the opportunity to examine the kinds of child-care arrangements used by Canadian parents with differing socioeconomic backgrounds. Few studies have examined child-care use with a nationally representative sample of children, because measures of child-care use, family characteristics, and children's developmental outcomes are rarely collected simultaneously. (For exceptions, see Ruopp, Travers, Glantz, & Coelen, 1979; Whitebook, Howes, & Phillips, 1989).

Our analysis also examines whether children's competencies differ across types of care arrangements, before and after adjusting for family structure and parents' socioeconomic status (SES). The adjusted estimates could be interpreted as *effects* of child-care arrangements on children's competencies, but we refrain from doing so, as there are undoubtedly selection processes determining parents' choices that are not captured by our control measures (see Raudenbush & Willms, 1995). For example, it may be that the parents of children with behaviour problems tend to prefer licensed daycare over family daycare, or perhaps they find it easier to place their child in a licensed daycare. If this were the case, our cross-sectional analyses of the NLSCY data would indicate that there was a disproportionate number of children with behaviour problems in licensed daycare centres, but it would be incorrect to infer that behaviour problems were due to attendance at a licensed daycare. This limitation is inherent to any study in which children are not randomly assigned to types of care arrangements. Stronger inferences regarding effects will be possible when the longitudinal data become available, but even then selection bias will remain a threat to validity. Therefore, the findings of this research need to be interpreted in conjunction with the findings of experimental studies of daycare quality. One of the strengths of this research is that it provides a description of the competencies of children across care arrangements in natural, rather than experimental, settings. The findings provide a foundation for a large-scale experimental study of daycare quality.

■ Method

The study entailed three sets of analyses. The sample for the first two was limited to children aged four and five, because it is for this group that we have scores on the Peabody Picture Vocabulary Test-Revised (PPVT-R). The PPVT-R has strong psychometric properties (Dunn & Dunn, 1981); it correlates well with measures of intelligence, particularly verbal subscales, and is a very good predictor of achievement. We excluded a small number of children who had already begun grade one. The third analysis includes all children from birth to age five.

The first analysis examines the kinds of child-care arrangements used by Canadian families with preschoolers. It distinguishes among *regulated daycare*, which is usually provided in a licensed daycare centre, but includes also licensed family daycare; *unregulated care in the home* by a sitter or nanny; *unregulated care outside the home*, such as a family daycare; and *care by a relative*, either inside or outside the home. The sample sizes in the NLSCY were too small to distinguish between in-home care by a brother or sister, rather than some other relative, or between care by a relative offered in the home versus someone else's home. The residual category, *no other care arrangement*, includes families where at least one parent was staying at home to provide care, as well as those families that did not require a care arrangement, even though one or both parents were working or studying.

The second set of analyses uses regression techniques to assess differences in children's competencies among types of daycare arrangements. Separate models are estimated for each of four outcomes: pro-social behaviour, PPVT-R scores, whether the child had a behaviour problem, and whether the child had a PPVT-R score at or below 85. The latter two variables are dichotomous, and therefore logistic regression was used.

These analyses are somewhat complicated because many children attend pre-kindergarten at age four in Ontario and Quebec, and kindergarten at age five in most of the other provinces. Pre-kindergarten and kindergarten could be treated as regulated care. We considered including them as a separate form of care arrangement, but we found that many parents used daycare centres, family daycare, and other care arrangements in conjunction with pre-kindergarten and kindergarten, so including them as a primary care arrangement was impractical. Consequently, rather than estimating the overall relationship for all provinces combined, we used hierarchical-linear modelling to estimate the relationships *within* each province and the average *within-province* relationship. In fitting the hierarchical regression models, we initially included

Table 15.1

Child-care arrangements for Canadian preschoolers

	Children in child care		Average family income	Years mother's education	Percent single parent	Number of hours in care
	Number	Percent				
Unregulated care						
• In the home	47,400	6.1	$60,800	14.5	9.5	24.4
• Outside the home	112,300	14.5	$58,200	14.4	9.4	22.0
Regulated daycare	94,700	12.2	$52,900	14.0	24.8	26.2
Care by a relative	56,300	7.3	$50,300	13.9	14.2	22.0
No other care arrangement	463,300	59.9	$41,600	13.5	16.8	

variables denoting attendance in pre-kindergarten and kindergarten. However, their inclusion did not substantially affect our estimates of differences among care arrangements, and therefore we excluded them from the model.

The findings from these regression analyses indicate that children from lower-income families who attend care facilities outside the home tend to have superior vocabulary scores than those cared for at home. Thus, the third set of analyses is concerned with the feasibility of providing licensed daycare to all families with incomes below $35,000. We include pre-kindergarten and kindergarten in this analysis, and provide separate estimates for Quebec, Ontario, and the other eight provinces combined.

■ The Use of Child-Care Arrangements

The number and percentage of children in various child care arrangements are displayed in Table 15.1. Only about four of every ten children at ages four or five are cared for on a regular basis by someone other than their parents or guardians. The majority of these children are cared for outside the home in unregulated daycare centres (14.5 percent of all children) or in licensed daycare centres (12.2 percent of all children). Unregulated care in the home (e.g., a babysitter or nanny) accounts for 6.1 percent of preschoolers; 7.3 percent of preschoolers are cared for by a relative.

Table 15.1 also shows the average family income, level of the mother's education, and the percentage of single parents for each type of care arrangement. Families using unregulated care in the home have the highest average family income — $60,800 for those using in-home care, and $58,200 for those using out-of-home care. The average income of those using regulated daycare is $52,900, which is about $5,300 above the average family income for the full population. Those who used care by a relative or who had no other care arrangement had the lowest levels of income, $50,300 and $41,600 respectively. Similarly, the average level of the mother's education was higher for families whose children were in either regulated or unregulated care, compared with children cared for by a relative, or by one or both of the parents.

The pattern was different, however, with respect to the percentage of single parents. Only 9.5 percent of the children in unregulated in-home care were from single-parent families, and 9.4 percent of those in unregulated care outside the home were from single-parent families. These results are consistent with the results pertaining to family income. The striking difference, though, is that nearly one in four children in regulated daycare settings were from single-parent families. Of children cared for by a relative, 14.2 percent were from single-parent families, and 16.8 percent of those cared for at home by a parent were from single parent families.

The last column of Table 15.1 displays the average number of hours per week in care arrangements other than "no care" arrangements. The time spent in care arrangements was highest for regulated daycare settings—on average 26.2 hours per week. The average time for unregulated in-home care was slightly lower—24.4 hours per week—and for unregulated care outside the home, and care by a relative, the average time was only 22 hours per week.

■ **Differences in Social and Cognitive Outcomes**

Table 15.2 displays differences among types of care arrangements in the average levels of children's pro-social behaviour and vocabulary skills, before and after adjusting for family background and the child's sex. In these analyses, *no other care arrangement* was used as the reference category, such that the regression coefficients indicate differences between no other care and the designated care arrangement.

The coefficients for pro-social behaviour (Model I) indicate that the lowest scores were for children in licensed daycare settings; the highest scores were for children in unregulated in-home care and in the care of a relative. The difference between regulated care and these other two types of arrangements was about half a point on the ten-point scale and was statistically significant. However, the difference between licensed daycare and no other arrangement

Table 15.2

Differences in social and cognitive outcomes by type of care arrangements

	Social and cognitive skills (regression coefficients)				Markers of vulnerability (likelihood ratios)			
	Pro-social behaviour		Preschool vocabulary		Behaviour problem		Low vocabulary	
	I	II	I	II	I	II	I	II
Socioeconomic status								
• Income		-0.02		**1.15**		1.02		**0.86**
• Income-squared		0.02		**-0.13**		1.02		0.86
• Mother's education		**0.04**		**1.10**		0.95		**0.84**
Family structure, sex								
• Single parent		-0.27		-0.12		**1.63**		1.19
• Number of siblings		**-0.19**		**-1.54**		0.91		**1.21**
• Female		**0.65**		0.29		1.07		0.92
Type of care (no other)	5.72	5.72	98.98	102.00				
• Unregulated care								
- In the home	0.24	0.20	**3.31**	0.16	0.97	1.07	**0.64**	1.01
- Outside the home	-0.01	-0.10	**2.78**	-0.35	0.87	0.96	**0.64**	1.08
• Licensed daycare	-0.23	-0.33	**1.81**	-1.09	1.21	1.16	**0.60**	0.98
• Care by a relative	0.24	0.18	**1.68**	-0.40	0.88	0.92	**0.73**	0.88

Note: Reported estimates are the average within-province estimates derived from fitting hierarchical linear models. In these models, the reference category is "No other care arrangement," against which other care arrangements are compared. Coefficients that are statistically significant (p<0.05) appear in boldface. For preschool vocabulary skills, significant interaction terms with income (and income-squared) indicate that the effects associated with these types of care depended on family income. The estimated effects are shown in Figure 15.1.

was not significant, nor was the difference between no other arrangement and in-home care or care by a relative. These differences change only slightly when the controls for background are added to the regression (Model II).

In the case of preschool vocabulary skills as measured by the PPVT-R, children in all four types of care arrangements had superior vocabulary skills on average compared to those cared for at home by at least one parent. The differences are fairly large, ranging from 1.7 to 3.3 points. However, the pattern changes entirely when controls for SES and family structure are added to the model. On average, the vocabulary skills of children cared for at home did not differ significantly from those of children in other care arrangements, once family background was taken into account.

Figure 15.1

Preschoolers' vocabulary scores by family income and child-care arrangement

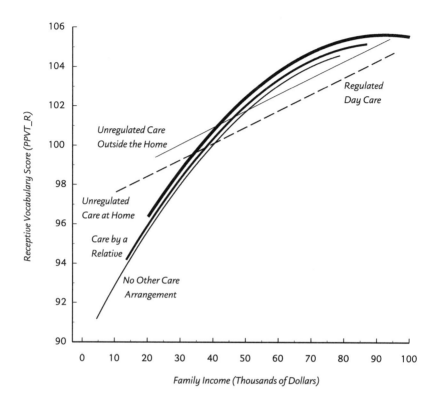

However, we found that the differences associated with regulated daycare and unregulated care outside the home depended on family income. Therefore the model was extended to include interaction terms for income and income-squared. The findings of this analysis are displayed in Figure 15.1. The figure shows that children from families with incomes below $35,000, who are cared for in either regulated or unregulated settings outside the home, tend to have superior vocabulary skills to those who are either cared for at home by a relative or one of the parents. (Relatively few children from families with incomes below $35,000 were in the care of someone at home other than a relative or parent.)

The pattern of results for the two markers of vulnerability were similar in most respects. There were no statistically significant differences across the various types of care arrangements in the likelihood of a child being considered to have a behaviour problem. However, children who did not participate in care arrangements were significantly more likely to have a PPVT score below 85 than those cared for in some other arrangement. These differences were small and not statistically significant, once family background was taken into account.

■ Children's Participation in Regulated Care

There are at least two plausible explanations for the results displayed in Figure 15.1. One is that low-income families whose children have lower verbal skills are more likely to care for their children at home than to place their child in family daycare or in a licensed facility. The other possibility is that attendance at a daycare centre has a positive effect on their vocabulary skills.

Either way, it suggests that many vulnerable children may lack sufficient exposure to the quantity and quality of language necessary to develop their verbal skills. Two important policy questions are whether the widespread provision of subsidized daycare and pre-kindergarten for children from low-income families would reduce the extent of vulnerability among young children, and if so, how much would it cost. Table 15.3 provides estimates of the percentages of children participating in licensed care for children from infancy to age five. Quebec offers state-funded pre-kindergarten in certain areas for children in low-income families; in Ontario, pre-kindergarten is offered in many school districts. Thus, the analysis is conducted separately for these two provinces.

In Quebec, about seven percent of infants and babies from low income families participated in some form of licensed care, and the percentage is only slightly higher for families with incomes above $35,000. For children aged 2 and 3, 11.6 percent of those in low-income families participated in licensed care, compared with 21 percent for families with higher incomes. At age four, the percentage increases because of pre-kindergarten. Among low income families, 31.4 percent participated in licensed daycare or kindergarten, and the percentage is almost double that for families with higher incomes. At age 5, 22.2 percent of the children from low-income families do not participate in licensed care, either in kindergarten or in a licensed daycare. About 9.2 percent of children from higher-income families do not participate in licensed care or kindergarten. These results are based on data collected in 1994–95. We expect that these patterns would look different today because of the Quebec initiative to offer daycare at five dollars per day.

In Ontario, the percentages of infants and babies in licensed care is similar to Quebec. But at ages two and three, a higher proportion of low-income fami-

Table 15.3

Percentage of children receiving regulated care by child's age and family income

	Quebec				Ontario			
	0–1	2–3	4	5	0–1	2–3	4	5
Family income $35,000 or less								
• No regulated care	92.9	88.4	68.6	22.2	92.4	83.6	24.9	0.5
• Licensed daycare[1]	7.1	11.6	11.4	3.1	7.6	16.4	2.1	0.5
• Kindergarten[2]			20.0	74.7			73.0	99.1
Number of children (000s)	81	85	39	42	109	116	65	44
Family income above $35,000								
• No regulated care	91.3	79.0	42.5	9.2	91.6	87.0	26.3	4.3
• Licensed daycare[1]	8.7	21.3	18.0	5.0	8.4	13.0	4.6	
• Kindergarten[2]			39.4	85.7			69.1	95.7
Number of children (000s)	97	104	61	46	176	178	95	95

Note 1: Does not include children who were also in pre-kindergarten or kindergarten.

Note 2: Includes children who were in either pre-kindergarten or kindergarten.

lies participated in licensed care in Ontario than in Quebec, and a lower proportion of higher income families participated in licensed care. At age four, about three-quarters of the children in Ontario were participating in some form of licensed care, and nearly all of these were in a pre-kindergarten rather than a licensed daycare setting. This attendance pattern was similar for both income groups. By age 5, only 1 percent of the children from low-income families and 4.3 percent of the children from higher-income families were not attending licensed daycare or kindergarten programs.

The results for the rest of Canada stand in sharp contrast to those of Quebec and Ontario. Among children from low-income families, the proportions of infants, babies, and toddlers participating in licensed care does not differ substantially from the proportions for Quebec and Ontario. But the results differ dramatically for children aged four and five. Over 80 percent of children aged 4 did not participate in licensed care or kindergarten. At age 5, 16.6 percent of children from low-income families and 9.4 percent of children from higher-income families did not participate in licensed care or kindergarten programs.

Table 15.3 (*cont.*)

Percentage of children receiving regulated care by child's age and family income

	Rest of Canada			
	0–1	2–3	4	5
Family income $35,000 or less				
• No regulated care	95.7	90.1	81.3	16.6
• Licensed daycare[1]	4.3	9.9	11.6	1.5
• Kindergarten[2]			7.1	81.9
Number of children (000s)	126	124	67	63
Family income above $35,000				
• No regulated care	94.1	85.7	83.4	9.4
• Licensed daycare[1]	5.9	14.3	11.8	2.0
• Kindergarten[2]			4.8	88.6
Number of children (000s)	147	160	81	75

Note 1: Does not include children who were also in pre-kindergarten or kindergarten.
Note 2: Includes children who were in either pre-kindergarten or kindergarten.

■ Summary and Policy Implications

Research on quality in daycare centres has emphasized the importance of three factors: low child-to-adult ratios, highly educated staff with specialized training, and the availability of resources to provide stimulating activities. High-quality daycare centres increase children's linguistic, cognitive, and social competencies, and has long-lasting benefits for children from low-income families. Investments in daycare for vulnerable children have large returns over time because they can result in less unemployment and dependence on social welfare, increased tax revenue, and reduced crime.

This study examines the child-care situations of Canadian children and asks whether children in different types of care arrangements differ in their social and cognitive skills. The NLSCY asked parents about their primary care arrangement. From their answers, we can determine the characteristics of children and parents in different child-care arrangements. Our analysis provides estimates of differences among children who received different types of care, both before and after taking account of the children's family background. Three important findings emerged from the analysis.

1. *Forty percent of Canadian children aged four and five spend part of their week in some type of care arrangement while their parents study or work outside the home. Unregulated care outside the home (i.e., family daycare) is the most prevalent form of care arrangement (see Table 15.1).* Only about 12.2 percent of Canadian preschoolers attend a licensed daycare, compared with 14.5 percent in unregulated care outside the home. About 6.1 percent are cared for at home by a non-relative and 7.3 percent are cared for by a relative. Canadians' preference for unregulated care may be driven by several factors, including cost, availability, size, and flexibility. Although licensing does not ensure quality care, it mandates safety standards and ensures that facilities meet criteria for child-to-adult ratios, staff training, and resources. Licensed daycare centres normally have a prescribed curriculum for developing children's cognitive, motor, and social skills. If we are to improve the overall quality of daycare provision in Canada, we need to increase the number of licensed daycares and ensure these centres can compete equally with family daycare.

2. *Children from low-income families who are cared for in facilities outside the home, either regulated or unregulated, have superior vocabulary skills to those who do not participate in care arrangements (see Figure 15.1).* This study cannot determine whether these differences are a direct result of children's attendance in child care programs or are due to subtle selection processes on the part of either parents or early childhood educators. However, given the results of controlled studies on the effects of quality daycare centres for disadvantaged children, and the findings in Chapter 3, which emphasize the importance of exposure to language, we expect that at least some of these differences are attributable to attendance at daycare centres.

    The differences are substantial: for families with incomes of $15,000, the difference is about 4 points on the PPVT-R test. In the acclaimed High/Scope Perry Preschool Program, children who had participated in the two-year program had, at age six, IQ scores five points above children in the control group. Although gains in IQ did not persist beyond age fourteen, the preschool children had higher achievement tests scores and lower failure rates throughout school. The estimate in this study is probably a lower bound on the effects of quality care, because it is the average effect associated with many different types of daycare centres. There is undoubtedly large variation among daycare centres in their quality, just as there is among elementary and secondary schools (Goelman et al., 2000; Willms, 2001).

3. *Despite the importance of quality care for disadvantaged children, less than half of Canadian four-year-olds from low-income families attend licensed daycare centres or pre-kindergarten programs. The provision of kindergarten for five-year-old children varies by province and is far from being universal (see Table 15.3).* There are about 100,000 4-year-olds and 20,000 5-year-olds in low-income families who do not receive any form of regulated care. If the annual cost of regulated care is about $4000 per child, then achieving universal care for low-income families would cost about half a billion dollars annually.

All children need rich and stimulating experiences, particularly in early childhood, to support healthy development. The findings from this study suggest the importance of making high-quality care arrangements available to all Canadian children who need them, particularly as the number of dual-earner families continues to increase. Controversies between maternal care versus organized care for children continue to rage. At present, many families cannot choose the care arrangements they would prefer for their young children, particularly if both parents work outside the home. There are not enough spaces at high-quality daycares to accommodate all children, and waiting lists are common. Quality care arrangements need to be made accessible and affordable so that all children can participate, regardless of race, ethnic background, level of competence, or ability to pay.

Universal programs of high-quality care would offer certain advantages (Offord, Kraemer, Kazdin, Jensin, & Harrington, 1998), including an established and consistent level of quality, the ease of obtaining public support (as opposed to targeted programs aimed at helping vulnerable children or children from poor families), and the potential for all children to participate. Scandinavian countries have set an example. In Sweden, 86 percent of women with children are employed, and child-care services are regulated, supervised, and standardized by the government. As a result, child care is provided to nearly half (47 percent) of all children prior to commencing formal education at age 7. In Sweden, participation in child care is associated with benefits for children, and early participation shows the most extensive benefits (Andersson, 1989; 1992). Some provinces, such as Quebec and BC, are phasing in funding models that should make high-quality care programs available to all children by offering affordable care arrangements. Since data for the present study is from 1994, prior to the implementation of these changes, our comparisons do not take the Quebec initiative into account. Future work will examine these changes more closely.

To achieve a national standard of quality and universal access to child care for those Canadian families who require or choose to use them, we need to coordinate the development and implementation of child care services across the provinces. This goal includes establishing consistent training and educational requirements for caregivers and consistent licensing requirements for high-quality care environments, as well as making a commitment to monitoring programs and collecting information in a coherent and coordinated way.

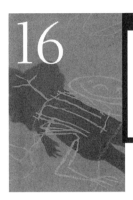

Can School Quality Compensate for Socioeconomic Disadvantage?

GEORGE FREMPONG
& J. DOUGLAS WILLMS

EDUCATORS AND RESEARCHERS have long directed their attention at improving schooling systems to ensure positive outcomes for all students. They believe that the skills and experiences needed for success in life require basic school knowledge such as reading and mathematics. The equitable distribution of this knowledge among the general population, especially among groups with differing socioeconomic status, is essential for a society's overall productivity and cohesion. Educators have emphasized the learning opportunities schools provide for students to acquire this knowledge. They contend that "quality schools" can make a difference in children's outcomes.

Educational researchers have attempted to identify quality schools by asking whether some schools are more effective than others on children's learning and, if so, what factors contribute to a school's success. In the late 1960s, a landmark study of educational opportunity in the US suggested that most of the variation in the academic achievement of schools was attributable to students' family background (Coleman, Campbell, Hobson, McPartland, Mood, Weinfeld, & York, 1966). The press popularized the findings, stating that "schools don't make a difference." This spawned a small industry of educational research aimed at examining whether some schools were more effective than others. Researchers attributed the findings to weaknesses in the design and analytical approach (Bowles & Levin, 1968). During the 1970s and 1980s, advances in educational measurement, research design, and statistical modelling enabled researchers to claim conclusively that schools do indeed differ significantly in their effect on children's outcomes (Raudenbush & Willms, 1991). Research during the 1990s was devoted to discerning why some schools perform better than others.

In an attempt to improve the quality of their schools, local and national governments have developed programs to monitor the effectiveness of their schools and schooling systems. Monitoring typically entails annual or biennial achievement testing at particular grade levels. In the US, these efforts have been supported by legislation which calls for "standards-based reform": states are required to prescribe standards in all subject areas, specify in detail the skills and curricular content that students are expected to learn, and measure students' performance against these standards (Rothman, 1995; Rothman & Elmore, 1998; Willms, 2001). In Canada, there is no national government body responsible for education. The provinces and territories have constitutional jurisdiction over education; the federal role is limited to transfer payments to the provinces. Thus, each province has its own assessment system. In most cases, these entail some form of province-wide testing at two or three grade levels in mathematics, science, and the language arts. Demographic data are usually limited to the child's sex. The aim of these systems is to assess whether the achievement of learning outcomes in a province is changing over time, whether there are specific aspects of the curriculum that are not being implemented success-fully, and how individual schools and school districts are performing relative to provincial norms. Such information can be useful to school, district, and provincial administrators for making day-to-day decisions about the allocation of resources, the efficacy of certain programs, and the strengths and weak-nesses of their systems. However, as is the case with performance-based assessment, routine monitoring is believed to encourage a process of self-exam-ination and to motivate educators to provide a better education (Willms, 1992).

The federal government has provided impetus to realize a national assess-ment of school achievement by supporting the efforts of the Council of Ministers of Education, Canada (CMEC) in the development of the Student Achievement Indicators Program (SAIP) (CMEC, 1997). However, like the provincial monitoring systems, the SAIP does not include demographic data on students' ethnicity or family background. Consequently, the data have been used largely to make interprovincial comparisons. The SAIP also does not provide a means to assess the extent of variation among Canadian schools in their performance or address questions about why some schools or schooling systems outperform others.

The National Longitudinal Survey of Children and Youth (NLSCY) can provide some indication of the variation among Canadian schools in their academic achievement, but it is limited because the sample design was not based on a random sample of schools. The measure of academic achievement in the first wave included only a brief test of mathematical computation skills, which does not adequately cover the mathematics curriculum. In 1994, when the baseline data for the NLSCY were collected, Canada also participated in the Third International Mathematics and Science Study (TIMSS; Robitaille, Taylor, & Orpwood, 1996) and the International Adult Literacy Survey (IALS; OECD & Statistics Canada, 1995). The TIMSS sample design was school-based and covered three populations of students: grades three and four (referred to as Population A), grades seven and eight (Population B), and the final year of high school, which in most provinces is grade twelve (Population C). The strengths of the TIMSS are that the mathematics test is comprehensive (Schmidt et al., 1996), covering several achievement domains, and the questionnaires administered to the principal and classroom teacher include a number of school and classroom factors (Gonzalez & Smith, 1997). Its weakness as a study of school effects is that only one classroom was sampled per grade level, and therefore estimates of school effects are less accurate. The IALS was not designed as a study of school effectiveness either; however, because it includes a general, less curriculum-specific measure of quantitative literacy skills, it can indicate the distribution of skills after students have completed their formal schooling.

Despite the limitations of these various national and international studies, together they can provide a portrait of successful schools and schooling systems in Canada. This study has five aims. First, it asks whether the prevalence of vulnerable children varies significantly among classrooms, schools, and provinces, before and after adjusting for students' family background. Second, it examines the extent of variation among provinces in their mathematics achievement, based on data from the NLSCY, the SAIP, the TIMSS, and the IALS. In this analysis, the emphasis is on average levels of mathematics achievement rather than the prevalence of children scoring below the threshold set to define vulnerability. Third, it asks whether schools and classrooms vary in their average levels of mathematics achievement, and if so, whether some of this variation is attributable to the family background characteristics of the students enrolled in them. This analysis also provides a test of the hypothesis of converging gradients, and the hypothesis of double jeopardy (see Chapter 2). Fourth, it asks whether some of the variation among schools and classes can be accounted for by various school and classroom factors, including structural features of the schools and teaching practices. Finally, the analysis assesses whether some of the interprovincial variation in mathematics achievement can be accounted for by the school and classroom processes measured in this study.

■ Review of the Literature

The research on why student outcomes vary among schools has been based on the theory of economic production functions (Bridge, Judd, & Moock, 1979; Lau, 1979; Levin, 1980). The theory presumes that schooling outcomes are largely determined by family influences and children's experiences at school, and that the latter are the result of school resources, structural features of the schooling system, school policies, and classroom practice (Raudenbush & Willms, 1995). The aim of a production function analysis is typically to estimate the proportion of variance associated with factors pertaining to the quality of schooling, separate from factors associated with students' family background. The tacit belief is that if researchers can identify the most important factors affecting student learning, school districts and governments will be able to improve academic achievement by investing in these factors (Willms, 1992).

The early studies of school effectiveness based on economic production functions used traditional multiple regression techniques (see Coleman et al., 1966; Jencks et al., 1972). These techniques are limited in that they do not provide an estimate of the effects associated with particular schools or their socioeconomic gradients, which are essential to the assessment of excellence and equity in schooling. The recent advances in statistical modelling provide a framework for estimating "school effects" and "gradients," and discerning which factors contribute to excellence and equity (Raudenbush & Bryk, 1988; Willms & Raudenbush, 1994). The term "school effect" is used to denote the difference between a school's mean level of achievement and some standard, after taking account of the initial ability and the socioeconomic background of students attending the school (Raudenbush & Willms, 1995). The standard is typically the average score for a district or the provincial or national average. The term "gradient" is used to refer to the relationship between a schooling outcome and socioeconomic status (SES).

The approach to analysis is to address four questions: to what extent schools vary in their outcomes, to what degree schooling outcomes vary for pupils of differing status, which school policies and practices improve levels of schooling outcomes, and which school policies and practices reduce inequalities in outcomes between high- and low-status groups (Willms, 1992, p. 120). The first question can be extended to ask to what extent schools vary in their attainment of schooling outcomes, after adjusting for pupils' SES and prior ability—that is, how large are school effects? The second question can be extended to ask whether gradients vary among schools, and if so, whether the gradients converge at higher levels of SES.

Research in several countries has shown that the schools children attend make a difference to their academic achievement, even after account is taken of the child's family background and ability upon entering school (Gray, 1989; Raudenbush & Willms, 1991). What is less clear is the magnitude of this difference. Results from the US National Longitudinal Study of Children and Youth for grade-eight students suggest that when schools with similar levels of mean SES are compared, there is a range of at least one full standard deviation between the best- and worst-performing schools (Ho & Willms, 1996). At this grade level, one standard deviation is equivalent to about one and a half to two years of schooling (for example, see Martin & Hoover, 1987). Willms and Jacobsen (1990) examined children's rate of growth in mathematics skills between grades three and seven for an entire cohort of students attending thirty-one elementary schools in one BC school district. The rate at which students acquire academic skills is a strong indicator of school performance (Willms, 2001). They found that by the end of grade seven, a student with average ability attending one of the three best-performing schools in the district was more than a full year of schooling ahead of comparable children attending one of the three worst-performing schools. Taking these findings together, we could conclude that the school a child attends makes a difference of at least one grade level by the end of elementary school.

Researchers have been relatively successful in determining why some schools achieve better outcomes than others. Their research has emphasized the importance of the learning environment in the classroom, rather than general school-level factors. For example, Lee and Smith (1993) found that variation in levels of middle-school performance was partially attributable to aspects of the school associated with "restructuring," such as reduced departmentalization, heterogeneous grouping, and team teaching. Ho & Willms (1996) found that parents' participation in school activities had a positive effect on the achievement scores of eighth-grade students in the US; Willms and Somers (2001) found similar effects associated with the disciplinary climate of the school. Other research has emphasized the concept of "academic press," which describes schools where principals and teachers project the belief that all students can master the curriculum. Their high expectations are manifest in a number of teaching practices and school routines, including homework practices, the content and pace of the curriculum, and how time and resources are used in the classroom (Anderson, 1985; Dreeben & Gamoran, 1986; Plewis, 1991; Scheerens, 1992). The literature does not offer strong support for more general school-level factors, such as teachers' credentials or school resources.

Willms (2001) used 1996 data for New Brunswick from the Elementary School Climate Study to examine the extent of variation in schooling outcomes among classrooms, schools, and school districts. These data were derived from questionnaires administered to the full population of grade-six students and to all elementary and middle-school teachers. The student questionnaire included measures of four affective schooling outcomes: self-esteem, general well-being, sense of belonging, and general health. The questionnaire data were merged with students' test scores in mathematics, reading, science, and writing, which were based on provincially standardized tests administered biennially by the NB Department of Education. The findings indicated that the majority of variation was among pupils within classrooms; that is, students' scores within classes tend to be relatively heterogeneous compared with the variation from class to class, or school to school. What was striking, though, is that for every outcome measure, there was considerably more variation among classrooms within schools than among schools within school districts. For example, 7 percent of the variation in mathematics scores was among classrooms, compared with only 4.7 percent among schools and 1.8 percent among school districts. The results for science and writing scores were similar, with slightly more variation among classrooms and less variation among schools. In the case of reading, over 90 percent of the variation was among pupils within classrooms; of the remaining variance, the majority was at the classroom level. The same results were evident for the four affective measures. These results are consistent with the findings of other studies of school effectiveness, which suggest that what goes on in a child's classroom is far more important than features of the school or school district.

Relatively few studies have examined variation among schools in their socioeconomic gradients. Part of the problem is that most studies do not collect data from enough students within schools to estimate gradients accurately. Lee and Bryk (1989) examined variation among US secondary schools in their gradients. They found that schools not only varied in their socioeconomic gradients but also in the achievement gap between minority and non-minority students. The variation was associated with various aspects of academic organization.

School size was also important: small schools with less "differentiation in mathematics course taking" tended to have shallower gradients. As part of an investigation of the effects of parental involvement, Ho and Willms (1996) constructed a nationally standardized measure of SES, and estimated the within-school socioeconomic gradients for mathematics and reading across more than 1000 middle schools. The average slope of the socioeconomic gradients for reading was 0.25. In schools with high levels of parental involvement, the average gradient was relatively gradual—0.21—compared with 0.29 for schools with low levels of parental involvement. However, parental involvement did not have a comparable effect for mathematics. Willms and Kerckhoff (1995) used hierarchical linear models to estimate the socioeconomic gradients for 148 Local Education Authorities (LEAs) in the UK, based on data from the National Child Development Study (NCDS) describing pupils' reading and mathematics achievement and their overall level of examination attainment. They found some significant positive effects associated with lower pupil–teacher ratios and less selective LEAs, but the factors were unrelated to socioeconomic gradients. Taken together, these studies provide convincing evidence that gradients vary among schools and school districts, but it is difficult to achieve a powerful enough research design to discern why gradients are steep or shallow in particular schools. The hypothesis that socioeconomic gradients converge at higher levels of SES has not been systematically examined.

A number of studies have shown that the ability and SES of a child's classmates can have a substantial effect on the child's learning outcomes, over and above the effects associated with the child's own ability and socioeconomic background. When children are segregated, either between schools through residential segregation or by the "creaming" of the most able pupils into selective schools (e.g., private schools or charter schools), between classes through tracking or streaming, or within classes through ability grouping, children from advantaged backgrounds do better, while those from disadvantaged backgrounds do considerably worse.[1] Sociologists initially attributed these "contextual effects" to peer interactions; however, other factors likely contribute to this phenomenon. Schools with a high proportion of advantaged students tend to receive greater support from parents, and it is much easier for teachers to maintain high expectations and establish the kind of learning environment conducive to high academic achievement—a positive disciplinary climate, a fast-paced curriculum, and an effective use of learning time. What is less clear is whether the effects of the school and classroom context are equally strong for advantaged and disadvantaged students alike. The concept of double jeopardy suggests that when children from low-SES families are segregated in school settings where the majority of other children also have low SES, they are doubly disadvantaged: their academic achievement tends to be low because of their individual family background, and it is further hampered by their classroom or school context. It may also be that when students with high ability or SES are placed in low ability or low-SES settings, their schooling outcomes suffer. The strength of contextual effects, and the extent to which they interact with students' individual characteristics, is extremely important as it affects the manner in which students are allocated to schools, classrooms, and instructional groups.

■ Methods and Results

The research methods and analyses in this chapter are relatively complex compared with those in most other chapters, as they involve several data sets and the use of hierarchical linear modelling with both dichotomous and continuous outcome measures. Thus, to simplify the presentation, we have organized the chapter according to the five questions set out in the introduction and have presented the methods and results together for each topic (refer to Chapters 3 and 4 for a discussion of methods).

Does the prevalence of vulnerable children vary significantly among classrooms, schools, and provinces?

To answer this question, we used data from the NLSCY and the Third International Mathematics and Science Study (TIMSS; see Sidebar 16.1). The research questions look at children who are vulnerable because they have exceeding low mathematics scores. In the case of the NLSCY, vulnerability was defined as those who had scored at least 75 points below their peers, which is roughly the same as being one and a half years behind in schooling (see Chapter 3). For the TIMSS, we set vulnerability as being below the tenth percentile on the full mathematics test.

We used a logistic regression analysis to assess the magnitude of differences among the provinces in the proportion of children deemed vulnerable, before and after controlling for SES, gender, and immigrant status. The outcome was a dichotomous measure denoting whether or not the child had an exceedingly low mathematics score. The independent variables used for the NLSCY included SES, sex of the child, and immigrant status (the construction of these

Sidebar 16.1

The Third International
Mathematics and Science Study

Our analysis used data from the Third International Mathematics and Science Study (TIMSS), drawing from the Population B sample for Canada, which includes information describing more than 16,000 students and their teachers and principals. The data were collected in Spring 1995, at the same time as the NLSCY data were collected. The achievement test in mathematics includes 128 multiple-choice items and 23 constructed-response items, which cover a broad range of mathematical concepts. In order to examine a breadth of content while minimizing testing time, the TIMSS developed eight test booklets (i.e., rotated forms); each student completed one booklet. Six provinces (BC, Alberta, Ontario, Quebec, New Brunswick, and Newfoundland) participated as "member countries" in the TIMSS. For further details, see Beaton et al. (1996) and Robitaille et al. (1996).

variables is described in Chapter 4). The same set of independent variables was used for the TIMSS; however, the measure of immigrant status was not separated into categories describing the length of time the family had been in Canada. The measure of SES was a statistical composite of the level of education of the child's parents and a count of the number of educationally related materials in the home, such as books and computers.

Table 16.1 presents the results of the multilevel regression analysis. First, we consider the unadjusted results. Each school (or classroom, in the case of the TIMSS) has a certain prevalence of vulnerable children, which could range from zero to one hundred percent. The estimate of the average prevalence across all schools in the NLSCY is 10.1 percent; for the TIMSS, it is 10.6 percent. These results reflect the pre-defined criteria established for vulnerability in each study. The research question, however, is whether prevalence varies significantly among schools. The statistical modelling provides estimates of the variance components, which include an estimate of the variance of the prevalence estimates among schools. However, for a multilevel logistic regression, these are difficult to interpret. Thus, we used the results to estimate a "low prevalence," which is the estimated prevalence for a school that was one standard deviation below the average for all schools, and a "high prevalence," which is the estimated prevalence for a school which was one standard deviation

Table 16.1

Variation among schools in the prevalence of children with low mathematics scores

	NLSCY (297 schools)		TIMSS (775 classes)	
	Unadjusted	Adjusted	Unadjusted	Adjusted
Average likelihood (%)	10.1	9.6	10.6	9.7
Child level (odds ratio)				
• Socioeconomic status		**0.66**		**0.62**
• Female		0.89		1.05
• Immigrant				**1.64**
- Less than 5 years ago		0.80		
- 5 to 10 years ago		0.47		
- More than 10 years ago		1.19		
Variation among schools				
• Low prevalence (%)	7.1	6.7	5.2	5.1
• High prevalence (%)	14.4	13.6	20.5	17.6

Note: Odds ratios that differ significantly from 1.0 (p<0.05) appear in boldface.

above the average for all schools. Roughly two-thirds of schools would fall between these extremes. The range of prevalence estimates for these extremes ranges from 7.1 percent to 14.4 percent for schools in the NLSCY, and from 5.2 percent to 20.5 percent for classes in the TIMSS. This variation is statistically significant and clearly important in substantive terms.

The adjusted models in Table 16.1 include SES, sex of the child, and immigrant status as covariates. These factors reduce the range of prevalence estimates, but only slightly. The adjusted ranges are 6.7 percent to 13.6 percent for the NLSCY, and 5.1 percent to 17.6 percent for the TIMSS. This means that the variation in the prevalence of vulnerable children that we observe from school to school, or class to class, is only attributable to SES to a small degree.

The model also furnishes estimates of the odds ratios associated with the covariates. The odds ratio associated with an increase of 1 standard deviation in SES was 0.66 for the NLSCY, and 0.62 for TIMSS, indicating that children from low-SES families are more likely to have exceedingly low achievement in mathematics. This is remarkably consistent; however, the results for the two studies differ in their estimates associated with immigrant status. In the

Table 16.2

Variation among provinces in the prevalence of children with low
mathematics scores

	NLSCY		TIMSS	
	Unadjusted	Adjusted	Unadjusted	Adjusted
Average likelihood (%)	9.1	8.7	9.9	8.8
Variation among provinces				
• Newfoundland	11.8	9.3	14.8	12.2
• Nova Scotia	10.8	9.7		
• Prince Edward Island	9.5	7.8		
• New Brunswick	11.6	9.8	13.1	11.9
• Quebec	7.6	6.8	3.2	2.3
• Ontario	9.6	9.7	13.2	11.9
• Manitoba	10.2	9.2		
• Saskatchewan	10.8	9.7		
• Alberta	8.8	8.8	7.9	7.4
• British Columbia	7.9	7.7	9.7	9.2

Note: The estimates of prevalence have been adjusted for socioeconomic status, gender, and
immigrant status.

NLSCY, there was no significant effect associated with immigrant status, whereas in TIMSS, immigrants were significantly more likely to have low mathematics scores.

Table 16.2 displays the variation among provinces in the prevalence of children with low mathematics scores. The prevalence of vulnerable children, when averaged across the provinces, is 9.1 percent for the NLSCY and 9.9 percent for the TIMSS. However, the prevalence in the provinces varies considerably. The first and third columns show the unadjusted prevalences. The results for the NLSCY indicate that Saskatchewan, Manitoba, Ontario, and the four Atlantic provinces had prevalences above the national average, whereas BC, Alberta, and Quebec had prevalences below the national average. The TIMSS results for the six provinces that participated substantiate the NLSCY results. The variation among provinces is much more stark, however, ranging from only 3.2 percent for Quebec to more than 13 percent for Ontario, New Brunswick, and Newfoundland.

The second and fourth columns provide estimates of prevalence adjusted for children's SES, gender, and immigrant status. The adjusted scores indicate the likelihood of being vulnerable for a group of "nationally average children"—that is, a group with average SES and a representative mix of males and females, immigrants and non-immigrants. The average expected prevalence is 8.7 percent for the NLSCY and 8.8 percent for the TIMSS. The prevalence estimates were between 1.0 and 2.5 percentage points lower in the Atlantic provinces and about 1 percentage point lower in Saskatchewan and Manitoba. The results for Ontario, Alberta, and British Columbia were not significantly affected by the statistical adjustment. Consequently, the statistical adjustment for students' characteristics and family background resulted in a wider gap between Ontario and Quebec, which is expected given the disparities in their average SES.

To what extent do provinces vary in their mathematics achievement?

This analysis examines whether interprovincial comparisons derived from the NLSCY are consistent with those from the TIMSS, Student Achievement Indicators Program (SAIP), and International Adult Literacy Survey (IALS) (see Sidebars 16.2 and 16.3). We began by converting the measure for the mathematics outcomes for each study into a scale measured in "years of schooling," to make a common measure for purposes of comparison. For example, for the TIMSS data, the difference between the mean scores for children in grades seven and eight was considered equivalent to one year of schooling. Therefore, we scaled the scores so the mean score for students in grade 7 was 7.0, and the mean scores for students in grade 8 was 8.0. This conversion assumes that the growth in mathematics skills, as measured by the TIMSS tests, is linear across a fairly large range of grades, say from about grades four through eleven. This is a rather liberal assumption, and we do not have data to substantiate, for example, that the mean score of Canadian students in grade 3 is close to a score of 3.0 on our re-expressed scale. However, we expect it is fairly accurate within the range of grades six through nine, which renders it useful for expressing differences among provincial means. This scaling does not affect the statistical significance of any observed differences among provinces or other groupings of children; it only provides a re-expression of the magnitude of the difference from the scale used in TIMSS to a years-of-schooling measure.

The analysis used the full sample of children in grades two through six of the NLSCY (the scaling of the mathematics scores for the NLSCY is described in Chapter 3). Figure 16.1 shows the mean scores for each province. Our intention is to show the extent of variation among provinces derived from the various

We used data from the 1993 and 1997 School Achievement Indicators Program (SAIP) assessments (Council of Ministers of Education, Canada, 1997). These assessments involved testing representative samples of Canadian children aged thirteen (most of whom were in grade eight) and sixteen (most of whom were in grade eleven); the samples included more than 20,000 students at each age.

The assessments included tests in mathematics, science, and language. The mathematics test assessed students' general knowledge in mathematics and their skills in mathematics problem-solving. Students were examined in their use of strategies to solve mathematics problems in four domains: numbers and operations, algebra and functions, measurement and geometry, and data management and statistics. These areas of mathematics are covered in the curricula of all provinces and in the curriculum standards document of the National Council of Teachers of Mathematics (NCTM, 1989). Educators from each province assessed the tests to ensure that the items were consistent with their curriculum objectives.

SAIP describes students' skills on a scale with five levels, which are intended to represent a continuum of knowledge and skills acquired over their entire elementary and secondary school careers. In mathematics, for example, Level 1 denotes competency in the early stages of mathematics, such as computation skills using adding, subtracting, dividing, and multiplying; Level 5 denotes advanced competency, such as the ability to solve problems requiring the use of algebraic expressions and geometric principles that are normally taught during the last two years of secondary school. In scaling the SAIP results, we used a technique recommended by Mosteller and Tukey (1977) which re-expresses the categorical results (i.e., the five levels) into a continuous measure. The technique assumes the categorical results were derived from an underlying logit distribution (similar to a normal distribution but with fatter tails). We then re-scaled the results so that the achievement gap between an average thirteen-year-old and an average sixteen-year-old represented three years of schooling.

Sidebar 16.3

International Adult Literacy Survey

The International Adult Literacy Survey (IALS) was conducted by the Organization of Economic Cooperation and Development (OECD) and Statistics Canada in 1994 to determine the level and distribution of literacy skills among the adult population of eight OECD countries, including Canada. The study has now been extended to include about 30 countries. The survey involved interviews and testing of a representative sample of adults and youth in each country. The realized sample in Canada included 5,660 adults aged 16 to 90. The IALS test was designed to assess literacy skills in three domains: prose, document, and quantitative. (For a description of the tests, see OECD & Statistics Canada, 1995).

Our analyses are based on scores from the quantitative test, which required respondents to locate, comprehend, and use mathematical ideas embedded in text. Willms (1999) estimated a standardized score for the full international population of youth aged 16 to 25 and constructed a "years-of-schooling" metric by regressing young people's standardized scores on their level of education.

studies; the question of whether these differences are statistically significant is taken up in the subsequent, more detailed analyses of the NLSCY and TIMSS data.

Three important findings are evident from these results. First, the variation among provinces in their mathematics results increases at higher grade levels. At grade two, the gap between high- and low-achieving provinces is only a few months of schooling. By grade four, the gap increases to more than six months of schooling, and by the middle school years (grades six to eight), it is equivalent to nearly one and a half years of schooling. At age thirteen, when most children are in either grade eight or grade nine, the variation among provinces is equivalent to about two full years of schooling, and it remains large throughout the secondary years. The results for IALS suggest that the variation is even greater after students leave school, but we believe the IALS scores are not as closely linked to schooling as the curricular-specific tests used in TIMSS and SAIP.

The second finding is that the results are remarkably similar across the four studies. We found this surprising, given the diverse nature of the tests: the NLSCY is based on a very short test covering only one domain, the TIMSS

Figure 16.1

Inter-provincial differences in mathematics scores

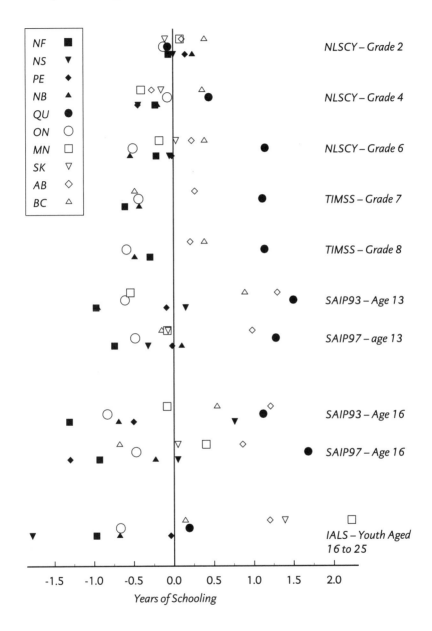

test is curriculum-specific but relevant to some universal curriculum, the SAIP is more closely related to the Canadian curriculum, and the IALS covers a more general set of quantitative literacy skills. The sampling strategy also varies across the four studies. The consistency of the results speaks to the validity of the NLSCY measure of cognitive vulnerability, which is considered one of the weaknesses of the first wave of the NLSCY (see Chapter 3).

The third finding is that some provinces consistently outperform others. Quebec anchors the top end of the distribution, with the highest scores by the end of grade four, and it maintains its advantage through to the end of secondary school. (Quebec's results for the IALS are somewhat anomalous. The results presented in Figure 16.1 are not adjusted for family background, and the IALS results may be more closely related to SES and literacy experiences in the home and workplace, whereas the results from the other studies are more closely related to children's school experience.) Ontario, the largest province, anchors the bottom end of the distribution. With a few exceptions, BC and the prairie provinces score above the national average, while the average scores of the Atlantic provinces hover around those of Ontario. The findings presented in Figure 16.1 are provincial means and do not include statistical adjustment for SES; we examine the variation in overall mathematics scores later.

Do schools and classrooms vary in their average levels of mathematics achievement?

Beyond this question, we also wanted to know whether variation was attributable to the family background characteristics of the students. The analyses in this section assess the magnitude of school effects, provide tests for the hypotheses of converging gradients and double jeopardy, and discern whether particular school and classroom process variables are related to mathematics achievement. The outcome measure for the NLSCY is the "relative mathematics score"—that is, the child's mathematics score relative to his or her same-age peers, expressed in years of schooling. The outcome measure for the TIMSS is the child's mathematics score, also expressed in years of schooling. (A dummy variable denoting grade seven versus grade eight was included in the model to account for the effects of an extra year of schooling.) The analysis includes four hierarchical linear models.

1. The first model is a null model, which simply partitions the mathematics scores into within- and among-school components. This model

addresses whether schools vary in their levels of academic achievement, before account is taken of students' characteristics or family background.

2. The second model introduces the three student-level family background variables—SES, sex, and immigrant status—to gauge the extent of variation among schools after controlling for student characteristics and family background. To some extent, it tests whether schools make a difference. The model also yields a test of the hypothesis of converging gradients.

3. The third model adds school mean SES to the model, to test the hypothesis of double jeopardy. This model, and the fourth model, were examined only for the TIMSS data, as these data include much more reliable indicators of school-level factors.

4. The fourth model added eight variables describing various schooling processes.[2]

Table 16.3 presents the results of the analysis. (The models in Table 16.3 are similar to those in Table 16.2, except that the outcome variable is the continuous mathematics score, rather than the dichotomous variable indicating vulnerability.) The first model tests the hypotheses that schools and classrooms differ in their unadjusted scores. The results indicate that they do differ: 19.1 percent of the variance is among schools (and therefore 80.9 percent is within schools) in the NLSCY; 19.2 percent of the variance is among classrooms in the TIMSS. The model also yields estimates of the magnitude of the within- and between-school components. Within schools, the standard deviation for the NLSCY is about 1.16 years. This suggests that in a typical elementary school, at each grade level, about two-thirds of all children would have scores within about 1.2 years of the average for their age. But about sixteen percent of all children fall above or below that range. What this means for most elementary-school teachers is that in a class of 25 pupils, they can expect to have 4 students whose scores are at least 1 year behind those of their peers and 4 students whose scores are at least 1 year above those of their peers. The estimates for the TIMSS suggest that the within-classroom components are nearly double those estimated for the NLSCY. Thus, the typical middle-school classroom teacher can expect to have about 4 students who score more than 2 years below their peers and 4 students who score at least 2 years above their peers.

Similarly, school mean scores at the elementary level vary considerably. The results indicate that about two-thirds of schools have average scores that fall

Table 16.3

Variation among schools in children's mathematics scores

	NLSCY (297 schools)		TIMSS (775 classes, grades 7 and 8)			
	I	II	I	II	III	IV
Within-school effects						
• Socioeconomic status		**0.34**		**0.52**	**0.50**	**0.50**
• Female		0.15		**-0.15**	**-0.15**	**-0.16**
• Immigrant				**-0.36**	**-0.36**	**-0.34**
- Less than 5 years ago		0.23				
- 5 to 10 years ago		-0.26				
- More than 10 years ago		-0.34				
Variance components						
• Variation among school (%)	**19.1**	**16.7**	**19.2**	**18.2**	**17.9**	**13.6**
• Correlation intercepts/gradients		**-0.10**		**-0.14**		
• Within schools (SD)	1.16	1.10	2.20	2.13	2.13	2.13
• Among schools (SD)	0.56	0.49	1.07	1.00	0.99	0.84
Effects on mean achievement						
• School mean SES					**0.47**	**0.38**
• Students grouped						**-0.10**
• Traditional approach						-0.12
• Use computers						**-0.15**
• Use calculators						**0.26**
• Amount of homework						**0.15**
• Disciplinary problems						**-0.36**
• Teachers specialize						**0.61**
• Pupil–teacher ratio						**-0.02**
• Topic covered this year						0.31
• Topic covered last year						0.18
Effects on SES gradients						
• School mean SES					**0.14**	**0.09**
• Students grouped						**0.08**
• Traditional approach						-0.08
• Amount of homework						**0.08**
• Teachers specialize						-0.14
• Pupil–teacher ratio						**0.02**

Note: Figures that are statistically significant appear in boldface.

within half a year of the national average, and that nearly all schools fall within one year of the national average. As with the within-classroom variation, the variation among schools at the middle-school level was nearly twice as large as at the elementary level.

The second model in Table 16.3 asks whether there is variation among schools and classrooms at these levels after taking account of students' characteristics and family background. The covariates accounted for only about 12.6 percent of the variance among schools (reducing it from 19.1 percent to 16.7 percent) and 5.2 percent of the variance among classes (reducing it from 19.2 percent to 18.2 percent). Thus, we cannot claim that schools vary in their mathematics scores mainly because of the types of students they enroll. This model also provides a test of converging gradients. The socioeconomic gradients were found to vary significantly among schools in the NLSCY and among classes in the TIMSS. The intercepts were correlated negatively with the gradients in both studies, providing evidence of converging gradients. However, the magnitude of the correlation was small: -0.10 for the NLSCY and -0.14 for the TIMSS.

The third model, which was fit to the TIMSS data only, provides a test of double jeopardy. The estimate of the effect for classroom mean SES is 0.47, which is comparable to the effect associated with the SES of the child. In practical terms, this means that if a child's SES is one standard deviation below the national average, he or she is likely to have a mathematics score that is the equivalent of about six months below that of his or her peers. But if this child also attends a classroom that has a low average SES, say one where the average for the classroom is also one standard deviation below the national average, the child is likely to be a full year (i.e., 0.50 + 0.47) below national norms. In this case, double jeopardy truly means double. The classroom mean SES was also positively related to the SES gradient, indicating that the SES gradient is more gradual in low mean SES classrooms and steeper in high mean SES classrooms.

Why do classrooms vary in their achievement?

The last model in Table 16.3 includes several variables that describe school and classroom variables. These were modelled on both the intercepts and the gradients, although the model for the gradients was reduced as most of the processes did not have a significant effect. The results indicate that the most successful classrooms are those where less grouping is practised, calculators are used but computers are not, there is regular homework, there are few discipline problems, teachers specialize, and there are small classes. The results provide some support for an effect associated with a faster-paced curriculum, but the coefficients were not statistically significant. Results for the model describing socioeconomic gradients indicate that classrooms have more equitable results (i.e., more gradual slopes) when less grouping is practised, there is less homework, and there are smaller classes.

Why do some provinces have higher scores than others?

An important aspect of a multilevel analysis is that it provides estimates of how each school or classroom fares relative to the national average. These residuals differentially "shrink" the estimates for each classroom, according to how accurately the mean score for that classroom was estimated. We aggregated the residuals from each of the four models to assess the extent to which the models accounted for variation among the provinces. These are displayed in Figure 16.2. Results for Model I, which do not include any statistical adjustment, indicate that on average the achievement levels of classrooms in Quebec scored more than one year above the national average, whereas classrooms in Alberta and BC scored about three months above the national average, and classrooms in Newfoundland, New Brunswick, and Ontario scored about two months below the national average. Model II includes adjustment for student characteristics and family background. The figure indicates that the adjustment only slightly reduces the variation among the four provinces that score close to the national mean, whereas the adjusted score for Quebec is slightly higher. Model III includes students' background characteristics and mean SES, and again, the scores for the five provinces close to the national average are only slightly affected and the score for Quebec is higher. The final model includes adjustment for the variables in the previous model, plus the set of school process variables. In this case, the variation among the provinces diminishes considerably. The provinces close to the national average are virtually indistinguishable, and the average score for Quebec is pulled down about a third of the way towards the national average (from about 1.2 to 0.8). We conclude that the classroom process variables included in our model account for most of the interprovincial variation, with the exception of Quebec. Factors such as having specialized mathematics teachers and a lower pupil-teacher ratio account for some of the Quebec advantage, but not all of it.

Figure 16.2

Variation among provinces in their average residuals for different models

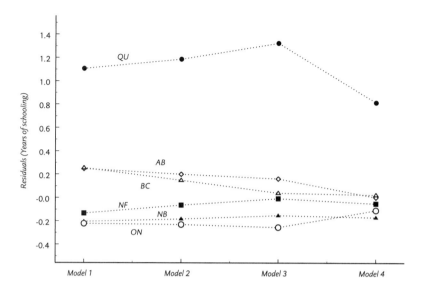

■ Discussion and Policy Implications

Using data from four national and international studies, we have gleaned important findings concerning the effectiveness of schools and schooling systems in Canada. Five of the most important findings emerging from our study are discussed below.

1. *There are large and statistically significant differences among the Canadian provinces, both in their levels of academic achievement in mathematics and in the prevalence of children with very low mathematics scores.* By the end of grade two, children in Quebec score slightly above the national average on the NLSCY mathematics test, while Ontario scores slightly below the national average. As children get older, the differences between the two provinces increase, and by the time children enter secondary school, the gap is more than one full year of schooling. Children in the four western provinces tend to score above the national average, but not as significantly as those of Quebec; children in the Atlantic provinces tend to have results similar to those of Ontario. The disparities among the provinces at the end

of the middle-school years are evident in the results of the NLSCY, the TIMSS, and the SAIP. The prevalence of children who have particularly low scores also varies among provinces, and is consistent with the findings evident in the comparisons of average levels of achievement. Moreover, these disparities are apparent even after controlling for SES and the proportions of immigrants in each province.

2. *There are large and statistically significant differences among schools and classrooms in their levels of achievement and in the prevalence of children with very low mathematics scores.* Consider two families who both have a child entering kindergarten. The children have similar levels of ability and the families are both of average SES. The findings in this study suggest that if one family chooses a school with above-average performance and the other chooses a school with below-average performance, by the time the children enter secondary school the child in the better school will be at least one full grade level ahead of the other child in mathematics. These are large differences and, given the importance of mathematics, could have important consequences for their entry to post-secondary education and the labour market.

3. *Socioeconomic gradients vary significantly among schools and classrooms, and there is some evidence that gradients converge at higher levels of SES.* Socioeconomic gradients are markers of how well a school achieves an equitable distribution of outcomes for children with differing socioeconomic backgrounds. Steep gradients indicate large disparities between advantaged and disadvantaged students within a school, whereas gradual gradients indicate a more equitable distribution of outcomes. Equity and excellence need to be considered hand in hand; that is, gradients need to be considered alongside absolute levels of achievement. Schools and districts need to strive to achieve equity by bolstering the achievement levels of less-advantaged students. School policies and practices that achieve equity but result in lower achievement levels for certain groups are undesirable.

Some schools are successful in achieving both excellence and equity (e.g., see Lee & Bryk, 1989; Willms, 1998). The findings in this study, evident in both the NLSCY and the TIMSS, indicate that gradients vary significantly among schools and that there is a modest relationship between excellence and equity. The most successful schools and classrooms tend to be those which have relatively high achievement levels for students from lower socioeconomic backgrounds.

4. *On average, the most successful schools and classrooms were those where less grouping was practised, calculators were used but computers were not, there were fewer disciplinary problems, teachers specialized in mathematics, and class sizes were smaller.* The finding related to grouping runs contrary to the literature, at least with respect to practices whereby teachers form groups strategically so that students lacking certain skills can learn them from their peers (Cohen & Lotan, 1995). However, if teachers tend to group students by ability, they could produce the effects observed in this study; our data did not allow us to distinguish what type of grouping was practised. This outcome may also be a matter of degree: perhaps the best results accrue when there is good mix of direct instruction and group activities. The results indicating that computer use results in lower mathematics achievement run contrary to what some might expect. Our conjecture is that in classes where computers are currently being used, too much instructional time is spent teaching the mechanics of using a computer rather than the fundamentals of mathematics. This may not be the case in a decade or so, when a larger proportion of students have basic computing skills and there are more computers in the classroom. The finding about disciplinary climate is consistent with the literature. The TIMSS data did not include a strong measure of classroom discipline, which we expect would have yielded even stronger effects.

Achievement scores tended to be higher in classes where the teachers specialize in mathematics. Gradients were not associated with teacher specialization; thus, it seems this factor has equal benefits for students from differing socioeconomic backgrounds. The issue of teacher specialization and how teachers are organized for instruction is quite complex (Bryk, Lee, & Smith, 1990), and neither the NLSCY nor the TIMSS data are adequate for addressing this issue in detail.

Other studies have indicated that reducing class size leads to higher achievement levels, but in most cases the effects have been relatively small (e.g., Hedges, Laine, & Greenwald, 1994; Nye, Hedges, & Konstantopoulos, 1999; Willms & Kerckhoff, 1995; Willms & Somers, 2000). The results in this study indicate that a reduction in class size by five students would lead to an increase in overall achievement equivalent to about one month of schooling. This is a small effect, but on the positive side, reducing class size seems to also reduce inequities. Some researchers have warned that the likely benefits resulting from wide-scale class-size reductions need to be assessed relative to the likely effects of other reforms which are potentially less costly (Brewer, Krop, Gill, & Reichardt, 1999; Ehrenberg, Brewer, Gamoran, Willms, 2001).

We would expect that regular homework assignments would bolster achievement. Our findings suggest this is the case but also indicate that students of lower SES benefit less, perhaps because they do not complete assigned homework as regularly as high-SES students. Cross-sectional studies of the relationship between the number of hours children spend doing homework and their academic achievement have revealed a negative relationship (e.g., Ho & Willms, 1996; Stevenson & Baker, 1987). The explanation is that children who are struggling academically tend to spend more time outside of class completing their work and preparing for examinations. This finding stresses the need for longitudinal research to assess how gains in achievement are related to particular school policies and practices.

5. *The average SES of a classroom has an effect on student achievement, over and above the effects associated with a child's own background.* This finding is consistent with a considerable body of literature pertaining to the contextual effects associated with one's peer group, and it has important implications for policy-makers at district and provincial levels because of the effects of policies that tend to segregate students according to ability or SES. A number of researchers have noted that when students are segregated through residential segregation, private schooling, or choice arrangements within the public sector, advantaged students benefit slightly but disadvantaged students do considerably worse.

The analyses of the TIMSS results pertain to classrooms; however, because the sample design did not include two classrooms per school, it is not possible to assess the effects of policies that might contribute to the segregation of students with varying ability within the same school. This question is especially relevant in New Brunswick and Ontario, where French immersion programs have been implemented in many school districts. The concern is that if students who are vulnerable, either because of cognitive difficulties or behavioural problems, are less likely to enroll in French immersion, then we would expect to see lower levels of achievement among less-advantaged students. The results in Chapter 3 suggest that more than a quarter of Canadian students are vulnerable. If specialized programs within a school result in most vulnerable children being segregated in one classroom, then the teacher would have to meet the needs of twelve to fourteen vulnerable children, instead of six or seven.

When we embarked on this work, we expected to find that the content and pace of the curriculum in each province would account for the differences between Ontario and Quebec, and between the Atlantic and western provinces. Willms (1996) previously noted that similar disparities were evident in two international studies conducted during the 1980s and suggested that the Quebec advantage could be due to a faster-paced, more centralized curriculum and to cultural differences in the emphasis placed on mathematics. The TIMSS data are especially well suited to testing the curriculum hypothesis, and this study did find some interprovincial differences associated with curriculum coverage. However, it was certainly not the most important factor and could not explain the large disparities among provincial results. Rather, the differences seem to be attributable to a myriad of factors that have to do with the culture of school life, the way students are organized for instruction, and to some extent school resources. In large-scale national studies, it is difficult to measure such ephemeral concepts as school climate. Nevertheless, these results indicate that even with fairly cursory measures, we could account for some of the Quebec advantage and nearly all of the variation among the other provinces.

Our only national monitoring system, the SAIP, is not well suited to monitoring the effectiveness of schools. One problem is that, for political reasons, the CMEC has been reluctant to collect data on children's SES, which is a prerequisite for understanding socioeconomic gradients and discerning why certain schools or provinces outperform others. Another problem is that neither the SAIP or the large international studies follow a cohort of students longitudinally. Such study is essential, because our primary interest when studying school effectiveness is learning gains, not students' achievement at a particular grade level. We maintain that a national monitoring activity that meets these criteria needs to be conducted by Statistics Canada; it has the capacity to do so and could guarantee confidentiality of micro-data.

A good starting point would be for it to develop and administer a comprehensive school climate questionnaire to a representative sample of teachers and to all principals, annually or biennially. This questionnaire would ultimately reduce the burden on school staff because the data could be used for the NLSCY, the forthcoming Youth-in-Transition Survey (YITS), the Program of Indicators of Student Achievement (PISA) being conducted by the OECD, and other national and international surveys. On top of this, we need a comprehensive school-based study in which children are tested regularly as they progress through the schooling system. We are already part of the way there, as the necessary infrastructure has been developed for the NLSCY and the YITS. A Canadian school-level database would yield useful comparative information for schools and school districts, which is currently lacking. Nationally collected student achievement data, which included information on student background and schooling processes, would provide a solid base for monitoring the effectiveness of our schools. Moreover, if the monitoring branches within each province used some of the items from the national tests and questionnaires in their own monitoring programs, they would be able to anchor their results for individual schools to a national standard.

NOTES

1   See Brookover et al., 1978; Henderson, Mieszkowski, & Sauvageau, 1978; Rumberger & Willms, 1992; Shavit & Williams, 1985; Summers & Wolfe, 1977; and Willms, 1985, 1986 regarding between-school segregation. See Gamoran, 1991, 1992; and Kerckhoff, 1986, 1993 regarding tracking and streaming. See Dar & Resh, 1986; Dreeben & Gamoran, 1986; Rowan & Miracle, 1983; Slavin, 1987; Sorensen & Hallinan, 1984; and Willms & Chen, 1989 regarding within-classroom segregation.

2   The set of school and classroom process variables included the following factors:

    a. whether students were grouped for instruction: this was the mean score on a 4-point scale (0 = never, 1 = once in a while, 2 – often, 3 = always) indicating whether students worked in pairs or in small groups in class, or for problems or projects;

    b. whether computers were used for instruction: a 4-point scale indicating degree of use;

    c. whether calculators were used for instruction: a 4-point scale indicating degree of use;

    d. regular homework: a 4-point scale indicating frequency of assignments;

    e. extent of discipline problems: a scale derived from four items describing school discipline;

    f. whether teachers specialized in mathematics teaching within the school: the proportion of the teachers' assignment devoted to mathematics instruction;

    g. pupil–teacher ratio: total school enrollment divided by full-time teacher equivalents (FTE) of the school;

    h. curriculum coverage: teachers responded to questions about their coverage of 37 curriculum content topics in mathematics, which asked whether each topic was covered during that school year, the previous year, or had not been covered. We constructed two variables describing the proportion of topics covered that year, and the proportion covered the previous year.

In preliminary models we also included variables describing the frequency of quizzes, the extent to which the teacher emphasized problem-solving during lessons, and whether there was a remedial program in the school. However, the relationships of these factors to achievement were not statistically significant, even with relaxed p-values, and thus were dropped the model. We initially included the square of the pupil–teacher ratio (PTR) in the model. However, the squared term was not statistically significant, so it was also excluded from the model.

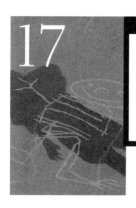

Pre-Adolescent Girls and the Onset of Puberty

CHRISTA JAPEL, RICHARD TREMBLAY,

PIERRE MCDUFF, & J. DOUGLAS WILLMS

EARLY ADOLESCENCE is a period of important emotional, social, and cognitive transition. Most striking, however, are the rapid and dramatic biological changes that occur during this period. Pubertal maturation signals impending fertility and an important milestone in an adolescent's life.

The age when puberty begins and the rate at which it progresses vary greatly among individuals (Brooks-Gunn, 1988; Eveleth & Tanner, 1990), and maturing earlier or later than one's peers can have negative effects on an adolescent's social adaptation. Most of the effects associated with maturational timing have to do with being early, not late (Brooks-Gunn, 1988), and appear to be stronger for girls than for boys (Alsaker, 1995; Brooks-Gunn, Petersen, & Eichhorn, 1985). Whereas early maturation seems to be a social asset for boys, for girls it is associated with emotional and behaviour problems and with earlier sexual activity (Graber, Brooks-Gunn, & Warren, 1995; Stattin & Magnusson, 1990). Younger adolescents are less likely to use contraception, and early sexual activity places them at high risk for pregnancy (Furstenberg, Brooks-Gunn, & Chase-Lansdale, 1989). The results in Chapter 14 of this volume indicate that early pregnancy may entail a life trajectory of teenage motherhood, compromising educational attainment and resulting in disadvantaged socioeconomic circumstances (see also Miller & Heaton, 1991).

The first cycle of the National Longitudinal Survey of Children and Youth (NLSCY) included children up to eleven years old. In the self-report questionnaire, children aged ten and eleven were asked about their pubertal development. Thus, it is possible to examine the relationship of puberty to several factors describing family background and discern whether early maturation is associated with childhood vulnerability. That is the aim of this investigation.

Until recently, researchers thought the timing of pubertal maturation depended on the genetic predisposition of the individual. However, we now realize that it may be related to family socioeconomic status (SES) and affected by a number of psychosocial factors. Eveleth and Tanner (1990) presented an array of studies providing evidence that on average, in both low- and high-income countries, girls from more advantaged socioeconomic backgrounds reached the onset of first menstruation (menarche) earlier than girls from less advantaged backgrounds. However, a Norwegian study (Brundtland, Liestol, & Walloe, 1980) and a Canadian study (Jenicek & Demirjian, 1974) produced contradictory findings, suggesting that girls from lower social-class backgrounds reach menarche at an earlier age.

The Norwegian and Canadian findings are consistent with other research that suggests early pubertal development is associated with stressful family environments. For example, Steinberg (1988) studied pubertal development among adolescents from a predominantly white, socioeconomically heterogeneous background. He found the rate of pubertal development for girls was accelerated for those who were emotionally distant from their parents, especially their mothers; for boys it was unaffected by their relations with their parents. Ellis (1991) reported similar findings for a large sample of adolescents from a wide range of socioeconomic backgrounds. A study of more than 1000 Canadian adolescents found that menarche was about four to five months earlier for girls in father-absent families than for those in two-parent families (Surbey, 1990). Moreover, for the girls living in families with both parents present, stressful life events were associated with earlier menarche. These differences were evident even after controlling for family size, birth order, weight, and SES.

An evolutionary theory of socialization was proposed by Belsky, Steinberg, and Draper (1991a, 1991b) to explain these effects. They argued that girls living in stressful conditions, such as father-absent families or families with marital discord and unstable employment, receive less adequate parenting and develop insecure and mistrustful models of their self, others, and relationships. This inadequacy renders them prone to developing internalizing behaviour problems, including anxiety and emotional disorders, which can result in lower metabolic rates and an accumulation of body fat, thereby stimulating menarche and setting the stage for sexual activity and procreation.

A New Zealand study of 416 girls followed from birth to age 16 found that family conflict or living in a father-absent family were related to early menarche; however, these relationships were not mediated by behaviour problems or weight (Moffitt, Caspi, Belsky, & Silva, 1992). Other smaller-scale studies have found that girls in single-parent families, or families with a high level of marital discord, experience earlier menarche (Graber, Brooks-Gunn, & Warren, 1995; Wierson, Long, & Forehand, 1993). They suggest that negative affect is related to early puberty, thus lending support to Belsky et al.'s theory.

However, the theory is not supported by the findings of research on the relationships among a stressful environment, negative affect, and hormonal levels. Studies of gonadal and adrenal hormone levels have found that psychosocial stressors result in the activation of the adrenal axis, which is accompanied by suppression of the gonadal axis, endocrinological processes which appear to be associated with slower pubertal development (Nottelmann, Inoff-Germain, Susman, & Chrousos, 1990; Susman et al., 1985; Susman et al., 1987; Susman, Dorn, & Chrousos, 1991; Susman, Nottelmann, Dorn, Gold, & Chrousos, 1989). Nottelmann et al. (1990) noted, however, that these findings offer stronger support for a stress model for boys than for girls; but because their research was based on a sample of only 108 adolescents, they emphasized the need to test the stress theory with data from a large longitudinal study.

Some of the discrepancies in the research results may be attributable to differences in methodology. The majority of studies have relied on retrospective data, which provide only a rough indication of pubertal maturation and exclude the early changes of puberty. Given the wide variation in the sequence of pubertal changes, and the possible independence of some of the changes, measures considering only a single aspect of pubertal maturation should be avoided when general pubertal development is assessed (Alsaker, 1995). Only a few studies have included socioeconomic conditions, and they did not uncover a significant relationship (Moffitt et al., 1992; Surbey, 1990). However, these studies were based on retrospective reports of pubertal development.

Our study uses the cross-sectional data from the first cycle of the NLSCY to contribute to this literature in two significant ways. First, we examine the relationship of pubertal development to a wide range of factors describing family structure, SES, and family processes. Second, we ascertain the extent to which early pubertal development is associated with internalizing and externalizing behaviour problems, as well as mathematics achievement, self-esteem, and peer relations. Some of the strengths of the NLSCY are that the data are nationally representative and include a wide range of outcomes and family-related factors. Another is that pubertal development is assessed prospectively, rather than retrospectively, and it is possible to control statistically for adolescents' height and weight. However, because the data are cross-sectional, we cannot make strong causal inferences about the effects of family stressors or behaviour problems on pubertal development. One could hypothesize, for example, that early puberty results in friendships with older peers, leading to emotional problems or deviant behaviours. When data from subsequent cycles of the NLSCY become available, we will be able to provide a much stronger test of the theory of Belsky et al. The need will remain for studies that examine the relationship between stressful environmental conditions and the endocrinological processes of pubertal maturation.

■ Method

This study examined data describing girls aged ten and eleven, and their families; it included data for 1,583 girls. The majority of the data was collected from the person most knowledgeable (PMK) through the parent questionnaire. Data describing the extent of pubertal development were obtained from the adolescent self-report questionnaire and included responses from 1,347 of the 1,583 girls. The realized sample with complete data on all variables used for the main regression analyses included 1279 cases.[1]

The first set of analyses were ordinary least-squares regressions of pubertal development on the child's age in months, body mass index (BMI; i.e., the ratio of weight to height-squared), SES, the mother's employment status, whether the mother was a teen parent or single parent, whether the child was the first- or second-born, and a set of family process variables including family functioning, maternal depression, and parenting practices. The measure of pubertal development was based on three items developed by Petersen et al. (1988). The questionnaire asked girls to report on a scale from one to four the extent of growth of their body hair and breasts, and to indicate whether or not they had begun to menstruate. Consistent with the other scales used in this volume, we used the data from these items to construct a scale with values ranging from zero to ten, with high scores indicating advanced pubertal development.[2] The mean score for the full sample was 2.67, with a standard deviation of 2.02. The 85th and 95th percentiles for this measure were 4.44 and 7.78 respectively.

The second set of analyses employed a logistic regression model to discern the effects that early puberty might have on the various markers of vulnerability used throughout this volume (see Chapter 3). Because we had data for this age group from the self-completed questionnaire, we could extend the set of outcomes to include self-esteem (both general self-esteem and specific to personal appearance) and several variables describing the behaviours of their peers. The measures of self-esteem were each based on four items, and for each we constructed a dichotomous variable which indicated whether a child's level of self-esteem was below the 15th percentile. The logistic regressions provided for each marker of vulnerability an estimate of the odds ratio associated with a one-point increase on the pubertal development scale. In the first model, we included only pubertal development. We then extended the model to include BMI and the set of variables describing family background and family structure. Although pubertal development is related to some of the family-process variables, their inclusion in these models did not appreciably affect the estimates for pubertal development, and thus we did not include them as controls.

The literature regarding the Belsky et al. theory calls for analyses that treat behavioural variables such as anxiety and emotional disorders as predictor variables in a model predicting early puberty. However, because we do not have prior measures of behaviour, we cannot infer a causal relationship. Thus, in keeping with the structure of the analyses reported in earlier chapters, we treat the behavioural variables as outcomes, and estimate whether pubertal development is associated with behaviour problems.

In preliminary analyses, we also included variables describing the girls' self reports of whether they had ever smoked, drunk alcohol, or used drugs. We found that very few girls reported they participated in these activities, and puberty was unrelated to participation, except for smoking, which had a negative relationship with pubertal development. However, our analyses which examined whether their friends participated in these activities revealed important and significant relationships with puberty. In this survey, adolescents were asked to complete it in the privacy of their own room or elsewhere, then put it in an envelope and seal it. Nevertheless, some adolescents may have been reluctant to report their own activities accurately on a questionnaire completed in their own home, and therefore their responses regarding their friends' behaviours may be more valid. In addition, girls with advanced pubertal development probably tend to have older friends, which would account for the discrepancies between their own behaviours and those of their friends.

Table 17.1

The relationship between pubertal development and age, body mass index, family background, and family processes for females aged ten and eleven

	I	II	III	IV	V
Age of child (months)	**0.114**	**0.006**	**0.112**	**0.107**	**0.109**
Body mass index			**0.085**	**0.082**	**0.086**
• (missing body mass index)			-0.268	-0.260	-0.258
Family background					
• Socioeconomic status		**-0.123**	-0.091	-0.041	-0.035
• Mother works part-time				-0.247	**-0.268**
• Mother at home				0.200	0.150
• Single parent				0.034	-0.012
• Teen mother				**0.464**	0.426
• Second child				**-0.830**	**-0.927**
• Only child				**0.461**	**0.479**
Family Processes					
• Family functioning					-0.001
• Depressed					0.235
• Parenting practices					
- Rational					-0.017
- Responsive					**-0.081**
- Firm approach					**0.092**
- Reasons with child					0.014
R-squared	0.154	0.158	0.174	0.193	0.203

Note: Coefficients that are statistically significant (p<0.05) appear in boldface.

■ Results

Table 17.1 displays the results of the multiple regression analysis with pubertal development as the dependent variable. The first model includes only the age of the child in months, and as expected, the results indicate that the pubertal development of older children is more advanced. The results suggest that on average, scores on the 10-point scale increase by about 0.11 points per month as a girl matures. This is a useful statistic as it helps to place the other estimates in context. The second model includes age of the child and SES. The coefficient is -0.123, which indicates that an increase of 1 standard deviation in SES is associated with a decrease of 0.123 points on the 10-point pubertal development scale. This is not a large effect—roughly equivalent to the girl reaching puberty one month later.

The third model adds BMI to the child's age and SES. The findings suggest that a 1-point increase in BMI is associated with an increase of 0.09 points on the pubertal development scale. For this sample of children, the average height was 1.44 metres (approximately 4 feet, 9 inches), and the average weight was 38.59 kilograms (about 85 pounds). For a child of average height, a gain of about 2.08 kilograms (about 4.6 pounds) results in a 1-point increase in BMI. These results indicate that a 1-point increase in BMI is associated with a 0.09 increase in pubertal development, and pubertal development scores increase about 0.11 points per month; therefore, a rough estimate is that children who are 5 kilograms (about 12 pounds) above the average weight for their height are likely to experience puberty 2 months earlier. The results also show that BMI mediates some of the relationship between pubertal development and SES, such that the relationship with SES is no longer statistically significant. Moreover, the increase in R-squared achieved by adding BMI suggests that it is a much more important predictor than SES.

The fourth model added the set of family background variables to the model. The inclusion of these family background variables increased the proportion of variance explained by about 2 percent, from about 17.4 to 19.3 percent. Three of the variables were statistically significant. The children of teen mothers were more likely to have advanced puberty than those of mothers who had their first child at a later age. This effect is substantial— approximately equivalent to a child starting puberty four months earlier. The pubertal development of first-born children, on average, was faster than that of second-born children. The results suggest that first-born girls experience puberty about seven months earlier than their younger sisters. Similarly, only children had a faster rate of development, which suggests that it is not only birth order that matters but also the presence of a sibling.

The results suggest that there is no relationship between pubertal development and SES, which is not accounted for by the other variables in the model. The two variables pertaining to the mother's employment status suggest that girls whose mothers are working outside the home, either full-time or part-time, experience puberty later than those living with mothers who are at home full-time. The effect is equivalent to about two to four months, but is not statistically significant. (In the final model, the variable denoting working part-time is significant.) Overall, the results of this model suggest that the significant effects of SES on pubertal development observed in Model II are to some extent mediated through BMI, but also attributable to whether the mother was a teen when she had the child, and to a limited extent her employment status.

Table 17.2

Odds ratios associated with advanced pubertal development for markers of vulnerability during adolescence

	Unadjusted	Adjusted
Low mathematics score	**1.19**	**1.19**
Behaviour problems		
• Anxiety	**0.99**	**0.96**
• Emotional disorder	**0.87**	**0.82**
• Physical aggression	**0.67**	**0.53**
• Indirect aggression	**0.74**	**0.61**
• Hyperactivity	**0.87**	**0.85**
• Inattention	**0.82**	**0.83**
Low self-esteem		
• General	0.99	0.98
• Personal appearance	1.02	0.99
Peers with errant behaviour		
• Friends smoke	**1.24**	**1.22**
• Friends drink	**1.44**	**1.45**
• Friends use drugs	**1.26**	**1.33**
• Member of bad group	**1.12**	**1.12**
• Friends get in trouble	1.01	1.01

Note: Odds ratios are adjusted for child's age, body mass index, SES, mother working part-time, mother at home, single parent, teen parent, second child, and only child. Odds ratios that differ significantly from 1.0 ($p < 0.05$) appear in boldface.

The last model presented in Table 17.1 extends the previous model to include three important family processes: family functioning, maternal depression, and parenting style. These factors increased the proportion of variance explained by about 1.4 percent. Two of the parenting variables were statistically significant and indicated that girls were less advanced in their pubertal development if they lived in families where the parents were more responsive to their needs and less firm in their approach. In both cases, the effects were small—equivalent to about one month. The effects of maternal depression were in the expected direction, suggesting that girls whose mothers are suffering depression are more likely to reach puberty at an earlier age.

Table 17.2 presents the results for fourteen separate logistic regression analyses that explore the correlates of pubertal development. Each analysis included two models. The first regressed the dichotomous outcome on the continuous measure of pubertal development, with control for the child's age. The odds ratios for pubertal development are in the first column. (Due to space limitations, we do not display the full set of regression parameters for each outcome.) The second model includes pubertal development and all of the covariates used in Model III above. For example, for low mathematics scores, the results indicate that a 1-point increase on the pubertal development scale is associated with an increase in the odds of having a low mathematics score by a factor of 1.19. The effect is statistically significant and remains the same after taking account of family background.

These cross-sectional results are inconsistent with previous research that suggests that pubertal development is related to behaviour problems. With the exception of anxiety problems, these findings suggest that advanced pubertal development is associated with fewer behaviour problems. For example, a 1-point increase in pubertal development was associated with a decrease in the odds ratio by about 17 percent after taking account of family background. This relationship was particularly strong for physical and indirect aggression.

The results also indicate that there is virtually no relationship between pubertal development and self-esteem. However, there is strong evidence that girls with advanced pubertal development are more likely to associate with other children who smoke, drink alcohol, or use drugs, or are members of a group that frequently gets into trouble. The only peer-related outcome for which pubertal development was not significant was the variable denoting the PMK's assessment of whether the child's friends get into trouble. The effects associated with the four variables derived from the girls' reports were large and statistically significant, with odds ratios ranging from 1.12 to 1.45 after taking account of family background.

■

This study explored the relationship between pubertal development and a number of socioeconomic factors and family processes for a nationally representative sample of preadolescent girls. It also examined whether advanced maturation was associated with the developmental outcomes used to define childhood vulnerability in this volume. Four significant findings emerged from the analysis.

1. *Pubertal development is negatively related to SES; however, the relationship is not strong and is mediated through the child's BMI.* The negative association with SES is consistent with an earlier Canadian study conducted in Montreal (Jenicek & Demirjian, 1974) and with research conduced in Norway (Brundtland, Liestol, & Walloe, 1980). However, it is inconsistent with several studies that suggest girls with higher SES tend to reach puberty at an earlier age. The role of BMI as a mediator of socioeconomic gradient may account for this discrepancy. It may be, for example, that in low-income countries pubertal development is delayed by insufficient nutrition, whereas in countries like Canada and Norway, the problem is reversed. Tremblay, Inman, and Willms (2000) found that pre-adolescents in New Brunswick who were from lower-socioeconomic backgrounds tended to have a high BMI and were less physically active. Tremblay and Willms (2000) also found dramatic increases in the prevalence of childhood obesity in Canada over the past two decades. Therefore, in Canada it may be a lack of physical exercise, rather than poor nutrition or an insufficient amount of food, that causes adolescent girls to become overweight, thereby affecting pubertal development.

2. *Pubertal development tends to proceed more slowly for children whose mothers delayed child-bearing until after their teen years and in families where the parents were more responsive to the girls' needs and less firm in their approach.* These findings are consistent with earlier research that suggests that a stressful family atmosphere and a less-nurturing environment increase the rate of pubertal development. Our results also indicated that children of mothers with depressive symptoms and mothers who were not working outside the home were more likely to mature at a faster pace, although the relationships were not statistically significant. We did not find a significant association between family functioning and pubertal development. It may be that some of the effects of these factors are also mediated through BMI.

We also found that first-born children, especially those without siblings, were more likely to reach puberty early. Previous research has also shown that the presence of siblings delays menarcheal age (Brooks-Gunn, 1988), but the processes underlying this association are not understood. A limitation of this study is that there is no information on the mother's maturational pattern. Previous studies have reported highly significant correlations between mothers' and daughters' ages at menarche, suggesting that menarche is partly genetically determined (Alsaker, 1995; Campbell & Udry, 1995; Treloar & Martin, 1990).

3. *Advanced pubertal development was not associated with behaviour problems, as earlier literature suggests. In fact, our findings suggest that girls who mature early are less prone to certain types of behaviour problems.* We do not have a good explanation for this discrepancy. The NLSCY subjects were still relatively young, whereas most other research has been based on older adolescents. It may be that certain behaviour problems do not become apparent until later, when the stressful transition to high school accentuates certain behavioural problems (Caspi & Moffitt, 1991). Younger teens may also receive more attention from their parents than older teens. When the longitudinal data become available, it will be possible to examine the effects of school transition on behaviour. Moreover, because the age of transition to high school varies among provinces, and to some extent among school districts within provinces, it will be possible to determine whether the effects of school transition on behaviour interact with pubertal development.

4. *Girls with advanced pubertal development are more likely to be members of a group with anti-social behaviours and to have friends who smoke, drink alcohol, and use drugs.* We expect that at least some of this relationship is attributable to early-maturing girls associating with older peers, rather than socially deviant peers per se. Our analyses did not uncover a relationship between advanced puberty and smoking, drinking, or the use of drugs amongst the pre-adolescent girls themselves. This lack of a relationship may in fact be the case, or it may stem from a bias due to non-response or inaccurate reporting.

Taken together, these findings suggest that pre-adolescent girls from lower socioeconomic backgrounds tend to have a higher BMI, which is related to early maturation. Children from lower socioeconomic backgrounds tend to have a higher dietary fat intake (Bergstrom, Hernell, & Persson, 1996) and are more likely to be overweight or obese (Kimm et al., 1996). This places them at an increased risk for cardiovascular disease, diabetes, and generally poor health later in life (Bouchard & Johnson, 1988). Being overweight or obese is also related to the onset of menarche; and although advanced pubertal development does not appear to be related to academic or behavioural problems at this age, it is related to the type of friends they choose. Thus, early maturity may be a precursor to early sexuality and dropping out of school, thereby compounding the problems associated with being overweight or obese. With respect to social policy, therefore, this study stresses the important roles that activity and nutrition play in children's development. For example, efforts to improve nutrition and increase physical education in the schools are likely to reduce childhood vulnerability and promote children's health and well-being.

NOTES

1   One of the important variables in the analyses was "body mass index" (BMI), which is the ratio of a person's weight in kilograms divided by the square of his or her height in metres. Data pertaining to the girls' BMI was obtained from parents' reports of the girls' height and weight; about twenty percent of the data on this variable were missing. We replaced missing data for BMI with the mean BMI for the sample and computed a dummy variable which indicated whether or not data were missing for BMI. The missing data indicator was included in the analysis alongside BMI. This technique, recommended by Cohen and Cohen (1983), is especially useful when considerable data are missing for only one or two variables in a regression analysis. The estimate of the regression coefficient for the relevant variable (in this case, BMI) pertains only to those cases with available data, and the estimate for the missing data indicator indicates the magnitude of the differences in the outcome variable for those with and without missing data. We found that in all cases the coefficient for the missing data indicator was statistically insignificant.

2   The responses pertaining to body hair growth and breast development were coded as follows: "has not yet started growing" = 0; "has barely started growing" = 3.33; "is definitely underway" = 6.67; and "seems complete" = 10. The item pertaining to menstruation was coded "Yes = 10", and "No" = 0. The scores for the three items were averaged for each child.

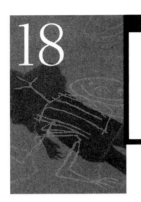

The Role of the Peer Group in Pre-Adolescent Behaviour

18

WENDY M. CRAIG, RAY DEV. PETERS,

& J. DOUGLAS WILLMS

PEERS PLAY A CENTRAL ROLE in the social development of children and adolescents. During early adolescence, there are significant changes in the importance and structure of peer groups. First, adolescents spend less time with their parents and more time with their peers than during early childhood. By age ten, children spend on average forty percent of their day with peers, and when adolescents are asked to name the most important people in their lives, more than fifty percent of the individuals named are of the same age (Hartup, 1996). Second, during early adolescence, the peer group functions more often without adult supervision than during childhood (Brown, 1990). There is also an increase in contact with the opposite sex and an emergence of larger collectives of peers.

The quality of adolescent peer groups has long-term consequences. Researchers have linked positive peer relationships to positive mental health outcomes at midlife (Hightower, 1990), while negative peer interactions, such as peer rejection, are related to internalized behaviour problems, such as anxiety, and externalized behaviour problems, including drug use and delinquency (Dishion, 1990; Kandel, 1978). Thus, peers play an important role in shaping adolescents' psychological and social development. The aim of this study is to examine adolescents' social competence and peer relationships, and determine whether these factors are related to adolescents' socioeconomic background and to the likelihood of displaying internalizing or externalizing behaviour problems.

■ Friendship and Its Implications for Mental Health

Hartup (1996) argues that it is important to distinguish between having friends, the identity of the friends, and the quality of the friendship. Generally, the research indicates that children who have friends tend to be more socially competent and less troubled than those who do not, and that having friends supports adaptation during key developmental periods such as adolescence (Hartup 1983; Newcomb & Bagwell, 1995). Having friends means having good, supportive friends, and thus it is important to discern the identity of the friends and the quality of the friendship.

Whether a friendship is developmentally advantageous or disadvantageous seems to derive mainly from the identity of the friends and the quality of the relationships. Supportive relationships between socially skilled individuals appear to be developmentally advantageous: they help children build relationships and develop socially acceptable norms of behaviour. In contrast, coercive and conflict-laden relationships are developmentally disadvantageous, especially among anti-social children. A number of studies have shown that friends tend to be similar to one another in their behaviour and attitudes, with respect to both pro-social and anti-social behaviours (Cairns, Cairns, Neckerman, Gest, & Gariepy, 1988; Haselager, Hartup, Van Lieshout, & Riksen-Walraven, 1995). These similarities among friends, called "behavioural concordance," may be a function of the socio-demographic conditions that bring individuals in proximity to one another; social selection processes whereby individuals tend to socialize with those who have similar behaviours and attitudes; or mutual socialization processes whereby friends become similar to one another over time. An ethnological perspective of behavioural development situates relationships within a social nexus, whereby factors within the individual shape relationships, and relationships in turn shape the individual (Hinde, 1989). From an ethnological perspective, understanding the characteristics of peer groups is critical to explaining the development of behaviour problems in early adolescence.

The role of peers in externalizing behaviour problems

Peer influence on anti-social behaviour peaks during adolescence. Researchers hypothesize that peers supply the adolescent with the attitudes, motivation, and rationalizations to support anti-social behaviour, as well as the opportunity to engage in specific delinquent acts. Researchers have examined the influence of deviant peer associations (Simons et al., 1993), the formation of networks (Cairns et al., 1988), and the influence of peers with deviant values (Agnew, 1989).

Researchers have found that aggressive and anti-social children are often rejected by their peer group (Dodge, 1983) and lack the basic skills necessary for developing a supportive friendship network (Giordano, Cerkovitch, & Pugh, 1986). Once these children are rejected by their classmates, their rejection and status are relatively stable and resistant to change (Bierman, 1989). Furthermore, when rejected children interact with their peers on the playground, the interaction is likely to be significantly more aversive than that of their classmates (Walker et al., 1987; Pepler, Craig, & Roberts, 1995). Thus, aggressive and anti-social children lack the basic skills and social competence to form positive friendships.

Most anti-social children do develop friendships, however, but at the cost of escalating problem behaviours during adolescence (Giordano et al., 1986). Aggressive children tend to form friendships with marginalized children who are similar to themselves in terms of aggressive and anti-social behaviours (Cairns & Cairns, 1991), a pattern that Patterson et al. (1989) refer to as the "shopping" hypothesis. These children tend to share similar anti-social values, attitudes, and behaviours (Cairns et al., 1988) and therefore comprise a deviant peer group. Association with deviant peers is highly correlated with peer conflict, indicating that these friendships reinforce coercive and aggressive patterns of interaction and fail to teach children the pro-social skills necessary for positive relationships (Dishion, 1990). The deviant peer group is presumed to provide a training ground for delinquent behaviours and drug and alcohol use in later childhood (Patterson et al., 1989, 1992). This limited opportunity for positive peer interaction places aggressive children at risk for continuing to learn and employ aggressive behaviours (Parker & Asher, 1987). For aggressive children, rejection by peers and association with deviant peers seem to be critical factors in setting the course towards maladjustment in adulthood. In longitudinal analyses comparing violent and non-violent adults, Farrington (1991) reported that adolescent involvement in group violence and vandalism was associated with the maintenance of anti-social behaviours into adulthood.

The role of family demographics

Demographic variables describing the child's neighbourhood and family, including parental education, income, and occupation, are related to the incidence of anti-social behaviour (Elliot et al., 1985; Wilson & Hernstein, 1985).

This relationship is particularly strong for children with extreme anti-social behaviour problems (Elliot et al., 1985). Researchers have consistently found an association between poverty and high levels of violence. Epidemiological research suggests that individuals with behavioural problems tend to cluster in neighbourhoods and that behavioural problems and their negative consequences echo throughout neighbourhoods (Wilson & Hernstein, 1994). Sampson et al. (1993) hypothesize that children growing up in neighbourhoods with limited social resources, weak inter-generational ties, low levels of participation in community life, and easy access to guns and drugs are likely to model their behaviours on those around them; children learn and incorporate the behavioural norms embodied in their community. In such economically disadvantaged communities, aggressive values and behaviours can even increase an adolescent's social status.

Garbarino and Gillian (1980) referred to this process as a "concentration effect." They found that the most disadvantaged neighbourhoods lacked a critical mass of stable, achievement-oriented families to provide neighbourhood cohesion, sanctions against maladaptive behaviours, and support for basic community institutions. Stressed and discouraged families are surrounded by others in similar circumstances, resulting in a concentration of poor, unskilled, and unemployed individuals. In such neighbourhoods, high-risk families compete for limited resources, thereby compounding their problems. For many adolescents living in poor neighbourhoods, violence is perceived as an effective method for overcoming the many barriers to advancement (Coie & Jacobs, 1993).

Although these patterns may be the norm in many poor areas, the results in Chapter 4 provide evidence that children's outcomes vary substantially among neighbourhoods and communities. Indeed, within all communities there are parents who do not contribute to violence and chaos, and have deep concerns about the negative influences of their neighbourhood on their children. And even though living in an economically disadvantaged neighbourhood may contribute to the development and maintenance of problematic behaviour, the majority of children with internalizing and externalizing behaviour ✳ problems do not live in poor areas.

While the literature identifies a relationship between socioeconomic status (SES) and behaviour problems, it is likely that this relationship is mediated by family and community processes. For example, stressors related to unemployment, marital discord, and divorce are related to children's behaviours (Farrington, 1987; Garmezy & Rutter, 1983), but researchers hypothesize that these effects are mediated through factors such as inadequate parenting and family management skills, which tend to break down during times of stress (Patterson, 1982, Dishion et al., 1995). In addition, a number of studies have cited parental rejection of the child and a lack of parental involvement as predictors of later aggressive behaviour problems and delinquency (e.g., Farrington, 1991; Loeber & Stouthamer-Loeber, 1986; Olweus, 1979). Monitoring a child's activities seems to be particularly important, as unsupervised time after school is correlated with exposure to deviant peers and susceptibility to peer pressure (Patterson, 1986).

A full understanding of the mechanisms that propel children on an anti-social trajectory requires better comprehension of the relationships among individual factors, inter-individual interactions, social networks, inter-network relations, and the wider economic, cultural, and social conditions of the neighbourhood and community (Cairns & Cairns, 1991). This understanding requires both qualitative and quantitative research with approaches from various research traditions. Our study stands to contribute to the body of the research in that it is national in scope, with a large sample of males and females, and comprehensive measures of SES, internalizing and externalizing behaviours, the social competence of adolescents, and the nature of their relationships with peers. The analysis first examines the relationships between family demographic variables and sex with externalizing and internalizing behaviour problems, and then assesses whether social competence or having anti-social friends mediates these relationships.

■ Method

This study was based on the responses of 3,404 10- and 11-year-old children and their parents. The measures of SES and internalizing and externalizing behaviour problems are described in Chapter 3. We used the composite measure of SES, as well as mother's employment (working part-time or working at home versus working full-time), family structure (single- versus two-parent family), whether or not the mother was a teen parent, and the number of children in the family. Sex was coded 0 for males, 1 for females. The outcome measures included anxiety, emotional problems, physical aggression, indirect aggression, hyperactivity, and conduct disorder, which were based on parents' assessments of the child's behaviour, and scaled with latent class scaling (outlined in Chapter 3).

Social competence was assessed by adolescents' responses to four items: "I have a lot of friends," "I get along with others easily," "Other kids want me to be their friend," and "Most kids like me." It was scaled such that higher scores indicated greater social competence. The reliability coefficient (Cronbach's alpha) was 0.77. Anti-social friends was made up of two dichotomous variables. The first was based on adolescents' reports of whether they were part of a group that did bad things, and was coded 1 if they did and 0 if they did not. The second was derived from parents' responses to the question, Does the child hang around with others who frequently get into trouble? It was scaled either 0, indicating the child did not hang around friends who got into trouble, or 1, indicating that the child's friends did get into trouble.

The analysis involved estimating three sets of regression models, following a procedure recommended by Baron and Kenny (1986) for assessing mediating effects. In the first set of regressions, the potentially mediating variables were regressed on the demographic variables to discern whether the mediating variables were related to socioeconomic factors or sex. Because social competence is a continuous variable, an ordinary least-squares regression model was fitted to the data; for the two dichotomous measures of anti-social friends, we used logistic regression models. The second set of regressions, also based on logistic regression models, fit the dichotomous measures of internalizing and externalizing behaviour problems on the set of family background variables and sex. The third set of regression models extended the first set to include the mediating variables social competence and anti-social friends.

■ Social Competence, Anti-Social Friends, and Family Background

Table 18.1 presents the results for the regressions of social competence, and the two indicators of anti-social friends, on SES, family structure, mother's employment status, teen parenthood, number of siblings, and sex of the child. Females rated themselves as being less socially competent than males, as did children in single-parent families. Social competence was also negatively related to having a mother who was not working outside the home. Children with more brothers and sisters also rated themselves lower on this scale. Overall, however, the relationship was weak; the model accounted for less than two percent of the variance.

Although females rated themselves lower in social competence, they were less likely to be members of an anti-social group or to have friends that got into trouble. Children who lived in single-parent families were more likely to have anti-social friends. Children whose mothers did not work outside the home were more likely to have friends that got into trouble.

Table 18.1

Relationship between social competence, association with misbehaving peers, and family background

	Social competence (regression coefficients)	Members of a bad group (odds ratios)	Friends get in trouble (odds ratios)
Mean score	**7.962**		
Socioeconomic status	-0.060	**0.628**	**0.771**
Mother works part-time	-0.089	0.921	1.160
Mother at home	**-0.222**	0.769	0.770
Single parent	**-0.330**	**2.064**	**1.626**
Teenage mother	-0.267	0.955	1.136
Number of siblings	-0.071	0.968	0.929
Female	**-0.369**	**0.670**	**0.536**
R-squared	**0.019**	**0.027**	**0.043**

Note: Coefficients that are statistically significant (p<0.05) appear in boldface.

The effects of peer relationships

Table 18.2 displays the results for the regressions showing the effects of the family background, sex, and peer variables on children's behaviour problems. The effects associated with family background and sex are consistent with findings in earlier chapters. Consistent with our hypothesis, children with low social competence were more likely to display behaviour problems. The odds ratios were of similar magnitude across the six behaviour problems, ranging from 0.62 to 0.85, and with the exception of conduct disorders were statistically significant.

The odds ratios associated with being a member of a bad group ranged from 1.03 to 2.26, indicating that youth who were members of a bad group were more likely to experience behaviour problems. With the exception of indirect aggression, however, these were not statistically significant. In contrast, the odds ratios associated with parents' assessments as to whether their children associated with anti-social peers ranged from 1.49 to 6.29, which in all cases were statistically significant. The effects were largest for physical aggression and conduct disorders.

Table 18.2

Relationship between behavioural problems, social competence, and association with misbehaving peers (odds ratios)

	Anxiety		Emotional problems		Physical aggression	
	I	II	I	II	I	II
Socioeconomic status	0.93	0.95	0.88	0.91	1.01	1.14
Mother works part-time	1.21	1.10	1.45	1.37	**5.75**	**5.81**
Mother at home	**1.58**	**1.58**	**2.18**	**2.17**	**5.04**	**5.30**
Single parent	1.25	1.00	**2.40**	**2.12**	**7.61**	**7.46**
Teenage mother	1.34	1.18	**3.41**	**3.36**	**3.54**	**4.05**
Number of siblings	0.90	0.88	1.01	0.99	**1.60**	**1.67**
Female	**1.44**	**2.05**	**1.42**	**1.94**	1.02	1.71
Social competence		**0.70**		**0.70**		**0.62**
Member of bad group		1.27		1.56		1.03
Friends get in trouble		**2.27**		1.62		**2.94**
R-squared	0.009	0.064	0.036	0.073	0.028	0.043

Note: Odds ratios that differ significantly from 1.0 (p<0.05) appear in boldface.

Peer relationships as a mediator of the effects of SES

Table 18.2 provides estimates of the effects of the components of SES on children's outcomes, before and after controlling for the peer variables (i.e., Model I versus Model II). The results generally suggest that the mediating role of social competence and peer relationships is rather weak. This is not surprising, given the findings presented in Table 18.1, which indicated that these peer-related variables did not have a strong association with SES or other demographic variables. An interesting finding stemming from comparisons of the two models is that, in the case of anxiety, emotional problems, physical aggression, and hyperactivity, the variables describing peer relationships played a stronger role in explaining variation among adolescent behaviours than did the measures of family background.

■ Summary and Policy Implications

The results generally indicate that behavioural problems among ten- and eleven-year-old children were more prevalent among single-parent mothers and mothers who were not working outside the home. Emotional problems,

Table 18.2 (*cont.*)

Relationship between behavioural problems, social competence, and association with misbehaving peers (odds ratios)

	Indirect aggression		Hyperactivity		Conduct disorders	
	I	II	I	II	I	II
Socioeconomic status	**0.49**	**0.49**	**0.84**	**0.86**	**0.37**	**0.40**
Mother works part-time	**4.71**	**4.58**	1.27	1.25	0.00	0.00
Mother at home	**3.86**	**3.83**	**1.65**	**1.61**	0.69	0.86
Single parent	**5.51**	**4.55**	**1.80**	**1.59**	**17.81**	**9.66**
Teenage mother	**3.30**	**3.44**	1.45	1.39	0.00	0.00
Number of siblings	**1.36**	**1.37**	**0.82**	**0.81**	1.29	1.25
Female	**2.54**	**3.46**	**0.50**	**0.59**	**0.17**	0.45
Social competence		0.85		0.78		0.79
Member of bad group		2.26		1.29		2.07
Friends get in trouble		2.03		1.49		**6.29**
R-squared	0.043	0.049	0.029	0.057	0.016	0.020

Note: Odds ratios that differ significantly from 1.0 ($p<0.05$) appear in boldface.

physical aggression, and indirect aggression were more prevalent among mothers who were teenagers when the child was born. Female adolescents tended to suffer more often than males from anxiety and emotional problems, and were more likely to be indirectly aggressive. Males were more likely to be hyperactive and display conduct disorders. Socioeconomic status was weakly related to indirect aggression, hyperactivity, and conduct disorders, and was not related to physical aggression, anxiety, or emotional problems. Moreover, the full set of family background variables accounted for only about one to three percent of the variance.

Adolescents' self-reported social competence was significantly related to five of the six behaviour problems, as was parents' reports of whether the child had friends who tended to get into trouble. These variables tended to have fairly strong independent relationships with behaviour problems; they only weakly mediated effects associated with SES. Two important findings relevant to social policy emerge from this study.

1. *Social competence plays an important role in determining whether an adolescent suffers from behavioural problems.* Early adolescence can be a precarious period because the problem behaviours that characterize childhood can

become consolidated, grow more serious, and have more significant implications. Friendships with peers become more important during this period and play a significant role in shaping values and determining behaviour. Although parents and educators recognize the importance of social skills, relatively little time is spent in directly teaching these skills; we generally rely on the broader socialization that occurs during the elementary years. However, there are good programs for adolescents that foster skills in forming and maintaining positive relationships, dealing with conflict, and understanding their own feelings and behaviours. These results suggest that placing greater emphasis on social skills would reduce the number of behaviour problems adolescents exhibit. We believe that it might also result in better school performance.

2. *Forming friendships with peers who frequently get into trouble is associated with both internalizing and externalizing behaviour problems.* An intriguing finding of this study is that parents' assessments of whether their children associate with friends who get into trouble have a strong relationship with behaviour problems. That is, parents seem to have a good sense as to whether their child's friendships are positive or negative. Yet as adolescents mature, parents have relatively few means to guide their children and help them learn pro-social skills. Similarly, many teachers recognize when children are forming harmful relationships, but feel they have relatively few means to intervene.

Children are most likely to establish meaningful friendships when they are engaged with others in enjoyable activities. Thus, an important role for both parents and teachers is to increase children's involvement in supervised activities. School programs that provide youth with skills in athletics, arts, and music are important. Similarly, communities that provide opportunities for youth to engage in organized activities in community centres, youth groups, sports clubs, and extended school programs provide a forum for youth to establish positive relationships. Adults can also provide opportunities for youth to become involved as volunteers. Training programs for teachers, counsellors, and other professionals who work with youth need to provide strategies for prevention and intervention. It may be, for example, that teachers could use different strategies for grouping children to increase their social skills.

This research shows that it is possible to measure social competence and identify children who have anti-social friends as early as age ten, and to discern the effects these factors have on their behaviour. Early adolescence marks the beginning of a critical transition in children's development. As such, it provides a unique opportunity to provide support. A limitation of cross-sectional research such as this study is that we cannot make strong causal inferences. It may be, for example, that children with behavioural problems are more likely to associate with delinquent peers because they are isolated from the mainstream. The research also does not inform us whether the manifest behaviour problems become worse over time as a result of poor social skills or contact with anti-social peers. Therefore, the findings in this study call for smaller, longitudinal studies, ideally with control and treatment groups. There is relatively little evidence, for example, of the effects of broad-based community interventions or of training programs designed to increase children's social skills.

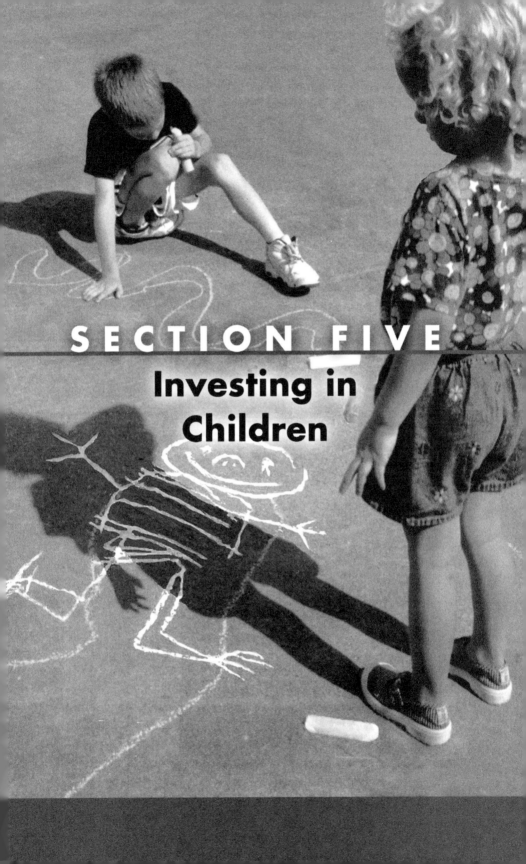

SECTION FIVE
Investing in
Children

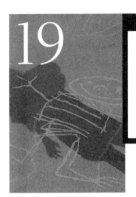

Research Findings Bearing on Canadian Social Policy

19

J. DOUGLAS WILLMS

■ Social Policy for Canadian Children

THE SOCIAL POLICY of a nation reflects its values and political ideology. An overarching value of Canada's social policy is that equality of social outcomes is desirable. There is an underlying premise that equality of social outcomes can never be attained but that as a society we must strive for equality of opportunity. The belief is that if people are afforded equality of opportunity to meet their basic needs and receive high-quality medical care and education, then other important outcomes such as creativity, culture, and productive work will follow. The government might tolerate variation in social outcomes due to differences in individual talents and abilities, but would seek to even out variation across jurisdictions, among social class and ethnic groups, and between the sexes, while striving to improve desirable outcomes. Indeed, Canadians have considerable pride in the equality of opportunity afforded by our medical and educational systems.

The importance of social policy directed to achieving equality of opportunity for families with children is well accepted at all levels of government. Moreover, there is a growing awareness that there are critical periods during the first few years of life, when children's brains are developing, that establish a foundation for learning, behaviour, and health over the life cycle. To achieve optimal brain development, children must receive adequate nutrition and be cared for in nurturing and stimulating environments. Children who do not get a good start in life have difficulties rebounding and achieving their potential. Thus, the support of families in the effort to provide the best possible environments for children is a critical investment. It could be considered the foundation of social policy.

Ten years ago, the federal government explicitly made the eradication of child poverty a goal for Canada. National policies focussed on increasing income assistance and family support to achieve this objective. In addition to improving income security programs, such as social allowance and employment assistance, it developed the National Child Benefit (NCB) in concert with the provinces and territories. The NCB includes a federal tax benefit for families with low incomes, and provincial and territorial reinvestments in services for children in low-income families. The federal government also achieves a redistribution of tax revenue through the Canada Health and Social Transfer (CHST), which provides cash payments and tax transfers to the provinces and territories for health care, post-secondary education, social assistance, and social services.

More recently, the federal government has taken an active role in the direct provision of services for children and their families. Recent efforts have been directed mainly toward ensuring that every child enters school "ready to learn." In 1997, the government announced the National Children's Agenda (NCA), establishing its commitment to work with the provincial and territorial governments to improve the health and well-being of Canadian children. The NCA included two federal initiatives that were already underway: the Canada Prenatal Nutrition Program (CPNP) and the Community Action Program for Children (CAPC), an intervention aimed at improving the health and well-being of children prenatally to age six by providing additional support to families within communities. The federal government recently extended the parental-leave provision of employment insurance to a full year, in recognition of the importance of the first year of a child's life. It is also piloting an initiative called Understanding the Early Years (UEY), designed to help communities assess the outcomes of their preschool children and plan to meet their needs.

Despite these efforts, social policy concerned with the delivery of services for children is largely a provincial matter because provincial governments have constitutional jurisdiction over health, education, and social services. The nature of programs for children and families, and the populations for which they are targeted, varies considerably among the provinces, and every province has a unique mix of programs. For example, Quebec introduced subsidized licensed daycare for preschool children. Manitoba has such programs as Baby

First and Early Start. New Brunswick developed an Early Childhood Initiative that provides a suite of interventions to families with children considered at risk. Within every province, special groups such as First Nations children and children with disabilities receive special education and extra support. However, despite this variation among provinces, a majority of provincial programs are targeted, either directly or indirectly, to children from low-income families, based on the assumption that poverty is the primary determinant of childhood vulnerability.

The public education system is the primary universal vehicle for achieving equality of opportunity. The legal authority for education is highly centralized provincially, with authority delegated to each province's department of education through its minister of education. The mandate of a department is set out in various legislative regulations and acts—mostly called school acts—and the administration of schools is carried out by school districts, or in some cases smaller administrative units. Schools have traditionally emphasized the achievement of cognitive outcomes as their primary goal, but over the past twenty years their mandate has broadened and increasingly emphasizes the development of social and behavioural outcomes. Educators have strived to make schools more responsive to the needs of children and their families by increasing parental involvement in school governance (McKenna & Willms, 1998) and by "restructuring" schools in ways that give teachers, parents, and students greater autonomy (Fullan, 1992).

Municipal governments are largely responsible for the quality of the neighbourhoods within their boundaries. Their expenditures cover not only infrastructure elements—such as roads, public transportation and garbage collection—but also qualitative amenities—such as parks, playgrounds, swimming pools, community centres, and libraries. Thus, municipalities play an important role in delivering services and amenities, and improving the quality of the residential environment. The revenue for municipalities is based on property tax and in many cases affluent neighbourhoods have better amenities.

The research in this volume bears directly on Canadian social policy. It is based on data from the first cycle of the National Longitudinal Survey of Children and Youth (NLSCY), which were collected in 1994-95 from a representative sample of Canadian children and their families. A primary aim of this research was to determine the prevalence of vulnerable children in Canada, based on children's cognitive and behavioural outcomes, and determine the extent to which there are disparities in outcomes among children from differing family backgrounds. Knowing which citizens are vulnerable and how vulnerability is related to family income and other socio-demographic characteristics is fundamental to the policy-making process. This research is also concerned with whether we can relieve the burden of suffering experienced by many Canadian children. Another aim, then, is to identify aspects of family, school, and community life that are related to vulnerability and to discern whether some of these factors explain why children from particular family backgrounds are especially prone to being vulnerable. Achieving this aim can help us understand the extent to which policies are likely to reduce vulnerability and provide a basis for determining what kinds of public services and benefits might be most effective.

This chapter summarizes the key findings that bear on social policy and provides suggestions for further research. Each of the previous chapters includes a summary of the important findings derived from detailed analyses covering each topic. They are not repeated here. Instead, this chapter presents a new set of analyses, synthesizing the main findings that bear directly on social policy. These analyses are a consolidated account of the relationships described in more detail in the volume; their aim is to capture the essence of the results and serve to explain the findings in simpler terms. The chapter concludes with a discussion of the kind of research on childhood development that will be possible as the NLSCY proceeds apace.

■ An Index of Childhood Vulnerability

Our approach to the study of childhood development and vulnerability emphasizes outcomes rather than risk factors. Instead of thinking about "children at risk" as those from low-income or single-parent families, we consider the learning and behavioural outcomes of children at different ages. In Chapter 3, I developed a vulnerability index that considers a child to be vulnerable if he or she had poor outcomes in either the cognitive or behavioural domains. The vulnerability index is intended to identify children whose chances of leading healthy and productive lives are somewhat reduced unless there is a concerted and prolonged effort to intervene on their behalf. Children were classified as being vulnerable in the cognitive domain if they had a low score on a standardized test of motor and social development at ages zero to three, a low score on a test of receptive vocabulary at ages four or five, or a low score on a standardized mathematics test at ages six to eleven. Children were considered vulnerable in the behavioural domain if they were rated by their parents as having a difficult temperament at ages zero or one, or were classified as having any one of six behaviour disorders (i.e., anxiety, emotional disorder, hyperactivity, inattention, physical aggression, or indirect aggression) at ages two to eleven.

At least one out of every four Canadian children is vulnerable

Our analysis revealed that 28.6 percent of Canadian children were vulnerable. This finding is rather troubling, and one could argue that the criteria used to define vulnerability were too liberal. However, a case can be made that they should not be more stringent. They were based on well-established cut-off points for the cognitive measures and, in the case of behaviour problems, by determining empirically which children clustered in groups with very low behaviour ratings. The prevalence of children with behaviour problems estimated in this study—19.1 percent—is comparable to findings from the Ontario Child Health Study (Offord et al., 1987). And in 1993, the year before the collection of the first cycle of data for the NLSCY, 29.2 percent of Canadian youth had dropped out of secondary school before graduation (Organisation for Economic Co-operation and Development, 1996; see Table R11.1). These earlier results suggest that a figure of 28.6 percent is realistic. But whether or not the criteria established are too lenient or too stringent, the vulnerability index provides a useful means for making comparisons among jurisdictions such as provinces and communities and among children from different types of families.

Childhood vulnerability is only weakly associated with family income

One of the surprising findings of the study was that the relationship between childhood vulnerability and family income was not as strong as we previously believed. Figure 19.1 shows the prevalence of vulnerable children in families at varying levels of family income. Families were categorized into four groups, or quartiles, according to their income, with each group representing 25 percent of Canadian families. Each bar on the graph represents the percentage of children for the corresponding income group who were classified as vulnerable. Families in the lowest quartile had incomes below $27,930. While the Statistics Canada low-income cut-offs require consideration of family size, family structure, and region, the low-income cut-off for a family of four in a medium-sized city in 1994 was about $26,000 (Statistics Canada, 1999). Given this, along with the objective of the National Child Benefit of providing increased benefits for families with net incomes below $30,000, we could roughly consider the lower

Figure 19.1

The prevalence of vulnerable children by family income

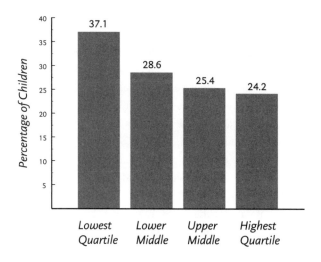

quartile group to be families living in poverty. Our findings show that this group does have a higher prevalence of vulnerable children—about 37 percent—but this also means that about 63 percent of the children living in poor families had average or above-average scores on the cognitive measures and were not exhibiting major behaviour problems. The figure also shows clearly that the majority of vulnerable children were in families with incomes above the poverty threshold. In fact, even among families in the highest quartile, nearly 25 percent had either cognitive or behavioural difficulties. These results confront the stereotype that the majority of children who have problems at school or display behaviour problems are from poor families: it is simply not the case.

Our findings confront two other stereotypes regarding vulnerable children. One is that cognitive difficulties and behaviour problems necessarily go hand in hand. About 12.8 percent of the children in the study were vulnerable in the cognitive domain, while 19.1 percent had one or more behaviour problems; only 3.0 percent had both. Another stereotype belied by the findings is that it is mainly boys who have difficulties. Although the prevalence of childhood vulnerability was significantly greater for boys than for girls—31.1 percent compared to 26.0 percent—the differences were not as large as we might expect. Boys were more likely to display "externalizing" behaviour problems, such as hyperactivity and physical aggression, but many girls were prone to "internalizing" behaviour problems, including emotional disorders and anxiety. Children who act out or are fidgety or aggressive often create a great deal of stress for teachers and fellow classmates, and thus receive considerable attention. However, children with internalizing disorders often suffer in silence and receive little attention, yet their problems can also have implications for their future health and well-being.

■ Childhood Vulnerability and the Socioeconomic Gradient

Successful social policy means raising and flattening socioeconomic gradients

In providing a portrait of the social outcomes of Canadian children, our analyses emphasize socioeconomic gradients rather than simply the average level of outcomes. The term *socioeconomic gradient* refers to the relationship between some developmental outcome and socioeconomic status (SES). It summarizes the bivariate relationship between an outcome variable and SES. The outcome can be any social outcome, and in this research, we include several cognitive and behavioural measures. SES refers to the relative position of a family or individual on an hierarchical social structure, based on their access to, or control over, wealth, prestige, and power (Mueller & Parcel, 1981). As in most studies of this type, SES is operationalized with a composite measure comprising family income and the level of education and occupational prestige of the child's parents.

Gradients are a simple, straightforward policy device for shifting attention away from risk factors towards desired social outcomes and inequalities in outcomes, and Figure 19.2 provides an example. The gradient represents the best-fitting line through the data describing children's outcomes and SES. In this case, it is a straight line and can be summarized with three components: the average level, the slope, and the variation of scores above and below the line. Comparisons of gradients across jurisdictions, among ethnic groups, between the sexes, or across time can provoke questions about why some groups do better than others. They especially prompt us to ask, Can we alter socioeconomic gradients?

Most social policies aim to raise the gradient for one or more social outcomes. A successful social policy could (a) raise outcome levels evenly across the socioeconomic distribution, as in Figure 19.3a; (b) raise outcomes more for those with high SES than for those with low SES, as in Figure 19.3b; or (c) raise outcomes more for those of low SES than for those of high SES, as in Figure 19.3c. If Canadian social policy aims to achieve equality of opportunity

Figure 19.2

A socioeconomic gradient

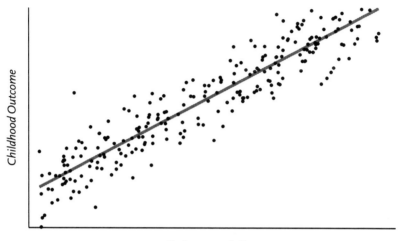

for children, then generally we are striving to raise and flatten gradients, as in Figure 19.3c. A particular policy might improve outcomes for low-SES children at the expense of high-SES children, thereby flattening the gradient without raising average levels of outcomes. This would not be considered a successful policy, as equity is achieved at the expense of excellence. The same argument would apply to a policy that steepened the gradient without raising average levels of outcomes, as equity would be compromised to achieve excellence.

Chapter 1 sets out ten central questions regarding gradients. The first four of these relate mainly to the relationship between childhood outcomes and SES. The last six questions pertain to factors that mediate the gradient and to variation among communities in their gradients.

Socioeconomic gradients are evident at birth

The findings indicate that even very early markers of vulnerability, such as a low birth weight or a difficult temperament during infancy, are related to SES. These are examined in detail in Chapters 4, 5, and 7. Table 19.1 presents a relatively simple analysis indicating the approximate magnitude of the relationship. In

Figure 19.3

A social policy with positive effects could (a) raise outcome levels evenly across the SES distribution, (b) raise outcomes more for those with high SES than those of low SES, or (c) raise outcomes more for those of low SES than those of high SES.

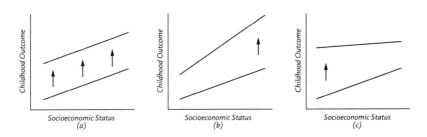

this analysis, and others, I divided families into three groups: low-SES families, who were in the bottom 25 percent of the SES distribution; average-SES families, who were in the middle two quartiles; and high-SES families, who were in the top 25 percent of the SES distribution. The analysis employed a logistic regression to determine the odds ratio associated with a child being vulnerable if he or she were in a low-SES family compared with an average SES family, or a high-SES family compared with an average family.[1]

The results indicate that the odds of a child in a low-SES family being born with a low birth weight was 1.21 times that of a child in an average-SES family. The corresponding odds ratios for difficult temperament and low motor and social development were 1.22 and 1.18 respectively. Similarly, children in high-SES families were less likely to have had a low birth weight (odds ratio of 0.67), a difficult temperament (0.95), or low motor and social development (0.87). These odds ratios are not especially large and were statistically significant only for difficult temperament in the case of low-SES children and for low birth weight for high-SES children. Nevertheless, they do provide evidence that socioeconomic gradients become evident at an early age.

Socioeconomic gradients become stronger as children get older

During infancy (ages zero and one) and the toddler years (ages two and three), the pattern of socioeconomic gradients varied depending on the measures

Table 19.1

Markers of vulnerability and family SES for infants and toddlers (odds ratios)

	Low birth weight	Difficult temperament	Low motor and social development
Low SES	1.21	**1.22**	1.18
High SES	**0.67**	0.95	0.87

Note: Odds ratios that differ significantly from 1.0 (p < 0.05) appear in boldface.

considered. On the marker of difficult temperament, the gradient was stronger for infants than for toddlers, whereas on the marker of behaviour problems, the gradient was particularly strong for toddlers and relatively weak for preschoolers (ages four and five). However, after children reach school age, the evidence suggests there is a steady increase in the strength of the socioeconomic gradient for both behaviour problems and cognitive performance. The more detailed analyses presented in Chapter 4 also reveal that the strength of the gradient for income per se becomes stronger for cognitive and behavioural outcomes during the school years.

Socioeconomic gradients vary depending on the outcome considered

Table 19.2 displays the odds ratios associated with SES for the cognitive and behavioural markers of vulnerability. These were estimated separately for children aged zero to five and six to eleven. The odds of a child from a low-SES family being vulnerable were about a third higher than for a child from an average-SES family, for both age groups and in both the cognitive and behavioural domains. However, the pattern is not consistent for children from high-SES families. For the younger cohort, the odds of having cognitive difficulties were about three-quarters that of an average-SES child, and of displaying behaviour problems the odds were about seventy percent that of an average-SES child. For older children growing up in high-SES families, the odds of having cognitive difficulties were less than half that of children in average-SES families. However, the odds of a high-SES child displaying behaviour problems remained unchanged at about 70 percent. Thus, it seems that living in a high-SES family may have a stronger buffering effect for cognitive difficulties as children get older than it does for behaviour problems.

Table 19.2

Markers of cognitive difficulties and behaviour problems and family SES (odds ratios)

	Cognitive difficulties	Behaviour problems
Ages 0 to 5		
• Low SES	**1.36**	**1.33**
• High SES	**0.74**	**0.69**
Ages 6 to 11		
• Low SES	**1.36**	**1.31**
• High SES	**0.46**	**0.70**

Note: Odds ratios that differ significantly from 1.0 ($p < 0.05$) appear in boldface.

Mother's education has a dominant effect compared with other aspects of SES

The measure of SES used in the study is a statistical composite comprising family income, the level of the mother's and father's education, and the prestige of the mother's and father's occupations (see Chapter 4). The analysis above shows the overall effects of living in a low- or high-SES family; however, one of the important questions in this study concerned whether certain components of SES had larger effects than others. Table 19.3 presents the results of an analysis of the effects of living in a family with low income, low parental education (parents had not completed secondary school), and low parental occupation (more than one standard deviation below the mean, which is approximately the bottom fifteen percent).

For younger children (aged zero to five), the effects associated with mother's education were considerably larger than those associated with family income. The odds of a child being vulnerable in either domain were nearly 50 percent higher if the child's mother had not completed secondary school; living in a low-income family increased the odds by about 20 percent for cognitive difficulties and 30 percent for behaviour problems. The mother's occupation played a significant role for cognitive difficulties, and father's occupation played a significant role for behaviour problems; the other effects were relatively small and not statistically significant. For older children (ages six to eleven), the effects of family income were larger than for younger children: the odds ratios

Table 19.3

Markers of cognitive difficulties and behaviour problems and the factors comprising family SES (odds ratios)

	Cognitive difficulties	Behaviour problems
Ages 0 to 5		
• Low family income (<$25,000)	**1.18**	**1.31**
• Mother's education < secondary	**1.49**	**1.45**
• Father's education < secondary	1.06	1.11
• Mother's occupation low	**1.35**	0.97
• Father's occupation low	0.95	**1.18**
Ages 6 to 11		
• Low family income (<$25,000)	**1.30**	**1.61**
• Mother's education < secondary	**1.66**	**1.50**
• Father's education < secondary	**1.30**	**1.12**
• Mother's occupation low	0.96	1.00
• Father's occupation low	1.10	1.05

Note: Odds ratios that differ significantly from 1.0 (p < 0.05) appear in boldface.

were 1.30 for cognitive difficulties and 1.61 for behaviour problems. The father's level of education played a more significant role at this age, especially for cognitive difficulties. The effects of the mother's education did not diminish; in fact, the odds ratios were slightly larger: 1.66 for cognitive difficulties and 1.50 for behaviour problems.

This decomposition of the effects of SES suggests that the level of education of the mother has a dominant effect throughout the early years and after the child enters school, while income and the level of education of the father increase in their importance as children get older.

■ A Challenge to the Culture of Poverty Thesis

Research has consistently shown that parenting practices influence a range of childhood outcomes such as academic achievement, pro-social behaviour, and high-school completion. Some studies have argued that children of poor parents have worse schooling outcomes because of inadequate parenting. The research in this volume challenges this "culture of poverty" thesis and the widespread belief that children from poor families do not fare well because of

Figure 19.4

Models of the influence of variables

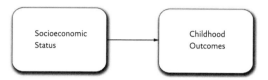

A. Path diagram for a socioeconomic gradient

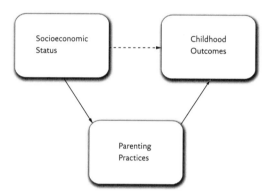

B. The mediation model underlying the "culture of poverty" thesis

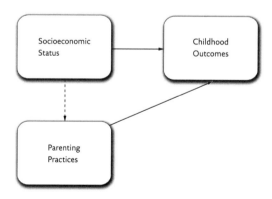

C. Socioeconomic status and parenting practices as independent influences

inadequate parenting. A primary aim of this research is to determine which factors mediate the relationships between childhood outcomes and SES.

Mediating factors describe the underlying processes through which one variable influences another. I will use path diagrams and a simple example to explain the concept, and then extend the analysis presented in Table 19.3 to provide a summary of the important relationships uncovered in this research. Figure 19.4a depicts the socioeconomic gradient as a path diagram with childhood outcomes and SES represented as single constructs.[2]

A mediating factor explains why one variable influences another. For example, if poor parenting is the underlying mechanism through which SES influences childhood outcomes, we would expect a strong relationship between SES and parenting practices and between parenting practices and childhood outcomes. This is the model underlying the culture of poverty thesis, which is depicted in Figure 19.4b. One criterion for a factor to be a mediator is that it must significantly explain the primary relationship, in this case the relationship between SES and childhood outcomes. Thus, the arrow between SES and outcomes is portrayed with a dashed arrow, to indicate that the "mediated" relationship is very weak or even non-existent.

The effects of good parenting far outweigh the effects of income

Previous research on parenting styles has found that children have superior schooling outcomes when their parents monitor their behaviour, are responsive to their needs, and encourage independence with a democratic approach. This style of parenting, referred to as *authoritative* parenting, is contrasted with an *authoritarian* style, which typifies parents as being highly controlling; or a *permissive* style, which typifies parents as overly nurturing and providing few standards for behaviour. The findings in Chapter 8 used parents' responses to a set of 25 questions regarding their child-rearing practices to classify parents into 4 groups. Three of the groups corresponded to the three styles of parenting, and a fourth group, referred to as inadequate parenting, comprised parents who scored low on all aspects of parenting skills.

Table 19.4 presents the results of a simple analysis that examines the potentially mediating effects of parenting styles on the relationship between SES and behaviour problems for children aged two to eleven. More detailed analyses of these findings are presented in Chapters 8 and 9. The first model includes the two variables denoting high- and low-SES families. The results indicate that children in a high-SES family are 32 percent less likely (or 0.68

Table 19.4

Parenting practices as a potential mediator of the socioeconomic gradient for children's behaviour problems (odds ratios)

	I	II
Socioeconomic status		
• Low-SES family	**1.34**	**1.29**
• High-SES family	**0.68**	**0.74**
Parenting practices		
• Authoritarian		**2.09**
• Permissive		**1.65**
• Inadequate		**2.83**

Note: Odds ratios that differ significantly from 1.0 (p < 0.05) appear in boldface.

times as likely) to exhibit behaviour problems as those in an average-SES family, whereas children in a low-SES family are 34 percent more likely to exhibit behaviour problems. The second model includes variables denoting parents who are either authoritarian, permissive, or ineffective, which yields odds ratios relative to parents who have an authoritative style. The most striking result is that these effects far outweigh the effects of living in either a low- or high-SES family: the odds ratios range from 1.65 to 2.83.

However, what is also evident, is that the parenting variables do not substantially affect the odds ratios for SES: the protective effect of living in a high-SES family was reduced from 32 percent to 26 percent, and the detrimental effect of living in a low-SES family was reduced from 34 percent to 29 percent. The results in Chapter 8 also show that the relationship between parenting practices and SES is very weak. Thus, rather than the mediator model displayed in Figure 19.4b, the findings support a model where SES and parenting practices independently influence childhood outcomes. This model is shown in Figure 19.4c.

Children living in single-parent and teen-parent families are prone to exhibiting behaviour problems

Two chapters are concerned with particularly vulnerable families: those headed by single parents (Chapter 13) and teen mothers (Chapter 14). Do children

Table 19.5

Relationship between children's vulnerability and family background, child characteristics, family environment and neighbourhood support (odds ratios)

	Ages 0 to 5				Ages 6 to 11			
	Cognitive difficulties		Behaviour problems		Cognitive difficulties		Behaviour problems	
	I	II	I	II	I	II	I	II
Family background								
• Low SES	**1.26**	**1.14**	**1.20**	1.11	**1.32**	**1.30**	**1.16**	**1.08**
• High SES	**0.73**	**0.86**	**0.73**	**0.84**	**0.46**	**0.47**	**0.75**	**0.84**
• Mother at home	**1.43**	**1.41**	0.93	0.92	**1.11**	**1.10**	1.09	1.08
• Single parent	1.03	0.88	**1.53**	**1.25**	1.00	1.01	**1.77**	**1.67**
• Teenage mother	0.91	0.87	**1.36**	**1.33**	1.15	1.14	**1.65**	**1.69**
• Number of siblings	**1.07**	1.05	0.93	0.87	**1.10**	**1.10**	0.95	0.91
• Recent immigrant	**2.20**	**1.96**	1.06	0.99	0.76	0.73	**0.31**	**0.29**
Child characteristics								
• Female	**0.70**	**0.72**	0.96	0.99	**0.78**	**0.78**	**0.60**	**0.61**
• First child	**0.77**	**0.80**	**0.76**	**0.74**	**1.44**	**1.45**	**1.21**	**1.20**
Family environment								
• Authoritarian style		**1.53**		**2.01**		0.88		**1.87**
• Permissive style		**1.23**		**1.80**		0.92		**1.43**
• Inadequate parenting		**1.85**		**2.14**		0.91		**2.75**
• Maternal depression		**1.21**		**1.77**		0.92		**1.56**
• Poor family functioning		**1.38**		**1.32**		1.02		**1.51**
• Parents read to child		0.92		0.96				
Neighbourhood support		**0.93**		1.00		**0.95**		1.07

Note: Odds ratios that differ significantly from 1.0 (p < 0.05) appear in boldface.

living in single-parent families or families with young mothers have worse cognitive and behavioural outcomes than other children, after account is taken of their socioeconomic circumstances? Table 19.5 extends the analyses presented earlier in this chapter to include other aspects of a child's background and other mediating factors. The first model for each domain and age group (Model I) provides estimates of the effects of SES and other background factors. The second model extended the first estimates to include family environment and neighbourhood support as potentially mediating factors.

There is an interesting pattern evident in the results for both single parents and teen mothers. First, the children of these parents do not appear to have an increased risk of experiencing cognitive difficulties compared with their peers. One should note, however, that these are odds ratios that have been adjusted for all other variables in the model. Thus, they are assessing whether children living in families headed by single parents and teen mothers are at increased risk compared with children in families with similar levels of SES. Because single parents and teen mothers tend to have lower levels of education and considerably lower family income, their children are at increased risk. What these results indicate is that their children are not more likely to have cognitive difficulties compared with other children living in families with similar socioeconomic circumstances. The second pattern is that children living in families headed by a single parent or teen mother are more likely to exhibit behaviour problems, and the magnitude of the effect far outweighs the effects associated with living in a low-SES family. Moreover, the risk increases as children get older.

Children with behaviour problems are moderately concentrated within families

Chapter 6 asked whether children with behaviour problems tended to be concentrated in certain families. The results indicated only a moderate degree of concentration—about ten percent of children with behaviour problems are concentrated in five percent of all families with children who have behaviour problems. The concentration was somewhat higher for physical aggression than other types of behaviour problems, and the odds of a second child being highly physically aggressive if the first child was aggressive was found to be about three to four times higher than if the first child was non-aggressive. The results in Figure 19.5 also indicate an interesting pattern with respect to birth order. First-born children were much less likely to experience either cognitive difficulties or behaviour problems during the early years, but were more likely to have problems in both domains after they entered school.

The effect associated with the number of children in the family is also interesting. The findings indicate that having more brothers and sisters increases the likelihood of a child having cognitive difficulties—each additional sibling increases the odds by about five to ten percent. However, children with more brothers and sisters are less likely to display behaviour problems—each additional sibling decreases the odds by about five to ten percent.

Children who had immigrated within the last ten years were more likely than non-immigrant children to have cognitive difficulties, but this result is probably an artifact of the nature of the tests and was not evident for school-age children. Children who had immigrated were much less likely to exhibit behaviour problems.

Working outside the home does not increase childhood vulnerability

There is considerable debate in the literature (and certainly within many families) as to whether children whose mothers work outside the home fare better or worse than those whose mothers do not work outside of the home. The results in Table 19.5 suggest that children whose mothers are at home are at increased risk of displaying cognitive difficulties during the early years, but this diminishes after their children enter school. The more detailed analyses in Chapter 4 suggest that this increased risk is primarily associated with poorer motor and social development among toddlers. There are no apparent effects of either working or not working outside the home on children's behaviour outcomes. There is a trade-off: mothers who do not work outside the home have more time to be engaged with their child, and this has positive effects (see Chapter 10). But stay-at-home mothers generally have a lower family income, and thus their children do not benefit from some of the effects associated with increased income. Stay-at-home mothers also tend to be slightly more prone to depression, which can have detrimental effects on their child's development (see Chapter 12). On balance, however, there are minimal long-term effects of either working or not working outside the home. What matters most is that a child is cared for throughout the day by warm and responsive caregivers, in an environment rich with opportunities to learn.

The family environment is the strongest determinant of childhood vulnerability. Model II in Table 19.5 presents a summary analysis of the effects associated with family environment and neighbourhood support. These are presented alongside the results of Model I so that one can assess the mediating effects of these factors. The factors include parenting styles (as in Table 19.4), maternal depression, family functioning, whether the parents read regularly to the child, and neighbourhood support. More detailed analyses of the effects of these factors are presented in Chapters 8, 9, 10, 11, and 12.

All of the family environment factors have strong significant effects on childhood vulnerability in both domains during the early years. What is impressive is the magnitude of these effects: the odds ratios for parenting styles, maternal depression, and poor family functioning range from 1.21 to 2.14, which far outweigh the effects attributable to living in a low-SES family. Reading to a child also significantly reduced the likelihood of a child having cognitive difficulties or displaying behaviour problems, and although the effect is small compared with the effects of parenting, maternal depression and family functioning, it is noteworthy in that these are the effects net of all other variables in the model. Neighbourhood support also had a small positive effect on cognitive outcomes, but curiously, not for behavioural outcomes.

The results also indicate that after children enter school, these family environment variables continue to have a profound effect on children's behavioural outcomes but not on their cognitive outcomes. The measure of cognitive problems at this age derives solely from a short test of mathematics, which we acknowledge as a limitation of this study (see the discussion in Chapter 4). Family environment may have an effect on other aspects of cognitive development, which we can assess when a broader array of cognitive measures become available in subsequent cycles of the NLSCY. Neighbourhood support had a positive effect on cognitive outcomes but a negative effect on behaviour problems. The anomalous result for behaviour probably stems from the relationships between neighbourhood support and the various family environ- ✓ ment variables.

The findings present a serious challenge to the "culture of poverty" thesis

If the "culture of poverty thesis" holds, then we would expect to find a strong relationship between poverty and parenting styles and other aspects of family life. We would also expect the full set of family variables to explain the effects of poverty. However, the findings indicate that parenting styles, engagement, family functioning, and maternal depression are only weakly related with income or SES. The results presented in Table 19.5 allow us to address the question of mediating effects for the full set of family environment variables. The results for young children suggest that about half of the increased risk associated with living in a low-SES family is accounted for by the environment variables (the risk reduced from 26 percent to 14 percent for cognitive difficulties and from 20 percent to 11 percent for behaviour problems). About half of the protective effects associated with living in a high-SES family are also attributable to family environment (the risk of 27 percent diminished to 14 percent for cognitive difficulties and from 27 percent to 16 percent for behaviour problems.) The "one-half" result also applies to behaviour problems for the school-age cohort: the increased risk associated with living in a low-SES family decreased from 16 percent to 8 percent and the protective effect associated with living in a high-SES family decreased from 25 percent to 16 percent. The family environment variables did not substantially mediate the effects of SES for cognitive difficulties among the school-age children.

An important implication of this research is that poor families and single-parent mothers are unfairly characterized as lacking parenting skills and being less engaged with their children. Both positive and negative practices are found in rich and poor families alike, and in single- and two-parent families. Moreover, the effects of parenting and family functioning far outweigh the effects associated with living in a low-income family. Again, what matters most is that a child is cared for throughout the day by warm and responsive care-givers, in an environment rich with opportunities to learn.

■ Schools and Communities Make a Difference

Children from low-income families appear to benefit most from daycare

Chapter 15 examined the effects associated with attending a preschool or daycare compared with other forms of care arrangements. The findings indicate that about 40 percent of Canadian children aged 4 and 5 spent part of their week in some form of care arrangement, and of those, only about 30 percent (12 percent overall) were in a regulated daycare. The results indicated that attending a daycare, irrespective of whether it was regulated, had a positive effect on the vocabulary skills of children living in low-income families. For high-income families, attending a daycare did not seem to have either a positive or a negative effect compared with other forms of care arrangements.

Children's cognitive development is substantially affected by their classroom and school environment

The research on successful schools and classrooms presented in Chapter 16 indicates that provinces vary considerably in their mathematics achievement. Perhaps the most remarkable finding is the dramatic success of Quebec compared with the other provinces. Quebec's superior performance in mathematics achievement is apparent in the results for grade-two students, and its relative advantage increases steadily throughout the elementary school years. The findings indicate that by the end of the middle-school years, students are on average about one full grade level above the national average. In contrast, Ontario scored below the national average, as did the Atlantic provinces.

Children in British Columbia and the prairie provinces scored above the national average, but their results were not as impressive as those of Quebec. These disparities were evident not only in the data from the NLSCY, but also in the data from a number of other surveys. The disparities were not attributable to family SES or the proportions of immigrants in each province.

The findings also indicate that schools and classrooms vary considerable in their mathematics results, even after taking account of SES and immigrant status. On average, schools and classrooms tended to be more successful when class sizes were small and students were taught by teachers who specialized in mathematics instruction. Achievement scores were also better for teachers who did not practice ability grouping and were able to successfully maintain classroom discipline.

The prevalence of vulnerable children varies among communities

The school-based analyses in Chapter 16 found that the prevalence of children with exceedingly low mathematics scores varied significantly among provinces and among schools. More generally, analyses of the variation in childhood vulnerability indicated that the prevalence of vulnerable children varied significantly among neighbourhoods, ranging from about 25 percent to 35 percent, and among cities, ranging from 25 percent to 32 percent. The prevalence of vulnerable children also varied considerably among provinces. Taken together, this research provides strong evidence that "communities" vary in their prevalence of vulnerable children. We have observed statistically significant variation in prevalence rates among provinces, schools, cities, and neighbourhoods, even after account is taken of family SES.

We found it much more difficult to determine why communities vary. Using "provinces" as a unit of analysis for community has limited use, in that there are too many factors that might contribute to observed differences. Enumeration areas were used as a proxy for neighbourhoods, but these units were too small to achieve accurate estimation of prevalence rates. We achieved a better grasp of why communities varied when we used schools and classrooms as a unit of analysis, but we had to rely on data collected as part of another study. Using cities as a unit of analysis, or neighbourhoods defined as larger entities than enumeration areas (EAs), is suitable for assessing community effects. However, the NLSCY does not afford much information on resources or practices at these levels. This problem is being addressed with the development of the UEY project.

Successful communities are those that succeed in bolstering the outcomes of their least-advantaged children

A study of youth literacy in Canada and the US suggests that some provinces and states are more successful than others in achieving high levels of literacy for all citizens (Willms, 1999). In other words, they have high and gradual gradients. The pattern evident in this work, and in other research that has compared gradients across several countries, is that gradients converge at high levels of SES. Studies of school and classroom effects on children's academic achievement also reveal a pattern of converging gradients (e.g., Lee & Bryk, 1989; Willms, 1999). This pattern has important implications for social policy: it suggests that children and youth from high-SES families tend to do well in any community, but the outcomes of those from low-SES families vary substantially among communities.

The analyses of gradients in Chapter 16 lend support to this hypothesis of converging gradients: the successful schools and classrooms tend to be those that have relatively high achievement levels for students from lower socioeconomic backgrounds. However, the analysis of gradients at the levels of provinces, cities, and neighbourhoods did not afford a strong test of the hypothesis. At the levels of provinces and cities, there was relatively little variation in the slopes of the gradients. The analyses detected significant variation among neighbourhoods in their gradients, but the sample sizes within neighbourhoods were too small to significantly discern whether gradients converged.

When children are segregated by SES, those from disadvantaged families are even more prone to being vulnerable

A number of studies of school achievement have found that children who are less able academically and who attend mixed-ability schools tend to have higher achievement levels than children with similar ability who are segregated in schools with other children of low ability. Similarly, when children are segregated among schools or classrooms along socioeconomic lines, either indirectly through residential segregation or through policies that support selective schooling, children from low-SES backgrounds tend to do considerably worse, while those from high-SES backgrounds tend to do marginally better (see the review in Chapter 16). More generally, the hypothesis of double jeopardy holds that children with low ability or from low-SES families are vulnerable, but when these children also live in low-SES communities, they are especially vulnerable (Willms, 2000). A critical question for this study, therefore, was whether this hypothesis held at the level of neighbourhood, school, and city.

The results of our analyses of mathematics achievement found strong evidence of double jeopardy: the average SES of a classroom was strongly related to student achievement, even after taking account of the child's own family background. In fact, the effects of the average SES of a child's classmates were as strong as the SES of the child's family in determining the child's mathematics outcome. About a quarter of the double-jeopardy effect was attributable to the measures of school and classroom processes available in the data. The analyses at the levels of neighbourhood and city neither supported or refuted the hypothesis. As with the assessment of converging gradients, the study lacked statistical power to detect the effects of community-level variables.

■ Future Research on Childhood Development

The design of the NLSCY entails biennial data collection on the sample of children examined in this study. At each data collection period, a new sample of children under two years of age is drawn. For example, in 1996–97, data were collected for the children who participated in the 1994–95 study, who were then aged two through thirteen. Together with the new sample of infants for that period, the resulting data set covers ages zero through thirteen. This design will enable researchers to conduct two types of longitudinal analyses, which are at the heart of social policy research. One type uses the longitudinal data for children: as the 1994–95 cohort is followed, we will have developmental data describing the same set of individuals for several points. The second type use longitudinal data for higher units of analysis, such as provinces, cities, and schools. As the survey proceeds, we will have monitoring data describing successive cohorts of children at a given age. These two kinds of data will enable us to understand the causal mechanisms that lead to desirable social outcomes, to monitor changes in children's outcomes at the national and provincial levels, and to discern whether particular social policies are successful in raising and flattening socioeconomic gradients.

As the NLSCY children get older, we will have data covering the adolescent period and eventually extending into adulthood. Chapter 18 suggests that forming friendships with peers who frequently get into trouble is associated with both internalizing and externalizing behaviour disorders. This foreshadows the importance of understanding the role of peer groups on developmental outcomes during the adolescent period.

Developmental data

The longitudinal developmental data will afford the opportunities for investigations focussed on the long-term trajectories of children's outcomes and how these are related to individuals' characteristics and experiences. While there are countless questions that researchers interested in child development might pursue, most of them would conceive development as a continuous or transitional process (Boyle & Willms, 2001). The term *child development* connotes the continuous acquisition or loss of functional characteristics, such as language, academic achievement, or life skills. With the NLSCY, for example, we will soon have measures of children's academic skills for several occasions covering the elementary school period. Even though achievement is assessed at two-year intervals, the underlying process is considered to be continuous, with skills increasing or decreasing gradually over time. Other questions pertain to the occurrence and timing of major life experiences, which occur as discrete events. These can be either positive or negative experiences; some prominent examples for children and youth include grade repetition, puberty, pregnancy, high-school graduation, and transition to post-secondary schooling or the labour market. For these questions, development is viewed as a marked change in status—that is, as a transitional process. Entering or leaving periods of vulnerability, as defined in this study, can also be viewed as a transitional process. The two types of developmental processes require different approaches to analysis. Two of the prevailing methodological approaches are discussed in detail by Boyle and Willms (2001).

A major limitation of the research reported here is that it is difficult to make strong causal inferences based on cross-sectional data. For example, the analyses indicate a strong relationship between parenting styles and vulnerability, even after taking account of children's family demographic characteristics. We naturally infer, therefore, that better parenting would cause better childhood outcomes, and the case for a causal relationship is bolstered by theory and previous research. With longitudinal data, one can examine whether changes in developmental outcomes (e.g., growth in academic achievement) or the occurrence or timing of some event (e.g., dropping out of school) are related to changes in parenting style. If so, we have a stronger case for a causal relationship.

An even stronger case could be made for a causal relationship with a true experiment. For example, one could randomly assign families with ineffective parenting styles to treatment and control groups and provide parent training for parents in the treatment group. If children in the treatment group improved their cognitive and behavioural outcomes while children in the control group did not, we would have strong evidence of a causal relationship. However, even such controlled studies do not provide the final word on the subject: people often react differently when they are being studied or even react negatively if they are assigned to a control group; sometimes the success of a treatment occurs because of a particularly charismatic leader; and often it is difficult to generalize the findings from a small sample in one locale to the national population. What is required is a number of small experimental studies that piggy-back on the NLSCY by using some of the same measurement instruments. Richard Tremblay and his colleagues have launched a study of infants in three Quebec communities that will serve as a good example of an experimental study piggy-backing on the NLSCY.

One of the problems with longitudinal research is that it takes several years before one has the necessary data to describe a developmental process for a cohort of individuals. For example, the research on the effects of puberty (Chapter 17) suggests that girls with advanced pubertal development are more likely to associate with members of a group with anti-social behaviours and have friends who smoke, drink alcohol, and use drugs. But with the current data, it is impossible to determine the long-term consequences of these relationships. Similarly, the research on children with teenage mothers (Chapter 14) suggests that they are more prone to behaviour problems and have poor vocabulary skills on entry to school. We do not know, however, whether these problems are usually overcome as the children age with their parents. Research aimed at understanding these relationships requires longitudinal data.

A strategy to overcome the long waiting time required to amass longitudinal data is to employ an accelerated longitudinal design (Raudenbush & Chan, 1992). The idea is to string together the growth trajectories for three or more different cohorts to discern what the long-term growth trajectory for the present cohort might look like. For example, in the NLSCY, we will soon have several four-year growth trajectories for children covering the periods 1994–95 to 1998–99. To take a simple example, we could estimate the growth trajectory in height between zero and four for children born in 1994, and between one and five for children born in 1993, and so on through to the trajectory between eleven and fifteen for children born in 1983. If we plotted each of these four-year trajectories on a graph of height versus age, we would have a series of four-year lines that overlapped at certain points. These lines could be joined together to form one long straight line, which would constitute our estimate of the likely growth trajectory from age zero to eleven for children born in 1994.

The lines may not overlap because of measurement error or because of period effects (e.g., there may be a secular trend for children to be getting taller). Whether these disjunctures are statistically significant can be formally tested (see Raudenbush & Chan, 1992).

When longitudinal data become accessible, an important agenda will be to examine some of the primary relationships reported above. For example, we will be especially interested in the effects of a short-term versus long-term exposure to poverty. Are children's outcomes susceptible to changes in parenting styles, family functioning, or whether or not the mother is suffering from depression? Analyses addressing these questions will not only be strengthened by having longitudinal data, but also by having data for more than one child per family. For example, as the 1994–95 cohort ages, some of the children will encounter certain negative life experiences, such as parents who separate or divorce, parents who become unemployed, or the death of a family member. These data will allow us to model whether these experiences have differing short- and long-term effects on the growth trajectories of children within the same family, thereby providing a way of determining whether some of these experiences have worse consequences for children at different ages.

One of the exciting aspects of this research has been to examine the effects of family, neighbourhood, and community contextual variables on children's outcomes. With longitudinal data, we will be able to estimate the effects of factors such as neighbourhood support on developmental outcomes, conceived as either continuous or transitional processes. These require more complex multilevel statistical models, but they will give us a much stronger purchase on their effects than was possible in this study. The research in this vein will be strengthened with the community-level data being collected through the UEY project, which can be viewed as a multi-site piggy-back study to the NLSCY.

Monitoring data

A fundamental concern of social policy is whether gradients are changing over time. The NLSCY design will yield comparable data on successive cohorts of children every two years, enabling us to examine secular trends in children's outcomes as the study progresses. For example, we will soon have data describing three cohorts of infants aged zero to one. We could ask whether the prevalence of low birth weight is increasing or decreasing, and whether the relationship between low birth weight and SES is become weaker or stronger.

These relationships can be assessed at the national level as well as at provincial or local levels. To follow this example, if the socioeconomic gradients for low birth weight were becoming higher and flatter in some provinces, but lower and steeper in others, we would want to examine the policies potentially affecting these changes. A recent assessment of the potential effects of New Brunswick's Early Childhood Initiative provides an example. It examines whether changes in the socioeconomic gradients for early childhood outcomes between 1994–95 to 1995–96 were statistically significant for New Brunswick and how these changes compared with changes in the gradients for the other provinces (Willms, 2000).

Even stronger models for monitoring change will be possible when data from three cycles of the survey are available. Raudenbush and I set out an hierarchical model, referred to as the stability model, that can be used to assess whether gradients are changing over time and whether changes in gradients are related to changes in community-level factors (Willms & Raudenbush, 1989). This model offers a powerful test of whether certain provincial or local policies are having their intended effect.

Finally, social-policy research employing both developmental data and monitoring data will be strengthened by merging the NLSCY data with data from other sources. During the past ten years, Human Resources Development Canada and Statistics Canada have been successful in developing a "unified and coherent system of social statistics," aimed at providing "a framework for the study of causes, effects and outcomes, and the roles and possible impacts of policies" (Fellegi & Wolfson, 1999). This system is based on a suite of large national studies pertaining to children's education and health, the transition of youth from school to the labour market, youth and adult literacy, and population health. Using these data to establish a comprehensive monitoring system for educational and health outcomes is important because it can provide a framework for conducting policy research, evaluating particular reforms, and assessing the strengths and weaknesses of the schooling and health systems. A comprehensive monitoring system can provide a means for discerning whether there are inequalities in social outcomes among people with differing socioeconomic backgrounds, among ethnic groups, and between males and females, and to some extent determine whether inequalities in outcomes stem from inequalities in opportunity. Thus, it can encourage a process of self-examination and renewal of national, provincial, and local policies based on research evidence.

NOTES

1   An odds ratio, as the name suggests, is simply the ratio of the odds of an event occurring for a particular group (in this case, for example, children living in either a low- or high-SES family) to the odds of the event occurring for the reference group (in this case, children living in a family of average SES). For example, in low-SES families the prevalence of children with low birth weight was 6.83 percent. The odds of a child being low birth weight is the ratio of the likelihood of the event (6.83 percent) to the likelihood of "not the event" (100 - 6.83 = 93.17 percent), or 0.0733. Among children born to families in the middle of the SES distribution, the prevalence of low birth weight was 5.70 percent, which corresponds to an odds of (5.70/94.3 =) 0.0604. Thus, the ratio of these two odds is 0.0733 to 0.0604, or 1.21. Researchers would say that the chances of a child being low birth weight is 1.21 times higher for children in low-SES families compared with those in average-SES families, but technically, one should say the *odds* of low birth weight for children in low-SES families is 1.21 times the *odds* for those in average SES families.

2   The arrow from SES to outcomes implies that SES influences childhood outcomes but not vice versa. One could hypothesize that in some instances children who are particularly vulnerable affect their parents' SES, in which case the arrow would be bi-directional. There are powerful statistical techniques for estimating very complex models in the social sciences, which include such reciprocal relationships (e.g., Bollen, 1989), but for our purposes we assume a simple unidirectional model.

Implications of the Findings for Social Policy Renewal

J. DOUGLAS WILLMS

■ A New Era in Canadian Social Policy

WE ARE ENTERING A NEW ERA in Canadian social policy. At all levels of government, there is a growing awareness that social policy and economic policy are inextricably linked: improving the quality of life of a nation's citizens requires sustained economic growth, but this in turn requires investments in human and social capital. The "human capital" of a society—embodied in the knowledge, competencies and health of its members (Alexander, 1997; Becker, 1993)—requires investments in education, health, and nutrition. Moreover, countries with greater equality of income have superior economic growth because more families can afford to educate their children, and the state is less burdened by the "defensive necessities" of preventing crime and providing welfare subsidies (Osberg, 1995; van der Gaag, & Tan, 2000). Recent research has also provided compelling evidence that learning and health depend on relationships among people, both within communities and organizations and among them. Sociologists have used the term "social capital" to describe the nature of these relationships and the extent to which they facilitate collective action, the strength of social networks, and the norms and values of a community (Coleman, 1988). Research in this vein has been concerned with the nature of social support and collective action, and how it affects people's trust, trustworthiness, and sense of security and well-being.

Governments are increasingly called upon to base policy decisions on empirical evidence. They commission studies to tackle specific policy issues and support research on social policy. They devote considerable resources to monitoring social outcomes, understanding the causal mechanisms that lead to desirable outcomes, and testing the efficacy of various policy strategies. Despite these efforts, it is difficult to keep social policy abreast of social changes, which are increasingly shaped by global forces. Social policy is built upon an infrastructure that resists change, and while governments may have effective "levers" for redistributing income and providing social programs, building social and human capital is less straightforward. For example, should governments maintain their programs targeted to particular groups? What kinds of programs are sustainable? How can successful pilot programs be brought to scale? How can governments integrate social and economic policy more successfully? Maxwell (1996) contends that, during the 1960s and '70s, economic policy was characterized by accommodation: citizens were protected from increases in the costs of living, and industry was protected from competitive pressures through subsidies and trade barriers. In the 1990s, economic policy shifted to a new regime that emphasized free trade, new markets for Canadian exports, and deficit reduction. During this period, however, little attention was paid to social policy, leaving us with a system based on old values and perceptions. Maxwell argues that the old social safety net does not offer the right kinds of support and does not meet the current needs of Canadian families (see also Maxwell, 1995; Peters, 1995).

Bringing research evidence to bear on social policy is not straightforward. Research in the social sciences seldom produces unequivocal findings that can be used to make objective judgements to form public policy. Moving from research findings to policy implications requires researchers to make a giant leap; where they land is determined by their culture, experiences, and values. Moreover, policy-making is a political process that occurs within a political context. But research findings can shape public opinion, provoke public dialogue, cause legislative debate, and inform the policy process—gradually creating a new framework of understanding.

While this research was proceeding, we had the opportunity to present preliminary results to an audience made up of a broad cross-section of the Canadian policy community. The Applied Research Branch of Human Resources Development Canada (HRDC) hosted a national conference that included representatives from the federal government, provincial and municipal governments, non-government and voluntary organizations, social workers, educators, parents, and youth. The discussion ensuing from the research was summarized in the document *Investing in Children: Ideas for Action* (Human Resources Development Canada, 1999).

An over-arching theme of the discussion was how difficult it is to be a "good" parent, especially for people who are marginalized in society. Another theme was that research does not adequately capture the problems faced by children who fall through the holes in our social safety net, such as those who have been abused, those whose parents are addicted to alcohol, and those who have lost a parent. Participants were unanimous in their call to increase co-operation across levels of government, across departments at each level of government, and among organizations in the public, private, and voluntary sectors.

Some of our research findings generated considerable debate, as they were disturbing to some participants. The most controversial issue was the notion that vulnerability and poverty are not synonymous. Some participants were especially concerned that the research would convey a message that poverty does not matter, which might lead to policies that reduce benefits to poor families. Others expressed fears that the emphasis on early childhood outcomes would take resources away from the problems of adolescents, and that a call for universal programs would take away from effective targeted programs. Therefore, I begin with these issues in the next two sections. But the findings in this volume indicate that eliminating poverty will not in itself substantially reduce vulnerability. The last section, therefore, calls for a renewal of Canadian social policy by building an infrastructure for a family-enabling society.

■ Poverty Matters

No child should live in poverty. Aside from any other issue, it is a matter of human rights. The results of this research emphatically do not suggest that the federal or provincial governments should reduce benefits to needy families. Nor do they suggest that poverty is not a significant risk factor. What they do reveal is that the majority of vulnerable children are not living in poor families, and that about two-thirds of children who are living in poor families have cognitive and behavioural outcomes that are in the average range or better. The findings also provide strong evidence that what matters most is the kind of family environment a child lives in: the benefits of good parenting skills, a cohesive family unit, and parents with good mental health far outweigh the negative effects associated with poverty. Moreover, these factors do not have a strong relationship with family income. Thus, it is unfair to stereotype single parents or parents with low incomes as inadequate parents, or to presume that most children from disadvantaged families are vulnerable.

This said, I must also caution readers that this research may have understated the effects of poverty on children's outcomes. There are several reasons. First, a few recent studies of US children have indicated that those who live in poverty for sustained periods are more likely to be vulnerable than children who experience poverty for relatively short periods (Duncan, Brooks-Gunn, & Klebanov, 1994; McLeod & Nonnemaker, 2000). Indeed, our findings do indicate that the effects of income on both cognitive and behavioural outcomes increase as children get older. It may be, therefore, that the cumulative effects of living in poverty have a much stronger effect than our cross-sectional findings suggest. Future analyses, based on the longitudinal data from the National Longitudinal Survey of Children and Youth (NLSCY), will provide information on the long-term consequences of poverty on children's outcomes.

Second, because of the size and nature of the NLSCY sample, the data do not allow us to estimate the effects of extreme poverty. The US research has found a dramatic increase in vulnerability associated with extreme poverty (Duncan, Yeung, Brooks-Gunn, & Smith, 1998). Thus, if benefits to poor families in Canada were reduced, we would likely have more families living in extreme poverty, leading to a substantial increase in the number of vulnerable children.

Third, we expect many of the children being followed in the NLSCY will move in and out of vulnerability. Many children are likely to experience negative life events that cause them to become vulnerable, at least for a period, while others will likely overcome their difficulties through their own efforts and with the support of their families and immediate communities. As we follow the NLSCY children, we may find that those living in poor families have more episodes of vulnerability or are vulnerable for longer periods. Finally, family income may play a more dominant role in determining whether a child makes a successful transition from middle to secondary school, or from secondary school to post-secondary education and the labour market. Adolescents who have experienced prolonged periods of poverty may be especially vulnerable to becoming involved in criminal activities.

A dominant argument of recent studies in the US has been that childhood vulnerability is caused by pre-existing differences between poor and non-poor parents in their social and emotional functioning. Therefore, programs aimed at alleviating poverty have limited benefits (Mayer, 1997; Duncan et al., 1998).

However, this argument presumes that such psychological factors are immutable and are not affected by improved economic circumstances. Its emphasis is also on the characteristics of the individual, principally the mother, without attention to the structural features of a society that can contribute to, and interact with, the well-being of parent and child. For example, an adolescent girl with low self-esteem may be prone to early sexuality and child-bearing, and thereafter she and her baby are destined to live with low income, poor housing, and few opportunities for quality child care. The child eventually enters a school with few resources and low-quality instruction. The local community affords few opportunities for the child to participate in sports and recreational activities. These structural features of the school and community contribute to the low self-esteem of the mother and lead to chronic depression, thereby further reducing the child's chances for success. The point is that the characteristics of the parents and the context in which they live are interdependent and dynamic: context affects parents' psychological well-being and vice versa. It may be that cash benefits to the poor have relatively small effects by themselves, but if they are coupled with efforts to reduce social exclusion and provide social support, they could have dramatic, enduring effects.

■ Intervene Early and When Needed

During the past decade, researchers have advanced a strong case for early intervention, derived from new evidence in neurobiology about how the brain develops and from research documenting the long-term success of early childhood programs for economically deprived children. The neurobiological research has shown that brain development from conception to age one is rapid and extensive, much more so than previously believed, and is heavily influenced by the infant's environment (Carnegie Corporation of New York, 1994). A newborn has billions of neurons, which, during the course of development, form connections called synapses. These synapses are formed in response to environmental stimuli; while this is occurring, many of the neurons that are not being used are pruned away. This process of synapse formation and neuron pruning is often referred to as the "sculpting" or "wiring" of the brain. Moreover, there are critical periods, especially during the first three years, when particular areas of the brain are sculpted (McEwan & Schmeck, 1994; Cynader & Frost, 1999). While this evidence from neurobiology has been mounting, longitudinal studies that have followed children who have received intensive interventions aimed at increasing stimulation and providing parent training and support have demonstrated long-lasting effects on their social, behavioural, and educational outcomes (e.g., Andersson, 1992; Olds et al., 1997, 1998; Osborn & Milbank, 1987; Schweinhart, Barnes, & Weikart, 1993; Wasik & Ramey, 1990). Recent studies have also suggested that children's environments during the early years contribute substantially to the development of their endocrine and immunological systems (Gunner, 1998; McEwan, 1998). Taken together, these strands of research provide compelling evidence that care and stimulation during the early years are critical to establishing a foundation for learning, behaviour, and health over the life cycle (McCain & Mustard, 1999).

The neuroscience story has not been without its critics. Bruer (1999) argues that it has engendered a myth that a child's long-term prospects for health and well-being are wholly determined during the first three years—that kindergarten is too late, because the window of opportunity has already "slammed shut." He argues that neuroscientists have also shown that the brain is remarkably plastic and develops throughout life, continually affected by a person's environment and experiences. Moreover, he maintains that most learning does not occur during critical periods in the first three years of life, but throughout the schooling years and into adulthood. He also says that the findings of the longitudinal research have been overstated and that early gains in intelligence are not sustained into adolescence. This assertion is consistent with research examining the long-term effects of Head Start programs in the US (Lee, Brooks-Gunn, Schnur, & Liaw, 1990). Bruer's overriding concern is that the early-years message will cause policy-makers to reduce or eliminate spending on many worthwhile programs targeted to adolescents and adults in favour of spending on early childhood. His concern is shared by many families who have children with mental or physical handicaps, as their children's development depends critically on sustained, continuous effort to support their education and social development throughout early childhood and the schooling years.

The findings from this research could be taken to support either side of this debate. On the one hand, they indicate that socioeconomic gradients are evident during the first three years, and that by the time children enter kindergarten there is significant variation in their language skills that is related to their family socioeconomic background, the environment in which they were raised, and for some children, whether they had attended a daycare or were cared for at home. The findings also show that we can identify "vulnerable children" with some degree of reliability during the early years and demonstrate that vulnerability is associated with the child's environment. Although this research is cross-sectional, the results from other longitudinal studies provide compelling evidence that these vulnerable children have relatively poor long-term prospects unless concerted intervention and support is brought to bear. On the other hand, this research also demonstrates that development does not stop at age three. Parenting, family functioning, and maternal depression, on balance, appear to be equally strong determinants of children's behaviour for children aged zero to five as for those aged six to eleven. Our findings also show that the school a child attends, and the teaching methods and learning environment of the classroom, can have a dramatic effect on a child's learning. It may well be that prolonged exposure to good schooling and community support is enough to overcome the problems exhibited by many children who have had less than ideal environments during the early years.

My view, therefore, is that we cannot ignore the weight of evidence from neuroscience that supports the need for early intervention, but there is also substantial evidence indicating that child development does not end at age three, or age five, or even later. Much like the nature–nurture controversy, this debate is not productive. Nearly everyone would agree that ensuring all children get a good start in life is important, and most would also agree that we need to provide the necessary support for those who do not get a good start. The important question is how we can achieve both aims, and the findings of this research bear on this issue. Our findings suggest that, during the early years, it is more difficult to discern which children are vulnerable and that vulnerability is not strongly associated with socioeconomic status (SES). As children get older, it is easier to assess their cognitive and behavioural development, and the relationship with SES becomes stronger. Therefore, these findings suggest that universal and preventive interventions would likely be more effective during the early years, from zero to age five, but thereafter we need to support successful schooling—as a universal intervention—and complement the efforts of parents and teachers with successful, targeted interventions for those who require additional support. From a social-policy perspective, this direction allows us to recast the early-versus-late debate as a call for action: we need to ensure that all children have the best possible start, while ensuring that those who have chronic difficulties, or who encounter difficult experiences later in life, receive the support they need.

■ Building an Infrastructure for a Family-Enabling Society

The primary message of this research is that the nature of children's environments within the family, and in their schools, neighbourhoods, and communities, has a very strong effect on children's cognitive and behavioral development and on the prevalence of childhood vulnerability. This finding requires us to shift our thinking from childhood vulnerability as a problem stemming from poverty and single parenting to vulnerability as a problem arising from the environments in which children are raised. It requires us to focus less on ameliorating risk factors and more on creating environments that support children's development.

The research indicates that the important factors are parenting skills, the cohesiveness of the family unit, the mental health of the mother, and the extent to which parents engage with their children; and that these features affect and are affected by the neighbourhood, the school, and the wider community. The social-policy mandate is much broader, therefore, than simply offering parenting programs, increasing counselling for adolescents and parents, or building more parks and playgrounds. We need to envisage a family-enabling society and renew social policy such that families and communities receive the support they need to raise their children. There are numerous challenges inherent in this call, organized under four themes below. I consider these the cornerstones of a family-enabling society.

Share responsibility for social policy

Governments can bring pressure to bear on agencies to effect changes that would enable families. For example, they can legislate minimum maternal-leave benefits and set standards for employee benefits. They can require schools to be accountable through testing programs. They can pass legislation restricting the use of toxic materials. Governments can also provide support, not only financially but also by providing guidance and technical assistance aligned with their objectives. They can also take a lead role in influencing agencies to change their practices. However, the success of government interventions depends on the capacity and will of local communities (McLaughlin, 1987). Schorr (1997) argues that successful community-rebuilding initiatives draw on outside resources and expertise, but they rely on the communities' own resources and strengths to effect change. Community-building is a process that combines actions in economic, education, service, and health domains. Building the infrastructure for a family-enabling society requires committed and charismatic community leaders, material resources, and a collective will and synergy among community members.

Many community-builders, especially those working at the grassroots, have correctly argued that top-down reforms, with standards and processes rigidly prescribed by experts and policy-makers, do not usually work. Many reformers would also argue that governments have been slow to learn this lesson. But the reverse is also true: communities that try to achieve renewal without seeking outside resources are less successful in achieving their aims. In Chapter 1, I introduced the concept of social capital, which is acquired "through changes in the relations among persons that facilitate action" (Coleman, 1988). It is embodied in the strength of social networks, information channels, and strong community norms. Woolcock (2000) has elaborated on the concept, distinguishing between bonding social capital (the relations among family members, close friends, and neighbours), bridging social capital (social ties with more distant friends, associates, and colleagues), and linking social capital (alliances with those in power that enable one to leverage resources, ideas, and information). Increasing social capital therefore requires collaboration and co-operation among families within neighbourhoods, between families and schools, across neighbourhood and regional boundaries, among public, private, and voluntary organizations, and across levels of government. From this perspective, the distinction between top-down versus bottom-up reforms is an unhelpful dichotomy, and debate about their relative merit is unlikely to be productive. What is required is a truly collaborative process that builds consensus across levels, allowing each to contribute according to its strength. This process must seek to strike the right balance between pressure and support from outside the community, and the capacity and will of those working within. The "right" balance depends on the nature of the reform and the assets of the community.

To achieve a shared responsibility for social-policy renewal, federal and provincial administrators and politicians must confront a number of issues about the constitutional jurisdiction over education and health, which is jealously guarded by the provinces. A salient issue that has impeded progress in the past is that many policy-makers consider child development during the early years to be an educational and health issue, and therefore federal involvement in this area has been challenged by the provinces. This issue has arisen in a context of strained relations between the federal and provincial governments, following several years of cutbacks in transfer payments to the provinces for education and health. Relationships among the provinces have also been strained because of disagreements over the extent to which federal social policy should reallocate funds from the so-called have to have-not provinces. However, there are signs that these strained relationships are changing. One such sign is the federal–provincial–territorial early childhood development initiative, arising from the September 2000 First Ministers Meeting on Health Renewal and Early Childhood Development. The First Ministers, with the exception of Quebec, agreed to build on existing services and supports for children, with a focus on four areas: promotion of healthy pregnancy, birth, and infancy; improvement of parenting and family supports; strengthening early childhood development, learning, and care; and strengthening community supports. They also agreed to make these services and supports more co-ordinated and widely available (Government of Canada, 2000).

Another problem resulting from provincial jurisdiction over education and health is that there is considerable duplication of effort across provinces. For example, each province develops its own educational curricula and sets standards for success, even in areas such as mathematics and science where international curricula are gradually becoming accepted. At times, it seems the provinces go to great lengths to be different from one another. The results in this volume provide overwhelming evidence that students in Quebec have better results in mathematics, which has been evident in national comparative studies for at least two decades. Yet there has not been a concerted effort to learn why Quebec students have better results. Now Quebec is launching a universal system of low-cost daycare, and there is a significant opportunity to build on and learn from this initiative.

To overcome some of these current problems, we need governments and corporations to strengthen networks that facilitate action—that is, invest in linking social capital by creating and supporting alliances that will enable communities "to leverage resources, ideas, and information." For at least a few years, governments could spend less money on pilot programs and new initiatives, and be more assertive in amassing, synthesizing, and disseminating local knowledge. For example, although we have some very successful early childhood education centres across the country, we do not have a good sense of the common or community-specific elements that make them successful, even though these programs are known to be successful within their communities. We are also not very good at bringing successful programs to scale (see Elmore, 1996) or ensuring that successful programs can be sustained. When George Soros was trying to modernize and improve schooling in Eastern Europe, he identified within each country 100 educational leaders who were willing to undertake training and be responsible for disseminating new knowledge within their local areas. For the first five years, these leaders were provided with training from western experts, but thereafter the emphasis was on bringing new knowledge to bear to improve schools within each country. This kind of network-building is effective because it goes beyond the sharing of ideas, which happens routinely in national conferences and workshops, and to some extent through the Internet, to establishing networks that facilitate action across communities.

Governments, unions, and corporations can also play a role by establishing standards, disseminating information on successful models, and celebrating the accomplishments of successful social entrepreneurs. The term "family-friendly workplaces" has recently become popular to describe corporations that have generous and flexible family-enabling policies. Yet we do not have a good sense of the costs and benefits of these policies, nor do we have a set of standards that corporations should strive to meet. In the same vein, we need to broaden the idea to include family-friendly neighbourhoods, family-friendly schools, and family-friendly communities.

Invest in human capital that enables families

Societies derive economic and social benefits from investing in people. The investments considered as "human capital" normally include expenditures on education, health, and nutrition (Sweetland, 1996). Human capital has become a dominant theme of the Organization for Economic Cooperation and Development (OECD), and there is widespread agreement among OECD countries that building a knowledge economy will increase employment and economic prosperity and abate the polarization of incomes (Alexander, 1997). Several recent studies have shown that investments in human capital have non-market effects as well, on adults' health and well-being, and on the educational and health outcomes of children. Investing in human capital is associated with efficient consumer choices, reduced crime, and the low prevalence of non-marital childbearing. (See Behrman & Stacey, 1997 and Wolfe & Haveman, 2000 for recent reviews.) Investment in education, both formal and informal, is usually considered foremost because of its relatively close link with economic productivity. The OECD's agenda has heavily emphasized lifelong learning for all, with learning defined broadly to encompass learning that occurs formally in educational institutions and informally at home, at work, or through various media (OECD, 1996).

The results of this study indicate that the mother's level of education is one of the strongest predictors of children's cognitive and behavioural outcomes during the early years, and remains strong throughout the elementary school years. Successful graduation from secondary school is also an important threshold for predicting childhood vulnerability and has many ramifications for a youth's long-term prospects in the labour market. Canada's dropout rate, hovering around 28 percent, is alarmingly high, especially compared with many other OECD countries (OECD, 2000).[1] Thus, a key strategy for investment in human capital must be to improve high-school graduation rates. Perhaps the most important predictors of whether a youth will complete secondary school are cognitive ability and prior academic achievement. However, recent research has shown that students are also prone to dropping out if they suffer low self-esteem, have a poor attitude towards school, or experience feelings of alienation.

Students who are engaged are less likely to drop out. Engagement refers to the extent to which students participate in academic and non-academic school activities, identify with school, and accept school values (e.g., Finn, 1993; Goodenow & Grady, 1993; Voelkl, 1997; Wehlage, Rutter, Smith, Lesko, & Fernandez, 1989; see Audas and Willms, 2000, for a review). The literature on dropping out also notes important factors outside school, particularly the effects of the peer networks. Many students become detached from their school friends, motivating a quiet withdrawal from school, or have conflicts that lead to expulsion (Kelly, 1993). At the same time, they develop friendships with peers who have already dropped out of school (Ellenbogen & Chamberland, 1997). Engagement and dropping out are especially important with respect to investing in human capital, because they provide a focus for community development in which the broad policy community can participate and achieve tangible, easily measured results.

Although improving graduation rates is important, it does not embrace the concept of lifelong learning for all. In the fullest sense, this concept means embracing learning in all its forms, including informal learning that occurs outside of formal institutions, which is linked to work, leisure pursuits, nutrition and health, and civic participation. In a more limited sense, with respect to enabling families, we require a concerted effort to increase the skills of all community members in ways that will enable families and improve children's life chances. Such an effort could involve, for example, the development and provision of parenting programs, or helping people attend courses on recreational leadership, first aid, or interpersonal counselling. It could also entail providing more opportunities for families to receive counselling.

There are two major barriers to people's access to lifelong learning, both well recognized in the literature. First, the majority of adult education and training is financed by employers, and the likelihood of receiving employer-sponsored training is lower for females and minorities, especially those with lower formal educational attainment. Most women who undertake education and training finance it themselves (e.g., OECD & HRDC, 1997; Rubenson and Willms, 1993). Second, employers are more likely to invest in adult education and training if they perceive the investment will yield returns through increased employer productivity. Thus, they prefer to invest in training that is more directly related to the aims of the firm (see Xu, 2000 for a review). Social reformers find it difficult to convince employers that investing in general education and training, such as courses on parenting or leadership, will increase profits. Becker (1964) concluded that employers are unlikely to support general education and training unless the employee is paying the costs. Moreover, parents who are not working outside the home and parents who work in lower-paying jobs are less likely to receive this family-enabling education and training. Thus, a concerted effort to increase human capital in this area will require public funding.

The findings of this study, and indeed much of the research in this area over the past decade, support the call for a comprehensive system that would have nurses visit the mothers of newborns at home; early childhood development centres would form part of the system. A large-scale study of home visitations in New York demonstrated that home visits by trained nurses can reduce the incidence of child mistreatment and the frequency of hospital visits (Olds et al., 1997). This study found that the mother's mental health plays a key role in child development, not only post-partum but throughout childhood. However, "well-baby" clinics need to embrace "well moms" as well, and be extended to cover a period much longer than the first year of a child's life. "Well-baby, well-mom" services are likely to improve the physical and mental health of the mothers as well as their babies.

The link between the mother's nutritional habits and a child's later health is well established (Barker, 1997), and some programs aimed at reducing smoking among pregnant women have lowered the incidence of low birth weight (Central West Planning Information Network, 1998). We need to reconceive daycares as "early childhood development centres" (McCain & Mustard, 1999), aimed not only at providing care and stimulation for young children, but also at providing the necessary training and support for parents. In short, we need a seamless, universal system of support for families, from conception to kindergarten, designed to promote learning and human development.

Increase social inclusion

When we embarked on this research, we believed we would be able to identify the most important socioeconomic factors affecting children's development, and then use census data and geographical analyses to determine where there were vulnerable communities in Canada. This information would lead to further research that evaluated programs suited for "ghettoed" communities. But our findings did not support this model. First, we found that socioeconomic factors have relatively weak effects on children's outcomes compared with parenting styles, engagement, family functioning, and maternal depression, and these factors are only weakly related to socioeconomic conditions. Second, when we examined the distribution of neighbourhoods with particularly low SES, these were distributed much more evenly across and within provinces and cities than we expected. This was not the case for affluent neighbourhoods, however, most of which are concentrated in a few of the major cities. In many respects, therefore, Canada is more gated than ghettoed.

We did find, however, that the socioeconomic characteristics of a classroom or school have an effect on children's development over and above the effects of the socioeconomic circumstances of the child's family. Thus, if children from poor families are concentrated in settings with other children from poor families, they are even more likely to be vulnerable. There are also schools and communities that demonstrate that it is possible to have positive outcomes for children from poor families without compromising the outcomes of children from affluent families. Indeed, the research has shown that the most effective schooling systems are those in which the schools have heterogeneous intakes (see review in Chapter 16).

Taken together, the findings in this volume convey a powerful message for social policy: we need to tackle social exclusion head on. The term "social exclusion" (or its opposite, "social inclusion") has roots in the movement towards integrating children with physical and mental handicaps, but it has recently become popular in Europe to encompass people who are marginalized from society for whatever reason. I am using it in this general sense, but am concerned in particular with ways that certain children, especially those who are vulnerable, are segregated in certain neighbourhoods and schools, or among classes within schools.

Consider, for example, a small city that has ten to fifteen elementary schools. If this city had the average number of vulnerable children, in the sense used in this study, then about 28 percent of the children would be vulnerable. If vulnerable children were evenly distributed among schools and classrooms—

that is, if there were no social exclusion—then a classroom teacher with 25 students would have about 7 children who were vulnerable. But suppose there is a pocket of affluence in the city, and the majority of children in this area attended a particular public school or the city's only private school. This concentration would raise the average number of vulnerable children in all other classrooms and schools. A French-immersion program that did not enroll a representative proportion of children with learning disabilities, mental and physical handicaps, and behaviour disorders would further increase the extent to which vulnerable children were segregated from other children. District or school programs for the gifted and charter schools could have the same effect. Finally, there could be less-subtle selective forces within schools, such as the placement of children with relatively poor cognitive skills into split classes, or other forms of streaming. With such forces at play, there would be many classrooms where the classroom teacher had to cope with 10 to 12 vulnerable children, instead of 7. Moreover, there would be fewer children who served as role models for acceptable behaviour and engagement in academic pursuits. I believe most teachers would agree that under these conditions it is nearly impossible to meet the needs of all children.

There are powerful social, economic, and political forces that move us inexorably towards a more socially exclusive society for our children. These cannot be easily confronted. Imagine the resistance, for example, if a province proposed replacing tuition tax credits for parents sending their children to private schools with a tax benefit for parents whose children were enrolled in inclusive public schools. Or if an elected school board argued against the idea of parental choice of schools through open enrollments in favour of designated schools.

However, there are measures that provincial governments, school administrators, and community leaders can take. First, they can provide compensatory funding for schools in low socioeconomic areas. (The SES of families served by schools could be determined easily through the use of postal codes and census matching, as demonstrated in this study.[2]) Intervention could be undertaken directly by increasing funding for low-SES schools, or through a variety of other measures, such as ensuring that low-SES schools are the first to receive new equipment, providing in-service training and other benefits to teachers working in low-SES schools, and celebrating the successes of schools that serve a wide socioeconomic mix of families. Similarly, municipalities can strive to ensure that money spent on sports facilities, parks, playgrounds, family resource centres, and other facilities that enable families are allocated in ways that promote equitable access. For example, a well-equipped sports and recreation facility can dramatically change the nature of a poor community and, in the longer term, reduce residential segregation. Second, governments and school districts can examine alternatives to existing programs that contribute to segregation. With respect to French immersion for English-speaking students, for example, they could consider partial immersion programs for all children, whereby instruction in French is gradually increased while children are mastering English. Third, school districts can diversify offerings among and within schools, such that there are environments that accommodate family preferences and the diverse needs of students, while ensuring that there are no "low-status" options.

Tackling segregation within and between schools is probably the most direct way that governments and school districts can simultaneously raise and flatten gradients. Moreover, most measures to reduce segregation are not costly, and in some cases can even reduce costs. Ultimately, the best defense against forces leading to greater exclusion is to ensure that our public schools accommodate the needs of children with diverse abilities and interests, and are uniformly of high quality. All schools should be "charter" schools with a single mission: success for all.

Increase capacity for program evaluation, monitoring, and research

In 2000, for the first time, all of the provincial education ministers signed an agreement to participate in an international study of school achievement. Consequently, every province participated in the Programme of International Student Indicators (PISA), a study sponsored by the OECD that is examining the school achievement of fifteen-year-old youth in more than forty countries. The Canadian PISA sample also participated in the Youth in Transition Survey (YITS), a longitudinal survey that will follow young people into the labour market. Approximately 30,000 youth participated in the base-year data collection for the two surveys, making it the largest-ever school-based study of Canadian youth. The PISA/YITS is important because it complements the NLSCY study and provides a means for assessing socioeconomic gradients within and between Canadian communities, as well as for comparing them to the gradients of other countries. But perhaps more importantly, the PISA/YITS is a federal and provincial collaboration that involves Human Resources Development Canada (HRDC), Statistics Canada, and the Council of Ministers of Education Canada (CMEC).

The federal government is also making a concerted effort to increase the capacity of Canadian researchers to conduct quantitative research in the social sciences, based largely on a set of recommendations set forth in a report by a joint working group of the Social Sciences and Humanities Research Council and Statistics Canada on the advancement of research using social statistics (Bernard et al., 1998). These include the establishment of data research centres, which will support analysis of data from the major national longitudinal surveys; data training schools aimed at training new scholars in statistical methods; and a program of university research chairs and fellowships. HRDC has recently established five research centres that are concentrating on analyses of data from the NLSCY. These initiatives stand to make a substantial contribution to the infrastructure supporting research on children and families.

However, if this work is to be brought to bear at the level of communities and families, we also need to support program evaluation, monitoring, and "action research" at the provincial and local levels. Our findings suggest that some communities are more successful than others in reducing childhood vulnerability, but we do not understand very much about what makes a successful community. Across this country there are countless examples of highly successful programs for vulnerable children, but we do not understand very well how to replicate these programs or diffuse best practices. The provinces also lack monitoring systems to gauge the success of early childhood interventions. A step towards supporting research in this vein would be to establish a national steering committee, with support from the federal govern-ment through the National Children's Agenda. The committee could set out a program of research aimed at better understanding what family-friendly schools, family-friendly workplaces, and family-friendly neighbourhoods might look like, and how they can be achieved. It could also tackle pertinent policy issues such as how income security could be designed so that parents who have just become divorced receive the support they need, and fundamental qualita-tive issues such as "coping": what does it actually take for single parents or teen parents to cope, and what kinds of support really make a difference?

■ Concluding Remarks

I believe that most Canadians would agree that the health and well-being of our children needs to be the central element of our social policy. If we can invest our time and resources in ways that improve the quality of life for vulnerable children, and help all children achieve their full potential, we will certainly realize returns in economic prosperity and reduce the burdens associated with crime, social welfare, and health. But we also stand to create a society that is more tolerant and socially inclusive—in short, a better place for everyone to live. Many accounts of childhood vulnerability argue that governments need to spend more money to reduce the number of children living in poverty. This is true; we do. But we also need to make other kinds of investments as well. As we enter this new era in Canadian social policy, I hope that we can rethink our investment strategy, so that families are better able to provide the love, care, and support that are essential for healthy child development.

One of the important aims of the NLSCY is to monitor how well our children and families are doing. In this research, we have developed a "vulnerability index" for Canada, which considers a child to be vulnerable if he or she had poor outcomes in either the cognitive or behavioural domains. The index can be a useful policy device, because it provides a means for monitoring children's outcomes over time. The index also enables us to describe the extent of variation in childhood vulnerability among provinces, communities, and neighbourhoods. Understanding which jurisdictions are doing well, and which are doing poorly, is an important first step in understanding "what works" and how we might do things differently. But the research effort is largely wasted unless we take the next step. It will require provinces, communities, and families to grapple with the issues and find new ways of supporting child development. I hope that the research based on the NLSCY will engender numerous action-oriented research studies.

This research has provided convincing evidence that socioeconomic gradients in childhood outcomes vary among communities. But it leaves open the question of the extent to which gradients can be raised and levelled through people's efforts. My sense is that gradients are relatively stable, because societies maintain a certain tolerable equilibrium for inequalities, which is subtly kept in balance by economic and political forces. I am optimistic, however, that gradients are not immutable. We have ample evidence that schools and schooling systems can be altered through policy, practice, and reform. Better support for children is high on the policy agendas at both the federal and provincial levels, and there is a spirit among Canadians that change is possible.

NOTES

1 The secondary level graduation rate was about 72 percent in 1998. This was based on the number of people, at any age, who graduated for the first time from secondary school, divided by the number of youth at the age at which students typically complete secondary school. Thus, it takes into account students graduating at the traditional age, as well as those graduating at an older age. It does not include adults who later pass the General Educational Diploma (OECD, 2000).

2 This strategy would be preferable than a system that based compensation on poor test performance, which in effect would reward poor academic results. Similarly, trying to identify the prevalence of children with special needs is problematic, because the diagnosis of children with learning disabilities by school staff is unreliable and can lead to unnecessary labelling.

APPENDICES

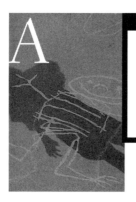

Outcome Measures
Used in the Study

J. DOUGLAS WILLMS

■ Motor and Social Development

The Motor and Social Development (MSD) scale was developed by the US National Center for Health Statistics to measure the motor, social, and cognitive development of children from birth to age three. The scale comprises 48 questions. Parents are asked a subset of 15 questions, depending on the age of their child. For example, for children aged zero to three months, parents are asked whether the children can turn their head when lying on their stomach, follow a moving object with their eyes, or turn their head around to look at something. The most difficult tasks are asked of parents with children aged 22 to 47 months. These include whether the children can speak in a partial sentence of three words or more, go to the toilet alone, pedal a tricycle at least ten feet, or count out loud up to ten. The reliability of the scale varies somewhat, depending on the age of the child; on average, it is about 0.80.[1] The scores were standardized to have a mean of zero and a standard deviation of fifteen, using data for one-month age groups. A cut-off score of 85—one standard deviation below the mean—was used to define "low MSD scores."

■ Peabody Picture Vocabulary Test (PPVT-R)

The Peabody Picture Vocabulary Test (PPVT-R) measures children's receptive vocabulary. Children are presented a set of pictures and are asked to identify the picture corresponding to the word read by the interviewer. The PPVT-R has been used in hundreds of research studies over the past forty years. Scores on the PPVT have a correlation of about 0.70 with both the full-scale intelligence quotient and the verbal intelligence quotient derived from the Wechsler Intelligence Scale (Dunn & Dunn, 1997). Correlations of PPVT scores with academic achievement tests range from 0.33 to 0.80 with tests of academic achievement (Williams & Wang, 1997). The reliability of the test for 4- and 5-year-old children ranges from 0.93 to 0.95 (both alternate forms reliability and Cronbach's alpha). The scores for the National Longitudinal Survey of Children and Youth (NLSCY) sample were standardized to have a mean of zero and a standard deviation of fifteen, using data for two-month age groups. A French version of the test was also developed and normed separately for children who took the test in French. The French version is called the Echelle de Vocabulaire en Images Peabody (EVIP); however, in this volume we will use the abbreviation PPVT-R to refer to both versions of the test. As with the MSD, a cut-off score of 85 was used to define "low PPVT-R scores."

■ Mathematics Computation Test

The mathematics computation test was designed to assess students' understanding of basic arithmetic operations. It is a shortened version of the computation sub-test of the Canadian Achievement Tests, Second Edition (CAT/2). The shortened version included three levels: Level 2, with 10 items, for children in grade 2; and Levels 4 and 6, each with 15 items, for children in grades 3 and 4, and grades 5 and 6, respectively. The test scores were scaled to a vertically equated scale, based on results from a separate norming sample selected by the Canadian Testing Centre. The idea underlying vertical equating is that the tests at each level include items that overlap in their content and difficulty with some of the items in the tests set for lower and higher grade levels. This makes it possible to map scores onto a long, continuous scale. In this case, the scores were placed on a scale that ranges from 1 to 999. In this survey, the Level 2 scaled scores ranged from 200 to 400; the Level 4 scores from 264 to 550; and the Level 6 scores ranged from 314 to 624.

In order to facilitate interpretation, we determined the relationship between scaled scores and age (and age-squared), and then recoded the scaled scores into age equivalents. For example, an age equivalent score of 120 is the average score achieved by children who are 120 months (i.e., 10 years) old. We then subtracted the children's actual ages in months from their age-equivalent mathematics scores to yield a measure that indicated whether children were above or below their same-age peers. For example, a score of -8.0 indicates that a child was lagging behind his or her same-age peers by about 8 months of schooling.

We encountered two problems with the test in the first cycle of the NLSCY. One is that the tests were too easy for many children, especially those in grades three and five. A disproportionate number of children at these grade levels achieved a perfect score. This problem, called a "ceiling effect," can result in biased estimates when comparisons are made across groups, because children with relatively high ability are unable to achieve scores that indicate their true ability. The second problem is that there was an inordinate amount of missing data, stemming from refusals by parents or school boards, teacher non-response, and various administrative problems (Human Resources Development Canada and Statistics Canada, 1996). Although these problems were addressed satisfactorily in Cycle 2 of the NLSCY, they needed to be taken into account in this study.

We used several approaches. First, we used preliminary Cycle 2 data to establish criteria for a cut-off score to classify children as having low mathematics ability.[2] The number of children in a group scoring below some threshold is not biased by ceiling effects in the same way that the mean score for a group is biased. Second, because we had extensive information on children's family background, we were able to impute mathematics scores for those children who did not complete the test.[3] These imputed scores are used only in the calculation of the vulnerability index. Third, in the analyses in Chapter 16, which are concerned primarily with school quality and comparisons among provinces and schools, we used data from the NLSCY and the Third International Mathematics and Science Study (TIMSS). The TIMSS data were collected from a different sample of students in 1994 and included a much more extensive mathematics test. We find that the NLSCY results are remarkably similar to those based on the TIMSS.

■ Children's Temperament

Children's temperament was derived from parents' responses to a set of questions pertaining to various aspects of their children's behaviour. The questions were taken from the Infant Characteristics Questionnaire (ICQ; Bates, Freeland, & Lounsbury, 1979), the Child Characteristics Questionnaire (CCQ; Lee and Bates, 1985), and the Preschool Characteristics Questionnaire (PCQ; Finegan et al., 1989). These questionnaires had only been used in small-scale studies prior to the NLSCY, and therefore we conducted several analyses to determine the factor structure underlying these scales and their psychometric properties. These are presented in Chapter 6. We identified five factors, which we labelled good-natured, independent, consistent, adaptable, and obedient; scores were scaled on a ten-point scale.

The full set of temperament items will not be administered in future cycles of the NLSCY, in order to reduce the respondent burden and make room for other questions. Thus, we defined vulnerability for temperament using the following set of items, which will be used in future cycles of the study.

- How easy or difficult is it for you to calm or soothe <child's name> when he/she is upset?
- How many times per day, on average, does <child's name> get fussy and irritable—for either short or long periods of time?
- How much does <child's name> cry and fuss in general?
- How easily does <child's name> get upset?
- When he/she gets upset (e.g., before feeding, during diapering, etc.), how vigorously or loudly does he/she cry and fuss? (Wording is slightly different for children one to three.)
- How changeable is <child's name>'s mood?
- Please rate the overall degree of difficulty <child's name> would present for the average parent?

The reliability coefficients for this scale were 0.77, 0.79, 0.79, and 0.79 for children aged 0, 1, 2, and 3 respectively. We conducted a principal components factor analysis (see Sidebar 3.4) on the seven items, separately for each one-year age group, and in each case one underlying factor emerged. We considered children to be vulnerable if they were more than one standard deviation below the mean on the underlying principal component.

◼ Pro-social Behaviour

The pro-social behaviour scale comprised five items for children aged two and three, and ten items for children aged four through eleven. The scale assesses whether children are empathetic (e.g., the child will try to help someone who is hurt), helpful (e.g., the child volunteers to clear up a mess someone else has made), and inclusive of other children (e.g., the child will invite bystanders to join in a game). The scores were also scaled on a ten-point scale. The scale has a reliability of 0.80 for children aged 2 and 3, and 0.79 for children aged 4 through 11.

◼ Behaviour Problems

Children's behaviour was based on assessments by the person most knowledge-able (PMK) about the child, which in most cases was the mother. The scales included several questions, each with the same format, e.g., How often would you say that <child's name> can't sit still? How often would you say that <child's name> is restless or hyperactive? There were three possible responses: "Never or not true," "Sometimes or somewhat true," and "Often or very true." The items were as follows.

ANXIETY

<child's name> seems to be unhappy, sad, or depressed

<child's name> is too fearful or anxious

<child's name> is worried

<child's name> cries a lot

<child's name> tends to do things on his/her own—is rather solitary (four- to eleven-year-olds only)

<child's name> appears miserable, unhappy, tearful, or distressed (four- to eleven-year-olds only)

EMOTIONAL DISORDER

<child's name> seems to be unhappy, sad, or depressed

<child's name> is not as happy as other children

<child's name> is too fearful or anxious

<child's name> is worried

<child's name> cries a lot

<child's name> is nervous, high strung, or tense

<child's name> has trouble enjoying himself/herself

HYPERACTIVITY

<child's name> child can't sit still, is restless, or hyperactive

<child's name> is distractible, has trouble sticking to any activity

<child's name> fidgets

<child's name> can't concentrate, can't pay attention for long

<child's name> is impulsive, acts without thinking

<child's name> has difficulty awaiting turn in games or groups

<child's name> cannot settle to anything for more than a few moments

INATTENTION

<child's name> can't concentrate, pay attention for long

<child's name> gives up easily

<child's name> stares into space

<child's name> is inattentive

PHYSICAL AGGRESSION

<child's name> gets into many fights

<child's name> when another child accidentally hurts him/her (such as bumping into him/her), assumes that the other child meant to do it, and then reacts with anger and fighting

<child's name> kicks, bites, hits other children

<child's name> physically attacks people (four- to eleven-year-olds only)

<child's name> threatens people (four- to eleven-year-olds only)

<child's name> is cruel, bullies or is mean to others (four- to eleven-year-olds only)

INDIRECT AGGRESSION (four- to eleven-year-olds only)

<child's name> when mad at someone, tries to get others to dislike that person

<child's name> when mad at someone, becomes friends with another for revenge

<child's name> when mad at someone, says bad things behind the other's back

<child's name> when mad at someone, says to others: let's not be with him/her

<child's name> when mad at someone, tells the other one's secrets to a third person

Children were assigned into one of three clusters ("extremely hyperactive," "somewhat hyperactive," and "not hyperactive") using latent class scaling. This scaling was done separately for boys and girls, by one-year age groups. In most analyses, we use dichotomous variables indicating whether or not a child was classified in the extreme group.

NOTES

1   Cronbach's alpha reliability coefficients for the NLSCY sample were as follows: age o to 3 months, 0.857; 4 to 6 months, 0.707; 7 to 9 months, 0.766; 10 to 12 months, 0.751; 13 to 15 months, 0.700; 19 to 21 months, 0.705; 22 to 47 months, 0.846.

2   Children were classified as having a low mathematics score if they scored more than 75 points below the predicted average score for other children of their age. The predicted scores were determined by regressing children's scaled scores on their age and age-squared. The standard deviation of the scaled scores at each age was approximately 50 points; therefore, children scoring below the threshold are approximately one and a half grade levels behind their peers.

3   The scores were imputed using the regression method in the SPSS^X missing values program. Imputation was based on the child's age (and age-squared), family income, and the mother's and father's occupation and level of education. On average, children who had not taken the test were from lower-SES backgrounds than those who had. Therefore, the prevalence of children considered to have low mathematics scores was slightly higher among those with imputed scores, thereby slightly increasing the overall prevalence of children with low mathematics scores. We expect this is a more accurate estimate of vulnerability than one based solely on children who had taken the mathematics test.

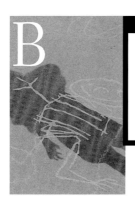

Provincial Maps Depicting Neighbourhood Types

JANE LAW & J. DOUGLAS WILLMS

THE AIM OF OUR ANALYSIS was to identify areas where there is likely to be a particularly high percentage of vulnerable children and to display these areas visually on maps of each province. We also wanted to discern whether characteristics of neighbourhoods have an effect on children's outcomes, over and above the effects associated with their individual family backgrounds. The analysis identifies "neighbourhood types," using enumeration areas (EAs) as an operational definition of "neighbourhoods." EAs are geographic areas comprising on average about 400 families. We appreciate that EA boundaries do not accurately capture the boundaries of neighbourhoods as local residents might perceive them, and thus we are likely to underestimate neighbourhood effects. However, the use of EAs is a practical and inexpensive means to determine whether research in this vein is productive.

We used cluster analysis, a statistical technique that forms clusters of objects or individuals based on how similar they are with respect to a number of defining characteristics (see Sidebar 3.3, page 62), to classify the 39,573 EAs described in the public data file of the 1991 Canadian census. Our clustering was based on six defining characteristics: median income, percentage of non-immigrants, percentage of two-parent families, average number of years of education, percentage of employed youth, and percentage of employed adults. We know from our analysis of the National Longitudinal Survey of Children and Youth (NLSCY) data that income, levels of education, and parents'

Table B.1

Numbers of EAs of each type by province

	NF	PE	NS	NB	QU	ON	MB	SK	AB	BC
1	160	11	58	102	394	130	48	92	63	179
2	380	24	148	190	759	356	91	110	129	262
3	32	16	96	91	1250	1004	158	107	227	353
4	11	16	117	71	1450	1958	253	218	567	821
5	175	75	424	346	2668	2905	299	286	695	1108
6	47	56	529	203	1720	2266	567	972	1073	889
7	50	31	132	80	1149	3765	271	443	999	1167
8	11	1	21	9	264	890	23	18	184	144

employment are significantly related to children's developmental outcomes. We also included immigrant status and family structure in the analysis, as these are related to family socioeconomic status (SES).

For most EAs, data were available to describe all six characteristics; however, data on media income were missing for many EAs. Thus, prior to the cluster analysis, we inputed missing data using an EM (conditional expectation/ maximum likelihood) method. We also identified those EAs for which there were no children and classified those EAs separately as Type o (i.e., "no children"). We then randomly sampled 500 EAs from the full set and used the unweighted pair-group method (UPGMA) of analysis to cluster them. We examined the pattern of minimum distances between clusters at each step to decide upon the appropriate number of clusters. We repeated this procedure ten times and found over repeated samples that eight clusters was an appropriate number of neighbourhood types. Finally, we mean k-means clustering, requesting eight clusters, to classify all of the EAs (except those with no children) into eight types.

The average scores on the six defining characteristics for each of the eight types are displayed in Table 3.4 (page 62). The eight types are ordered based on their average SES and were assigned a colour that is used in the maps reproduced below. Table B.1 displays the distribution of EA types by province. The geographical distribution of these neighbourhood types is displayed on maps for each province and for six Canadian cities: Vancouver, Edmonton, Winnipeg, Toronto, Montreal, and Halifax.

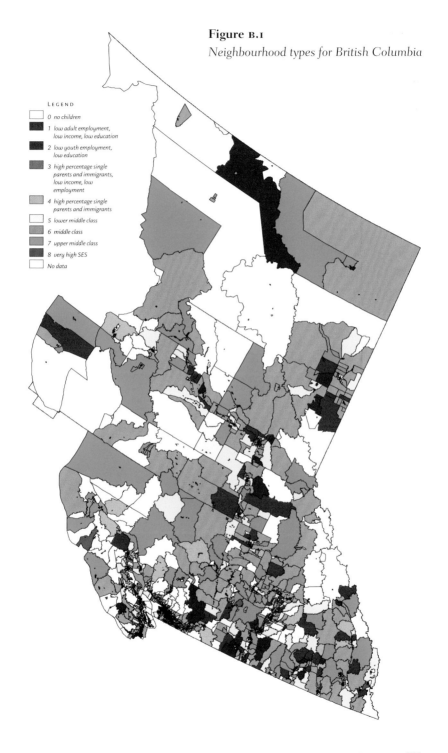

Figure B.1

Neighbourhood types for British Columbia

LEGEND

0 no children

1 low adult employment, low income, low education

2 low youth employment, low education

3 high percentage single parents and immigrants, low income, low employment

4 high percentage single parents and immigrants

5 lower middle class

6 middle class

7 upper middle class

8 very high SES

No data

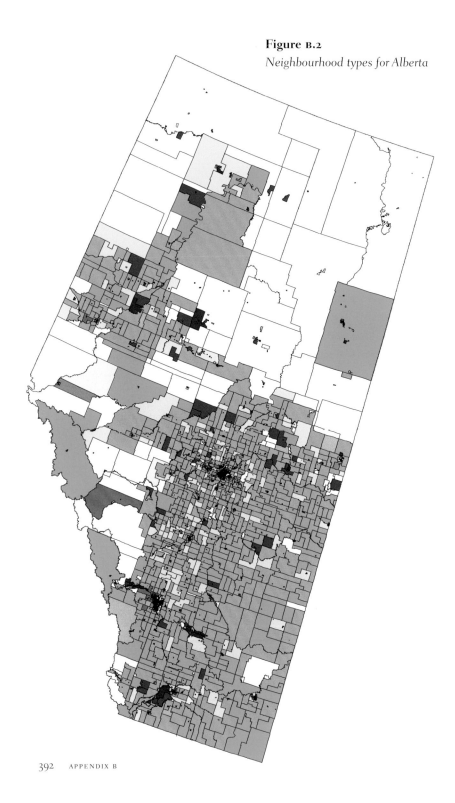

Figure B.2

Neighbourhood types for Alberta

Figure B.3

Neighbourhood types for Saskatchewan

LEGEND

- 0 *no children*
- 1 *low adult employment, low income, low education*
- 2 *low youth employment, low education*
- 3 *high percentage single parents and immigrants, low income, low employment*
- 4 *high percentage single parents and immigrants*
- 5 *lower middle class*
- 6 *middle class*
- 7 *upper middle class*
- 8 *very high SES*
- *No data*

Figure B.4

Neighbourhood types for Manitoba

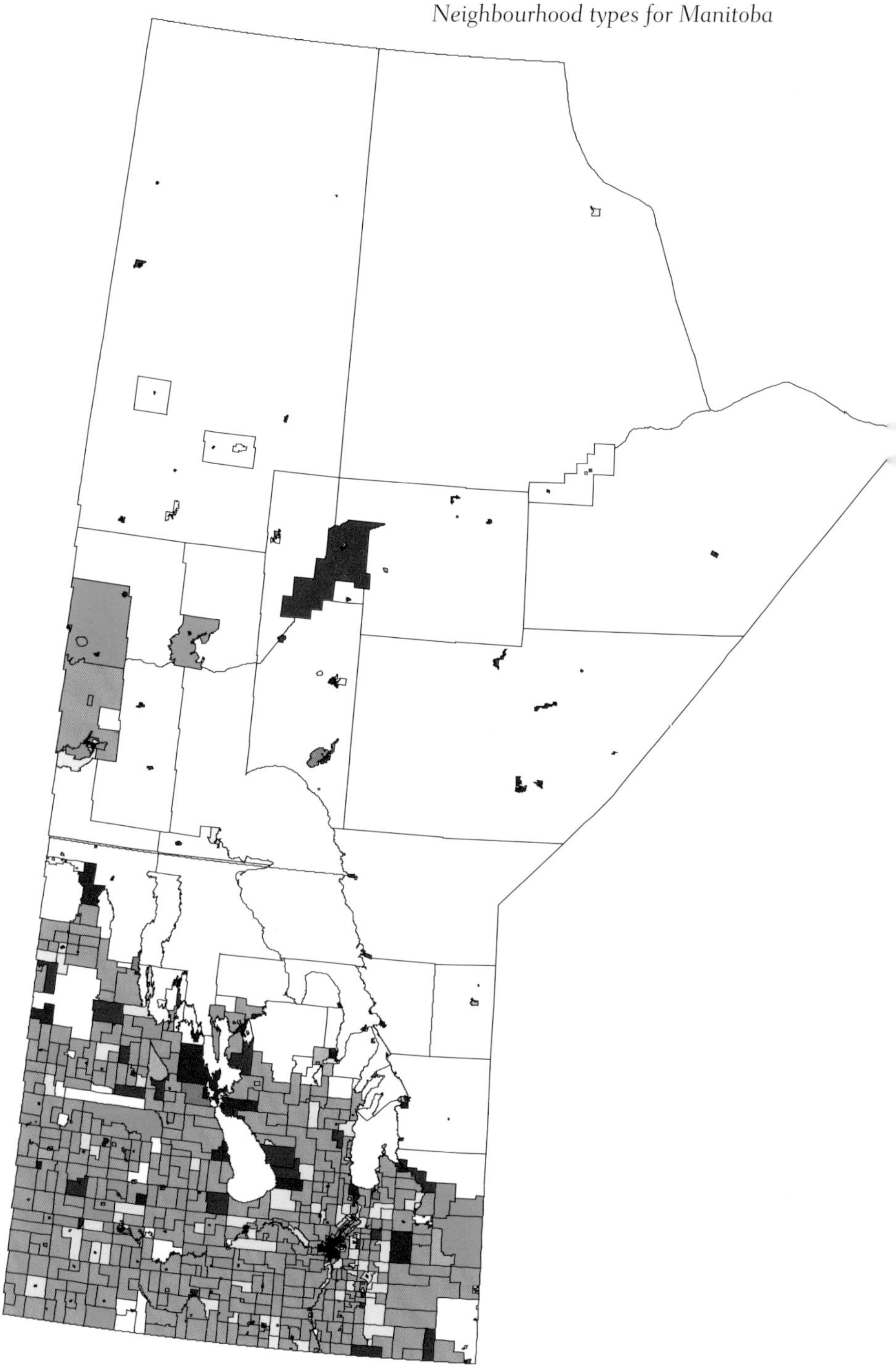

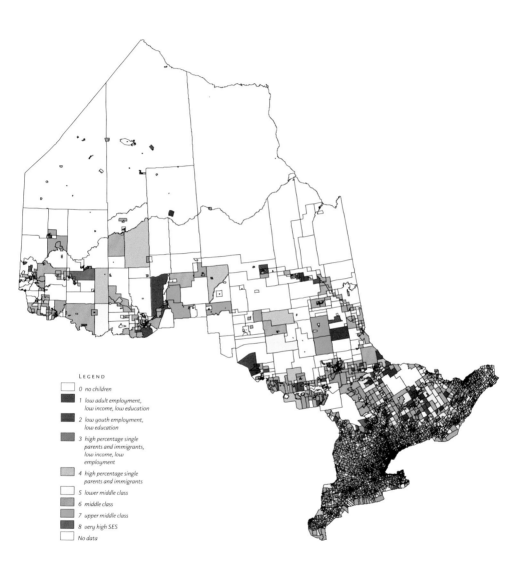

Figure B.5

Neighbourhood types for Ontario

LEGEND

0 *no children*

1 *low adult employment, low income, low education*

2 *low youth employment, low education*

3 *high percentage single parents and immigrants, low income, low employment*

4 *high percentage single parents and immigrants*

5 *lower middle class*

6 *middle class*

7 *upper middle class*

8 *very high SES*

No data

Figure B.6
Neighbourhood types for Quebec

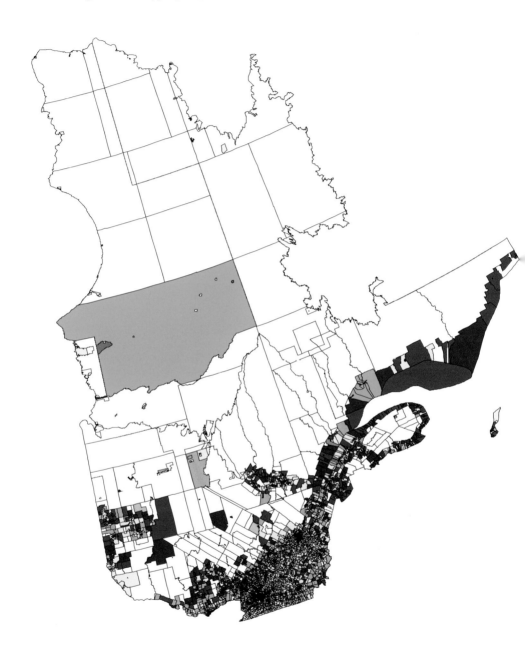

Figure B.7
Neighbourhood types for New Brunswick

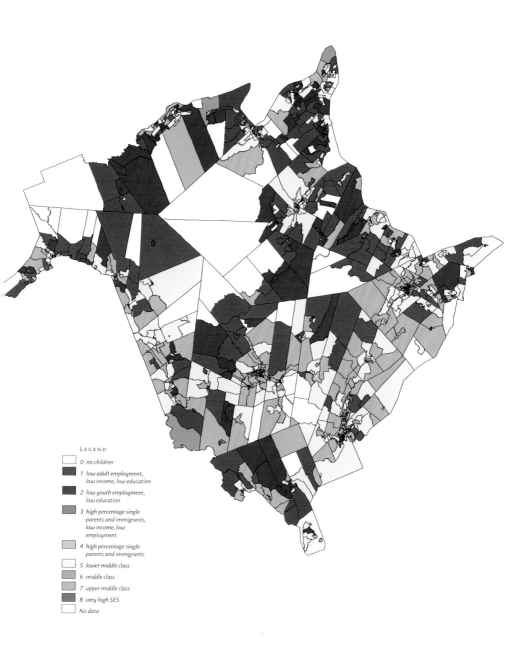

LEGEND

- 0 *no children*
- 1 *low adult employment, low income, low education*
- 2 *low youth employment, low education*
- 3 *high percentage single parents and immigrants, low income, low employment*
- 4 *high percentage single parents and immigrants*
- 5 *lower middle class*
- 6 *middle class*
- 7 *upper middle class*
- 8 *very high SES*
- *No data*

Figure B.8
Neighbourhood types for Nova Scotia

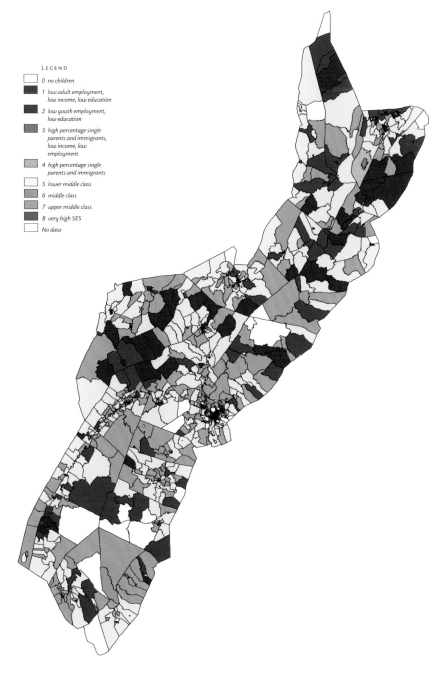

LEGEND

0 *no children*

1 *low adult employment, low income, low education*

2 *low youth employment, low education*

3 *high percentage single parents and immigrants, low income, low employment*

4 *high percentage single parents and immigrants*

5 *lower middle class*

6 *middle class*

7 *upper middle class*

8 *very high SES*

No data

Figure B.9
Neighbourhood types for Prince Edward Island

Figure B.10

Neighbourhood types for Newfoundland

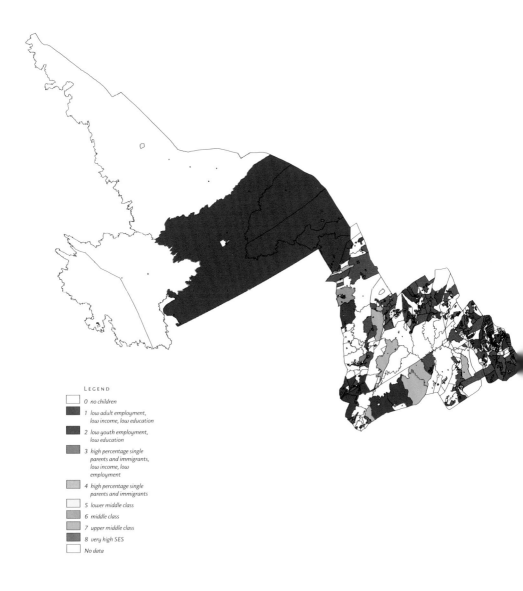

LEGEND

0 *no children*

1 *low adult employment, low income, low education*

2 *low youth employment, low education*

3 *high percentage single parents and immigrants, low income, low employment*

4 *high percentage single parents and immigrants*

5 *lower middle class*

6 *middle class*

7 *upper middle class*

8 *very high SES*

No data

Figure B.11

Neighbourhood types for Vancouver

Figure B.12

Neighbourhood types for Edmonton

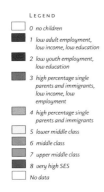

LEGEND

0 *no children*

1 *low adult employment,
   low income, low education*

2 *low youth employment,
   low education*

3 *high percentage single
   parents and immigrants,
   low income, low
   employment*

4 *high percentage single
   parents and immigrants*

5 *lower middle class*

6 *middle class*

7 *upper middle class*

8 *very high SES*

No data

Figure B.13

Neighbourhood types for Winnipeg

Figure B.14

Neighbourhood types for Toronto

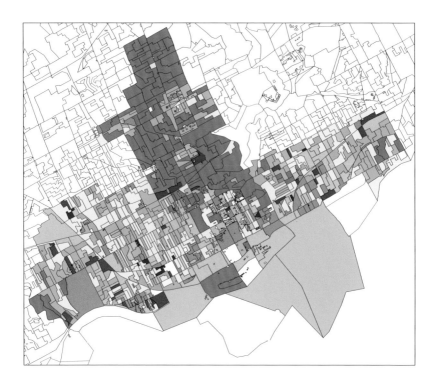

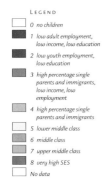

LEGEND

0 *no children*

1 *low adult employment, low income, low education*

2 *low youth employment, low education*

3 *high percentage single parents and immigrants, low income, low employment*

4 *high percentage single parents and immigrants*

5 *lower middle class*

6 *middle class*

7 *upper middle class*

8 *very high SES*

No data

Figure B.15

Neighbourhood types for Montreal

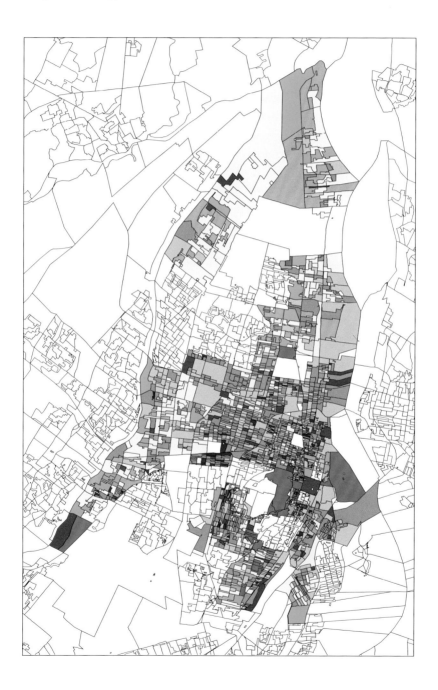

Figure B.16

Neighbourhood types for Halifax

LEGEND

0   *no children*

1   *low adult employment, low income, low education*

2   *low youth employment, low education*

3   *high percentage single parents and immigrants, low income, low employment*

4   *high percentage single parents and immigrants*

5   *lower middle class*

6   *middle class*

7   *upper middle class*

8   *very high SES*

No data

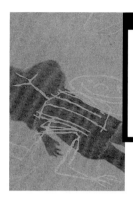

References

Abel, E.L. 1995. An update on incidence of FAS: FAS is not an equal opportunity birth defect. *Neurotoxicology and Teratology, 17*, (4), 437–43.

Achenbach, T.M. 1991. *Empirically based taxonomy: Profile types derived from the CBCL/4–18, TRF, and YSR.* Burlington, VM: University of Vermont, Department of Psychiatry.

Agnew, R. 1989. Delinquency as a creative enterprise: A review of recent evidence. *Criminal Justice and Behaviour, 16*, 98–113.

Alexander, T.J. 1997. Human capital investment: Building the "knowledge economy." *Policy Options*, July/August, 1997.

Alsaker, F.D. 1995. Timing of puberty and reactions to pubertal changes. In M. Rutter (Ed.), *Psychosocial disturbances in young people: Challenges for prevention* (pp. 37–82). Cambridge, MA: Cambridge University Press.

Anastasi, A. 1988. *Psychological testing (6th ed.).* New York: MacMillan Publishing Company.

Anderberg, M. 1973. *Cluster analysis for applications.* New York: Academic Press.

Anderson, C.S. 1985. The investigation of school climate. In G.R. Austin & H. Garber (Eds.), *Research on exemplary schools* (pp. 97–126). Orlando: Academic Press.

Andersson, B.E. 1989. Effects of day-care on cognitive and socio-emotional competence of thirteen-year-old Swedish schoolchildren. *Child Development, 63*, 20–36.

Andersson, B.E. 1992. Effects of public day-care: A longitudinal study. *Child Development 60* (4), 857–66.

Arnett, J. 1989. Caregivers in day-care centers: Does training matter? *Journal of Applied Developmental Psychology, 10*, 541–52.

Audas, R.P., & Willms, J.D. 2000. *Engagement and dropping out of school: A life course perspective.* Report prepared for Human Resources Development Canada.

Baillargeon, R., Tremblay, R.E., & Willms, J.D. 2000. *The prevalence of physical aggression in Canadian children: A multi-group latent class analysis of data from the National Longitudinal Study of Children and Youth.* Ottawa, ON: Applied Research Branch, Human Resources Development Canada and Statistics Canada.

Baldwin, C., Baldwin, A., & Cole, R. 1990. Stress-resistant families and stress-resistant children. In J. Rolf, A. Masten, D. Cicchetti, K. Neuchtherlin, & S. Weintraub (Eds.), *Risk and protective factors in the development of pychopathology* (pp. 257–80). New York: Cambridge University Press.

Barker, D.J. 1997. Fetal nutrition and cardiovascular disease in later life. *British Medical Bulletin, 53* (1), 96–108.

Barnett, W.S. 1992. Benefits of compensatory preschool education. *The Journal of Human Resources, 27* (2), 279–312.

Barnett, W.S. 1995. Long-term effects of early childhood programs on cognitive and social outcomes. *The Future of Children, 5* (3), 25–50.

Baron, R.M., & Kenny, D.A. 1986. The moderator–mediator variable distinction in social psychological research: Conceptual, strategic, and statistical considerations. *Journal of Personality and Social Psychology, 51* (6), 1173–82.

Bates, J.E. 1994. Parents as scientific observers of their children's development. In S.L. Friedman & H.C. Haywood (Eds.), *Developmental follow-up: Concepts, domains and methods* (pp. 197–216). New York: Academic Press.

Bates, J.E., & Bayles, K. 1984. Objective and subjective components in mothers' perceptions of their children from age 6 months to 3 years. *Merrill-Palmer Quarterly, 30* (2), 111–30.

Bates, J.E., Bayles, K., Bennett, D.S., Ridge, B., & Brown, M.M. 1991. Origins of externalizing behavior problems at eight years of age. In D.J. Pepler & K.H. Rubin (Eds.), *The development and treatment of childhood aggression* (pp. 93–120). Hillsdale, NJ: Erlbaum.

Bates, J.E., Freeland, C.A., & Lounsbury, M.L. 1979. Measures of infant difficultness. *Child Development, 50,* 794–803.

Bates, J.E., Maslin, C.A., & Frankel, K.A. (1985). Attachment security, mother–child interaction, and temperament as predictors of behavior problem ratings at age 3 years. *Monographs of the Society for Research in Child Development, 50* (1-2), 167–93.

Baumrind, D. 1967. Child care practices anteceding 3 patterns of preschool behavior. *Genetic Psychology Monographs, 75,* 43–88.

Beardslee, W.R., Versage, E.M., & Gladstone, T.R.G. 1998. Children of affectively ill parents: A review of the past 10 years. *Journal of the American Academy of Child and Adolescent Psychiatry, 37* (11), 1134–41.

Beaton, A.E., Mullis, I.V.S., Martin, M.O., Gonzalez, E.J., Kelly, D.L., & Smith, T.A. 1996. *Mathematics achievement in the middle school years: IEA's Third International Mathematics and Science Study (TIMSS)*. Chestnut Hill, MA: Boston College.

Beatson-Hird, P., Yuen, P., & Balarjan, R. 1989. Single mothers: their health and health service use. *Journal of Epidemiological Community Health, 43*, 385–90.

Bebbington, P., Hurry, J., Tennant, C., Sturt, E., & Wing, J.K. 1981. Epidemiology of mental disorders in Camberwell. *Psychological Medicine, 11*, 561–79.

Becker, G.S. 1964. *Human capital: A theoretical and empirical analysis with special reference to education*. New York: National Bureau of Economic Research.

Becker, G.S. 1981. *A treatise on the family*. Cambridge, MA: Harvard University Press.

Becker, G.S. 1993. *Human Capital* (3rd ed.). Chicago: University of Chicago Press.

Becker, G.S., & Tomes, H. 1986. Human capital and the rise and fall of families. *Journal of Labor Economics, 4* (2), S1–S139.

Behrman, J.R. & Stacey, N. (Eds.) 1997. *The Social Benefits of Education*. Ann Arbor: University of Michigan Press.

Belsky, J., Steinberg, L., & Draper, P. 1991a. Childhood experience, interpersonal development, and reproductive strategy: An evolutionary theory of socialization. *Child Development, 62*, 647–70.

Belsky, J., Steinberg, L., & Draper, P. 1991b. Further reflections on an evolutionary theory of socialization. *Child Development, 62*, 682–85.

Berger, M., Yule, W., & Rutter, M. 1975. Attainment and adjustment in two geographical areas. II. The prevalence of specific reading retardation. *British Journal of Psychiatry, 126*, 510–19.

Bergman, L.R., & Magnusson, D. 1997. A person-oriented approach in research on developmental psychopathology. *Development and Psychopathology, 9*, 291–319.

Bergstrom, E., Hernell, O., & Persson, L.A. 1996. Cardiovascular risk indicators cluster in girls from families of low socio-economic status. *Acta Paediatrica, 85* (9), 1083–90.

Berk, L.E. 1985. Relationship of caregiver education to child-oriented attitudes, job satisfaction, and behaviors toward children. *Child Care Quarterly, 14* (2), 103–29.

Bernard, P., Havens, B., Kuhn, P., Le Bourdais, C., Norris, D., Ornstein, M., Picot, G., Wilk, M., & Willms, J.D. 1998. *Final report of the Joint Working Group of the Social Sciences and Humanities Research Council and Statistics Canada on the advancement of research using social statistics*. Report prepared for Social Sciences and Humanities Research Council and Statistics Canada.

Beyer, S. 1995. Maternal employment and children's academic achievement: Parenting styles as mediating variable. *Developmental Review, 15*, 212–53.

Bielby, W.T. 1981. Models of status attainment. *Social Stratification and Mobility, 1*, 3–26.

Bierman, K. 1989. Improving peer relations of rejected children. *Advances in Clinical Child Psychology, 12*, 53–84. New York: Plenum Press.

Billings, A.G., & Moos, R.H. 1983. Comparisons of children of depressed and nondepressed parents: A social-environmental perspective. *Journal of Abnormal Child Psychology, 11* (4), 463-86.

Birch, D.M.L. 1998. The adolescent parent: A fifteen year longitudinal study of school-age mothers and their children. *International Journal of Adolescent Medicine and Health, 10,* 141–53.

Blashfield, R.K. 1984. *The classification of psychopathology* (pp.216–62). New York: Plenum Press.

Bloom, B.B. 1985. A factor analysis of self-report measures of family functioning. *Family Process, 24,* 225–40.

Bofill, J.A., Rust, O.A., Perry, K.G., Roberts, W.E., Martin, R.W., & Morrison, J.C. 1996. Forceps and vacuum delivery: A survey of North American residency programs. *Obstetrics & Gynecology, 88,* (4), part 1, 622–25.

Bollen, K.A. 1989. *Structural equations with latent variables.* New York: Wiley.

Bor, W., Najman, J. M., Andersen, M.J., O'Callaghan, M., Williams, G.M., & Behrens, B.C. 1997. The relationship between low family income and psychological disturbance in young children: An Australian longitudinal study. *Australian & New Zealand Journal of Psychiatry, 31* (5), 664–75.

Bouchard, C., & Johnston, F.E. (Eds.). 1988. *Fat distribution during growth and later health outcomes.* New York: A.R. Liss.

Bourdieu, P. 1977. Cultural reproduction and social reproduction. In J. Karabel and A. H. Halsey (Eds.), *Power and ideology in education.* New York: Oxford University Press.

Bowles, S., & Levin, H. 1968. The determinants of scholastic achievement — An appraisal of some recent findings. *The Journal of Human Resources, 3,* 3–24.

Boyle, M.H. & Willms, J.D. 1999. Place effects for areas defined by administrative boundaries. *American Journal of Epidemiology, 149* (6), 577–85.

Boyle, M.H., & Willms, J.D. 2001. Multilevel modelling of hierarchical data in developmental studies. *Journal of Childhood Psychology and Psychiatry, 42* (1), 141–62.

Boyle, M.H., Offord, D.R., Hofmann, H.G., Catlin, G.P., Byles, J.W., Links, P.S., Rae-Grant, N.I., & Szatmari, P. 1987. Ontario child health study. I. Methodology. *Archives of General Psychiatry, 44,* 449–56.

Boyle, M.H., Offord, D.R., Hofmann, H.G., Catlin, G.P., Byles, J.W., Links, P.S., Rae-Grant, N.I., & Szatmari, P. 1987. Ontario Child Health Study. I. Methodology. *Archives of General Psychiatry, 44,* 826–31.

Boyle, M.H., Offord, D.R., Racine, Y.A., & Catlin, G.P. 1991. Ontario Child Health Study Follow-up: evaluation of sample loss. *Journal of the American Academy of Child and Adolescent Psychiatry, 30,* 449–56.

Bradley, R.H., Caldwell, B.M., & Rock, S.L. 1988. Home environment and school performance: A ten-year follow-up and examination of three models of environmental action. *Child Development, 59,* 852–67.

Brewer, D., Krop, C., Gill, B.P., & Reichardt, R. 1999. Estimating the cost of national class size reductions under different policy alternatives. *Educational Evaluation and Policy Analysis, 21* (2), 179–92.

Bridge, R.G., Judd, C.M., & Moock, P.R. 1979. *The determinants of educational outcomes.* Cambridge, MA: Ballinger.

Broberg, A., Wessels, H., Lamb, M.E., Hwang, C. 1997. Effects of day care on the development of cognitive abilities in 8 year olds: A longitudinal study. *Developmental Psychology, 33* (1), 62–69.

Broidy, L., Nagin, D., & Tremblay, R.E. 1999. *The linkage of trajectories of childhood externalizing behaviors to later violent and nonviolent delinquency.* Paper presented at the Biennial Meeting of the Society for Research in Child Development, Albuquerque, NM.

Brookover, W.B., Schweitzer, J.H., Schneider, J.M., Beady, C.H., Flood, P.K., & Wisenbaker, J.M. 1978. Elementary school social climate and school achievement. *American Educational Research Journal, 15,* 301–18.

Brooks-Gunn, J. 1988. Antecedents and consequences of variations in girls' maturational timing. In M.D. Levine & E.R. McAnarney (Eds.), *Early Adolescent Transitions* (pp. 101–21). Toronto, ON: Lexington Books.

Brooks-Gunn, J., & Furstenberg, F.F. 1986. The children of adolescent mothers: Physical, academic, and psychological outcomes. *Developmental Review, 6,* 224–51.

Brooks-Gunn, J., Duncan, G.J., & Britto, P.R. 1999. Are socioeconomic gradients for children similar to those for adults?: Achievement and health of children in the United States. In D.P. Keating & C. Hertzman (Eds.), *Developmental health and the wealth of nations: Social, biological, and educational dynamics* (pp. 94–124). New York: Guilford Press.

Brown, B.B. 1990. The role of peer groups in adolescents' adjustment to secondary school. In T.J. Berndt & G.W. Ladd (Eds.), *Peer relationships in child development* (pp. 188–215). New York: Wiley.

Brown, G. & Harris, T. 1978. *Social origins of depression: A study of psychiatric disorder in women.* London: The Free Press.

Brown, G.W., & Rutter, M. 1966. The measurement of family activities and relationships. A methodological study. *Human Relations, 19,* 241–63.

Bruce, F.C., Adams, M.M., & Shulman, H.B. 1993. Alcohol use before and during pregnancy. *American Journal of Preventive Medicine, 9,* (5), 267–73.

Bruer, J.T. 1999. *The Myth of the First Three Years: A New Understanding of Early Brain Development and Lifelong Learning.* Riverside, NJ: Free Press.

Brundtland, G.H., Liestol, K., & Walloe, L. 1980. Height, weight and menarcheal age of Oslo schoolchildren during the last 60 years. *Annals of Human Biology, 7* (4), 307–22.

Bruvold, W.H. 1993. A meta-analysis of adolescent smoking prevention programs. *American Journal of Public Health, 83,* 872–80.

Bryk, A.S., Lee, V.E., & Smith, J.B. 1990. High school organization and its effects on teachers and students: An interpretative summary of the research. In W.H. Clune & J.F. Witte (Eds.), *Choice and control in American education. Volume 1: The theory of choice and control in education.* London: Falmer Press.

Bryk, A.S., and Raudenbush, S.W. 1987. Application of hierarchical linear models to assessing change. *Psychological Bulletin, 101* (1), 147–58.

Burchinal, M., Lee, M.W., & Ramey, C.T. 1989. Type of day-care and preschool intellectual development in disadvantaged children. *Child Development, 60,* 128–37.

Burchinal, M.R., Roberts, J.E., & Nabors, L.A. 1996. Quality of center child care and infant cognitive and language development. *Child Development, 67,* 606–20.

Byles, J., Byrne, C., Boyle, M.H., & Offord, D. 1988. Ontario Child Health Study: Reliability and validity of the general functioning subscale of the McMaster family assessment device. *Family Process, 27,* 97–104.

Byrne, C.M., Offord, D.R., & Boyle, M.H. 1992. *Family functioning and emotional/behavioral disorders in children: Results from the Ontario Child Health Study.* Ottawa, ON: Ministry of Community and Social Services.

Cairns, R.B., & Cairns, B.D. 1991. Social cognition and social networks: A developmental perspective. In D.J. Pepler, & K.H. Rubin (Eds.), *The development and treatment of childhood aggression* (pp. 249–78). Hillsdale, NJ: Erlbaum.

Cairns, R.B., Cairns, B.D., Neckerman, H.J., Gest, S.D., & Gariepy, J.L. 1988. Social networks and aggressive behaviour: Peer support or peer rejection. *Developmental Psychology, 24,* 815–26.

Campbell, B.C., & Udry, J.R. 1995. Stress and age at menarche of mothers and daughters. *Journal of Biosocial Science, 27* (2), 127–34.

Campbell, F.A. & Ramey, C.T. 1994. Effects of early intervention on intellectual and academic achievement: A follow-up study of children from low-income families. *Child Development, 65,* 684–98.

Canadian Council on Smoking and Health 1993. *A new start in life: About pregnancy and smoking.* [Brochure]. Ottawa, ON.

Canadian Mental Health Association. 1995. *Depression: An overview of the literature.* Ottawa, ON.

Carbonaro, W.J. 1999. Opening the debate on closure and schooling outcomes: Comment on Morgan and Sörensen. *American Sociological Review, 64* (5), 682–86.

Carnegie Corporation of New York. 1994. *Starting points: Meeting the needs of our youngest children.* New York: Carnegie Corp.

Case, R., Griffin, S., & Kelly, W.M. 1999. Socioeconomic gradients in mathematical ability and their responsiveness to interventions during early childhood. In D.P. Keating & C. Hertzman (Eds.), *Developmental health and the wealth of nations* (pp. 125–49). New York: Guilford Press.

Caspi, A., & Moffitt, T.E. 1991. Individual differences are accentuated during periods of social change: The sample case of girls at puberty. *Journal of Personality and Social Psychology, 61* (1), 157–68.

Caspi, A., & Silva, P.A. 1995. Temperamental qualities at age three predict personality traits in young adulthood: Longitudinal evidence from a birth cohort. *Child Development, 66,* 486–98.

Caspi, A., Henry, B., McGee, R., Moffitt, T.E., & Silva, P.A. 1995. Temperamental origins of child and adolescent behavior problems: From age three to age fifteen. *Child Development, 66,* 55–68.

Caspi, A., Moffitt, T.E., Newman, D.L., & Silva, P.A. 1996. Behavioral observations at age 3 years predict adult psychiatric disorders. *Archives of General Psychiatry, 53,* 1033–39.

Central West Planning Information Network 1998. *The Mandatory Health Prorgams and Services in Ontario: Overview of the Research Literature on the Effectiveness of Public Health Interventions.* Hamilton, Ontario.

Chao, R.K. 1994. Beyond parental control and authoritarian parenting style: Understanding Chinese parenting through the cultural notion of training. *Child Development, 65,* 1111–19.

Chassin, L., Presson, C.C., Sherman, S.J., & Edwards, D.A. 1992. The natural history of cigarette smoking and young adult social roles. *Journal of Health and Social Behaviour, 33,* 328–47.

Cheal, D., Wooley, F., & Luxton, M. 1998. *How families cope and why policymakers need to know.* Canadian Policy Research Network Inc., Study No. F 02, 75pp.

Clark, J.J., Sawyer, M.G., Nguyen, A-M.T., & Baghurst, P.A. 1993. Emotional and behavioural problems experienced by children living in single-parent families: A pilot study. *Journal of Paediatric Child Health, 29,* 338–43.

Clogg, C.C. 1979. Some latent structure models for the analysis of Likert-type data. *Social Science Research, 8,* 287-301.

Clogg, C.C., & Goodman, L.A. 1986. On scaling models applied to data for several groups. *Psychometrika, 51,* 123–35.

Cnattingius, S., Lindmark, G., & Meirik, O. 1992. Who continues to smoke while pregnant? *Journal of Epidemiology and Community Health, 46,* 218–21.

Cohen, E.G., & Lotan, R.A. 1995. Producing equal status interaction in the heterogeneous classroom. *American Educational Research Journal, 32* (1), 99–121.

Cohen, J. & Cohen, P. 1983. *Applied multiple regression/correlation analysis for the behavioral sciences (2nd Edition).* Hillsdale, NJ: Lawrence Erlbaum Associates.

Cohn, J.F., Campbell, S.B., Matias, R., & Hopkins, J. 1990. Face-to-face interactions of postpartum depressed and nondepressed mother–infant pairs at 2 months. *Developmental Psychology, 26* (1), 15–23.

Coie, J.D., & Jacobs, M.R. 1993. The role of social context in the prevention of conduct disorder. *Development and Psychopathology, 5,* 263–75.

– Coleman, J.S. 1988. Social capital in the creation of human capital. *American Journal of Sociology, 94,* supplement: s95–s120.

Coleman, J.S., Campbell, E.Q., Hobson, C.F., McPartland, A.M., Mood, A.M., Weinfeld, F.D., & York, R.L. 1966. *Equality of educational opportunity.* Washington, DC: Department of Health, Education, & Welfare.

Coley, R.L., & Chase-Lansdale, P.L. 1998. Adolescent pregnancy and parenthood. Recent evidence and future directions. *American Psychologist, 53,* 152–66.

Conger, R.D., Conger, K.J., Elder, G.H.Jr., Lorenz, F.O., Simons, R.L., & Whitbeck, L.B. 1992. A family process model of economic hardship and adjustment of early adolescent boys. *Child Development, 63,* 526–41.

Corcoran, J. 1998. Consequences of adolescent pregnancy/parenting: A review of the literature. *Social Work in Health Care, 27* (2), 49–67

Coulton, C.J., Korbin, J.E., Su, M., & Chow, J. 1995. Community level factors and child maltreatment rates. *Child Development, 66* (5), 1262–76.

Council of Ministers of Education, Canada. 1997. *School achievement indicators program: Mathematics assessment.* Toronto, ON: Council of Ministers of Education.

Crane, J. 1991. The epidemic theory of ghettos and neighborhood effects on dropping out and teenage childbearing. *American Journal of Sociology, 96* (5), 1226–59.

Crane, J. 1996. Effects of home environment, SES, and maternal test scores on mathematics achievement. *Journal of Educational Research, 89* (5), 305–14.

Cusson, R.M., & Lee, A.L. 1994. Parental interventions and the development of the pre-term infant. *Journal of Obstetric, Gynecological and Neonatal Nursing, 23,* 60–68.

Cynader, M.S., & Frost, B.J. 1999. Mechanisms of brain development: Neuronal sculpting by the physical and social environment. In D.P. Keating & C. Hertzman (Eds.), Developmental health and the wealth of nations (pp. 153–84). New York: Guilford Press.

D'Arcy, C., & Siddique, C.M. 1984. Social support and mental health among mothers of preschool and school age children. *Social Psychiatry, 19,* 155–62.

Dar, Y., & Resh, N. 1986. Classroom intellectual composition and academic achievement. *American Educational Research Journal, 23,* 357–74.

Dawson, G., Frey, K., Panagiotides, H., & Osterling, J. 1997. Infants of depressed mothers exhibit atypical frontal brain activity: A replication and extension of previous findings. *Journal of Child Psychiatry and Allied Disciplines, 38* (2), 179–86.

Deal, L.W., & Holt, V.L. 1998. Young maternal age and depressive symptoms: Results from the 1988 National Maternal and Infant Health Survey. *American Journal of Public Health, 88,* 266–70.

Deater-Deckard, K., Dodge, K., Bates, J.E., & Pettit, G. 1996. Physical discipline among African American and European American mothers: Links to children's externalizing behaviors. *Developmental Psychology, 32* (6), 1065–72.

Dedam, R., McFarlane, C., & Hennessy, K. 1993. A dangerous lack of understanding. *The Canadian Nurse, 89,* (6), 29–31.

Dejin-Karlsson, E., Hanson, B.S., Ostergren, P., Ranstam, J., Isacsson, S., & Sjoberg, N. 1996. Psychosocial resources and persistent smoking in early pregnancy—A population study of women in their first pregnancy in Sweden. *Journal of Epidemiology and Community Health, 50,* 33–39.

DiPietro, J.A., Hodgson, D.M., Costigan, K.A., & Johnson, T.R.B. 1996. Fetal antecedents of infant temperament. *Child Development, 67,* 2568–83.

Dishion, T.J., Andrews, D.W., & Crosby, L. 1995. Antisocial boys and their friends in early adolescence: Relationship characteristics, quality, and interactional process. *Child Development, 66,* 139–51.

Dishion, T.J. 1990. Peer context of troublesome behaviour in children and adolescents. In P. Leone (Ed.), *Understanding troubled and troublesome youth* (pp. 128–53). Beverly Hills, CA: Sage.

Dodge, K.A. 1983. Behavioural antecedents: A peer social class. *Child Development, 54,* 1354–99.

Dodge, K.A., Bates, J.E., & Pettit, G.S. 1990. Mechanisms in the cycle of violence. *Science, 250,* 1678–83.

Dodge, K.A., Pettit, G.S. & Bates, J.E. 1994. Socialization mediators of the relation between socioeconomic status and child conduct problems. *Child Development, 65,* 649–65.

Dohrenwend, B.P., Levav, I., Shrout, P.E., & Shwartz, S. 1992. Socioeconomic status and psychiatric disorders: The causation-selection issue. *Science, 255* (5047), 946–52.

Dolan-Mullen, P., Ramirez, G., & Groff, J.Y. 1994. A meta-analysis of randomized trials of prenatal smoking cessation interventions. *American Journal of Obstetrics and Gynecology, 171,* (5), 1328–34.

Donenberg, G., & Baker, B.L. 1993. The impact of young children with externalizing behaviors on their families. *Journal of Abnormal Child Psychology, 21,* 179–98.

Dooley, M.D. 1994. Women, children and poverty in Canada. *Canadian Public Policy, 20* (4), 430–43.

Dooley, M.D., Curtis, L., Lipman, E.L., Feeney, D.H. 1998. Child psychiatric disorders, poor school performance and social problems: the roles of family structure and low income in Cycle One of the National Longitudinal Survey of Children and Youth. In M. Corak (Ed.), *Labour markets, social institutions and the future of Canada's children.* Statistics Canada.

Dornbusch, S.M., Carlsmith, J., Bushwall, S., Ritter, P., Leiderman, H., Hastorf, A., & Gross, R. 1985. Single parents, extended households, and the control of adolescents. *Child Development, 56,* 326–41.

Dornbusch, S.M., Ritter, P., Liederman, P., Roberts, D., & Fraleigh, M. 1987. The relation of parenting style to adolescent school performance. *Child Development, 56,* 326–41.

Downey, D.B. 1994. The school performance of children from single-mother and single-father families: economic or interpersonal deprivation. *Journal of Family Issues, 15,* 129–49.

Dreeben, R., & Gamoran, A. 1986. Race, instruction, and learning. *American Sociological Review, 51,* 660–69.

Drews, C.D., Murphy, C.C., Yeargin-Allsopp, M., Decoufle, P. 1996. The relationship between idiopathic mental retardation and maternal smoking during pregnancy. *Pediatrics, 97, 4,* 547–53.

Dubrow, E.F., & Luster, T. 1990. Adjustment of children born to teenage mothers: The contribution of risk and protective factors. *Journal of Marriage and the Family, 52* (2), 393–404.

Duncan, G.J. & Brooks-Gunn, J. 1997. Income effects across the life span: Integration and interpretation. In G.J. Duncan & J. Brooks-Gunn (Eds.), *Consequences of growing up poor (pp. 596–610).* New York, NY: Russell Sage Foundation Press.

Duncan, G.J., & Brooks-Gunn, J. (Eds.) 1997. Consequences of growing up poor. New York: Russell Sage Foundation.

Duncan, G.J., Brooks-Gunn, J., & Klebanov, P.K. 1994. Economic deprivation and early child development. *Child Development, 65,* 296–318.

Duncan, G.J., Yeung, W.J., Brooks-Gunn, J., & Smith, J.R. 1998. How much does poverty affect the life chances of children? *American Sociological Review, 63,* 406–23.

Dunn, L.M. & Dunn, L.M. 1981. *Peabody Picture Vocabulary Test-Revised.* Circle Pines MN: American Guidance Service.

Dunn, L.M., & Dunn, L.M. 1997. *Examiner's Manual for the Peabody Picture Vocabulary Test — Third Edition (PPVT–III).* Circle Pines, MN: American Guidance Service.

Dunst, C., Trivette, C., & Thompson, R. 1991. Supporting and strengthening family functioning: Toward a congruence between principles and practice. *Prevention in Human Services, 9* (1), 19–43.

Durlak, J.A. 1997. Primary prevention programs in schools. *Advances in Clinical Child Psychology, 19,* 283–318.

Dutton, D.B., & Levine, S. 1989. Overview, methodological critique, and reformulation. In J.P. Bunker, D.S. Gomby, & B.H. Kehrer (Eds.) Pathways to health (pp. 29–69). Menlo Park, CA: The Henry J. Kaiser Family Foundation.

Echols, F.H., & Willms, J.D. 1995. Reasons for school choice in Scotland. *Journal of Education Policy, 10* (2), 143–56.

Ehrenberg, R.G., Brewer, D.J., Gamoran, A., & Willms, J.D. 2001. The class size controversy. *Psychological Science in the Public Interest, 2* (1), 1–30.

Elder, G.H., Conger, R.D., Foster, E.M., & Ardelt, M. 1992. Families under economic pressure. *Journal of Family Issues, 13* (1), 5–37.

Elder, G.H., Nguyen, T.V., & Caspi, A. 1985. Linking family hardship to children's lives. *Child Development, 56,* 361–75.

Ellenbogen, S., & Chamberland, C. 1997. The peer relations of dropouts: a comparative study of at-risk and not at-risk youths. *Journal of Adolescence, 20,* 355–67.

Elliot, D.S. Huzinga, D., & Ageton, S. 1985. *Explaining delinquency and drug use.* Beverly Hills, CA: Sage.

Ellis, N.B. 1991. An extension of the Steinberg accelerating hypothesis. *Journal of Early Adolescence, 11* (2), 221–35.

Elmore, R.E. 1996. Getting to scale with good educational practice. *Harvard Educational Review, 66,* 1–26.

Entwisle, D.R., & Alexander, K.L. 1990. Beginning school math competence: minority and majority comparisons. *Child Development, 61,* 454–71.

Entwisle, D.R., & Alexander, K.L. 1995. A parent's economic shadow: family structure versus family resources as influences on early school achievement. *Journal of Marriage and Family, 57,* 399–407.

Epelbaum, M. 1990. Sociomonetary patterns and specifications. *Social Science Research, 19,* 322–47.

Epstein, B., Baldwin, L., & Bishop, D. 1983. The McMaster Family assessment device. *Journal of Marital and Family Therapy, 9,* 171–80.

Epstein, N.B., Bishop, D.S., & Levin. S. 1978. The McMaster model of family functioning. *Journal of Marriage and Family Counseling, 5,* 19–31.

Ershoff, D., Quinn, V.P., & Mullen, P.D. 1995. Relapse prevention among women who stop smoking early in pregnancy: A randomized clinical trial of a self-help intervention. *American Journal of Preventive Medicine, 11,* 178–84.

Essen, J. 1979. Living in one-parent families: attainment at school. *Child: Care, Health and Development, 5,* 189–200.

Evans, W.N., Oates, W.E,. & Schwab, R.M. 1992. Measuring peer group effects: A study of teenage behavior. *Journal of Political Economy, 100* (5), 966–91.

Eveleth, P.B., & Tanner, J.M. 1990. *Worldwide Variation in Human Growth,* (2nd ed.). London: Cambridge University Press.

examination results. *Oxford Review of Education, 11* (1), 33–41.

Farrington, D. P. (1987). Early precursors of frequent offending. In J.Q. Wilson & G.C. Loury (Eds.), *From children to citizens (vol. III). Families, schools and delinquency prevention* (pp. 27–50). New York: Springer-Verlag.

Farrington, D.P. 1991. Childhood aggression and adult violence: Early precursors and later life outcomes. In D. J. Pepler & K. H. Rubin (Eds.), *The development and treatment of childhood aggression* (pp. 5–30). Hillsdale, NJ: Erlbaum.

Farrington, D.P., Barnes, G.C., & Lambert, S. 1996. The concentration of offending in families. *Legal and Criminological Psychology, 1,* 47–63.

Fauber, R.L., & Long, N. 1991. Children in Context: The Role of the Family in Child Psychotherapy. *Journal of Consulting and Clinical Psychology, 59,* 813–20.

Fellegi, I., & Wolfson, M. 1999. Towards systems of social statistics: Some principles and their application in Statistics Canada. *Journal of Official Statistics, 15* (3), 373–93.

Field, T.M. 1984. Early interactions between infants and their postpartum depressed mothers. *Infant Behavior and Development, 7*, 517–22.

Field, T.M., Healy, B., Goldstein, S., Perry, S., Bendell, D., Schanberg, S., Zimmerman, E.A., & Kuhn, C. 1988. Infants of depressed mothers show "depressed" behavior even with nondepressed adults. *Child Development, 59*, 1569–79.

Field, T.M., Sandberg, D., Garcia, R., Vega-Lahr, N., Goldstein, S., & Guy, L. 1985. Pregnancy problems, postpartum depression, and early mother–infant interactions. *Developmental Psychology, 21* (6), 1152–56.

Field, T.M, Healy, B., Goldstein, S., & Guthertz, M. 1990. Behavior-state matching and synchrony in mother–infant interactions of nondepressed versus depressed dads. *Developmental Psychology, 26* (1), 7–14.

Finegan, J.A., Niccols, A., Zacher, J., & Hood, J. 1989. Factor structure of the Preschool Characteristics Questionnaire. *Infant Behavior and Development, 12*, 221–27.

Finn, J.D. 1993. *School engagement and students at risk.* National Centre for Education Statistics. Washington, DC: US Dept of Education.

Flynn, R. J. 1993. Effects of unemployment on depressive affect. In P. Cappeliez & R.J. Flynn (Eds.), *Depression and the social environment: Research and interventions with neglected populations* (pp. 185–217). Montreal, PQ and Kingston, ON: McGill — Queen's University Press.

Forehand, R., McCombs, A., & Brody, G.H. 1987. The relationship between parental depression mood states and child functioning. *Advanced Behavior Research Theory, 9*, 1–20.

Forehand, R., Wells, K.C., McMahon, R.J, Griest, D., & Rogers, T. 1982. Maternal perceptions of maladjustment in clinic-referred children: An extension of earlier research. *Journal of Behavioral Assessment, 4* (2), 145–51.

Fowles, E.R. 1998. The relationship between maternal role attainment and postpartum depression. *Health Care for Women International, 19*, 83–94.

Fraser, A.M., Brockert, J.E., & Ward, R.H. 1995. Association of young maternal age with adverse reproductive outcomes. *The New England Journal of Medicine, 332*, 1113–17.

Friedmann, M.S., McDermut, W.H., Solomom, D.A., Ryan, C.E., Keitner, G.I., & Miller, I.W. 1997. Family functioning and mental illness: a comparison of psychiatric and nonclinical families. *Family Process, 36* (4), 357–67.

Fullan, M.. 1992. *Successful school improvement: The implementation perspective and beyond.* Buckingham: Open University Press.

Fuller, B., Holloway, S.D., Liang, X. 1996. Family selection of child-care centers: the influence of household support, ethnicity and parental practices. *Child Development, 67*, 3320–37.

Furstenberg, F.F., Brooks-Gunn, J., & Chase-Lansdale, L. 1989. Teenage pregnancy and childbearing. *American Psychologist, 44* (2), 313–20.

Furstenburg, F.F., Brooks-Gunn, J., & Morgan, S.P. 1987. *Adolescent mothers in later life.* New York: Cambridge University Press.

Furstenberg, F.F. & Hughes, M.E. 1995. Social capital and successful development among at-risk youth. *Journal of Marriage and the Family, 57,* 580–92.

Future of Children, 1995. *Long term outcomes of early childhood programs, 5* (3). CA: David and Lucile Packard Foundation.

Galambos, N.L., & Silbereisen, R.K. 1987. Income change, parental life outlook, and adolescent expectations for job success. *Journal of Marriage and the Family, 49,* 141–49.

Gamoran, A. 1991. Schools, classrooms, and pupils: International studies of schooling from a multilevel perspective. In A. Gamoran (Ed.), *Schooling and achievement: Additive versus interactive models.* San Diego, CA: Academic Press.

Gamoran, A. 1992. The variable effects of high school tracking. *Sociology of Education, 57,* 812–28

Garbarino, J., & Gillian, G. 1980. *Understanding abusive families.* New York: Lexington Press.

Garmezy, N., & Rutter, M. 1983. *Stress, coping, and development in children.* New York: McGraw-Hill.

Garner, C., & Raudenbush, S.W. 1991. Neighbourhood effects on educational attainment: A multilevel analysis. *Sociology of Education, 64* (4), 251–62.

Geronimus, A.T., Korenman, S., & Hillemeier, M.M. 1994. Does young maternal age adversely affect child development? Evidence from cousin comparisons in the United States. *Population and Development Review, 20,* 585–609.

Giordano, P.C., Cernkovich, S.A., & Pugh, M.D. 1986. Friendships and delinquency. *American Journal of Sociology, 91,* 1170–1202.

Goelman, H., Doherty, G., Lero, D.S., LaGrange, A., Tougas, J. 2000. *Caring and Learning Environments: Quality in Child Care Centres Across Canada.* Centre for Families, Work, and Well-Being, University of Guelph, Ont.

Goelman, H. & Pence, A. 1987. The impact of day care, family and individual characteristics on children's language development. In D. Phillips (Ed.), *Predictors of quality child care.* NAEYC Monograph Series. Washington, D.C.: National Association for the Education of Young Children.

Goldberg, W.A., Greenberger, E., & Nagel, S.K. 1996. Employment and achievement: Mothers' work involvement in relation to children's achievement behaviors and mothers' parenting behaviors. *Child Development, 67,* 1512–27.

Goldstein, H. 1995. *Multilevel statistical models* (2nd ed.). London: Arnold.

Gonzalez, E.J. and Smith T.A., (Eds.) 1997. *User Guide for the TIMSS International Database — Primary and Middle School Years 1995 Assessment.* Chestnut Hill, MA: TIMSS International Study Center, Boston College.

Goodenow, C., & Grady, K. 1993. The relationship of school belonging and friends' values to academic motivation among urban adolescent students. *Journal of Experimental Education, 62* (1), 60–71.

Goodman, S., Adamson, L., Riniti, J., & Cole, S. 1994. Mothers' expressed attitudes: Associations with maternal depression and children's self-esteem and psychopathology. *Journal of the American Academy of Child and Adolescent Psychiatry, 33* (9), 1265–74.

Gottesman, I.I., & Goldsmith, H.H. 1994. Developmental psychopathology of antisocial behavior: Inserting genes into its ontogenesis and epigenesis. In C.A. Nelson, et al. (Eds.), *Threats to optimal development: Integrating biological, psychological, and social risk factors. The Minnesota symposia on child psychology.* Vol. 27 (pp. 69–104). Hillsdale, NJ: Lawrence Erlbaum Associates, Inc.

Government of Canada 2000. Centres of Excellence for Children's Well-Being Web Site (http://socialunion.ca/nca_e.html).

Graber, J.A., Brooks-Gunn, J., & Warren, M.P. 1995. The antecedents of menarcheal age: Heredity, family environment, and stressful life events. *Child Development, 66*, 346–59.

Gray, J. 1989. Multilevel models: Issues and problems emerging from their recent application in British studies of school effectiveness. In D.R. Bock (Ed.) *Multi-level analyses of educational data* (pp. 127–45). University of Chicago Press.

Greaney, V. 1986. Parental influences on reading. *Reading Teacher, 39* (8), 813–18.

Green, R., Kolevson, M., & Vosler, N. 1985. The Beavers–Timberlawn Model of family functioning and the Circumplex Model of family functioning: Separate but equal? *Family Process, 24*, 385–98.

Greenberger, E., O'Neil, R., & Nagel, S.K. 1994. Linking workplace and homeplace: Relations between the nature of adults' work and their parenting behaviors. *Developmental Psychology, 30*, 990–1002.

Grolnick, W.S., & Ryan, R.M. 1989. Parent styles associated with children's self-regulation and competence in school. *Journal of Educational Psychology, 81* (2), 143–54.

Guerin, D.W., Thomas, C.W., Oliver, P.H., & Gottfried, A.W. 1999. *Easy vs. difficult temperament in infancy: Long-term developmental outcomes.* Paper presented at the meeting of the Society for Research in Child Development, Albuquerque, NM.

Gunner, M. 1998. Stress physiology, health and behavioral development. In A. Thornton (Ed.), *The well-being of children and families: Research and data needs.* Institute for Social Research Report. University of Michigan.

Gupton, A., Thompson, L., Arnason, R.C., Dalke, S., & Ashcroft, T. 1995. Pregnant women and smoking. *The Canadian Nurse,* 26–30.

Halpern, R. 1993. Poverty and infant development. In C.H. Zeanah (Ed.), *Handbook of infant mental health* (pp. 73–86). New York: Guilford Press.

Hambleton, R.K., & Swaminathan, H. 1985. *Item response theory: Principles and applications.* Kluwer-Nijhoff Publishing.

Hampson, R., Beavers, R., & Hulgus, Y. 1988. Commentary: Comparing the Beavers and Circumflex Models of family functioning. *Family Process, 27,* 85–92.

Hanson, L.A., et al. 1985. Breastfeeding as protection against gastroenteritis and other infections. *Acta Paediatrica Scandinavia, 74,* 641–42.

Hanson, T.L., McLanahan, S. & Thomson, E. 1997. Economic resources, parental practices, and children's well-being. In G.J. Duncan & J. Brooks-Gunn (Eds.), *Consequences of growing up poor* (pp. 190–238). New York: Russell Sage Foundation.

Harold-Goldsmith, R., Radin, N., & Eccles, J.S. 1988. Objective and subjective reality: The effects of job loss and financial stress on fathering behaviors. *Family Perspective, 22,* 309–25.

Harris, K.M., & Marmer, J.K. 1996. Poverty, paternal involvement, and adolescent well-being. *Journal of Family Issues, 17* (5), 614–40.

Hartup. W.W. 1983. Peer relations. In M. Hetherington (Ed.) *Handbook of Child Psychology Vol IV: Socialization, personality, and social development.* New York: Wiley.

Hartup, W.W. 1996. The company they keep: Friendships and their developmental significance. *Child Development, 67,* 1–13.

Hasleager, G.J., Hartup, W.W., Van Lieshout, C.F., & Riksen-Walraven, M. 1995. *Friendship similarity in middle childhood as a function of sex and sociometric status.* Unpublished manuscript, University of Nijmegen.

Health Canada 1996. Joint Statement: *Prevention of fetal alcohol syndrome (FAS) and fetal alcohol effects (FAE) in Canada.* Internet address http://www.ccsa.ca/fasstmnt.htm.

Health Canada, Laboratory Centre for Disease Control. *Measuring up.* [Online]. Available: http://www.hc-sc.gc.ca/hpb/lcdc/brch/measuring/mu_ee_e.html [1999, November 26].

Hedges, L.V., Laine, R.D., & Greenwald, R. 1994. Does money matter? A meta-analysis of the effects of differential school effects on student outcomes. *Educational Researcher, 23* (3), 5–14.

Henderson, V., Mieszkowski, P., & Sauvageau, Y. 1978. Peer group effects and educational production functions. *Journal of Public Economic, 10,* 97–106.

Hertzman, C. 1999. Population health and human development. In D.P. Keating & C. Hertzman (Eds.), *Developmental health and the wealth of nations* (pp. 21–40). New York: Guilford Press.

Hess, R.D.,Holloway, S.D., Dickson, W.P., & Price, G.G. 1984. Maternal variables as predictors of children's school readiness and later achievement in vocabulary and mathematics in sixth grade. *Child Development, 55,* 1902–12.

Hightower, E. 1990. Adolescent interpersonal and familial precursors of positive mental health at midlife. *Journal of Youth and Adolescence, 19,* (3), 257–75.

Hinde, R.A. 1989. Temperament as an intervening variable. In G.A. Kohnstamm, J.E. Bates, and M. Klevjard Rothbart (Eds.), *Temperament in childhood* (pp. 27–33). New York, NY: John Wiley & Sons.

Ho, E. & Willms, J.D. 1996. The effects of parental involvement on eighth grade achievement. *Sociology of Education, 69,* 126–41.

Hoepfner, R., Wellisch, J., & Zagorski, H. 1977. *The sample for the sustaining effects study and projections of its characteristics to the national population.* Santa Monica: System Development Corporation

Hoff-Ginsberg, E., & Tardif, T. (1995. Socioeconomic status and parenting. In M.H. Bornstein (Ed.), *Handbook of parenting: Vol. 2. Biology and ecology of parenting* (pp. 161–88). Mahwah, NJ: Erlbaum.

Hofferth, S.L. & Kisker, E.E. 1992. The changing demographics of family day care in the United States. In D.L. Peters & A.R. Pence (Eds.), *Family day care: Current research for informed public policy* (pp. 28–57). New York: Teachers College Press.

Hoffman, L.W. 1989. Effects of maternal employment in the two-parent family. *American Psychologist, 44* (2), 283–92.

Hoffman, S.D. 1998. Teenage childbearing is not so bad after all ... or is it? A review of the new literature. *Family Planning Perspectives, 30,* 236–39, 243.

House, J., Kessler, R., Herzog, R., Mero, R.P., Kinney, A.M., & Breslow, M.J. 1990. Age, socioeconomic status, and health. *The Millbank Quarterly, 68,* 383–411.

House, J.S., Williams, D.R., & Kessler, R.C. 1987. *Social integration, social support, and the health effects of unemployment.* Ann Arbor, MI: University of Michigan, Survey Research Centre.

Howes, C., Phillips, D.A. & Whitebook, M. 1992. Thresholds of quality: Implications for the social development of children in center-based child care. *Child Development, 63,* 449–60.

Human Resources and Development Canada and Statistics Canada. 1996. *Growing up in Canada: National longitudinal survey of children and youth.* Ottawa, ON: Statistics Canada.

Human Resources Development Canada 1999. *Investing in Children: Ideas for Action.* Applied Research Branch, Ottawa: HRDC.

Jacobsen, B.K. & Thelle, D.S. 1988. Risk factors for coronary heart disease and level of education. *American Journal of Epidemiology, 127,* 923–32.

Japel, C., McDuff, P., & Tremblay, R.E. 1997. In M. Jetté, H. Desrosiers, & R.E. Tremblay (Dir.), *In 2001... I'll be 5 years old! — Survey of 5-month-old infants, Preliminary Report of the Longitudinal Study of Child Development in Québec.* Montreal: Ministère de la Santé et des Services sociaux, Government of Quebec.

Jencks, C.S., Smith, M., Acland, H., Bane, M.J., Cohen, D., Ginitis, H., Heyns, B., & Michelson, S. 1972. *Inequality: A reassessment of the effect of family and schooling in America.* New York: Basic Books.

Jenicek, M., & Demirjian, A. 1974. Age at menarche in French Canadian urban girls. *Annals of Human Biology, 1* (3), 339–46.

Jenkins, J.M., & Smith, M.A. 1990. Factors protecting children living in disharmonious homes: Maternal reports. *Journal of the American Academy of Child and Adolescent Psychiatry, 29,* 60–69.

Johnson, R.A., & Gerstein D.R. 1998. Initiation of use of alcohol, cigarettes, marijuana, cocaine and other substances in US birth cohorts since 1919. *American Journal of Public Health, 88,* 27–33.

Judge, K., & Benzeval, M. 1993. Health inequalities: new concerns about the children of single mothers. *British Medical Journal, 306,* 67–80.

Kabacoff, R.I., Miller, I.W., Bishop, D.S., Epstein, N.B., & Keitner, G.I. 1990. A psychometric study of the McMaster family assessment device in psychiatric, Medical and nonclinical samples. *Journal of Family Psychology, 3* (4), 431–39.

Kandel. D.B. 1978. Homophily, selections, and socialization in adolescent friendships. *American Journal of Sociology, 84,* 427–36.

Karoly, L.A., Greenwood, P.W., Everingham, S.S., Houbé J., Kilburn, M.R., Rydell, C.P., Sanders, M., & Chiesa, J. 1998. *Investing in our children: What we know and don't know about the costs and benefits of early childhood interventions.* Santa Monica, CA: Rand.

⌐Keating, D.P. & Hertzman, C. (Eds) 1999. *Developmental health and the wealth of nations.* New York: Guilford Press.

Keating, D.P. & Mustard, F.J. 1996. The National Longitudinal Survey of Children and Youth: An essential element for building a learning society in Canada. In *Growing up in Canada: National Longitudinal Survey of Children and Youth* (pp. 7-13). Ottawa, ON: Human Resources Development Canada and Statistics Canada.

Keitner, G.I., Miller, I.W., & Ryan, C.E. 1994. Family functioning in severe depressive disorders. In L. Grunhaus & J.F. Greden (Eds.), *Severe depressive disorders* (pp. 89–110). Washington, DC: American Psychiatric Press Inc.

Kellam, S.G., Ensminger, M.E., & Turner, J. 1977. Family structure and the mental health of children. Concurrent and longitudinal community-wide studies. *Archives of General Psychiatry, 34,* 1012–22.

Kelly, D.M. 1993. *Last chance high: How girls and boys drop into and out of alternative schools.* New Haven, CT: Yale University Press.

Kerckhoff, A.C. 1986. Effects of ability grouping. *American Sociological Review, 51* (6), 842–58.

Kerckhoff, A.C. 1993. *Diverging pathways: Social structure and career deflections.* New York: Cambridge University Press.

Kim, J.-O., & Mueller, C.W. 1978. Factor Analysis: Statistical methods and practical issues. In Eric. M. Uslaner (Ed.). *Quantitative Applications in the Social Sciences.* Beverly Hills: Sage Publications.

Kimm, S.Y., Obarzanek, E., Barton, B.A., Aston, C.E., Similo, S.L., Morrison, J.A., Sabry, Z.I., Schreiber, G.B., & McMahon, R.P. 1996. Race, socioeconomic status, and obesity in 9- to 10-year-old girls: the NHLBI Growth and Health Study. *Annals of Epidemiology, 6* (4), 266–75.

Kochanska, G., Kuczynski, L., Radke-Yarrow, M., & Welsh, J.D. 1987. Resolutions of control episodes between well and affectively ill mothers and their young children. *Journal of Abnormal Child Psychology, 15* (3), 441–56.

Kohn, M.L. 1977. *Class and conformity: A study in values, 2nd Edition*. Chicago: The University of Chicago Press.

Kohn, M.L. & Schooler, C. 1978. The reciprocal effects of the substantive complexity of work and intellectual flexibility: A longitudinal assessment. *American Journal of Sociology, 84* (1), 24–52.

Kolko, D.J., Kazdin, A.E., McCombs Thomas, A., & Day, B. 1993. Heightened child physical abuse potential. *Journal of Interpersonal Violence, 8*, 169–92.

Konarski, R. and Willms, J.D. 2000. *GEOCLUS: A Program for Contiguity-Constrained Hierarchical Cluster Analysis*. University of New Brunswick: Canadian Research Institute for Social Policy.

Koren, G. 1996. Motherisk update — Alcohol consumption in early pregnancy: How much will harm a fetus? *Canadian Family Physician, 42*, 2141–43.

Kraemer, H.C., Kazdin, A.E., Offord, D.R., Kessler, R.C., Jensen, P.S., & Kupfer, D.J. 1997. Coming to terms with the terms of risk. *Arch Gen Psychiatry, 54* (April), 337–43.

Kunst, A.E., & Machenbach, J.P. 1992. *An international comparison of socioeconomic inequalities in mortality*. Rotterdam: Erasmus University.

Lamborn, S.D., Dornbusch, S.M., & Steinberg, L. 1996. Ethnicity and Community Context as Moderators of the relations between family decision making and adolescent adjustment. *Child Development, 67*, 283–301.

Lamborn, S.D., Mounts, N.S., Steinberg, L., & Dornbusch, S.M. 1991. Patterns of competence and adjustment among adolescents from authoritative, authoritarian, indulgent, and neglectful families. *Child Development, 62*, 1049–65.

Lamont, M., & Lareau. A. 1988. Cultural capital: Allusions, gaps, and glissandos in recent theoretical developments. *Sociological Theory, 62*, 153–68.

Lareau, A. 1987. Social class differences in family–school relationships: The importance of cultural capital. *Sociology of Education, 60* (April), 73–85.

Lareau, A. 1989. *Home advantage: Social class and parental intervention in elementary education*. Philadelphia: The Falmer Press.

Lau, C.J. 1979. Educational production functions. In D.M. Windham (Ed.), *Economic dimensions of education*. Washington, DC: National Academy of Education.

Lazar, I., Darlington, R., Murray, H., Royce, J. & Snipper, A. 1982. Lasting effects of early education: A report from the Consortium of Longitudinal Studies. *Monographs of the Society for Research in Child Development*. Series No. 195, 47 (2–3).

Lee, C.L., & Bates, J.E. 1985. Mother–child interaction at age two years and perceived difficult temperament. *Child Development, 56*, 1314–25.

Lee, V.E., Brooks-Gunn, J., Schnur, E., & Liaw, F.-R. 1990. Are head start effects sustained? A longitudinal follow-up comparison of disadvantaged children attending head start, no preschool and other preschool programs. *Child Development, 61,* 495–507.

Lee, V.E., & Bryk, A.S. 1989. A multilevel model of the social distribution of high school achievement. *Sociology of Education, 62* (3), 172–92.

Lee, V.E., Bryk, A.S., and Smith, J.B. 1990. The Organization of Effective Secondary Schools. In L. Darling-Harmmond (Ed.), *Review of Research in Education* (pp. 171–267). Washington, DC: American Educational Research Association.

Lee, V.E. & Smith, J.B. 1993. Effects of school restructuring on the achievement and engagement of middle-grade students. *Sociology of Education, 66,* 164–87.

Lefkowitz, M.M., Eron, L.D., Walder, L.O., & Huesmann, L.R. 1977. *Growing up to be violent: a longitudinal study of the development of aggression.* New York: Pergamon Press.

Lempers, J.D., Clark-Lempers, D., Simons, R.L. 1989. Economic hardship, parenting, and distress in adolescence. *Child Development, 60,* 25–39.

Lerner, J.V., & Lerner, R.M. 1983. Temperament and adaptation across life: Theoretical and empirical issues. In P.B. Baltes & O.G. Brim, Jr. (Eds.), *Life-span development and behavior* (Vol. 5, pp. 197–231). San Diego, CA: Academic Press.

Levin, H. 1980. Education production theory and teacher inputs. In C.E. Bidwell and D.M. Windham (Eds.), *The analysis of educational productivity* (pp. 203–31). Cambridge, MA: Ballinger.

Levitt, C., Watters, N., Chance, G., Walker, R., & Avard, D. 1993. Low-birth-weight symposium: Summary of proceedings. *Canadian Medical Association Journal, 148* (5), 767–71.

Lipman, E.L., & Offord, D.R. 1997. Psychosocial morbidity among poor children in Ontario. In G. Duncan & J. Brooks-Gunn (Eds.), *Consequences of growing up poor* (pp. 239–87). New York: Russell Sage Foundation.

Lipman, E.L., Offord, D.R., & Boyle, M.H. 1994. Economic disadvantage and child psycho-social morbidity. *Canadian Medical Association Journal, 151,* 431–37.

Lipman, E.L., Offord, D.R., & Boyle, M.H. 1996. What if we could eliminate child poverty? The theoretical effect on child psychosocial morbidity. *Social Psychiatry and Psychiatric Epidemiology, 31,* 303–07.

Lipman, E.L., Offord, D.R., & Boyle, M.H. 1997. Single mothers in Ontario: socio-demographic, physical and mental health characteristics. *Canadian Medical Association Journal, 156,* 639–45.

Lipman, E.L., Offord, D.R., & Dooley, M.D. 1996. What do we know about children from single-mother families? Questions and answers from the National Longitudinal Survey of Children and Youth. In *Growing Up in Canada. National Longitudinal Study of Children and Youth* (Cat. No. 89-550-MPE). Ottawa, ON: Human Resources Development Canada, Statistics Canada.

Loeber, R., & Stouthamer-Loeber, M. (1986). Family factors as correlates and predictors of juvenile conduct problems and delinquency. *Crime and Justice, 7,* 29–149.

Loney, E.A., Green, K.L, & Nanson, J.L. 1994. A health promotion perspective on the house of commons' report "Foetal alcohol syndrome: A preventable tragedy." *Canadian Journal of Public Health, 85* (4), 248–51.

Longfellow, C. & Szpiro, S.Z. (1983, April). *Maternal depression: A source of stress for children.* Paper presented at the biennial meeting of the Society for Research in Child Development, Detroit, MI.

Luker, K. 1996. *Dubious conceptions. The politics of teenage pregnancy.* Cambridge, MA: Harvard University Press.

Lyons, J.J., True, W.R., Eisen, S.A., Goldberg, J., Meyer, J.M., Faraone, S.V., Eaves, L.J., & Tsuang, M.T. 1995. Differential heritability of adult and juvenile antisocial traits. *Archives of General Psychiatry, 52,* 906–15.

Ma, X., & Willms, J.D. 1995. The effects of school disciplinary climate on eighth grade achievement. Paper prepared for the annual meeting of the American Education Research Association.

Macleod-Clark, J., & Maclaine, K. 1992. The effects of smoking in pregnancy: a review of approaches to behavioural change. *Midwifery, 8,* 19–30.

Manski, C.F. 1993. Identification problems in the social sciences. *Sociological Methodology, 23,* 1–56.

Margolin, G. 1981. The reciprocal relationship between marital and child problems. *Advances in Family Intervention, Assessment and Theory, 2,* 131–82.

Marmot, M.G., Smith, G., Stansfeld, S., Patel, C., North, F., Head, J., White, L., Brunner, E., & Feeney, A. 1991. Health inequalities among British civil servants: The Whitehall Study. *Lancet, 337,* 1387–93.

Martin, D.J., & Hoover, H.D. 1987. Sex differences in educational achievement: A longitudinal study. *Journal of Early Adolescence, 7,* 65–83.

Maxwell, J. 1995. The social role of government in a knowledge-based economy. In P. Grady *et al.* (Eds.), *Redefining Social Security.* School of Policy Studies: Queen's University, Kingston.

Maxwell, J. 1996. *Social dimensions of economic growth.* (The Eric John Hanson Memorial Lecture Series, Vol. VIII.). University of Alberta: Department of Economics.

Mayer, S.E. 1997. *What money can't buy: Family income and children's life chances.* Cambridge, MA: Harvard University Press.

Maynard, R.A. 1997. The study, the context, and the findings in brief. In R.A. Maynard (Ed.), *Kids having kids: Economic costs and social consequences of teen pregnancy* (pp. 1–21). Washington, DC: Urban Institute Press.

Maziade, M., Bernier, H., Thivierge, J., & Coté R. 1987. The relationship between family functioning and demographic characteristics in an epidemiological study. *Canadian Journal of Psychiatry, 32,* 526–33.

Maziade, M., Boudreault, M., Thivierge, J., Capéraà, P., & Côté, R. 1984. Infant temperament: SES and gender differences and reliability of measurement in a large Quebec sample. *Merrill-Palmer Quarterly, 30* (2), 213–26.

Maziade, M., Capéraà, P., Laplante B., Boudreault, M., Thivierge, J., Côté, R., & Boutin, P. 1985. Value of difficult temperament among 7-year-olds in the general population for predicting psychiatric diagnosis at age 12. *American Journal of Psychiatry, 142,* 943–46.

McCain, Hon. M., & Mustard, F. 1999. *Reversing the real brain drain: Early years study.* Children's Secretariat, Toronto, ON.

McCartney, K. 1984. Effect of quality of day care environment on children's language development. *Developmental Psychology, 20* (2), 244–60.

McDonough, S.C. 1993. Interaction guidance: Understanding and Treating early infant–caregiver relationship disturbances. In C.H. Zeanah (Ed.), *Handbook of infant mental health* (pp. 414–26). New York: Guilford Press.

McEwan, B. & Schmeck, H. 1994. *The Hostage Brain.* New York: The Rockefeller University Press.

McEwan, B. 1998. Protective and damaging effects of stress mediators. *New England Journal of Medicine, 338* (3), 171–79.

McFarlane, A.H., Bellissimo, A., & Norman, G.R. 1995. Family structure, family functioning and adolescent well-being: The transcendent influence of parental style. *Journal of Child Psychology & Psychiary, 36,* 847–64.

McIntyre, L. 1996. Starting out. Growing up in Canada: National Longitudinal Survey of Children and Youth.

McKenna, M., & Willms, J.D. 1998. The challenges facing parent councils in Canada. *Childhood Education: Infancy Through Early Adolescents, 74* (6), 378–83.

McKie, C. 1993. An overview of lone parenthood in Canada. In J. Hudson & B. Galaway (Eds.), *Single parent families — perspectives on research and policy*, (pp. 54). Toronto, ON: Thompson Educational Publishing.

McLanahan, S., & Sandefur, G. 1994. *Growing up with a single parent: What hurts, what helps.* Cambridge, MA: Harvard University Press.

McLaughlin, M.W. 1987. Learning from experience: Lessons from policy implementation. *Educational Evaluation and Policy Analysis, 9* (2), 171–78.

McLaughlin, T.F. & Vacha, E.F. (1992). The at-risk student: A proposal for action. *Journal of Instructional Psychology, 19* (1), 66–68.

McLeod, J.D. & Nonnemaker, J.M. 2000. Poverty and child emotional and behavioral problems: Racial/ethnic differences in processes and effects. *Journal of Health and Social Behavior, 41* (2), 137–61.

McLeod, J.D. & Shanahan, M.J. 1993. Poverty, parenting, and children's mental health. *American Sociological Review, 58,* 351–66.

McLeod, J.D., Kruttschnitt, C., & Dornfeld, M. 1994. Does parenting explain the effects of structural conditions on children's antisocial behavior? A comparison of Blacks and Whites. *Social Forces, 73* (2), 575–604.

McLoyd, V.C. 1990. The impact of economic hardship on Black families and children: Psychological distress, parenting, and socioemotional development. *Child Development, 61,* 311–46.

McPherson, A.F., & Willms, J.D. 1986. Certification, class conflict, religion, and community: A socio-historical explanation of the effectiveness of contemporary schools. In A.C. Kerckhoff (Ed.), Research in sociology of education and socialization, Volume 6 (pp. 227–302). Greenwich, CT: JAI Press.

Michielutte, R., Ernest, J.M., Moore, M.L., Meis, P.J., Sharp, P.C., Wells, H.B., & Buescher, P.A. 1992. A comparison of risk assessment models for term and preterm low birthweight. *Preventive Medicine, 21,* 98–109.

Mijanovich, T. & Long, D. 1995. *Creating an alternative to welfare: First year findings on the implementation, welfare impacts, and costs of the self-sufficiency project.* Ottawa, ON: Human Resources Development Canada (Applied Research Branch, R-96-11E).

Millar, W.J., & Chen, J. 1998. Maternal education and risk factors for small-for-gestational-age births. *Health Reports* (Statistics Canada, Catalogue 82-003), 10(2), 43–51.

Miller, B.C., & Heaton, T.B. 1991. Age at first sexual intercourse and the timing of marriage and childbirth. *Journal of Marriage and the Family, 53,* 719–32.

Milne, A.M., Myers, D.E., Rosenthal, A.S., & Ginsburg, A. 1986. Single parents, working mothers, and the educational achievement of school children. *Sociology of Education, 59,* 125–39.

Mirowsky, J. & Hu, P. 1996. Physical impairment and the diminishing effects of income. *Social Forces, 74* (3), 1073–96.

Moffitt, T.E., Caspi, A., Belsky, J., & Silva, P.A. 1992. Childhood experience and the onset of menarche: A test of a sociobiological model. *Child Development, 63,* 47–58.

Moilanen, I., & Rantakallio, P. 1988. The single parent family and the child's mental health. *Social Science and Medicine, 27,* 181–86.

Moore, K.A., Morrison, D.R., & Greene, A.D. 1995. *Children born to teenage mothers: Analyses of the National Longitudinal Survey of Youth — Child Supplement and the National Survey of Children.* Washington, DC: Child Trends Inc. (ERIC Document Reproduction Service No ED 415 998)

Moore, K.A., Morrison, D.R., & Greene, A.D. 1997. Effects on the children born to adolescent mothers. In R.A. Maynard (Ed.), *Kids having kids: Economic costs and social consequences of teen pregnancy* (pp. 145–80). Washington, DC: Urban Institute Press.

Moore, M.L., Michielutte, R., Meis, P.J., Ernest, J.M., Wells, H.B., & Buescher, P.A. 1994. Etiology of low-birthweight birth: A population-based study. *Preventive Medicine, 23,* 793–99.

Moorehouse, M.J. 1991. Linking maternal employment patterns to mother–child activities and children's school competence. *Developmental Psychology, 27* (2), 295–303.

Morbidity and Mortality Weekly Report from the Centers for Disease Control and Prevention. 1995. Sociodemographic and behavioral characteristics associated with alcohol consumption during pregnancy — United Stated, 1988. *Journal of the American Medical Association, 273* (18). 1406–07.

Morgan, S.L., & Sᵌrensen, A.B. 1999. Parental networks, social closure, and mathematics learning: A test of Coleman's social capital explanation of school effects. American *Sociological Review, 64* (5), 661–81.

Mosley, W.H. & Cowley, P. 1991. The challenge of world health. *Population Bulletin, 46,* 1–39.

Mosteller, F., & Tukey, J.W. 1977. *Data analysis and regression.* Reading, MA: Addison-Wesley.

Mueller, C.W., & Parcel, T.L. 1981. Measures of socioeconomic status: Alternatives and recommendations. *Child Development, 52,* 13–30.

Muller, C. 1995. Maternal employment, parental involvement, and mathematics achievement among adolescents. *Journal of Marriage and the Family, 57,* 85–100.

Munroe Blum, H., Boyle, M.H., & Offord, D.R. 1988. Single-parent families: child psychiatric disorder and school performance. *Journal of the American Academy of Child and Adolescent Psychiatry, 27,* 214–19.

Murray, L. & Cooper, P.J. 1996. The impact of postpartum depression on child development. *International Review of Psychiatry, 8* (1), 55–63.

Nafstad, P., Botten, G., & Hagen, J. 1996. Partner's smoking: A major determinant for changes in women's smoking behaviour during and after pregnancy. *Public Health, 110,* 379–85.

Nagin, D., & Tremblay, R.E. 1999. Trajectories of boys' physical aggression, opposition, and hyperactivity on the path to physically violent and non violent juvenile delinquency. *Child Development, 70* (5), 1181–96.

Nanson, J.L. (1997, March 15). Binge drinking during pregnancy: Who are the women at risk? *Canadian Medical Association Journal, 156* (6), 807–08.

National Centre for Education Statistics. 1989. *National Education Longitudinal Study* (NCES Publication No. 90-482). Chicago: National Opinion Research Centre.

National Council of Teachers of Mathematics. 1989. *Curriculum and evaluation standards for school mathematics.* Reston, VA: National Council of Teachers of Mathematics.

Newcomb, A.F. & Bagwell, C. 1995. The developmental significance of children's friendship relations. In A.F. Newcombe & W.W. Hartup (Eds.), *The company they keep: Friendship in childhood and adolescence* (pp. 289–321). Cambridge: Cambridge University Press.

Ng, E., & Wilkins, R. 1994. Maternal demographic characteristics and rates of low birth weight in Canada, 1961 to 1990. *Health Reports, 6* (2), 241–52.

Normand, C.L., Zoccolillo, M., Tremblay, R.E., McIntyre, L., Boulerice, B., McDuff, P., Pérusse, D., & Barr, R.G. 1996. In the beginning: Looking for the roots of babies' difficult temperament. *Growing up in Canada*. Human Resources Development Canada and Statistics Canada, 57–68.

Norusis, M.J./SPSS Inc. 1992. SPSS/PC+: Advanced statistics (Version 5.0) [Computer software]. Chicago: SPSS Inc.

Nottelmann, E.D., Inoff-Germain, G., Susman, E.J., & Chrousos, G.P. 1990. Hormones and behavior at puberty. In J. Bancroft (Ed.), *Adolescence and puberty* (pp. 88–123). New York: Oxford University Press.

Nye, B., Hedges, L.V., & Konstantopolous, S. 1999. The long-term effects of small classes: A five-year follow-up study of the Tennessee class size experiment. *Educational Evaluation and Policy Analysis, 21* (2), 127–42.

Oberklaid, F., Sanson, A., Pedlow, R., & Prior, M. 1993. Predicting preschool behavior problems from temperament and other variables in infancy. *Pediatrics, 91* (1), 113–20.

Offord, D.R. 1989. Conduct disorder: risk factors and prevention.*Prevention of mental disorders, alcohol and other drug use in children and adolescents* (pp. 273–307). Rockville, MD: Alcohol, Drug Abuse & Mental Health Administration.

Offord, D.R., & Bennett, K. 1994. Conduct disorder: Long-term outcomes and intervention effectiveness. *Journal of the American Academy of child and Adolescent Psychiatry, 33* (8), 1069–78.

Offord, D.R., Boyle, M.H., & Jones, B.R. 1987. Psychiatric disorder and poor school performance among welfare children in Ontario. *Canadian Journal of Psychiatry, 32*, 518–25.

Offord, D.R., Boyle, M.H., Racine, Y.A., Fleming, J.E., Cadman, D.T., Monroe Blum, H., Byrne, C., Links, P.S., Lipman, E.L., MacMillan, H.L., Rae-Grant, N.I., Sanford, M.N., Szatmari, P., Thomas, H., & Woodward, C.A. 1992. Outcome, prognosis, and risk in a longitudinal follow-up study. *Journal of the American Academy of Child and Adolescent Psychiatry, 31* (5), 916–23.

Offord, D.R., Boyle, M.H., Szatmari, P., Rae-Grant, N.I., Links, P.S., Cadman, D.T., Byles, J.A., Crawford, J.W., Munroe Blum, H., Byrne, C., Thomas, H., & Woodward, C.A. 1987. Ontario child health study. II. Six-month prevalence of disorder and rates of service utilization. *Archives of General Psychiatry, 44*, 832–36.

Offord, D.R., Kraemer, H.C., Kazdin, A.E., Jensen, P.S., & Harrington, R. 1998. Lowering the burden of suffering from child psychiatric disorder: Trade-offs among clinical, targeted, and universal interventions. *Journal of the American Academy of Child and Adolescent Psychiatry, 37* (7), 686–94.

Offord, D.R., Kraemer, H.C., Kazdin, A.E., Jensen, P.S., Harrington, R., & Gardner, J.S. 1999. Lowering the burden of suffering: Monitoring the benefits of clinical, targeted, and universal approaches. In D.P. Keating & C.C. Hertzman (Eds), *Developmental health and the wealth of nations* (pp. 293–310). New York: Guilford Press.

- Offord, D.R., & Lipman, E.L. 1996. Emotional and behavioural problems. In *Growing up in Canada: National Longitudinal Survey of Children and Youth* (pp. 119–26). Ottawa, ON: Human Resources Development Canada and Statistics Canada.

Offord, D.R., & Waters, B.G. 1983. Socialization and its failure. In M.D. Levine, W.B. Carey, A.C. Crocker, & R.T. Gross (Eds.). *Developmental–Behavioural Pediatrics* (pp. 650–82). New York: John Wiley & Sons Inc.

Olds, D.L., Eckenrode, J., Henderson, C.R., Kitzman, H., Powers, J., Cole, R., Sidora, K., Morris, P., Pettitt, L.M., & Luckey, D. 1997. Long-term effects of home visitation on maternal life course and child abuse and neglect. Fifteen-year follow-up of a randomized trial. *Journal of the American Medical Association, 278* (8), 637–43.

Olds, D.L., Henderson, C.R., Cole, R., Eckenrode, J., Kitzman, H., Luckey, D., Pettitt, L., Sidora, K., Morris, P., & Powers, J. 1998. Long-term effects of nurse home visitation on children's criminal and antisocial behavior. *Journal of American Medical Association, 280* (14), 1238–73.

Olson, D.H., McCubbin, H.I., Barnes, H., Larsen, A., Muxem, M., & Wilson, M. 1985. *Family inventories.* St. Paul, MN: University of Minnesota, Family Social Science.

Olson, D.H., Russell, C.S., & Sprenkle, D.H. 1983. Circumplex Model VI: Theoretical update. *Family Process, 22,* 69–83.

Olweus, D. 1979. Stability of aggressive reaction patterns in males: A review. *Psychological Bulletin, 86,* 852–75.

Olweus, D. 1980. Familial and temperamental determinants of aggressive behavior in adolescent boys: A causal analysis. *Developmental Psychology, 16,* 644–60.

Ontario Ministry of Community and Social Services. 1986. *Ontario Child Health Study: Summary of initial findings.* Toronto, ON: Queen's Printer for Ontario.

Organisation for Economic Cooperation and Development. 1996. Education at a glance: OECD Indicators. Paris: OECD.

Organisation for Economic Cooperation and Development. 1996. *OECD Economic Surveys — Sweden: Implementing the OECD Jobs Strategy.* Paris: Author.

Organisation for Economic Cooperation and Development, Human Resources Development Canada, and Statistics Canada. 1997. *Literacy Skills for the Knowledge Economy.* Paris: OECD.

Organisation of Economic Cooperation and Development. 2000. *Education at a Glance: OECD Indicators 2000 Edition.* Paris: OECD.

Organisation for Economic Cooperation and Development & Statistics Canada. 1995. *Literacy, economy, & society: Results of the first international adult literacy survey.* Paris, France: Organization for Economic Cooperation and Development, and Ottawa, ON: Minister of Industry, Canada.

Osberg, L., 1995. The equity/efficiency trade-off in retrospect. *Canadian Business Economics, 3* (3), 5–19.

Osborn, A.F., & Milbank, J.E. 1987. *The Effects of Early Education: A Report from the Child Health and Education Study.* Oxford: Clarendon Press.

Pallas, A.M. 1988. School climate in American high schools. *Teachers College Record, 89* (4), 541–53.

Panaccione, V.F., & Wahler, R.G. 1986. Child behavior, maternal depression, and social coercion as factors in the quality of child care. *Journal of Abnormal Child Psychology, 14* (2), 263–78.

Panzarine, S., Slater, E., & Sharps, P. 1995. Coping, social support, and depressive symptoms in adolescent mothers. *Journal of Adolescent Health, 17,* 113–19.

Parke, R. & Buriel, R. 1998. Socialization in the family: Ethnic and ecological perspectives. *Handbook of child psychology: Social, emotional, and personality development, vol. 3.* New York: John Wiley & Sons.

Parker J.D., & Schoendorf, K.C. 1992. Influence of paternal characteristics on the risk of low birth weight. *American Journal of Epidemiology, 136* (4), 399–407.

Parker, J.G., & Asher, S.R. 1987. Peer relations and later personal adjustment: Are low-accepted children at risk? *Psychological Bulletin, 102,* 357–89.

Parks, P.L., & Arndt, E.K. 1990. Differences between adolescent and adult mothers of infants. *Journal of Adolescent Health, 11,* 248–53.

Passino, A.W., Whitman, T.L., Borkowski, J.G., Schellenbach, C.J., Maxwell, S.E., Keogh, D., & Rellinger, E. 1993. Personal adjustment during pregnancy and adolescent parenting. *Adolescence, 28,* 97–122.

Patterson, G.R. 1982. *Coercive family process.* Eugene, OR: Castilia.

Patterson, G.R. 1986. Performance models for antisocial boys. *American Psychologist, 41* (4), 432–44.

Patterson, G.R., DeBaryshe, B.D., & Ramsey, E. 1989. A developmental perspective on antisocial behavior. *American Psychologist, 44,* 329–35.

— Patterson, G.R., Dishion, T., & Reid, J. 1993. *Antisocial boys.* Eugene, OR: Castalia.

Peacock, J.L., Bland, J.M., & Anderson, H.R. 1995. Preterm delivery: Effects of socioeconomic factors, psychological stress, smoking, alcohol, and caffeine. *British Medical Journal, 311,* 531–35.

Peipert, J.F., & Bracken, M.B. 1993. Maternal age: An independent risk factor for cesarean delivery. *Obstetrics and Gynecology, 81,* 200–05.

Pence, A.R., Goelman, H., Lero, D.S., & Brockman, L. 1992. Family day care in a socioecological context: Data from the National Child Care Study. In D.L. Peters and A.R. Pence (Eds.), *Family Day Care: Current Research for Informed Public Policy.* New York: Teachers College Press.

Pepler, D.J., Craig, W.M., & Roberts, W.R. 1995. Aggression in the peer group: Assessing the negative socialization process. In J. McCord (Ed.), *Coercion and punishment in long-term perspectives,* (pp.213–28). New York: Cambridge University Press.

Pereira, A., Olsen, J., & Ogston, S. 1993. Variability of self reported measures of alcohol consumption: Implications for the association between drinking in pregnancy and birth weight. *Journal of Epidemiological and Community Health, 47,* 326–30.

Perosa, L.M., & Perosa, S.L. 1990. Convergent and discriminant validity for family self-report measures. *Educational and Psychological Measurement, 50*, 855–68.

Peters, S. 1995. *Exploring Canadian Values.* Canadian Policy Research Networks.

Petersen, A.C., Crockett, L., Richards, M., & Boxer, A. 1988. A self-report measure of pubertal status: Reliability, validity, and initial norms. *Journal of Youth and Adolescence, 17* (2), 117–32.

Peterson, C. & Peterson, R. 1986. Parent–child interaction and daycare: Does quality of daycare matter? *Journal of Applied Developmental Psychology, 7*, 1–15.

Pettit, G.S., & Bates, J.E. 1989. Family interaction patterns and children's behavior problems from infancy to 4 years. *Developmental Psychology, 25*, 413–20.

Pettit, G.S., Bates, J.E., & Dodge, K.E. 1997. Supportive parenting, ecological context, and children's adjustment: A seven-year longitudinal study. *Child Development, 68* (5), 908–23.

Phillips, D.A. 1987. Quality in child care: What does the research tell us? *Research Monographs of the National Association for the Education of Young Children: Vol. 1,* Washington, DC: NAEYC.

Phoenix, A. 1991. *Young mothers?* Cambridge, UK: Polity Press.

Pianta, R.C., López-Hernández, C., & Ferguson, J.E. 1997. Adolescent mothers and their children's early school performance. *Early Education & Development, 8,* 377–87.

Plewis, I. 1991. Using multilevel models to link educational progress with curriculum coverage. In S.W. Raudenbush & J.D. Willms, (Eds.), *Schools, classrooms, and pupils: International studies of schooling from a multilevel perspective* (pp. 149–66). San Diego: Academic Press.

Plomin, R., DeFries, J., McClearn, G., & Rutter, M. 1997. *Behavioral genetics.* New York: 3rd ed., Freeman.

Power, C., Manor, O., & Fox, A.J. 1991. *Health and class: The early years.* London: Chapman & Hall.

Price, R.H., Cioci, M., Penner, W. & Trautlein, B. 1993. Webs of influence: School and community programs that enhance adolescent health and education. *Teachers College Record, 94* (3), 487–521.

Prior, M., Smart, D., Sanson, A., & Oberklaid, F. 1993. Sex differences in psychological adjustment from infancy to 8 years. *Journal of the American Academy of Child and Adolescent Psychiatry, 32* (2), 291–304.

Pulkkinen, L., & Tremblay, R.E. 1992. Adult life-styles and their precursors in the social behaviour of children and adolescents. *European Journal fo Personality, 4* (3), 237–51.

Radloff, L.S. 1977. The CES-D scale: A self-report depression scale for research in the general population. *Applied Psychological Measurement, 1* (3), 385–401.

Raudenbush, S.W., & Bryk, A.S. 1988. Methodological advances in analyzing the effects of schools and classrooms on student learning. In E.Z. Rothkopf (Ed.), *Review of research in education Vol. 15* (pp. 423–75). Washington, DC: American Educational Research Association.

Raudenbush, S.W., & Chan, W.S. 1992. Growth curve analysis in accelerated longitudinal designs with application to the National Youth Survey. *Journal of Research in Crime & Delinquency,* 29 (4), 387–411.

Raudenbush, S.W., & Kasim, R.M. 1998. Cognitive skill and economic inequality: Findings from the National Adult Literacy Study. *Harvard Educational Review,* 68 (1), 33–79.

Raudenbush, S.W. & Willms, J.D. (Eds.). 1991. *Schools, classrooms, and pupils: International studies of schooling from the multilevel perspective.* New York: Academic Press.

Raudenbush, S.W., & Willms, J.D. 1995. The estimation of school effects. *Journal of Educational and Behavioural Statistics,* 20 (4), 307–35.

Raudenbush, S.W., & Bryk, A.S. 2002. *Hierarchical linear models: Applications and data analysis methods* (second edition). Thousand Oaks, CA: Sage.

Reesor, M., & Lipsett, B. 1997. Hours of work preference — Analysis of the 1995 Survey of Work Arrangements. Human Resources Development Canada, Applied Research Branch Working Paper, Ottawa, ON.

Reis, J.S., & Herz, E.J. 1987. Correlates of adolescent parenting. *Adolescence,* 22, 599–609.

Remkes, T. 1993. Saying no — completely. *The Canadian Nurse,* 89 (6), 25–28.

Richards, M.H., & Duckett, E. 1994. The relationship of maternal employment to early adolescent daily experience. *Child Development,* 65, 225–36.

Richman, N., Stevenson, J., & Graham, P.J. 1982. *Preschool to school.* London: Academic Press.

Rindskopf, D., & Rindskopf, W. 1986. The value of latent class analysis in medical diagnosis. *Statistics in Medicine,* 5, 21–27.

Robins, L.N., West, P.A., & Herjanic, B.L. 1975. Arrest and delinquency in two generations: A study of black urban families and their children. *Journal of Child Psychology and Psychiatry and Allied Disciplines,* 16, 125–40.

Robitaille, D.F., Taylor, A.R., & Orpwood, G. 1996. *The TIMSS–Canada Report.* Vancouver, BC: University of British Columbia.

Rodgers, B. 1990. Behavior and personality in childhood as predictors of adult psychiatric disorder. *Journal of Child Psychology and Psychiatry, 31* (3), 393–414.

Rootman, I. 1988. Inequities in health: Sources and solutions. *Health Promotion,* 26 (3), 2–8.

Rosenthal, R., & Vandell, D. (1996). Quality of care at school-aged child care programs: Regulatable features, observed experiences, child perspectives and parent perspectives. *Child Development,* 67, 2434–45.

Ross, C.E., & Mirowsky, J. 1988. Child care and emotional adjustment to wives' employment. *Journal of Health and Social Behaviour,* 29, 127–38.

Ross, C.E., & Willigen, M.V. 1997. Education and the subjective quality of life. *Journal of Health and Social Behavior, 38,* 275–97.

Ross, C.E., & Wu, C. 1995. The links between education and health. *American Sociological Review, 60,* 719–45.

Ross, D.P., Scott, K., & Kelly, M.A. 1996. Overview: children in Canada in the 1990s. *Growing Up in Canada: National Longitudinal Survey of Children and Youth.* Ottawa, ON: Human Resources Development Canada, Statistics Canada. 15–45.

Rothbart, M.K., & Ahadi, S.A. 1994. Temperament and the development of personality. *Journal of Abnormal Psychology, 103* (1), 55–66.

Rothbart, M.K., & Bates, J.E. 1998. Temperament. In W. Damon (Series Ed.) & N. Eisenberg (Vol. Ed.), *Handbook of child psychology: Vol. 3. Social, emotional and personality development* (5th ed.). New York: Wiley.

Rothbaum, F., & Weisz, J.R. 1994. Parental caregiving and child externalizing behavior in nonclinical samples: A meta-analysis. *Psychological Bulletin, 116,* 55–74.

Rothman, K. J., and Greenland, S. (1998). *Modern Epidemiology (2nd Edition).* Philadelphia: Lippincott, Williams, & Wilkins.

Rothman, R. 1995. *Measuring up: Standards, assessment, and school reform.* San Francisco: Josey-Bass.

Rothman, R., & Elmore, R.F. 1998. *Standards-based reform: The "theory of action."* Unpublished manuscript.

Rowan, B., & Miracle, A.W. Jr. 1983. Systems of ability grouping and the stratification of achievement in elementary schools. *Sociology of Education, 56* (2), 133–44.

Rubenson, K. & Willms, J.D. 1993. *Human Resources Development in British Columbia: An Analysis of the 1992 Adult Education and Training Survey in Canada.* Vancouver: Centre for Policy Studies in Education, University of British Columbia..

Rumberger, R. 1995. Dropping out of middle school : A multilevel analysis of students and schools. *American Educational Research Journal, 32* (2), 583–625.

Rumberger, R.W. 1990. Second chance for high school dropouts: The costs and benefits of dropout recovery programs in the United States. In D.E. Inbar (Ed.), *The second chance in education* (pp. 227–50). New York: Falmer Press.

Rumberger, R., & Willms, J.D. 1992. The impact of racial and ethnic segregation on the achievement gap in California high schools. *Educational Evaluation and Policy Analysis, 14* (4), 377–96.

Ruopp, R.R., Travers, J., Glantz, F., & Coelen, C. 1979. *Children at the center.* Cambridge, MA: Abt Associates.

Rutter, M. 1990. Commentary: Some focus and process considerations regarding effects of parental depression on children. *Developmental Psychology, 26* (1), 60–67.

Rutter, M., Cox, A., Tupling, C., Berger, M., & Yule, W. 1975. Attainment and adjustment in two geographical areas. I. Prevalence of psychiatric disorder. *British Journal of Psychiatry, 126,* 493–509.

Sacco, V.F. 1995. *Fear and personal safety.* Juristat Service Bulletin. Vol. 15. Ottawa: Statistics Canada.

Saigal, S., Feeny, D, Furlong, W., Rosenbaum, P., Burrows, E., & Torrance, G. 1994. Comparison of the health-related quality of life of extremely low birth weight children and a reference group of children at age eight years. *Journal of Pediatrics, 125* (3), 418–25.

Sameroff, A.J., Seifer, R., & Elias, P.K. 1982. Sociocultural variability in infant temperament ratings. *Child Development, 53,* 164–73.

Sampson, R.J., & Laub, J.H. 1994. Urban poverty and the family context of delinquency: A new look at structure and process in a classic study. *Child Development, 65,* 532–40.

Sampson, R.J., Morenoff, J.D., & Earls, F. 1999. Beyond social capital: Spatial dynamics of collective efficacy for children. *American Sociological Review, 64* (5), 633–60.

Sawyer, M.G., Sarris, A., Baghurst, P.A., Cornish, C.A., & Kalucy, R.S. 1990. The prevalence of emotional and behaviour disorders and patterns of service utilization in children and adolescents. *Australia and New Zealand Journal of Psychiatry, 24,* 323–30.

Sawyer, M.G., Sarris, A., Baghurst, P.A., Cross, D.G., & Kalucy, R.S. 1988. Family assessment device: Reports from mothers, fathers, and adolescents in community and clinic families. *Journal of Marital and Family Therapy, 14,* 287–96.

Scheerens, J. 1992. *Effective schooling: Research, theory, and practice.* London: Cassell.

Schmidt, W.H., McKnight, C.C., Valverde, G.A., Houang, R.T., & Wiley, D.E. 1996. *Many visions, many aims: A cross-national investigation of curricular intentions in school mathematics.* Dordrecht, Netherlands: Klwer Academic Publishers.

Schorr, L.B. 1997. Common Purpose: Strengthening Families and Neighbourhoods to Rebuild America. New York: Doubleday.

Schulsinger, C., Mednick, B.R., Klebanoff, M.A., Secher, N.J., Teasdale, T.W., & Baker, R.L. 1993. Delivery of preterm infants and small for gestational age infants across generations. *Acta Psychiatrica Scandinavica Supplementum 370,* 62–66.

Schultz, T.W. 1963. *The economic value of education.* New York: Columbia University Press.

Schwartz, C.E., Dorer, D.J., Beardslee, W.R., & Lavori, P. W. 1990. Maternal expressed emotion and parental affective disorder: Risk for childhood depressive disorder, substance abuse, or conduct disorder. *Journal of Psychiatric Research, 24* (3), 231–50.

Schweinhart, L., Barnes, H., & Weikart, D. 1993. Significant benefits: The High/Scope Perry Preschool Study through age 27. *Monographs of the High Scope Educational research Foundation, No. 10.*

Seeman, T.E. 1996. Social ties and health — the benefits of social integration. *Annals of Epidemiology, 6,* 442–51.

Sen, A. 1993. The economics of life and death. *Scientific American, 270,* 40–47.

Sewell, W.H., Hauser, R.M., & Featherman, D.R.(Eds.) 1976. *Schooling and achievement in American society.* New York: Academic Press.

Sexton, M., & Hebel, J.R. 1984. A clinical trial of change in maternal smoking and its effect on birth weight. *Journal of the American Medical Association, 251*, 911–15.

Sexton, M., Fox, N.L., & Hebel, J.R. 1990. Prenatal exposure to tobacco: Effects on cognitive functioning at age three. *International Journal of Epidemiology, 19*, 72–77.

Shapiro, L. (1997, May 12). The myth of quality time. *Newsweek*, 62–69.

Shavit, Y., & Williams, R.A. 1985. Ability grouping and contextual determinants of educational expectations in Israel. *American Sociological Review, 50*, 62–73.

Sigafoos, A., Reiss, D., Rich, J., & Douglas, E. 1985. Pragmatics in the measurement of family functioning: An interpretive framework for methodology. *Family Process, 24*, 189–203.

Simons, R.L., Johnson, C., Beaman, J., & Conger, R.D. 1993. Explaining women's double jeopardy: Factors that mediate the association between harsh treatment as a child and violence by a husband. *Journal of Marriage and the Family, 55*, 713–23.

Simons, R.L., Johnson, C., & Conger, R.D. 1994. Harsh corporal punishment versus quality of parental involvement as an explanation of adolescent adjustment. *Journal of Marriage and the Family, 56*, 591–607.

Simons, R.L., Whitbeck, L.B., Conger, R.D., & Chyi-In, W. 1991. Intergenerational transmission of harsh parenting. *Developmental Psychology, 27* (1), 159–71.

Sinclair, D., & Murray, L. 1998. Effects of postnatal depression in children's adjustment in school. *British Journal of Psychiatry, 172*, 58–63.

Slavin, R.E. 1987. Ability grouping and student achievement in elementary schools: A best-evidence synthesis. *Review of Educational Research, 57* (3), 293–336.

Smets, A.C., & Hartup, W.W. 1988. Systems and symptoms: Family cohesion/adaptability and childhood behavior problems. *Journal of Abnormal Child Psychology, 16*, 233–46.

Soliman, R.H., & Burrows, R.F. 1993. Cesarean section: Analysis of the experiences before and after the National Consensus Conference on Aspects of Cesarean Birth. *Canadian Medical Association Journal, 148* (8), 1315–20.

Sørenson, A.B., Hallinan, M. 1984. Effects of race on assignment to ability groups. In P.L. Peterson, L.C. Wilkinson, & M. Hallinan (Eds.) *The social context of education.* New York: Academic Press.

Spieker, S.J., Larson, N.C., Lewis, S.M., Keller, T.E., & Gilchrist, L. 1999. Developmental trajectories of disruptive behavior problems in preschool children of adolescent mothers. *Child Development, 70*, 443–58.

Stansfeld, S.A., Head, J., & Marmot, M.G. 1998. Explaining social class differences in depression and well-being. *Social Psychiatry and Psychiatric Epidemiology, 33* (1), 1–9.

Statistics Canada 1960. *Vital Statistics* (Catalogue 84–202).

Statistics Canada 1995. *Births and Deaths, 1995* (Catalogue 84 210 X1B).

Statistics Canada 1995. *Women in Canada: A statistical report.* Ottawa, ON: Minister of Industry.

Statistics Canada 1996. *Census families by presence of children, 1996 Census.* 1996 Census National Tables.

Statistics Canada 1997. *Births and Deaths, 1997* (Catalogue 84F0210XPB).

Statistics Canada 1998. Statistics Canada website for Canadian Statistics: Percentage of Dual Earner Families in Canada in 1998. http://www.statcan.ca/english/Pgdb/People/Families/ famillabor02a.htm

Statistics Canada 1999. *Low income cut-offs*, Catalogue # 13-551-XIB..

Statistics Canada, & Human Resources Development Canada. 1995. *National Longitudinal Survey of Children: Overview of survey instruments from 1994–95 data collection cycle 1.* Statistics Canada Catalogue no. 9502. Ottawa, ON: Minister of Industry.

Stattin, H., & Magnusson, D. 1990. *Pubertal maturation in female development.* Hillsdale, NJ: Erlbaum.

Steinberg, L. 1988. Reciprocal relation between parent–child distance and pubertal maturation. *Developmental Psychology*, 20 (4), 122–28.

Steinberg, L., Dornbusch, S.M., & Brown, B.B. 1992. Ethnic differences in adolescent achievement. *American Psychologist, 47*, 723–29.

Steinberg, L., Lamborn, S.D., Dornbusch, S.M., & Darling, N. 1992. Impact of parenting practices on adolescent achievement: Authoritative parenting, school involvement, and encouragement to succeed. *Child Development, 63*, 1266–81.

Steinburg, L. 1996. *Beyond the classroom: Why school reform has failed and what parents need to do.* New York: Simon and Schuster.

Sternberg, K.J., Lamb, M.E., Greenbaum, C., Cicchetti, D., Dawud, S., Cortes, R.M., Krispin, O., & Lorey, F. 1993. Effects of domestic violence on children's behavior problems and depression. *Developmental Psychology, 44*, 52.

Stevenson, D.L., & Baker, D.P. 1987. The family–school relationship and the child's school performance. *Child Development, 58*, 1348–57.

Stoppard, J.M. 1993. Gender, psychological factors, and depression. In P. Cappeliez & R.J. Flynn (Eds.), *Depression and the social environment: Research and interventions with neglected populations* (pp. 121–49). Montreal, PQ and Kingston, ON: McGill — Queen's University Press.

Summers, A.A., & Wolfe, Barbara L. 1977. Do schools make a difference? *American Economic Review, 67*, 639–52.

Surbey, M. 1990. Family composition, stress, and human menarche. In F. Bercovitch & T. Zeigler (Eds.), *The socioendocrinology of primate reproduction* (pp. 71–97). New York: Liss.

Susman, E.J., Dorn, L.D., & Chrousos, G.P. (1991). Negative affect and hormone levels in young adolescents: Concurrent and predictive perspectives. *Journal of Youth and Adolescence, 20* (2), 167–90.

Susman, E.J. Inoff-Germain, G., Nottelmann, E.D., Loriaux, D.L., Cutler, G.B., Jr., & Chrousos, G.P. 1987. Hormones, emotional dispositions, and aggressive attributes in young adolescents. *Child Development, 58*, 1114–34.

Susman, E.J., Nottelmann, E.D., Dorn, L.D., Gold, P.W., & Chrousos, G.P. 1989. The physiology of stress and behavioral development. In D.S. Palermo (Ed.), *Coping with uncertainty: Behavioral and developmental perspectives* (pp. 17–37). Hillsdale, NJ: Erlbaum.

Susman, E.J., Nottelmann, E.D., Inoff-Germain, G.E., Dorn, L.D., Cutler, G.B., Jr., Loriaux, D.L., & Chrousos, G.P. 1985. The relation of relative hormone levels and physical development and social-emotional behavior in young adolescents. *Journal of Youth and Adolescence, 14* (3), 245–64.

Sweet, J., Bumpass, L., & Call, V. 1988. *The design and content of the National Survey of Families and Households.* NSFH Working Paper No. 1, Centre for Demography and Ecology, University of Wisconsin-Madison.

Sweetland, S.R 1996. Human Capital Theory: Foundations of a Field of Inquiry. *Review of Educational Research, 66* (3), 341–59.

Taylor, L.C., Hinton, I.D., & Wilson, M.N. 1995. Parental influences on academic performance in African-American students. *Journal of Child and Family Studies, 4* (3), 293–302.

Thomas, A., & Chess, S. 1977. *Temperament and development.* New York: Brunner/Mazel.

Thomas, A., & Chess, S. 1982. Temperament and follow-up to adulthood. In *Temperamental differences in infants and young children* (CIBA Foundation symposium series: 89; pp. 168–75). London, UK: Pitman Books.

Thomas, A., Chess, S., & Birch, H.G. 1968. *Temperament and behavior disorders in children.* New York: New York University Press.

Thomson, E., Hanson, T.L., & McLanahan, S.S. 1994. Family structure and child well-being: economic resources vs. parental behaviours. *Social Forces, 73*, 221–42.

Touliatos, J., Perlmutter, B.F., & Straus, M.A. 1990. *Handbook of Family Measurement Techniques.* Newbury Park, CA: Sage.

Traub, R.E. 1983. *A priori considerations in choosing an item response model.* In R.K. Hambleton (Ed.), *Applications of item response theory* (pp. 57–70). Vancouver, British Columbia: Educational Research Institute of British Columbia.

Treloar, S.A., & Martin, N.G. 1990. Age at menarche as a fitness trait: Nonadditive genetic variance detected in a large twin sample. *American Journal of Human Genetics, 47*, 137–48.

Tremblay, M.S., Inman, J.W., and Willms, J.D. 2000. Relationships between physical activity, self-esteem, and academic achievement in ten- and eleven-year-old children. *Pediatric Exercise Science, 11* (3), 312–23.

Tremblay, M.S., & Willms, J.D. 2000. Secular trends in body mass index of Canadian children. *Canadian Medical Association Journal, 163* (11), 1429–33.

Tremblay, R.E. 1999. When social development fails. In D. Keating and C. Hertzman (Eds.), *Developmental health and the wealth of nations: Social, biological, and educational dynamics.* (pp. 55–71). New York: Guilford Press.

Tremblay, R.E., Boulerice, B., Harden, P.W., McDuff, P., Pérusse, D., Pihl, R.O., & Zoccolillo, M. 1996. Do children in Canada become more aggressive as they approach adolescence? In Human Resources Development Canada, Statistics Canada (Eds.), *Growing up in Canada: National Longitudinal Survey of Children and Youth* (pp. 127–37). Ottawa, ON: Minister of Industry.

Tremblay, R.E., & Craig, W. 1995. Developmental crime prevention. In M. Tonry & D.P. Farrington (Eds.), *Building a safer society: Strategic approaches to crime prevention, Volume 19* (pp. 151–236). Chicago: The University of Chicago Press.

Tremblay, R.E., Mâsse, B., Perron, D., LeBlanc, M., Schwartzman, A.E., & Ledingham, J.E. 1992. Early disruptive behavior, poor school achievement, delinquent behavior and delinquent personality: Longitudinal analyses. *Journal of Consulting and Clinical Psychology, 60* (1), 64–72.

Tremblay, R.E., Mâsse, L.C., Pagani, L., & Vitaro, F. 1995. From childhood physical aggression to adolescent maladjustment: The Montreal prevention experiment. In R.D. Peters & R.J. McMahon (Eds.), Preventing childhood disorders, substance abuse, and delinquency (pp. 268–98). Thousand Oaks, CA: Sage.

Turcot, L., Marcoux, S., Fraser, W.D., and the Canadian Early Amniotomy Study Group 1997. Multivariate analysis of risk factors for operative delivery in nulliparous women. *American Journal of Obstetrics and Gynecology, 176,* 395–402.

Turner, J.B., Kessler, R.C., & House, J.S. 1991. Factors facilitating adjustment to unemployment: Implications for intervention. *American Journal of Community Psychology, 19* (4), 521–42.

Tutty, L.M. 1995. Theoretical and practical issues in selecting a measure of family functioning. *Research on Social Work Practice, 5,* 80–106.

van den Boom, D.C. 1994. The influence of temperament and mothering on attachment and exploration: Experimental manipulation of sensitive responsiveness among lower-class mothers with irritable infants. *Child Development, 65,* 1457–77.

van der Gaag, J. & Tan, J. (2000, April). *The benefits of early childhood development programs: An economic analysis.* Paper presented for the Year 2000 Conference on Early Childhood Development sponsored by the World Bank. Washington, DC.

Vaughn, B.E., Bradley, C.F., Joffe, L.S., Seifer, R., & Barglow, P. 1987. Maternal characteristics measured prenatally are predictive of ratings of temperamental "difficulty" on the Carey Infant Temperament Questionnaire. *Developmental Psychology, 23* (1), 152–61.

Ventura, S.J., & Curtin, S.A. 1999. Recent trends in teen births in the United States. *Statistical Bulletin, 80* (1), 2–12.

Voelkl, K. 1997. Identification with school. *American Journal of Education, 105,* 294–318.

Wachs, T.D. 1992. *The nature of nurture.* Newbury Park, CA: Sage Publications.

Wadsworth, M.E.J. 1986. Effects of parenting style and preschool experience on children's verbal attainment: Results of a British longitudinal study. *Early Childhood Research Quarterly, 1,* 237–48.

Wakschlag, L.S., Chase-Lansdale, P.L., & Brooks-Gunn, J. 1996. Not just "Ghosts in the Nursery": Contemporaneous intergenerational relationships and parenting in young African-American families. *Child Development, 67* (5), 2131–47.

Walker, H.M., Shinn, M.R., O'Neill, R.E., & Ramsey, E. 1987. A longitudinal assessment of the development of antisocial behavior in boys: Rationale, methodology and first-year results. *Remedial and Special Education, 8,* 7-16, 27.

Walker, L.S., Ortiz-Valdes, J.A., & Newbrough, J.R. 1989. The role of maternal employment and depression in the psychological adjustment of chronically ill, mentally retarded, and well children. *Journal of Pediatric Psychology, 14* (3), 357–70.

Wasik, B.J., & Ramey, C.T. 1990. A longitudinal study of two early intervention strategies: Project CARE. *Child Development, 61* (6),1682–97.

Wasserman, R.C., DiBlasio, C.M., Bond, L.A., Young, P.C. & Colletti, R.B. 1990. Infant temperament and school age behavior: 6-year longitudinal study in a pediatric practice. *Pediatrics, 85* (5), 801–07.

Webster-Stratton, C. 1990. Stress: A potential disruptor of parent perceptions and family interactions. *Journal of Clinical Child Psychology, 19* (4), 302–12.

Wehlage, G.G., Rutter, R.A., Smith, G., Lesko, N., & Fernandez, R. 1989. *Reducing the risk: Schools as communities of support.* Philadelphia: Falmer Press.

Weissman, M., Leaf, P., & Bruce, J.L. 1987. Single parent women. *Social Psychiatry, 22,* 29–36.

Weitzman, M., Gortmaker, S., & Sobol, A. (1992). Maternal smoking and behavior problems of children. *Pediatrics, 90,* 342–49.

Wenk, D.A., Hardesty, C.L., Morgan, C.S., & Blair, S.L. 1994. The influence of parental involvement on the well-being of sons and daughters. *Journal of Marriage and the Family, 56,* 229–34.

Werner, E.E., & Smith, R.S. 1992. *Overcoming the odds: High risk children from birth to adulthood.* Ithaca, NY: Cornell University Press.

West, D.J., & Farrington, D. 1973. *Who becomes delinquent? Second report of the Cambridge Study in Delinquent Development.* New York, NY: Crane, Russak.

White, J.L., Moffitt, T.E., Earls, F., Robins, L., & Silva, P.A. 1990. How early can we tell?: Predictors of childhood conduct disorder and adolescent delinquency. *Criminology, 28* (4), 507–33.

Whitebook, M., Howes, C. & Phillips, D. 1989. *Who cares? Child care teachers and the quality of care in America.* Executive summary, National Child Care Staffing Study. Oakland, CA: Child Care Employee Project.

Wierson, M., Long, P.J., & Forehand, R.L. 1993. Toward a new understanding of early menarche: The role of environmental stress in pubertal timing. *Adolescence, 28* (112), 913–24

Wilkinson, R.G. 1992. Income distribution and life expectancy. *British Medical Journal, 304*, 165–68.

Williams, K.T., & Wang, J.J. 1997. *Technical references to the Peabody Picture Vocabulary Test — Third Edition (PPVT–III)*. Circle Pines, MN: American Guidance Service.

Willms, J.D. 1985. The balance thesis: Contextual effects of ability on pupils' o-grade examination results. *Oxford Review of Education, 11* (1), 33–41.

Willms, J.D. 1986. Social class segregation and its relationship to pupils' examination results in Scotland. *American Sociological Review, 51*, 224–41.

Willms, J.D. 1992. *Monitoring school performance: A guide for educators*. Washington, DC: Falmer.

Willms, J.D. 1992. Pride or prejudice? Opportunity structure and the effects of Catholic schools in Scotland. In A. Yogev (Ed.), *International Perspectives on Education and Society: A Research and Policy Annual, Vol. 2* (pp. 189–213). Greenwich, CT: JAI Press.

Willms, J.D. 1996. Indicators of mathematics achievement in Canadian elementary schools. In *Growing up in Canada: National longitudinal study of children and youth* (pp. 69–82). Ottawa, ON: Human Resources Development Canada and Statistics Canada.

Willms, J.D. 1997. *Literacy skills of Canadian youth*. Report prepared for Statistics Canada and Human Resources Development Canada.

Willms, J.D. 1998. Community differentials in adult literacy skills in Northern Ireland. In K. Sweeney, B. Morgan, & D. Donnelly (Eds.), *Adult literacy in Northern Ireland* (pp. 76–89). Belfast: Northern Ireland Statistics and Research Agency.

Willms, J.D. 1999. Basic concepts in hierarchical linear modelling with applications for policy analysis. In G.J. Cizek (Ed.), *Handbook of Educational Policy*. New York: Academic Press.

Willms, J.D. 1999a. *Inequalities in literacy skills among youth in Canada and the United States*. (International Adult Literacy Survey No. 6). Ottawa, ON: Human Resources Development Canada and National Literacy Secretariat.

Willms, J.D. 1999b. *Literacy skills in Poland*. Report prepared for Statistics Canada and the World Bank.

Willms, J.D. 1999c. Quality and inequality in children's literacy: The effects of families, schools, and communities. In D. Keating and C. Hertzman (Eds.), *Developmental health and the wealth of nations: Social, biological, and educational dynamics*. (pp. 72–93). New York: Guilford Press.

Willms, J.D. 2000. Have early childhood outcomes in New Brunswick improved? *ISUMA, 1* (2), 64–70.

Willms, J.D. 2001. Monitoring school performance for "standards-based reform." *Evaluation and Research in Education, 14*, (3&4), 237–53.

Willms, J.D., & Chen, M. 1989. The effects of ability grouping on the ethnic achievement gap in Israeli elementary schools. *American Journal of Education, 97* (3), 237–57.

Willms, J.D., & Jacobsen, S. 1990. Growth in mathematics skills during the intermediate years: Sex differences and school effects. *International Journal of Educational Research 14,* 157–74.

Willms, J.D. & Kerckhoff, A.C. 1995. The challenge of developing new social indicators. *Educational Evaluation and Policy Analysis, 17* (1), 113–31.

Willms, J.D., and Patterson, L. 1995. A multilevel model for community segregation. *Journal of Mathematical Sociology, 20* (1), 23–40.

Willms, J.D. & Raudenbush, S.W. 1989. A longitudinal hierarchical linear model for estimating school effects and their stability. *Journal of Educational Measurement, 26* (3), 209–32.

Willms, J.D. & Raudenbush, S.W. 1994. Effective schools research: Methodological issues. *International Encyclopaedia of Education,* (2nd Ed.).

Willms, J.D., & Shields, M. 1996. A measure of socioeconomic status for the National Longitudinal Study of Children. Report prepared for Statistics Canada.

Willms, J.D., & Somers, M.-A. 2001. Family, classroom, and school effects on children's educational outcomes in Latin America. *International Journal of School Effectiveness and Improvement, 12* (4), 409–45.

Wilson, J.Q. & Hernstein, R.J. 1985. *Crime and human nature.* New York: Simon and Schuster.

Wilson, J.Q. & Hernstein, R.J. 1994. A theory of criminal behaviour. In D.P. Farrington (Ed.), *Psychological explanation of crime.* Aldershot England; Dartmouth Publishing Company Limited.

Windsor, R.A., Lowe, J.B., Perkins, L.L., Smith-Yoder, D., Artz, L., Crawford, M., Amburgy, K., & Boyd, N.R. 1994. Health education for pregnant smokers: Its behavioral impact and cost benefit. *American Journal of Public Health, 83* (2), 201–06.

Winkleby, M.A., Jatulis, D.E., Frank, E., & Fortman, S.P. 1992. Socioeconomic status and health: How education, income, and occupation contribute to risk factors for cardiovascular disease. *American Journal of Public Health, 82,* 816–20.

Wolfe, B. & Haveman, R. 2000. Accounting for the social and non-market benefits of education. Report prepared for Organization for Economic Co-operation and Development and Human Resources Development Canada.

Wolfe, B.L., & Hill, S. 1992. *The health, earnings capacity, and poverty of single-mother families* (pp. 964–92). Madison, WI: Institute for Research on Policy.

Wolfson, M., Kaplan, G., Lynch, J., Ross, N., Backlund, E., Gravelle, H, & Wilkinson, R.G. 1999. Relation between income inequality and mortality: Empirical demonstration. *BMJ, 319,* 953–57.

Wolfson, M., Rowe, G, Gentleman, J.F., & Tomiak, M. 1993. Career earnings and death: A longitudinal analysis of older Canadian men. *Journal of Gerontology, 48* (4), S167-S179.

Wolk, S., Zeanah, C.H., Garcia-Coll, C.T., & Carr, S. 1992. Factors affecting parents' perceptions of temperament in early infancy. *American Journal of Orthopsychiatry, 62* (1), 71–82.

Woolcock, M. 2000. *Using social capital: Getting the social relations right in the theory and practice of economic development.* Princeton, NJ: Princeton University Press (forthcoming).

Xu, G. 2000. *Participation in Employer-Sponsored Adult Education and Training in Sweden (1975–1995).* Unpublished doctoral dissertation, University of British Columbia.

Young, M.A. 1982/83. Evaluating diagnostic criteria: A latent class paradigm. *Journal of Psychiatry Research, 17* (3), 285–96.

Zoloth, B.S. 1976. Alternative measures of school segregation. *Land Economics, 52* (3), 278–98.